D1477110

From Crisis to Creation

From Crisis to Creation

Lesslie Newbigin and the Reinvention of Christian Mission

MARK T. B. LAING

Foreword by
ANDREW F. WALLS

PICKWICK *Publications* · Eugene, Oregon

FROM CRISIS TO CREATION
Lesslie Newbigin and the Reinvention of Christian Mission

Pickwick Publications
An Imprint of Wipf and Stock Publishers
199 W. 8th Ave., Suite 3
Eugene, OR 97401
www.wipfandstock.com

ISBN 13: 978-1-61097-424-0

Cataloging-in-Publication data:

Laing, Mark T. B.

From crisis to creation : Lesslie Newbigin and the reinvention of Christian mission / Mark T. B. Laing ; foreword by Andrew F. Walls.

xxvi + y p. ; 23 cm. —Includes bibliographical references and index.

ISBN 13: 978-1-61097-424-0

1. Newbigin, Lesslie. 2. Missions—Theory. I. Walls, Andrew F. (Andrew Finlay). II. Title.

BV2063 .L21 2012

Manufactured in the U.S.A.

For my parents

Contents

Foreword by Andrew F. Walls | ix

Acknowledgments | xi

Introduction | xiii

Abbreviations | xxiii

1   The Making of an IMC General Secretary | 1

2   The Path Towards Integration | 32

3   Rolle and Willingen: A Theological Foundation for
Integration (and Mission) | 61

4   The IMC at Ghana: Debating Integration and Calling Newbigin | 87

5   Newbigin's Tenure as General Secretary of the
International Missionary Council | 110

6   Mission and Service: The Relationship between the IMC and the
Division of Inter-Church Aid | 138

7   Newbigin's Theology of Integration | 167

8   Integration and Secularization: The Quest for
Missionary Structures | 191

9   Secularization and the Missionary Structure of the Church | 218

10 Conclusion: The Outcome of Integration | 244

Appendix 1: A Chronology of Newbigin's Life with Other Key Events | 259

Appendix 2: Methodology | 261

Appendix 3: Interviews | 270

Bibliography | 271

Index | 287

Lesslie Newbigin and Rev. Lawrence McMaster being interviewed at the third assembly of the WCC, New Delhi, 1961 (used with permission of the World Council of Churches)

Foreword

GLOBAL THEOLOGY IS A topic increasingly canvassed as a result of those twentieth-century developments that have led to the realization that the majority of the world's Christians are now Africans, Asians, and Latin Americans. In many ways these developments reflect Christianity's reversion to type. The Church of the early centuries was widely spread across Asia, Europe and northern and eastern Africa. In the sixth century the Emperor of China and the King of Northumbria were studying expositions of the Christian faith at almost the same time; by the ninth century the faith could be found from the Steppes to Sri Lanka. Christianity has always been global in principle; it is now more fully global in extent than at any previous period of its existence. But its theological inheritance has to a large extent been shaped by the centuries of inter-action with the languages, cultures and intellectual history of Europe and North America. Recent years have seen a substantial flowering of African, Asian and Latin American theologies, and an intercontinental array of essentially local theologies. There is now a need to think theologically, comprehensively and globally.

A foundational thinker in this process is the late Lesslie Newbigin, one of the seminal theologians of mission of the twentieth century, and perhaps the most important in the English-speaking world. He always saw West and East as in interaction, and Christianity in relation both to other faiths and to the secular world. His thinking was anchored in the practice of Christian mission; he had himself been a missionary in India, a bishop of the Indian Church, a leading figure in the international structures of Church and Mission that emerged in the decades following the Second World War, a highly influential teacher and writer on mission, and, in his late years, pastor of a rundown English inner-city church. His theology emerged in dialogue with Hindu monism and Western secularism; his biblically-oriented thinking shows the gospel of the Triune God as public truth, entrusted to a Church of all nations that in principle is united in and with Christ, and in interaction with other faiths, societal structures, and cultures of East and West. His Trinitarian theology discourses both of love and of judgment, and takes seriously the "principalities and powers" behind the workings of the universe, represented by, but not identical with, political figures and institutions.

Dr. Mark Laing's rich book expounds all these themes as they evolved and were reflected in Newbigin's life as missionary, executive, theologian and prophet. In particular, it offers a valuable elucidation of Newbigin's involvement in the debates concerning the relation of Church and Mission that arose during his later years as Secretary of the International Missionary Council. This story is crucial to the understanding of the development of Christianity in the era since the Second World War, and until now has been substantially an untold story. Dr. Laing presents it in a clear narrative that holds the reader's interest, but also clarifies the theological and ecclesiological issues.

This is a book that goes to the heart of the relationship of Church and Mission among Christians of different backgrounds. Newbigin has attracted much attention in recent years and is bound to attract more; Dr Laing's careful researches and sympathetic exposition provide an invaluable route map for a journey that is abundantly worthwhile.

Andrew F. Walls
Honorary Professor in the University of Edinburgh
Professor of the History of Mission at Liverpool Hope University
Professor in the Akrofi-Christaller Institute, Ghana

Acknowledgments

THIS BOOK IS A revision of my PhD thesis that I submitted in 2010 to the University of Edinburgh. The writing of a thesis can be a difficult and solitary existence, yet I am aware of a host of helpers who enabled the completion of this work. Wise academic counsel and mentoring was unstintingly provided by my two supervisors, Dr. T. Jack Thompson and Professor Andrew Walls, to whom I am especially grateful. Professor Brian Stanley, my internal examiner, provided very helpful comments on how to revise my PhD for publication. The Reverend Murdoch Mackenzie was in many ways an unofficial third supervisor. I am grateful to Murdoch for the many conversations on Lesslie Newbigin, his personal reminiscence, his careful editing of my text, and for the introductions he furnished to a wide circle of friends who had worked with Newbigin. I am grateful for the help provided by librarians and archivists at New College, Edinburgh, The Special Collection of the University of Birmingham Library, the National Library of Scotland, the School of Oriental and African Studies, and the World Council of Churches. All archives are used with appropriate permission. I am also grateful to Christian Amondson and the staff at Wipf and Stock for their diligence in transforming a thesis into this book.

The most significant support I have received throughout this study has been from my wife, Helen. I remain profoundly indebted for the innumerable ways Helen has helped and encouraged me.

Introduction

Context

THE TWENTIETH CENTURY WITNESSED a major recovery of ecclesiology that brought to the fore the church's missionary nature and the church's calling to unity. These two concerns and the relationship between them were central to the life and work of Bishop Lesslie Newbigin as he sought to embody these theological convictions. The crucial attempt to embody the consensus on this relationship was the integration of the International Missionary Council (IMC) with the World Council of Churches (WCC) in 1961, as international symbols of a recovered relationship between mission and church. The post-colonial quest to reorganize and restructure missions led to the more fundamental questioning of how mission should be *redefined*. This is a study of Newbigin's involvement in this process.

In the twentieth century, the church has undergone a major revision of its ecclesiology challenging the assumptions inherited from a defective and ultimately redundant Christendom ecclesiology. What led to this recovery in ecclesiology during the twentieth century? Newbigin understood three reasons contributing to this recovery: the demise of Christendom, the missionary encounters of Western Christianity with the non-Western world, and the rise of the ecumenical movement.[1] These three factors will be (briefly) considered before turning to what was recovered: the church's concern for mission and for unity, and the relationship between them.

The breakdown of Christendom for Newbigin meant the dissolution of the synthesis between the gospel and Western culture.[2] With the acknowledgment of the rise of secularism as an ideology in the West, the upheavals of Communism in Orthodox Russia, and the lingering memory

---

1. Lesslie Newbigin, *The Household of God: Lectures on the Nature of the Church* (London: SCM, 1953) 1–25.

2. Ibid., 11.

of the blood and carnage from World War I—in which "Christian" nations battled against each other—the synonymous association of land with faith, of West with Christianity, was undermined.[3] Faced with such major theological challenges in its heartland, the inadequacy of the Western church's ecclesiology was exposed and the church was forced to re-examine its essential nature.

Foreign missions were important to nineteenth-century Western Christianity but in practice could never be considered as central to the life of the church. Instead, they were a peripheral activity of the church, growing out of her largesse and generosity. The voluntary spirit enthused many and this exuberance was to lead to the "fortunate subversion" of the Protestant church.[4] Missionary societies subverted and circumvented the church. For both missions and the church that was "fortunate" but it left an uneasy legacy of autonomous "foreign missions" divorced from the church "at home" which then incongruously related paternalistically to the "younger churches" planted overseas. Mission was practiced without adequate theological foundation and consequently "younger churches" were established with an inadequate ecclesiology. So the anomaly existed that "Protestant mission *societies*, having grown in isolation from the Western churches, were mainly responsible for the birth of younger *churches*, which now had to (indeed wanted to) enter into mature relationship with the *churches* of the West."[5] This gave impetus to the questions of how mission was related to the church and how, at an international level, relationships could be expressed between the various churches.

In Newbigin's practical experience in South India, it was the missionary practice of comity which particularly raised questions about the church's orientation. In South India the church had to constantly define itself against a dominant non-Christian culture. In such situations practical questions were raised about the church's relationship to the world, this in turn led to an appraisal of the true nature of the church.[6] Newbigin discerned a progression at work drawing the church together: "Out of this

---

3. Other factors also contributed to the demise of Christendom, ibid., 12–13. Lesslie Newbigin, *Foolishness to the Greeks: The Gospel and Western Culture* (Grand Rapids: Eerdmans, 1986) 30–34.

4. A. F. Walls, "Missionary Societies and the Fortunate Subversion of the Church," *Evangelical Quarterly* 60 (1988).

5. W. A. Saayman, *Unity and Mission: A Study of the Concept of Unity in Ecumenical Discussions since 1961 and Its Influence on the World Mission of the Church* (Pretoria: University of South Africa, 1984) 18.

6. Newbigin, *Household of God*, 14.

new missionary experience arose those forces by which the Churches were drawn from isolation into comity, from comity into cooperation, and—in some areas at least—from co operation into organic union."[7] Comity brought a simplification to understanding the church and its mission, as in each locale there was normally but one church. "One can also exhibit the connection between mission and unity by saying that missionary obedience puts the Church in a situation where its true nature is understood and disunity is seen for what it is."[8]

The third reason Newbigin gave for the recovery of ecclesiology, and thus concern for the relationship between unity and mission came from the rise of the ecumenical movement, which "was in large part the outgrowth of the missionary movement."[9] It has been conventional to regard the World Missionary Conference at Edinburgh in 1910 as the birthplace of the modern ecumenical movement. More correctly Edinburgh should be understood as "the culmination of a long tradition of pan-evangelical ecumenism."[10] And it is noteworthy that the "ecumenical movement as we here know it had its main impulse and its main achievements in what has organizationally been the most divided branch of the Church, Protestantism, but in one fashion or another it reached out to other forms of the Faith."[11] The very pragmatic Edinburgh conference, the founding inspiration for the IMC, explored avenues for better cooperation in mission. This was not from any theological impetus towards unity but from the compelling motive of evangelism, the conference delegates, under the influence of the chairman, John R. Mott, endorsing the Student Volunteer Movement for Foreign Missions slogan, "the evangelization of the world in this generation."

The main contribution of Edinburgh towards the relationship between mission and unity came from what Edinburgh constituted rather than from what actually took place at the conference. In establishing a continuation committee with J. H. Oldham as secretary and J. R. Mott as chairman, Edinburgh "ensured that international and inter-denominational missionary cooperation should move from the stage of occasional

7. Ibid., 18.

8. Ibid., 151.

9. Kenneth Scott Latourette, "Ecumenical Bearings of the Missionary Movement and the International Missionary Council," in *A History of the Ecumenical Movement, 1517–1948*, ed. Ruth Rouse and Stephen Neill (London: SPCK, 1954) 353.

10. Brian Stanley, ed., *The World Missionary Conference, Edinburgh 1910* (Grand Rapids: Eerdmans, 2009) 8.

11. Latourette, "Ecumenical Bearings," 401.

conferences to that of continuous and effective consultation";[12] this committee formally became the IMC in 1921.[13]

An adequate understanding of the interrelationship between mission and unity required the recovery of an adequate ecclesiology. The IMC, through several conferences, facilitated theological reflection. This was furthered by the founding of the journal the *International Review of Missions*, Oldham serving as the first editor. By the Jerusalem conference (1928) thinking had become increasingly church-centric, this tendency continuing at Tambaram (1938).[14] A consensus on the relationship between church, mission and unity gradually evolved. The highpoint of the expression of that relationship was in the integration of the IMC with the WCC at New Delhi in 1961.

A Recovery of Ecclesiology

Bishop Stephen Neill stated that "the problem of mission cannot be discussed *in abstracto*; it becomes intelligible only as the mission of the Church. Given a satisfactory ecclesiology, a satisfactory definition of the Church, the answer to all the main problems arising out of the Christian mission should lie ready to hand."[15]

For Newbigin, unity—a unity which was tangible and visible—belonged to the true nature of the church, and the demonstration of this unity was essential for the effective witness of the church. He understood the two as emanating from the heart of the Gospel and as therefore essential to the dual calling of the church: "That which makes the Church one is what makes it a mission to the world. . . . The connection between the movement for Christian reunion and the movement for world evangelization is of the deepest possible character. The two things are the two outward signs of a return to the heart of the Gospel itself."[16] Connecting them

12. Lesslie Newbigin, "Cooperation and Unity," *IRM* 59:233 (1970) 67.

13. The standard history is: W. R. Hogg, *Ecumenical Foundations: A History of the International Missionary Council and Its Nineteenth Century Background* (New York: Harper, 1952).

14. IMC, *Jerusalem Meeting March 24th–April 8th: The World Mission of Christianity: Messages and Recommendations* (London: IMC/Oxford University Press, 1928) 33. IMC, *Addresses and Other Records: Tambaram, Madras, December 12th to 29th, 1938*, vol. 7 (London: IMC/Oxford Univerity Press, 1939) 4.

15. S. Neill, *The Church and Christian Union*, The Bampton Lectures, 1964 (London: Oxford University Press, 1968) 319. Cf. Saayman, *Unity and Mission*, 112.

16. Lesslie Newbigin, *The Reunion of the Church: A Defence of the South India*

are Christ's promise that "if I be lifted up, I will draw all men to myself" (John 12:32) and the eschatological consummation of that promise, "to sum up all things in Christ" (Eph 1:10), themes which Newbigin would consistently return to.[17]

Importance and Contribution of This Study

Integration was the focal point for expressing the ecumenical consensus which developed in the twentieth century. This study takes that event and Newbigin's involvement in the process of integration as its centre. As such this study seeks to provide a theological history of an important incident. By the middle of the twentieth century it was acknowledged that mission needed to be rehabilitated and redefined. Central to that process was the role of the IMC as a vanguard of missionary thinking.

This book seeks to provide a unique contribution to the literature in several ways. There has been little prior study on integration of the IMC with the WCC.[18] This book is unique in showing Newbigin's crucial and substantial contribution to this process. As such the study demonstrates the evolution of Newbigin's missionary ecclesiology and details how Newbigin made the shift from examining the *structure* to the *substance* of mission, as he developed his trinitarian missiology.

A further claim to uniqueness lies in its substantial use of primary archival sources. Through the use of private correspondence, memos and numerous draft papers this book seeks to reveal the process through which Newbigin's theology evolved and then integrate that with the relevant published material from the Newbigin corpus. It seeks to provide a history of a theological process which demonstrates Newbigin in context, engaged and in tension with others.

Scheme (London: SCM, 1948, reprinted 1960) 11, 19.

17. E.g., "The Church's unity is the sign and the instrument of the salvation which Christ has wrought and whose final fruition is the summing-up of all things in Christ," Newbigin, *Household of God*, 149. See also Lesslie Newbigin, *Honest Religion for Secular Man* (London: SCM, 1966) 108; Lesslie Newbigin, "The Christian Layman in the World and in the Church," *NCCR* 72 (1952); Lesslie Newbigin, "The Mission of the Triune God," 1962 (WCC, Ecumenical Centre Library: Geneva).

18. An early study is: T. V. Philip, "Mission and Unity: Factors Contributing to the Integration of the International Missionary Council and the World Council of Churches" (PhD diss., Hartford Seminary Foundation, 1967).

Newbigin's working life can be divided into three periods:[19] his time as a missionary (and subsequently bishop) in South India; his involvement with the IMC and subsequently the WCC; and his "retirement" to the United Kingdom, in which he developed his missiological engagement with Western culture. Focusing on the middle period of Newbigin's life, this study argues that Newbigin's missionary experience (and his subsequent theological reflections) uniquely prepared him for integration. This book also demonstrates that the development of Newbigin's missiology of Western culture arose as a direct consequence of his involvement in integration. It thus started much earlier than 1974—the year of Newbigin's "retirement" and the starting point for most studies on his missiology to Western culture. Although not a major aspect of this book, this study shows hints of this aspect of Newbigin's missiology prior to the 1960s, becoming explicit during the 1960s as he engaged with secularization.

This study thus brings new knowledge to bear on Newbigin in three areas: history, biography, and theology. Historically, Newbigin's archives give insight into his thinking on the organizational expression of unity, and the relationship between the church and mission. Although not seeking to be a biographical study, this study also helps to elucidate material Newbigin alluded to in his autobiography.[20] And theologically, this study helps bridge the gap between Newbigin's systematic reflections and the organizational embodiment and articulations of those reflections.

The year 2009 was the birth centenary of Newbigin, 2010 marks the anniversary of Edinburgh 1910, and 2011 the jubilee of integration. Looking back enables us to move forward. After a century of the modern ecumenical movement, as Christianity continues its southern shift and becomes more diffuse, Andrew Walls anticipates that the "great issues of twenty-first-century Christianity are likely to be ecumenical."[21]

Research Questions

The purpose of this study is to examine Newbigin's role in the integration of the IMC with the WCC. The research is conducted with reference to

---

19. For a time line of Newbigin's life, see Appendix 1.

20. Lesslie Newbigin, *Unfinished Agenda: An Autobiography* (Grand Rapids: Eerdmans, 1985); Lesslie Newbigin, *Unfinished Agenda: An Updated Autobiography* (Geneva: WCC, 1993).

21. A. F. Walls, *The Cross-Cultural Process in Christian History: Studies in the Transmission and Appropriation of Faith* (Maryknoll, NY: Orbis, 2002) 96.

two main questions: 1) What was Newbigin's contribution to integration? 2) How did the process of integration affect Newbigin's theological reflection on the nature of mission? This study seeks to answer the first question in several ways:

1. How did Newbigin's background in India prepare him for his role as general secretary?

2. What theological foundation did Newbigin provide for integration?

3. What practical and administrative measures did Newbigin employ to facilitate integration?

4. What were the structural and organizational issues of integration, and how did Newbigin address these?

5. To what extent was integration of the two world councils a theological embodiment of the conviction that the church is missionary?

The second aspect of the research question, on how the process of integration affected Newbigin, is addressed in several ways:

1. How did Newbigin understand the theological relationship between mission and church?

2. How did Newbigin's thinking evolve from concerns about the structure of mission to focus on the substance of mission?

3. How was integration of mission and church to be expressed at the level of the local congregation?

4. How effective was integration at expressing a recovered ecclesiology?

5. What was Newbigin's assessment of the outcome of integration?

Outline of Chapters

The key leadership of Protestant missions recognized that by the middle of the twentieth century the missionary movement was in crisis. Colonial missions were discredited. The quest to reorganize and restructure missions became focused on the question of how the IMC should relate to the WCC, as international symbols of the relationship between mission and church. The two councils were "in association" with each other. But their relationship was more intimate and complex. The quest to express an adequate relationship between the two councils was driven, by some, with theological convictions regarding the missionary nature of the church. The desire to rehabilitate missions led to the more fundamental questioning of how mission should be *redefined*.

The purpose of this study is to ascertain an answer to two related questions: What was Newbigin's contribution to the integration of the IMC with the WCC; and secondly, how did the process of integration affect Newbigin's theological reflection on the nature of mission? In seeking to answer the first question, the book begins by examining how three formative factors in Newbigin's early career prepared him for the role as general secretary of the IMC (chapter 1). Newbigin's experience of the Student Christian Movement as a student at Cambridge; the Indian church as a young Church of Scotland missionary; and his role in the formation of the Church of South India are each examined to determine how they prepared Newbigin for integration.

As a prelude to Newbigin's direct involvement in the process of integration, the historical background is examined to answer these key questions (chapter 2): What was happening on the world stage to affect the relationship between the IMC and the WCC? What was happening internal to each council, and in the nexus of their relationships with each other? Why were conservative evangelicals so important to integration when they had distanced themselves from the ecumenical movement? What were their concerns about integration?

The WCC Central Committee meeting at Rolle in 1951, and the IMC Conference in Willingen in the subsequent year, provided a theological foundation for integration (chapter 3). Newbigin's role in both was critical. For Rolle he drafted the document "The Calling of the Church to Mission and to Unity," which provided an early foundation on which subsequent construction towards integration could be built. Newbigin then succeeded in having this document adopted at Willingen. Willingen was both a difficult and creative conference. Concepts such as the missionary nature of the church and the trinitarian basis for mission were established (and debated). In this Newbigin's role was critical in producing a statement the whole assembly could endorse. Willingen was a catalyst providing the theological agenda which would later fully occupy Newbigin beyond his theologizing on integration. The debate over the validity of the post-Tambaram, church-centric model of mission facilitated fruitful enquiry on the relationship between the church and the world, and the relationship between sacred and secular history.

The IMC leadership (and the WCC) was surprised at Ghana by the opposition expressed against integration (chapter 4). The key spokesperson representing those opposed to integration was Canon Max Warren. Whereas the WCC approved integration with little discussion, Ghana demonstrated the width and depth of conviction within the IMC against integration. Despite this opposition at the Ghana assembly the IMC eventually made two important decisions, to approve of the plan to integrate and second, to call Newbigin to facilitate integration, inviting Newbigin to become the next general secretary of the IMC.

Chapter 5 evaluates Newbigin's tenure as general secretary: What were the key issues for Newbigin in integration, what agenda did he pursue as general secretary, and how effective was he in implementing his goals? The chapter assesses the more immediate consequences of integration for mission.

During the 1950s Western mission boards were retracting from their historical involvement in service. Their place was being taken by powerful Western service agencies. In 1955 the mandate for the Division of Inter-Church Aid was expanded, making it "worldwide" and "permanent." The problematic overlap created between service agencies and traditional mission agencies was *the* central issue which gave impetus to the desire to integrate the IMC with the WCC. How was mission related to service and what was the best way to express that relationship in the structures of an integrated council? Newbigin argued, on theological and practical grounds, that as mission and church belong together so too do mission and service. Chapter 6 considers Newbigin's critical role in this debate.

Newbigin's theology of integration is the focus of chapter 7. Newbigin had already provided an earlier theological foundation for integration. But the discussion on integration became obsessed with structural questions. One of Newbigin's contributions as general secretary was to provide a subsequent theological "manifesto" for integration by writing various study papers. In the process of drafting research papers Newbigin made the significant shift from addressing the *structures* of mission to exploring the *substance* of mission. Returning to issues which he had first encountered at Willingen, Newbigin realized that there were considerable problems with the post-Tambaram church-centric model of mission. Newbigin's initial papers were critical of the inadequacies of this church-centric model, but limited in their construction of an alternative. In his subsequent papers he was more constructive, proposing a more adequate (and trinitarian) foundation for mission.

Integration of the two councils was enacted at the New Delhi assembly in 1961. At that time theological engagement with the processes of secularization was at its height. Secularization brought a critique to Christendom structures which failed to express the missionary nature of the church. In particular the parochial organization of the church and the form of ministry were challenged. To give "spiritual substance" to integration Newbigin argued that it was at the level of the local congregation that integration of mission and church must be made real. Recognizing the challenge of secularization the WCC initiated a study on the Missionary Structure of the Congregation. This important study and Newbigin's assessment of it are analyzed in chapter 8.

At the heart of integration was the desire to reunify church with mission, although the actual process raised fundamental questions on the accepted model for mission. It was Newbigin's hope that this would be expressed at all levels of the church's existence, the ecumenical movement serving as a sign and symbol for this process. By the time of integration of the IMC with the WCC there was convergence in Newbigin's critique of the structure of the congregation. His observation, from his experience, and experimentation within the Indian church, was now confirmed by his analysis of secularization. Chapter 9 focuses on Newbigin's particular contribution to these issues, namely his understanding of the impact of secularization upon society, and upon the church.

The study is concluded in chapter 10 where the overarching link between Newbigin's theology and the organizational embodiment of his convictions is re-examined. The long-term impact of integration and Newbigin's assessment of it is appraised. Collectively the chapters demonstrate Newbigin's contribution to integration and detail the evolution of his missiology as a consequence of his involvement in the process.

Abbreviations

BUL	Birmingham University Library
CCM	WCC Central Committee Minutes
CICCU	Cambridge Inter-Collegiate Christian Union
CofS	Church of Scotland
CSI	Church of South India
CWME	Commission of World Mission and Evangelism
DICA	Division of Inter-Church Aid
DICASR	Division of Inter-Church Aid and Service to Refugees
DICARWS	Division of Inter-Church Aid, Refugee and World Service
DWME	Division of World Mission and Evangelism
EACC	East Asia Christian Conference
EFMA	Evangelical Foreign Missions Association
ER	*Ecumenical Review*
FM	Foreign Mission of the Church of Scotland
FMC	Foreign Mission Committee of the Church of Scotland
IBMR	*International Bulletin of Missionary Research*
ICA	Inter-Church Aid
IFMA	Interdenominational Foreign Mission Association
IMC	International Missionary Council
IRM	*International Review of Mission(s)*
JAM	Joint Aid for Mission
JCM	Joint Committee Minutes (of the WCC and the IMC)

Abbreviations

MSC	The Study of the Missionary Structure of the Congregation
NCC	National Christian Council
NCCR	*National Christian Council Review*
NLS	National Library of Scotland
OBMR	*Occasional Bulletin of Missionary Research*
SCM	Student Christian Movement
SIS	South India Scheme for Church Union
SIUC	South India United Church
SOAS	School of Oriental and African Studies
WCC	World Council of Churches
WSCF	World Student Christian Federation

1

The Making of an IMC General Secretary

BY THE TIME OF the Ghana conference of the IMC (1957–58), New-bigin was *the* candidate of choice to lead the IMC, as the last general secretary, into integration with the WCC. What made Newbigin the unique and unanimous choice of the IMC? This chapter identifies three formative elements which shaped Newbigin's ecclesiology, the Student Christian Movement (SCM), the Indian church, and the formation of the Church of South India (CSI). Through the SCM Newbigin was introduced to Christianity and inducted into a form of Christianity which rather than being narrow and defensive was dynamic, experimental and ecumenical, having the world as its horizon.

As a young Church of Scotland missionary in South India, Newbigin experienced the dramatic growth of the village churches in rural Tamil Nadu. And, as a missionary, he was exposed to the dichotomous relationship that existed between mission and church expressed in the problematic relationship between the Church of Scotland's mission and the Indian church. Newbigin saw in the Indian church a church which was both missionary and profoundly concerned to regain its unity.

This was expressed in the negotiations for church union which concluded successfully with the formation of the Church of South India in 1947. Newbigin entered late in the negotiation process but rapidly assumed prominent responsibility, first in India and then internationally. Newbigin's theological reflections and apologetic for the South Indian union scheme enabled him to develop an ecclesiology in which the eschatological dimension was prominent. This gave credence to his claim that his experience of the Indian church was of relevance beyond the confines of South Asia.

Although Newbigin's experience of the SCM, the Indian church and the formation of the CSI are uniquely personal, his experience was not unparalleled in the lives of others. This chapter does not seek to provide an exhaustive list of the early factors which shaped Newbigin's theological outlook. Undoubtedly during his time of theological study at Westminster College he was particularly indebted to the influence of the college's principal, John Oman, and his successor Herbert Farmer.[1] However, at this early milestone on Newbigin's theological journey it can be acknowledged that whilst Newbigin's faith was "Christ-centered as to content, origin and effect" his ecclesiology was still incipient, "awaiting further development."[2]

What *is* being claimed in this chapter is that, besides Newbigin's general theological development, the SCM, his early Indian experience, and his role in the formation of the CSI, were critical in determining Newbigin's *ecclesiology*. Paul Löffler, who worked under Newbigin in the IMC, recalled how Newbigin would repeatedly refer to his Indian experiences "to an extent that I would judge them to be fundamental for his orientation."[3] This chapter seeks to show how these formative experiences prepared Newbigin for his future role in integration. As Newbigin reflected on the Indian church and sought to provide a rigorous theological defense for it he quickly rose, above his peers, to international prominence, making him the obvious choice as general secretary, who was prescient in the theological foundation he provided for integration.

The Influence of the Student Christian Movement

"Newbigin is most essentially an SCM man, he owes his Christianity . . . to the SCM."[4]

Newbigin's Involvement with the Student Christian Movement

From Newbigin's earliest publications it is evident that he understood his faith as a world faith, which, although of immense personal importance,

1. Newbigin, *Unfinished Agenda*, 28, 31.
2. Wainwright, *Newbigin*, 38.
3. Löffler was with the IMC from 1960, Löffler, email to Laing, 28/9/2007.
4. Andrew Walls, interview with Laing, 24/4/2009.

must also engage in the issues and concerns of the world.[5] Newbigin gained this perspective as an undergraduate at Cambridge University (1928–31) through the Student Christian Movement (SCM); and through his involvement with the SCM he was introduced to a wider network of Christian leaders with worldwide horizons.

The historian of the British evangelical movement, David Bebbington, notes that evangelicalism in Britain during the 1920s was marked by severe division. Although "[p]olarisation was by no means total, for co-operation between the wings, liberal and conservative, continued in a number of organizations. Yet division was sufficiently acute to cause schism in several Evangelical institutions."[6] Bebbington highlights several reasons for this division, chief being "conflicting estimates of the Bible," i.e. debate over the infallibility of scripture. It was over this issue that the Cambridge Inter-Collegiate Christian Union (CICCU) disaffiliated from the SCM in 1910.[7] Other issues driving division included the emergence of premillenialism, the holiness movement, responses to high Anglicanism, the ongoing debate on the relation between science and religion, the use of leisure—for some there was a need for "utter separation from everything that was questionable," and attitudes to the social dimension of the gospel—with many evangelicals repudiating their earlier engagement with social issues.[8] However, in contrast to the American situation the British response to these controversies was more tempered. "Fundamentalist controversies did exist in Britain, but they were storms in a teacup when compared with the blizzards of invective that swept contemporary America."[9] Unlike the stark polarization across the Atlantic, in Britain, "[t]he cleavage between conservative and liberals was far from absolute . . . There was therefore a broadening continuum of Evangelical opinion . . . rather than a simple separation into two camps."[10] But as the twentieth century

---

5. E.g., "In so far as the Church is not truly and deeply one the world over, demonstrating to the world a unity that can transcend all sectional aims, however lofty, it is not merely failing to take account of the plain facts of the world as it is to-day, it is also to that extent denying its own true nature and contradicting its own true witness." Lesslie Newbigin, "The Student Volunteer Missionary Union," in *The Christian Faith Today* (London: SCM, 1933) 98.

6. D. W. Bebbington, *Evangelicalism in Modern Britain: A History from the 1730s to the 1980s* (London: Routledge, 2002) 181.

7. Ibid., 188.

8. Ibid., 184–217.

9. Ibid., 227.

10. Ibid., 227–28.

progressed British evangelicalism became increasingly fragmented, and polarized between liberal and conservative wings as the influence of those able to hold a mediating position waned.[11]

One institutional expression of the disquiet amongst evangelicals was the division which occurred within the SCM with the InterVarsity Fellowship (IVF) forming as a consequence in 1927. Thus was as a result of the growing tension within the movement which had existed from the founding of the YMCA in 1844: "there had been among students an acute intellectual conflict between religious orthodoxy and a liberalism which sought accommodation with the claims of natural science."[12] The growing dissatisfaction which culminated in division "has been a tragic one, which has never been healed, and from which both sides have suffered. Gradually the positions have hardened, as they have become globalized, to the point where, all over the world today, the relation between liberals or ecumenists . . . on the one hand and evangelicals on the other is one of the most difficult there is."[13]

Whilst the trend was towards increasing polarization in the twentieth century, in the 1920s British evangelical responses were varied. David Goodhew's article on the history of the CICCU details the complexity of the institution's relationship with the SCM (and other bodies) at the time Newbigin went up to Cambridge to read economics.[14] During the 1920s the CICCU was wary of doctrinal compromise distancing itself from the SCM. Discord rumbled on, some seeking to take the CICCU in an increasingly conservative direction, whilst others sought its re-integration into the SCM fold. Goodhew's conclusion was the between the wars CICCU's main achievement "was to weather the storm" later benefiting from the new signs of life within evangelicalism.[15]

---

11. Ibid., 228, 253.

12. R. H. S. Boyd, *The Witness of the Student Christian Movement: "Church Ahead of the Church"* (London: SPCK, 2007) 25.

13. Ibid., 27. Newbigin likened the schism to that dividing the early church. Newbigin, "The Congregation as a Missionary Agency," 6/1972, BUL: DA29/4/3/12, 4. For a brief history of the CICCU-SCM division from the perspective of the CICCU, see O. R. Barclay and R. M. Horn, *From Cambridge to the World: 125 Years of Student Witness* (Leicester: InterVarsity, 2002) 130–33.

14. D. Goodhew, "The Rise of the Cambridge Inter-Collegiate Christian Union, 1910–1971," *Journal of Ecclesiastical History* 54:1 (2003).

15. Ibid., 72.

Earlier in the 1920s, when Stephen Neill and Max Warren were at Cambridge, both were able to hold office in both organizations.[16] However, such positions of dual allegiance were untenable by Newbigin's time, when the SCM was perceived as being increasingly liberal and the CICCU bolstering its credentials as an increasingly conservative body.[17] Gradually the CICCU reformed its organization to safeguard its conservative stance to the extent that it "was increasingly well adapted to withstand all suggestions of doctrinal shift."[18]

Newbigin recounts how, during his first year at Cambridge (in 1928) he was attracted to the SCM rather than to the evangelical CICCU. Friends made at Queens' College, who were in the SCM, were open about their faith but also open to difficult questions. This contrasted with the CICCU members, whom Newbigin sensed were trying to "get at" him.[19] And the SCM gave Newbigin a vision of a new world a "vision of something that could embrace the whole life of all the nations, that thrilled me and drew me to enquire about its source."[20]

"The SCM has always been a place where faith and doubt can struggle together," that is what attracted Newbigin to it: "I was brought to the Christian faith through the SCM, because it was willing to take me as I was, with all my doubts and questions, and to help me to wrestle with them as part of the fellowship."[21] After his first year at Cambridge, for part of his summer vacation Newbigin helped at a Quaker camp for miners in the south of Wales. Newbigin recalled a decisive event which was to shape his thinking for the remainder of his life. One night, whilst still awake Newbigin had a vision of the cross that was both cosmic and ecumenical, "the cross spanning the space between heaven and earth, between ideals and present realities, and with arms that embraced the whole world. I saw it as something which reached down to the most hopeless and sordid of human misery and yet promised life and victory. I was sure that night, in

---

16. Neill graduated from Cambridge in 1923, Warren in 1926. Barclay and Horn, *From Cambridge*, 130.

17. Goodhew, "CICCU," 66–67.

18. Ibid., 72.

19. Newbigin, *Unfinished Agenda*, 9–10.

20. Lesslie Newbigin, "An Address Given on the Occasion of the 75th Anniversary of the Formation of the Scottish Council of the SCM at Glasgow University Chapel, 15/2/1986," BUL: DA29/3/3/78, 2.

21. Ibid., 3.

a way I had never been before, that this was the clue that I must follow if I were to make any kind of sense of the world."[22]

Newbigin experienced the power of the cross both to save and to hold together in tension what often breaks down into polarities.[23] That event marked a decisive change in Newbigin from being "sceptical" and "unconvinced" to now being a "committed Christian" and an active member of the SCM.[24]

As Newbigin's commitment to the SCM grew he attended the SCM Swanwick conferences which were to open up a "new world" for him and showed him that he belonged to a "larger Christ" than he had ever imagined.[25] At his first Swanwick conference he accepted the invitation from Willie Tindal, the then national study secretary, to serve on the SCM staff on graduation. Newbigin served as the SCM Intercollegiate Secretary in Glasgow from 1931 until he took up theological studies at Cambridge in 1933. At the interview for this appointment he met Helen Henderson, who was working as a staff secretary for SCM covering Glasgow, Dundee and Aberdeen. They worked together in Glasgow and subsequently became engaged and then married on August 20th, 1936.

Whilst working in Glasgow Newbigin was influenced by the ministry of Archie Craig, the Chaplain of Glasgow University. Initially Newbigin stayed with Craig and through this an enduring friendship developed. Newbigin recorded how this was "the beginning of a friendship to which I owe more than I can ever say."[26] Through his almost daily visits to Craig, Newbigin records his debt stating that he received from Craig "a kind of theological training which was, I think, more significant than anything before or after."[27] Writing near the end of his own life Newbigin reflected on the impact that Craig's friendship had in shaping his theological perspective, stating that Craig was a "man whose importance in the lives of people was far greater than his tenure of public offices might suggest."[28] Craig's biographer understood their relationship as being that of a father

22. Newbigin, *Unfinished Agenda*, 11–12.

23. Paul Weston, interview with Laing, 11/9/2008.

24. Newbigin, *Unfinished Agenda*, 10, 13.

25. Newbigin, "75th Anniversary," 1.

26. Newbigin, *Unfinished Agenda*, 20.

27. Ibid., 21.

28. Newbigin, in his preface to the biography: E. Templeton, *God's February: A Life of Archie Craig, 1888–1985* (London: BCC/CCBI, 1991) ix.

to an adult son, "a relationship which meant an immense amount to him [Craig]."[29]

After his tenure in Glasgow Newbigin returned to Cambridge for theological studies (1933–36), and it was during this time that he became the president of the Cambridge SCM (1934–35). His ecumenical concerns were evident in his attempts to heal the ongoing rift between the SCM and the CICCU. Newbigin's perception was that the other side, the CICCU viewed SCM members as unbelievers and hence the SCM "was regarded as no legitimate part of the Christian scene."[30] In 1935, to commemorate the centenary of the "Cambridge Seven"—whose missionary service has inspired the formation of the Student Volunteer Missionary Union (SVMU)—special events were organized by the CICCU at Cambridge. Newbigin, as president of the SCM, pleaded that the SCM also be allowed to join the celebrations. But this attempt to heal old rifts was only met by "adamant refusal" from the CICCU president.[31] Whilst many Christians remained entrenched in their respective side of the ecumenical-evangelical divide Newbigin continued to demonstrate that he saw no dichotomy in his outworking of his understanding of the gospel. A belief that he held to consistently throughout his life.[32]

On the occasion of the seventy-fifth anniversary of the formation of the Scottish Council of the SCM, when Newbigin addressed the congregation of Glasgow University Chapel, he reflected on the form of Christianity the SCM had first introduced him to. He acknowledged his gratitude to the honest intellectual enquiry which was integral to the life of the SCM, where he was encouraged to ask fundamental questions.[33] Newbigin described how the creativity and intellectual rigor that the SCM fostered was due to the creative tension inherent in its structure. An organization can be defined by its boundary or by its centre. In the case of the SCM its boundary being the world and its centre being Christ. During some periods of its history the SCM was too focused on its centre, and became exclusively concerned with issues of personal piety. At other times the opposite extreme ensued when the SCM lost sight of its centre and, orientated towards the world, became simply another protest organization. But

29. Ibid., 166.

30. Newbigin, *Unfinished Agenda*, 14, 33.

31. Ibid., 33. During this time the CICCU were developing a clearer doctrinal basis as they sought to defend themselves from liberalism and high Anglicanism. Barclay and Horn, *From Cambridge*, chs. 6–7.

32. Newbigin, "Cross-Currents," 146.

33. Newbigin, "75th Anniversary," 3.

the SCM was at its best during the times when it held these two together, a vivid devotion to Christ with a concern for the world.[34] Newbigin was to imbibe these dual concerns from the SCM and to demonstrate throughout his life the creativity that comes from holding them together.

Ecumenical Introductions

The SCM was the incubator for the ecumenical leadership of Newbigin's generation. Newbigin commented, on reading Tissington Tatlow's history of the SCM,[35] "Almost every one of its leaders in all parts of the world had been nurtured in the SCM."[36] As president at Cambridge it was Newbigin's "joy to receive and entertain" a "great succession of Christian leaders"; and through the SCM Newbigin was introduced to the wider network of the World Student Christian Federation (WSCF):[37] "One of the joys of being born into the Christian faith through the SCM was that one was from the beginning part of an ecumenical family."[38]

Consequently Newbigin was personally influenced by such ecumenical leaders as John Mott, William Temple, Joe Oldham, Hendrik Kraemer, Hanns Lilje, Charles Andrews, John Groser, Leslie Weatherhead, Nathaniel Micklem, Nicholas Zernov, and HG Wood,[39] perhaps the most influential in this distinguished list being Mott,[40] Temple, and Oldham. According to Newbigin it was Archbishop Temple who was to have the greatest influence on his generation of students. Through these personal encounters Newbigin was to learn firsthand from Temple of his vision of the ecumenical movement and of the fledgling plans for a world organization of the churches to follow the Oxford and Edinburgh meetings of 1937.[41]

---

34. Newbigin, "75th Anniversary," 4.

35. T. Tatlow, *The Story of the Student Christian Movement of Great Britain and Ireland* (London: SCM, 1933).

36. Newbigin, "75th Anniversary," 1.

37. For a history of the WSCF, see P. A. Potter and T. Wieser, *Seeking and Serving the Truth: The First Hundred Years of the World Student Christian Federation* (Geneva: WCC, 1997).

38. Newbigin, *Unfinished Agenda*, 72.

39. Ibid., 33.

40. Mott's biography records how Mott visited Oxford and Cambridge during this time with "successful" results and "carried tremendous weight as a speaker and evangelist." C. H. Hopkins, *John R. Mott, 1865–1955: A Biography* (Grand Rapids: Eerdmans, 1979) 681.

41. Newbigin, *Unfinished Agenda*, 33.

Newbigin recounted how Oldham was a frequent visitor to Cambridge. At the Edinburgh Quadrennial of the SCM in 1933 Newbigin remembered the "profound and prophetic address" given by Oldham. Speaking at what was a missionary conference he made the audience aware—and perhaps Newbigin for the first time—that "Christian" Europe had made a radical departure from Christianity in the Enlightenment and was now to be regarded as a mission field itself.[42] Oldham continued to be in regular contact with Newbigin as he prepared for the Oxford Conference (1937) on 'Church, Community and State.' Through these encounters Oldham came to the realization that Newbigin would be a valuable asset for the conference[43] and made prolonged—but unsuccessful—efforts to recruit his help and dissuade him from missionary service with the Church of Scotland.[44]

Newbigin's developing ecumenical vision of the church was augmented by his precocious reading of the *International Review of Missions*, the first theological periodical he was to subscribe to. He also avidly read the volumes from the International Missionary Council (IMC) conference at Tambaram (1938).[45] Once in India the SCM was an obvious network through which Newbigin could develop friendships and "the influence of the SCM on the Plans of Union of both CSI and CNI was very great."[46]

The SCM Influence

The SCM, "the church ahead of the church," made a major contribution to Newbigin's ecclesiology giving him a vision of the church which was

42. Ibid., 26–27. J. H. Oldham, "Faith in God and Faith in Man," in *The Christian Faith Today* (London: SCM, 1933). This address by Oldham was one of the earliest challenges to develop a genuinely missionary encounter with post-Enlightenment European civilization, and one which Newbigin remembered for the rest of his life. K. W. Clements, *Faith on the Frontier: A Life of J. H. Oldham* (Edinburgh: T. & T. Clark, 1999) 279.

43. Newbigin's rise in prominence at this time led McCaughey to state that he "was to be one of the most influential figures in the British SCM." J. D. McCaughey, *Christian Obedience in the University: Studies in the Life of the Student Christian Movement of Great Britain and Ireland, 1930–1950* (London: SCM, 1958) 45.

44. Oldham's zeal to recruit Newbigin was such that he even pursued the Newbigins on their honeymoon: Newbigin, *Unfinished Agenda*, 37–38. Clements, *Oldham*, 311. But Oldham's efforts failed, and the Newbigins left for India on 26/9/1936.

45. Newbigin, "75th Anniversary," 2.

46. Robin Boyd noted that amongst Newbigin's Indian friends, M. M. Thomas, Chandran Devanesen, and Stanley Samartha were all members of the SCM. Boyd, email to Laing, 11/06/2007.

forward looking, dynamic, and engaged with the world. "Newbigin meets church, if not *the church*, in meaningful terms first in the SCM."[47] The SCM vision of the church contrasted with Newbigin's negative perception of the Western church. Subsequent to Newbigin's SCM days this vision of the church was confirmed in Newbigin's experience of the Indian church. Negotiating the formation of the Church of South India (CSI) gave New-bigin a framework to develop his ecclesiology. Key elements being the for-ward orientation of the church, the church being defined by the process of becoming, rather than looking backwards to Western traditions, and that the church is missionary in its essential nature.[48]

Another key lesson Newbigin learned from the SCM was on the rela tionship between mission and unity: "From the beginning of my disciple-ship the SCM taught me to see unity and mission as two sides of a single commitment."[49] This conviction was at the heart of Newbigin's theological justification for the integration of the IMC with the WCC: "The connec-tion between the movement for Christian reunion and the movement for world evangelization is of the deepest possible character. The two things are the two outward signs of a return to the heart of the Gospel itself."[50] Concerning the method for integration, as with the CSI formation, New-bigin repeatedly emphasized the importance of the local and regional over the national or international. Again this emphasis can be directly traced to the SCM: "I was still convinced of the truth I had learned in the Cam-bridge SCM—that the health of the body depends upon the health of the smallest units."[51]

But the SCM also exerted a negative influence upon Newbigin. The schism between the SCM and the IVF, between "ecumenicals" and "evan-gelicals," meant that Newbigin was firmly identified as belonging to the ecumenical camp, he was thus perceived with suspicion, even as a "figure of fear" by evangelicals.[52]

Through the SCM Newbigin became a "diligent student of the bible" to the extent that Wilbert Shenk remarked that Newbigin was

---

47. Walls, interview, 24/4/2009.

48. Newbigin, *Reunion*.

49. Newbigin, *Unfinished Agenda*, 251.

50. Newbigin, *Reunion*, 19.

51. Newbigin, *Unfinished Agenda*, 105.

52. Walls, interview, 24/4/2009. It was only towards the end of his life that Newbi-gin was embraced by evangelicalism.

incomparable as a "master of biblical theology."[53] Rather than be shaped by any theological system Newbigin "was thoroughly a biblical thinker," holding lightly to Calvinism.[54] The influences Newbigin imbued from the SCM were modified by Newbigin's self-directed theological study at Cambridge. By avoiding the Tripos exam he was able to pursue what really interested him. Most significant was his study of James Denney's commentary on Romans,[55] through which Newbigin developed a clear understanding of Christ's atonement. This study marked a "turning point" in his theological journey: "I began the study as a typical liberal. I ended it with a strong conviction about 'the finished work of Christ,' about the centrality and objectivity of the atonement accomplished on Calvary."[56] These convictions on the gospel led him to be "totally committed" as an ecumenist.[57]

Newbigin and the Indian Church

The second formative influence was Newbigin's introduction to the Indian church. As a young missionary Newbigin experienced the dramatic growth of village churches in rural Tamil Nadu. Already primed by the SCM, these experiences provided Newbigin with a definitive model of the church—orientated towards the world and missionary in its essential nature.[58] Through these churches Newbigin believed he was witnessing a recovery in the relationship between mission and church. This contrasted with the dichotomous and problematic relationship between the Indian church and Foreign Mission of the Church of Scotland (FM) which Newbigin faced as a missionary. These formative years in India imbued Newbigin with a vision of the church which he carried with him to integration. In contrast, he rarely spoke of the Western church except to reprimand it for abandoning its missionary nature and being woefully fragmented.

53. Wilbert Shenk, interview with Laing, 1/11/2006.

54. Ibid.

55. J. Denney, *St. Paul's Epistle to the Romans*, in vol. 2 of *The Expositor's Greek Testament* (London: Hodder & Stoughton, 1901). For Newbigin to read Denney was "unusual," and would not have been initiated by a college professor. Walls, interview, 24/4/2009.

56. Convictions which Newbigin maintained throughout his life. Newbigin, *Unfinished Agenda*, 30.

57. Weston, interview, 11/9/2008.

58. Newbigin would repeatedly return to this defining model of the church. E.g., Lesslie Newbigin, *Mission in Christ's Way: Bible Studies* (Geneva: WCC, 1987) 23.

The Newbigins were missionaries with the Church of Scotland (CofS), serving in the Madras district of South India from 1936.[59] For the majority of that time Newbigin served as the "district missionary" in Kanchipuram, Madras District until furlough in 1946. During this period there was considerable correspondence between Newbigin and the Rev Alexander S Kydd. Kydd served as the general secretary of the Foreign Mission Committee of the Church of Scotland (FMC) from 1931 until forced to retire due to illness in 1945.[60] This archival material—which to date has not been utilized—provides an early insight into Newbigin's developing vision of the church formed as India prepared for independence.

By way of background it is important to remember that this period was a difficult one for the international mission of the CofS. There was retrenchment, reduction in missionary numbers, problems in recruiting missionaries and accumulative financial deficits. These deficits, because of their persistent nature, caused the FMC to even consider the total abandonment of one of its fields, or alternatively across the board reduction to their work. Kydd lamented: "I do not want to be too gloomy, but I feel very doubtful about the financial position getting markedly better in the near future and by 'near' I mean within ten years . . . The truth about the situation into which the country and Empire has moved is only gradually dawning upon us."[61]

Living Epistles

Although he had just arrived in India, due to a serious leg injury Newbigin was invalided home in late 1937, and from June of 1938, *inter alia*, was working as the Candidates Secretary for the FMC during his recuperation. During this time he edited *Living Epistles*.[62] This report, based on the

59. For Newbigin's personal account, see Newbigin, *Unfinished Agenda*, chs. 5–8.

60. The 1945 FMC report records the committee's regret over Kydd's illness and an appreciation of his service. He was succeeded by the Reverend J. W. C. Dougall, "Report of the Foreign Mission Committee for 1945," in *Reports to the General Assembly of the Church of Scotland* (Edinburgh: W. Blackwood, 1946) 292–95. Kydd's obituary appeared in *The Scotsman*, 19/7/1950, p. 3; digital archive, online: http://edu.archive.scotsman.com/article.cfm?id=TSC/1950/07/19/Ar00307.

61. Kydd to Newbigin 3/2/1940, NLS: Acc7548/A23. For Kydd's annual report, see "Report of the Foreign Mission Committee," in *Reports to the General Assembly of the Church of Scotland* (Edinburgh: W. Blackwood, 1936–1946).

62. Lesslie Newbigin, *Living Epistles: Impressions of the Foreign Mission Work of the Church of Scotland in 1938* (Edinburgh: Church of Scotland Foreign Missions Committee, 1939). Although the report was compiled and edited by Newbigin, it was

annual reports of several hundred missionaries, was published for the General Assembly and for sale in the churches; its target audience being the grassroots supporters of the FM in the local congregations.

Although *Living Epistles* was written for a popular audience, the booklet demonstrated Newbigin's prescience in his assessment of the future relationship between missions and the indigenous churches. Newbigin's foreword in *Living Epistles* focused on the profound growth of the "indigenous church" rather than the FM—it is noteworthy that Newbigin used this term and refrained from using the accepted term "younger church." Newbigin, influenced by his reading of Hendrick Kraemer,[63] already understood the form of mission in which "the Church thought of the world in regional terms, and of missionary work as a kind of 'colonizing' activity" as being anachronistic, the thinking of a previous generation.[64] The redundancy of such a model was exposed in the decline of Christianity in the West: "the moral and spiritual unity of the West has been so shattered by the manifest departure of the majority of its inhabitants from any faith in God as He is revealed in Jesus Christ."[65] Already by 1939 Newbigin (in contrast to Kydd) has moved from understanding mission directionally, in terms of giving and receiving. After the IMC Tambaram conference it "became abundantly manifest that the problems facing the Church all over the world are identical. In every land, 'Christian' and non-Christian alike, the Church is in a minority."[66] Newbigin understood that, in the early twentieth century, a fundamental shift had taken place away from the association of land with Christian faith, the church wherever it was located, was in a missionary situation.

Newbigin thus spoke of a new "sense of community" with the indigenous church, aware of "this new perception of the old truth that we without them, and they without us, shall not be made perfect."[67] At the commencement of his missionary career Newbigin had moved beyond the prevalent paternalistic language of the "younger church" which was dependent upon the "older church," to return to the more fundamental Pauline image of mutuality, and co-dependency.

---

published as an official document from the FMC.

63. H. Kraemer, *The Christian Message in a Non-Christian World* (London: Edinburgh House Press, 1938).

64. Newbigin, *Living Epistles*, 3.

65. Ibid.

66. Ibid., 4.

67. Ibid., 6.

Newbigin's Church-Centric Approach

But how was that new relationship with the indigenous church to be worked out in practice? Back in India Newbigin was struck by the rapid church growth occurring in rural villages, which was seemingly independent of the FM. For example the birth and development of a church in a remote "outcaste" village called Thirupanamur in which, "from the first the initiative was taken by the villagers, not by us."[68] This repeated pattern of the "spontaneous" expansion of village churches profoundly influenced Newbigin: "In my mind at least there were visions of a new missionary movement reaching out from that village to the untouched areas round about it, based not on a new effort from the headquarters, but on the new-found faith and conviction of the village people themselves."[69] From these experiences Newbigin understood that his role as a missionary was to *respond* to the village initiative. His rationale being that the work of the gospel was being prosecuted by divine agency rather than through any human agency, centered in the local or international headquarters of the FM.[70]

Concerning Newbigin's own methodology in village evangelism, with hindsight he recognized similarities and his indebtedness to Karl Barth. Rather than seek some rational common ground between himself as a Westerner and Hindus in the villages by an appeal to an apologetic which sought stability external to the gospel, Newbigin instead was unapologetic about speaking from within the framework of the gospel, narrating the story of which he believed he was a part.[71]

Having recognized that the centers for church growth lay in the villages, Newbigin endeavored to facilitate that growth. Rather than extracting key Christian converts from their context to train them in mission compounds, Newbigin did the reverse. During the quieter (but hotter) part of the agricultural year, rather than retreat to the cooler climes of Kodaikanal in the Nilgiri Mountains—the missionary norm—Newbigin initiated village camps: "The whole thing aims at creating the conditions

---

68. Newbigin to Kydd, 28/1/1940, NLS: Acc7548/B130.

69. Ibid. A more generalized account of the growth of such churches, stripped of geographic references, can be found in Newbigin's influential work *A South India Diary* (London: SCM, 1951). This portrait of the non-Western church opened a new world for many in the West.

70. At this early stage in his career, Newbigin did not attribute his indebtedness to Roland Allen. Later, he acknowledged that he was attempting to apply Allen's ideas.

71. Weston, interview, 11/9/2008.

in which the village churches can be as far as possible self-supporting, by laying the maximum possible responsibility on the shoulders of the ordinary, barely literate, but often shrewd and sensible, subaiyan [village elder]. It means a conception of the Church which is extremely primitive as far as all the outward things go—but which at least is soundly based on the real condition of the people."[72]

For Newbigin, on the basis of his theological convictions, historical entities needed to be realigned. To this end he advocated a more general change in mission policy with new initiatives: "[in] training in worship for the Christian groups; training lay leadership by means of hot-weather retreat courses; [and] strengthening the evangelistic staff."[73] Fundamental to facilitating this change in emphasis was Newbigin's realization of the essential role of women, both missionary and national.[74]

These early missionary experiences were to be determinative for Newbigin. At both a practical and theological level Newbigin continued to maintain his church-centric focus. Early in the correspondence with Kydd it becomes evident that Newbigin was aware that the Indian church was growing in spite of, rather than because of, the efforts of the CofS. This led to protracted discussion with Kydd and more widely within IMC circles on the nature and priorities which should determine the inevitable devolution to the "younger church."[75]

For the FMC maintenance of prestigious institutions was a central priority. In contrast to prevalent missionary attitudes which saw the urban institutional work of the mission as being central, Newbigin took a different tack. He argued that the role of the district missionary should be abolished in non-pioneering situations as the perpetuation of this model was detrimental to the development of an indigenous church. Newbigin recognized that what was considered peripheral and insignificant—the village work—should be given central priority to facilitate "building up the church in the only place where it is growing."[76]

Newbigin reasoned that rather than the FM facilitating the growth of the church, its policy of city based institutions was profoundly detrimental to the village church. Through education and the promise of better job prospects the best and brightest from the village were lured into mission

72. Newbigin to Kydd 3/5/1940, NLS: Acc7548/B130.

73. Newbigin to Kydd 27/12/1939, NLS: Acc7548/ B130.

74. Ibid.

75. This correspondence is in NLS: Acc7548/A24–27; B130.

76. Newbigin to Kydd 27/12/1939, NLS: Acc7548/B130.

institutions. This was doubly detrimental, in that it drained leadership from the true centers of church growth and, having done so, then stunted their development by placing them in unhealthy city churches, where energy was dissipated in internal strife rather than harnessed for evangelism.[77] Paramount for Newbigin was the need to facilitate the growth of the village churches because: "[I]t does seem that the village Church is the place where a truly indigenous Christianity can come into being—not the indigenousness of Western enthusiasts for indigenousness, but the real indigenousness of Indian Christians slowly developing their own modes of expression."[78]

Newbigin recognized the problematic relationship between mission and church which the mission policy of the FMC, in their relationship with the Indian church, had established: "The Mission [Council] employs catechists and evangelists and runs big schools, hospitals etc. The [Indian] Church is poor and pays small salaries. The Mission is rich and pays big ones. The missionaries are the most powerful people in the Christian community. They accept the authority of the Mission over themselves, but not the authority of the Church. The Mission controls the livelihood of most of the leading members of the Church, but has no official relationship to the courts of the Church."[79]

Newbigin argued that the historical reality of the missionary movement, in this case the FM, had produced and then perpetuated this dichotomy between mission and church. Newbigin understood this to the outworking of a defective ecclesiology: "The fundamental reason is that it is based on a false doctrine of the Church. The idea of a permanent dichotomy of Church and Mission as two separate organizations is totally foreign to the NT and destructive of any growth in Churchmanship."[80] This dichotomy was alien to Newbigin's reading of the NT which held the church as central: "The life of the Church is radically corrupted if it is separated from the missionary task, and evangelistic effort is corrupted if it does not spring from the Church and lead back into the Church."[81] Determinative for Newbigin was his theological understanding that: "The Church exists by mission and mission is a function of the Church. A per-

---

77. Newbigin to Kydd 26/7/1941, NLS: Acc7548/B130.

78. Ibid.

79. Lesslie Newbigin, "Relation of Older and Younger Churches in India: Uncensored Remarks," 1947, NLS: Acc7548/B43, 1.

80. Ibid.

81. Ibid.

manent organizational dichotomy of Church and Mission is [therefore] intolerable."[82]

Here Newbigin, from his firsthand experience is focusing on the dichotomy that mission organizations have created on the "mission fields." The outcome of a dichotomous relationship between foreign missions and the Indian church occurred regardless of the actual organization of the mission organization.

In the case of the CofS the mission remained wholly accountable to the church, this being expressed in the FMC's total subservience to the General Assembly. This contrasted with English or American voluntaryist societies which operated largely independently from the "home church." Regardless of a mission's relationship to its "home church" Newbigin was critical of all agencies in perpetuating a dichotomy *on the field* between their mission work and the indigenous church.

Newbigin identified several consequences from the separation of mission from the church. First, the "Development of a type of self-sufficient, introverted congregation, lacking all sense of the Church catholic, priding itself chiefly on its ability to pay its pastor, and disclaiming responsibility for missionary work around it."[83] Newbigin was critical of the prevalent assumption in mission theory that the objective of a mission organization was to establish churches according to the three-selfs principle:[84] "Our thought of the Church was wrong because we began from the principle of self-support and produced an emaciated affair with many of the full functions of a Church reserved for the Mission, instead of starting with the biblical and apostolic ideal of one catholic Church in which we and they are one."[85] The church, the world over, is one, and together shares a common orientation of facing outwards towards the world. Newbigin argued that the Pauline model was for churches to cooperate in partnership rather than aim at disparate and isolating self-sufficiency.

82. Ibid., 3.

83. Ibid., 1.

84. History attributes Henry Venn and Rufus Anderson with independently formulating that newly established churches should become self-supporting, self-governing, and self-propagating. W.R. Shenk, "Rufus Anderson and Henry Venn: A Special Relationship?" *IBMR* 5:4 (1981). Missionary commitment to this *principle* continued into the Edwardian period. B. Stanley, "The Remedy Lies with Themselves: Edinburgh 1910 on the Self-Supporting Indigenous Church," in *Yale-Edinburgh Group on the History of the Missionary Movement and Non-Western Christianity* (Edinburgh: July 2004) 1.

85. Newbigin, "Uncensored Remarks," 2.

The second consequence Newbigin cited was the failure to develop an adequate ministry. The mission policy of the CofS was actually undermining the ministry of the indigenous church. The "organizational dichotomy" between church and mission was expressed by the office of the district missionary who operated independently of the Indian church. The result of this was that key positions sought after by the best educated and most able Indian Christians were not as pastors but as administrators and mission employed managers. Newbigin asserted that, "This is understandable, for we missionaries have been predominately not pastors and evangelists, but administrators, and the typical position of a missionary is not in a pulpit but behind a big desk."[86] Newbigin maintained that a minister's central focus should be to do pastoral work and evangelism rather than become a kind of "office-wallah that most district missionaries become"; that the "district missionary [wa]s an anachronism who ought to be abolished."[87] The bureaucratization that missions brought had a disastrous impact on the pastorate: "Consequently all the Pastors have this ambition, to get out of the Pastorate—which is very much a slave's job—into the position of the Circle Chairman [of the mission]."[88] Newbigin was concerned to recover the importance and biblical understanding of the scope of the ordained ministry which he proposed would enable these organizational problems to be overcome.

Third, Newbigin was critical of the "'Overseas Presbyteries' of the CofS [operating] alongside the courts of the Indian Church."[89] CofS missionaries understood themselves to be under the authority of the CofS through the Overseas Presbytery of the CofS, rather than being accountable to the Indian church. This parallel, independent existence undermined the authority of the Indian church. Newbigin had personally witnessed the authority of the Indian church being disregarded by a CofS missionary colleague who stated that he was only under the jurisdiction of the CofS— an incident which profoundly affected his attitude to the authority of the Indian church.[90]

At a time when mission agencies were devolving responsibility and authority to the Indian church Newbigin argued that all foreign personnel should also be under the full authority of the indigenous church. Acting

---

86. Newbigin to Kydd 13/6/1943, NLS: Acc7548/B130.

87. Newbigin to Kydd 11/6/1942, NLS: Acc7548/B130.

88. Newbigin to Kydd 13/6/1943, NLS: Acc7548/B130.

89. Newbigin, "Uncensored Remarks," 1.

90. Newbigin, *Unfinished Agenda*, 72.

upon this conviction, in an unprecedented and pioneering move Newbigin—with Revs. Ellis O. Shaw and Robert P. Mackenzie—applied for full membership of Indian church and relinquished any anomalous claims to simultaneously be accountable to a "higher jurisdiction"—the Overseas Presbytery of the CofS. In the dichotomy that existed between the mission and the church, Newbigin as a *missionary*, was aligning himself with the indigenous church rather than to his mission. As this was unprecedented, the actual process of this change of allegiance was a rather protracted affair passing through several CofS committees and being discussed at the General Assembly before CofS approval was finally given.[91] Newbigin's initiative demonstrated that missionaries were prepared to recognize the authority of the Indian church, that the proper place of mission (and missionaries) was in *subservience* to the national church. For the Indian church it demonstrated a new era in missionary deployment which coincided with Indian independence from colonial rule.

The fourth consequence of the dichotomy, according to Newbigin, was the current stalemate in the process of devolution. Newbigin argued that although the FM, in principal, proposed to be church-centric, in reality the FM: "shrank from handing over a fine well-run institution to a body so weak and unimpressive as this 'Indian Church.' We thought in terms of 'Us' and 'Them,' and 'they' were clearly inadequate for the job."[92] Newbigin posited that the source of this dichotomous thinking again stemmed from a defective ecclesiology.

This early correspondence shows that Newbigin, from the *outset* of his missionary career was articulating a missionary ecclesiology, in which the church was central to his thinking. Newbigin started from the *theological* presupposition that mission and church belonged together. From that premise he asserted that the historical divorce between them on the mission field was fundamentally due to an errant ecclesiology. His missionary experience, in which he wrestled with the historical legacy of the dichotomy between mission and church, served to reinforce and clarify these presuppositions as he sought an organizational expression of his theological convictions.[93] The seemingly insignificant and unimport-

91. A Special Committee was established to confer with the General Administration Committee, the Inter-Church Relations Committee and the FMC, with a view to the matter being brought before the General Assembly for decision. Minute 7279, 21/3/1944, NLS: Dep298/Box191.

92. Newbigin, "Uncensored Remarks," 2.

93. That Newbigin acknowledged this in his ecclesiology at the *start* of his missionary career contradicts the assertion made by Michael Goheen. Goheen argues that

ant village churches gave Newbigin an enduring vision of the church—a non-Western missionary church which he contrasted with the stagnant, introverted Western church. In his emphasis on decentralized control, and the vitality of the village church one is reminded of the recurring refrain Newbigin imbued from formative SCM influences: "that the health of the body depends upon the health of the smallest units."[94] Newbigin would bring these early experiences and convictions to his work in integrating the IMC with the WCC, where his vision emphasized decentralization and regionalization rather than a burgeoning administration centered in Geneva.

The Formation of the Church of South India

The third factor preparing Newbigin for his international leadership of the IMC was his involvement in the Church of South India (CSI) negotiations. The formation of the CSI in 1947 was looked upon with great interest around the world, particularly as it pioneered the reunion of episcopal with non-episcopal churches. It not only affected India but reverberated globally, and especially it challenged old assumptions within the Western church. At the formation of the CSI there was the bright hope that the scheme would prove to be a catalyst for other reunion schemes: "I vividly remember how firmly we believed in those exciting days that our union in India would open the way for similar unions all over the world."[95]

Newbigin, in his young maturity, hit the crest, coming late to the CSI negotiations. Newbigin's ecclesiology was very much shaped by the CSI, an Asian church which has no equivalent in Western experience. The CSI was forward looking, always in the process of formation. Newbigin himself is a product of these developments. His experience and ideas of the church are formed first through the SCM and secondly by his experiences in South India.

Newbigin's model of the church, formed in the non-Western world, clashed with those holding to the historical church, his greatest difficulty being with Anglo-Catholic ecclesiology. His experience (and defense) of the Indian church prepared him for the ecumenical agenda on a world

Newbigin's ecclesiology shifted "paradigm" from that of a Christendom to a missionary ecclesiology *during* his missionary career. Goheen, *As the Father*, ch. 2.

94. Newbigin, *Unfinished Agenda*, 105.

95. Lesslie Newbigin, "The Basis and the Forms of Unity," *Mid-Stream: The Ecumenical Movement Today* 23 (1984) 1.

scale. The Indian church, which was missionary and profoundly committed to unity, provided Newbigin with a starting point on these key themes on which he later built his theology for the integration of the IMC with the WCC.

His experience of the formation of the CSI and his subsequent reflections on that led him to believe that, in South India, beyond the abnormal ecclesiology of Christendom, he was partaking in a recovery of ecclesiology. He could discern two key aspects in this recovery. First, that the church was missionary, the church was orientated towards the world, rather than towards itself. The second aspect recovered was that churches orientated towards the world also recovered a profound concern to overcome their divisions and become organically united—one visible body in each location.

Newbigin's Involvement in the South India Scheme

Newbigin entered into the South India Scheme for Church Union (SIS) late in its history and at a time when the process was languishing. Although a relatively young and inexperienced missionary he was quickly entrusted with considerable responsibility. In 1942 Newbigin was invited to succeed Rev. Dr. J. H. Maclean[96] as convener of the Union Committee of the Madras Church Council, Maclean nominating Newbigin as his successor.[97] A year later Newbigin was elected convener of the Union Committee for the whole of the South India United Church (SIUC) at a time of weariness and general despondency about the scheme.[98]

As chairman of the SIUC committee on union Newbigin was aware, that for the scheme to succeed, he must fight for it on three fronts: first, in India, the arguments for union needed to be disseminated to the level of the grassroots of the church, shifting the centre of gravity away from missionary domination, second, the importing of Western ecclesiastical debate into India needed to be curtailed, and third, internationally, the "propaganda" of Anglo-Catholic opposition to the scheme needed to be countered.

To enable the scheme to succeed, Newbigin appealed to the Church of Scotland and the American Board of Commissioners for Foreign

96. Maclean was a CofS missionary and Newbigin's predecessor as district missionary at Kanchipuram.

97. Maclean to Newbigin, 15/10/1942, BUL: DA29/2/4/16.

98. Newbigin, *Unfinished Agenda*, 74.

Missions for funds to allow the reports of the proposed union to be translated into Tamil and Telugu in preparation for the SIUC assembly in 1944. To support his case he cited the result from the Madras Church Council: "We badly lack machinery for adequate discussion of the Scheme in the vernaculars. The Scheme itself has never ever been translated. The discussion has therefore been dominated by missionaries. At last year's Madras Church Council I created a record by giving the entire report in Tamil and having the debate on it in Tamil. We got, as you know, a thumping majority for union, and several Indians told me it was the first time they had ever understood what the issues were. I know that this is symptomatic of a much wider situation."[99]

Newbigin's chairmanship was decisive in enabling the debate to move beyond the confines of English to reach ordinary South Indian Christians. Early calls for union had been Indian initiatives.[100] But subsequent missionary involvement had entangled the debate in problems inherent within Western ecclesiology; in particular, the relation between episcopally and non-episcopally ordered churches, and how they could be united to the satisfaction of the parent churches. The CSI was the pioneer in bringing together episcopal and non-episcopal churches, overcoming the biggest division that had beset the Protestant church.

One of the tactics of attack against the union scheme, employed by the Anglo-Catholics, was to ridicule it as being theologically insufficient: "A certain amount of somewhat lofty scorn seems to be being sprinkled on the Scheme of Union by those in the West who regard it as theologically inadequate."[101] Whilst in India Newbigin called for international support to combat Anglo-Catholic attacks on the union scheme.[102] Later he was to enter the fray, becoming the main international advocate of the scheme, representing the scheme at various Anglican conferences and consultations.[103] Newbigin's role effectively became that of international ambassador for the SIS.

---

99. Newbigin to Kydd, 13/9/1943, NLS: Acc7548/B130.

100. For a history, see B. Sundkler, *Church of South India: The Movement towards Union, 1900–1947* (London: Lutterworth, 1954).

101. Newbigin to "Dear Friends" [circular letter], October 1944, NLS: Acc7548/C1.

102. For details, see M. T. B. Laing, "The Advocates and Opponents of Church Union in South India: Perceptions and Portrayals of 'the Other,'" in *Yale-Edinburgh Group on the History of the Missionary Movement and Non-Western Christianity* (New College, University of Edinburgh: 2008).

103. Described in Newbigin, *Unfinished Agenda*, ch. 11.

The Reunion of the Church

In response to Anglo-Catholic opposition, Newbigin developed his theological defense of the SIS, in *The Reunion of the Church*,[104] in which he mainly dealt with the struggle to reconcile Catholic and Protestant ecclesiologies.

Newbigin observed the impetus for mission and unity that emerged, unexpectedly, from the missionary practice of comity.[105] The emergence of those concerns in the South Indian church led Newbigin to believe that he was partaking in a recovery of ecclesiology. If the events in South India were truly a "recovery of the heart of the gospel" as Newbigin understood them to be, then they had implications beyond the remit of South India, they were of import for the global church. The recovery of these twin concerns enabled Newbigin to critique the abnormal ecclesiology of Christendom which had grown complacent about both mission and unity.

For Newbigin church unity had to be organic: "As the Body of Christ, the church is an organism 'joined and knit together by every joint with which it is supplied when each part is working properly' (Eph 4:16). Its unity is therefore properly described as organic."[106] This was a conviction that he held throughout his life: "for so long as I have breath, I must continue to confess my belief that God intends his Church to be—in the words of the Lambeth Appeal—'an outward, visible and united society.'"[107]

Unity was never to be understood as a goal in and of itself, but was for the purpose of mission. Newbigin's "primary concern in developing, articulating, and defending this view of unity was that the church might remain true to its missionary nature."[108] The form of organic unity embodied in the CSI was, for Newbigin, the best recovery of unity that had yet been devised; other alternative forms of union such as the Ceylon scheme and the North India scheme proffered more problematic solutions, particularly to the question of how to unite episcopal with non-episcopal

---

104. Newbigin, *Reunion*.

105. The following are the main references in Newbigin's writing on comity: Ibid., 1–25; Newbigin, "Unity and Mission," *Covenant Quarterly* 19 (1961); Newbigin, "Missions in an Ecumenical Perspective," 1962 (WCC, Ecumenical Centre Library: Geneva); Newbigin, "Cooperation and Unity."

106. Lesslie Newbigin, "Union, Organic," in *Dictionary of the Ecumenical Movement*, ed. N. Lossky, J. M. Bonino, and J. Pobee (Geneva: WCC, 1991) 1028.

107. Newbigin, *Unfinished Agenda*, 253.

108. Goheen, *As the Father*, 201.

churches.[109] Newbigin's advocacy of the SIS scheme led him into prolonged debate with the Anglican Church on the best solution to disunity. His dual concern for unity *and* mission undergirded and was foundational to his detailed defense of the SIS.

For the "younger churches" not to respond to the theological impetus for unity that comes from the practice of comity, but rather ape Western denominationalism would "be the public denial of the Gospel which we preach, the good news of Him who, being lifted up, will draw all men to Himself."[110] "It is not possible to account for the contentment with the divisions of the Church except upon the basis of a loss of the conviction that the Church exists to bring all men to Christ. There is the closest possible connection between the acceptance of the missionary obligation and the acceptance of the obligation of unity. That which makes the Church one is what makes it a mission to the world."[111]

Newbigin argued that a static definition of the church which only states what the church *is* without also proposing what the church is *becoming* sustains this impasse between God's will for episcopacy and the reality of non-episcopal church traditions. A central method in Newbigin's argument for reconciliation is to apply Paul's theology of justification by faith collectively to the church. "Only in terms of the mystery of justification by faith, of the God who calleth things that are not as though they were, is the dilemma to be resolved. The central purpose of this book [*Reunion of the Church*] was to place the discussion of the question of Church union in that perspective."[112]

In the age of the *eschaton*, the Spirit enables the church to witness, to the ends of the earth, and until the end of time. The perspective of the *eschaton* enables the church to live with the inherent tension of being holy and sinful; and of defining itself in terms of what it is, and *also* in terms of what it is becoming. "This acceptance of a real end means that the dimension of time is a reality within the life of the Church."[113] This theology of time was reflected in the constitution of the CSI which explicitly con-

109. The Church of North India and the Church of Pakistan were inaugurated in 1970; negotiations to unite the Ceylon Church collapsed.

110. Newbigin, *Reunion*, 21.

111. Ibid., 11.

112. Ibid., xvi, xxvii, xxxiv. This critical point was missed by all reviewers of the 1948 edition, except for one, who complained that it did not belong to a book on the church. Newbigin thus felt justified in publishing a second edition, hoping that, this time, his central thesis would be understood.

113. Newbigin, *Household of God*, 133.

fessed that the church is not what it ought to be—it is in process.[114] The CSI constitution acknowledged the theological principle that the church was provisional, a temporary construct.[115] The church, caught up in the dynamic work of the Spirit, accepted that it was incomplete and open to change: "If the Church is the sign and fruit and instrument of Christ's purpose to draw all men to Himself; . . . and if the ultimate purpose is the union in one fellowship of all who accept Christ as Lord; then movement belongs to the very nature of the Church. It is, in its very nature, a pilgrim people."[116]

The Household of God

Encouraged by others, Newbigin sought to release the theology implicit in his defense from the particularity of the South Indian situation, and develop it to give support for the ecumenical movement, which, he perceived, was progressing without an adequate ecclesiological foundation.[117] The invitation to deliver the Kerr Lectures at Trinity College in Glasgow gave Newbigin the impetus to further develop his argument. He sought to "wrestle with the issues raised" on the doctrine of the church at the first assembly of the WCC, reflecting on what answers the formation of the CSI might contribute.[118] The lecture series subsequently was published as *The Household of God*.[119]

Central to Newbigin's thesis (and the book) was the question, "By what is the Church constituted?" Although "[w]e are all agreed that the Church is constituted by God's atoning acts in Christ Jesus," the question the church faced throughout history was, "how are we of the subsequent generations made participants in that atonement? *What is the manner of our engrafting into Christ?*"[120] Newbigin moved beyond the polarity of the Protestant-Catholic ecclesiologies to offer three answers: first "that we are incorporated in Christ by hearing and believing the Gospel," this was the Protestant answer; the second was the Catholic answer that "we are

114. Ibid., 25.

115. This was manifest in "The Pledge" and "The Thirty-Year Period" as means to gradually unite the ministry. Newbigin, *Reunion*, 107, 114–19.

116. Ibid., xxx.

117. Newbigin, *Unfinished Agenda*, 136–37.

118. Newbigin to Dr. Millar Patrick, 9/8/1950, BUL: DA29/1/6/113.

119. Newbigin, *Household of God*.

120. Ibid., 30. Italics in original.

incorporated by sacramental participation in the life of the historically continuous Church"; the third, what Newbigin hesitatingly called the Pentecostal answer, was that "we are incorporated by receiving and abiding in the Holy Spirit."[121] Each of these answers, which Newbigin explored in subsequent chapters, had dominated traditions of the church's self-understanding and definition, possessing an aspect of the church's essence, but each in and of itself was incomplete. And in relation to other traditions it was problematic if one tradition maintained an exclusive definition of the church, which thus negated dissenting ecclesiologies, as "none of us can be said to possess the *esse* of the Church."[122] This created an impasse in reunion movements as each tradition was unable to give up an aspect of what it considered was the *esse* of the church. Each tradition was rooted in the gospel, and "the denial of any of them leads to the disfigurement of the Church and the distortion of its message."[123] Whilst each tradition sought to remain true to its self-understanding of the essence of the church, yet there was the acknowledgement that, "We are drawn to one another by a real working of the Holy Spirit which we dare not resist."[124]

As "[t]he Church is not merely a historical reality but also an eschatological one," it can be rightly understood only in an eschatological perspective:[125] "The meaning of this 'overlap of the ages' in which we live, the time between the coming of Christ and His coming again, is that it is the time given for the witness of the apostolic Church to the ends of the earth. The end of all things, which has been revealed in Christ, is . . . held back until witness has been borne to the whole world . . . The implication of a true eschatological perspective will be missionary obedience . . ."[126]

As before, Newbigin maintained that two implications emerge from the *eschaton*, that the church is concurrently called to organic unity and to mission, the relationship between them emanating from the heart of the gospel, and animated by the gift of the Holy Spirit. It is by the Holy Spirit that the church is incorporated into Christ; "that we are made participants in the victory yet to be revealed"; and we are empowered for mission.[127]

121. Newbigin, *Household of God*, 30.

122. Ibid., 134.

123. Ibid., 111.

124. Ibid.

125. Ibid., 135.

126. Ibid.

127. Newbigin, *Household of God*, 142.

Missionary obedience of the church orientated the church outwards towards the world, "Evangelistic work places the Church in a situation in which the stark contrast between Christ and no-Christ is constantly being faced. In such a situation other matters necessarily fall into second place."[128] This had been Newbigin's shared experience as the CSI was formed. The mission experience of the church had forced critical examination of the disunity of the church and inspired efforts to recover unity. This recovery in the key themes of mission and unity, which the Western church had neglected, "must be prosecuted together and in indissoluble relation one with the other."[129]

Newbigin explored those implications from his reading of John 17:21. Unity is missional, "in order that the world may believe": "The Church's unity is the sign and the instrument of the salvation which Christ has wrought and whose final fruition is the summing-up of all things in Christ."[130] The organic unity of the church demonstrated the efficacy of Christ's salvation to make us one. And conversely, the disunity of the church was a contradiction of the gospel, undermining the credibility of Christ's prayer and his ability to reconcile all things in himself.

A crucial question was *how*; in progress from disunity to union, how were the disunited churches to be brought together? Newbigin, as one of the fourteen original bishops in the CSI, urged others contemplating union to look to the SIS, as a model for full organic union of the visible church, the first of its kind which had actually come to fruition. Newbigin's insistence on the SIS path towards unity, as opposed to other schemes which were more palatable to Anglicans, led him into prolonged theological debate which impacted the heart of the ecumenical movement and the outcome of other union schemes.[131]

Later Newbigin reflected on how the Lambeth Conferences of 1948 and 1958 had been *kairos* moments in the history of the church, which provided rare opportunities for dramatic progress. Rather than the

128. Ibid., 151.

129. Ibid., 144, 152.

130. Ibid., 149.

131. For details of this debate, see M. T. B. Laing, "The International Impact of the Formation of the Church of South India: Bishop Newbigin Versus the Anglican Fathers," *IBMR* 33:1 (2009). "The Faith and Order 'survey of church union negotiations 1959–1961' reported on the progress of some fifty sets of conversations and plans toward unity that were being conducted or drawn up at national and regional levels on every continent." Wainwright, *Newbigin*, 113. Of all those schemes only those in the Indian subcontinent succeeded in uniting with episcopal churches.

opportunity being embraced, it had been squandered. Newbigin expected that if Lambeth had responded positively to the CSI, "I am sure that the whole worldwide movement for unity among the Churches would have gone forward. . . . [Instead] That opportunity was lost, and is not likely to come again."[132]

Newbigin was a task theologian; his theological reflection emerged, not *in abstracto*, but out of the particular struggles the church faced and the organizational solutions he proposed to those problems. Newbigin's theology of time links the history of reunion with the theology which informed it and the reflection it produced. The church in eschatological perspective is not a static entity, but is in process and must, at certain junctures, make decisions which will have profound repercussions. Newbigin was well aware that the process of union created a tension between the theological formulation upon which union was based and the time lag of the organizational expression of that union. Thus, in the case of the CSI, ecclesiological expression was founded upon provisional theological formulations. The new united church needed to be defined in terms of what it was becoming rather than in static formulations. Newbigin insisted that "God demands decisions in time."[133] In 1947 a vote had to be taken for the CSI to become a reality. To demand at that time yet another delay to allow for a reformulation of the basis of union would be a *de facto* rejection of the scheme.[134]

From these experiences Newbigin understood the church's concern with mission and unity to be a recovery of the "heart of the gospel." In his work with the ecumenical movement he sought the proper embodiment of the relationship between mission and unity which was coupled with a sense of urgency, that "God demands decisions in time."

Conclusion

This chapter has argued that three factors were determinative in shaping Newbigin for the crucial responsibility of integrating the IMC with the WCC. The chapter has sought to detail the particular contribution each made to Newbigin's ecclesiology.

132. Newbigin, *Unfinished Agenda*, 114.

133. Newbigin cited in Hollis to Newbigin, 2/11/1958, BUL: DA29/2/8/17.

134. Newbigin to Archbishop Fisher, 15/4/1961, BUL: DA29/2/8/52. Lesslie Newbigin, "Anglicans, Methodists and Intercommunion: A Moment for Decision," *Churchman* 82:4 (1968) 282.

The SCM provided several key introductions for Newbigin. First and most fundamentally through the SCM Newbigin was introduced to Christianity. This was a form of Christianity which was centered on Christ but had an ecumenical vision of the world as its boundary. The creative and dialectical tension between the core, Christ, and the boundary, the world, characterized Newbigin's life. And he was acutely aware of the danger of capitulating to either pole. His introduction to Christianity through the SCM also introduced him to emerging fault-lines, fracturing in Britain what had been a broad continuum within evangelicalism. As the century progressed the ability of moderate evangelicals to sustain a mediating position was weakened and the rift between ecumenical and conservative evangelicals hardened as it became increasingly institutionalized. This was especially true in American. The role conservative evangelicals played in their association with the IMC (and suspicion of the WCC) would be a major concern for Newbigin, as the last general secretary.

The SCM introduced Newbigin to the ecumenical movement, to influential elder statesmen and to future friends in India. And through "the church ahead of the church" Newbigin developed an ecclesiology rooted in mission *and* unity, which insisted that both were inextricably linked. Newbigin imbued the crucial concern for the health of each smallest unit of an organization. This emphasis would later influence his priorities on integration.

As a young CofS missionary in Tamil Nadu Newbigin was introduced to the "intolerable dichotomy" between mission and church. He experienced this in the problematic relation between the CofS mission and the Indian church, the quest for devolution bringing this into sharp focus. Newbigin's correspondence with Kydd reveal his methodology: to always start from theological assumptions derived from his reading of the New Testament, and on that basis to then seek to re-align historical structures. This was the basis for his arguments on devolution and his later argument for integration.

His early missionary correspondence also reveals his church-centricism in which he argued for the realignment of the mission to effectively serve the rural and rudimentary village churches. The vision of these churches expanding "spontaneously" provided Newbigin with a model of the church to which he would often return. Through Kraemer Newbigin recognized that a new epoch had dawned in the relationship between mission organizations and indigenous churches. Newbigin's correspondence with Kydd reveals his prescience—in contrast to Kydd's intransigence—which was demonstrated in his own personal commitment to be accountable to the Indian church.

Facing the practical issues of how the Indian church should relate to the CofS mission led Newbigin to a more fundamental theological assessment of the importance of the church in general. He became aware that his theological position on the church had changed when he was drafting the book, *Sin and Salvation*:[135] "I found as I wrote that book that my thinking had changed in a significant way. Twenty years earlier [at Cambridge] in writing on this theme I had referred to the Church only in a very marginal way at the end of the essay. . . . Now I found that I had to begin with the Church—the point at which the unbeliever first comes into contact with the redemptive work of Christ."[136] The reason for this profound shift in thinking Newbigin attributed to his missionary experience: "I did not make that switch easily but I found that the experience of missionary work compelled me to make it. I saw that the kind of Protestantism in which I had been nourished belonged to a 'Christendom' context. In a missionary situation the Church had to have a different logical place."[137]

Newbigin's late entry into the practical negotiations of the SIS gave him a wealth of experience in committees and then of defending the scheme against critics—experience he would draw upon for integration. But more importantly the formation of the CSI gave Newbigin the task of formulating a theological defense. Newbigin argued that the CSI, rather than being an Indian oddity, was a demonstration of a recovered ecclesiology. The church's dual call to mission and unity was inextricably linked and emanated from the heart of the gospel. In India the impetus for these factors had emerged as a consequence of comity agreements. Newbigin argued that the church's call to mission and unity must also be understood in eschatological perspective. An eschatological perspective had to take a theology of time seriously. The church was defined not just in static terms of its essence, but also in terms of what it was *becoming*. The prospect of the *eschaton* universalized the need for these concerns to be recovered, particularly by the Western church. The success of the CSI was a universal sign to the churches that reunion was possible.

Newbigin, in his transition from the arena of the CSI to the larger ecumenical movement, carried these concerns. As the CSI was a sign to the churches that reunion was possible, he understood integration in an

---

135. Lesslie Newbigin, *Sin and Salvation* (London: SCM, 1956).

136. Newbigin, *Unfinished Agenda*, 146.

137. Ibid.

analogous way as a sign to the world. For Newbigin the basis of world unity was reconciliation in Christ mediated through the church, the new community, which, in reunion, demonstrated Christ's efficacy to make us one and, in mission, declared this to the world. Thus integration for New-bigin had an inherent logic.

There was a need to act upon the growing consensus in the ecumeni-cal movement that the church is missionary and called to unity. As he had succeeded with the CSI Newbigin took up his role as general secretary of the IMC with a similar sense of purpose and divine calling—that events in the ecumenical movement was being providentially ordered, and that he must play his part in this divine orchestration. Before concentrating on Newbigin it is necessary to consider the larger context of integration, the focus of chapter 2.

2

The Path Towards Integration

THIS STUDY SEEKS TO understand what Newbigin contributed to the integration of the two world councils, and to learn how Newbigin's engagement with this process affected his personal theological reflection on the nature of mission. Before the study can focus on Newbigin in particular it is necessary to understand the bigger picture, to place Newbigin in context. What was happening on the world stage to affect the relationship between the IMC and the WCC? What was happening internal to each council, and in the nexus of their relationships with each other? Outside the ecumenical movement, and profoundly wary of it, the conservative evangelicals looked on. Why were they so important to integration when they had distanced themselves from the ecumenical movement? What were their concerns about integration? And would increasing intimacy with the WCC compromise the IMC, such that evangelicals would disassociate themselves from the council? This chapter seeks to address these questions as a prelude to Newbigin's direct involvement in the process of integration.

The integration of the International Missionary Council (IMC) with the World Council of Churches (WCC) took place at the third assembly of the WCC in New Delhi in 1961. But integration was not just an event but also a process. From the inception of the WCC there were forces within both councils, drawing them beyond mere "association," to a more intimate relationship. For many involved in this process of integration, uniting the council concerned with "mission" with the council concerned with the "church" was the fitting organizational embodiment of more fundamental theological certainties.[1] Whilst the majority in both councils favored integration, within the IMC there were also strong voices of dissent, and even more strident protest from conservative evangelicals.

At one level the debate on integration was about organizational structures. But beyond structural obsessiveness lay more searching theological questions on the relationship between mission and church. By the middle of the twentieth century there was the realization that the Protestant missionary movement had reached a crisis. Factors within and outwith the movement forced those engaged in missions to the realization that missions not only needed to be reorganized, the concept of mission itself required rehabilitation. Those engaged in Protestant missions interpreted world events as turning against them. The theological foundation for their praxis was exposed as inadequate. What were the factors which led to this re-evaluation of missionary structures and, more fundamentally, of mission theology?

Factors Affecting the Relationship between the IMC and the WCC

The IMC and the WCC were intimately related from the inception of the WCC. When the IMC met in Tambaram (1938) they were faced with the question of how they should relate to the embryonic WCC. A Joint Committee was created with a mandate to explore this relationship. With the IMC operating "in association" with the WCC the incongruity was recognized of having two international Protestant[2] organizations, one ostensibly dealing with mission, the other, with the unity of the church. In the history of the Protestant missionary movement the theological relationship between mission and church, structurally expressed by mission organizations on the one hand and churches on the other, had been problematic. This was becoming increasingly apparent as the result of the missionary movement, the "younger church," became more influential. New patterns of relationship were demanded which would reflect a recovered biblical

---

1. Of course this is a caricature, as both councils had overlapping concerns.

2. The IMC remained exclusively Protestant. At its inception the WCC was predominantly (but not exclusively) Protestant. At the first assembly (1948) various Orthodox Churches joined, including the Ecumenical Patriarchate and the autonomous churches of Finland, Cyprus, Greece, and the "Oriental Orthodox" of Ethiopia and South India. More joined at the second assembly (1954). At the third assembly (1961) a large number of Orthodox Churches joined, thus significantly changing the WCC constituency. Martin Conway to Laing, email, 06/09/2008.

understanding of the mission of the church, and old assumptions were challenged. Various factors affected the relationship between the IMC and the WCC. External to them, but impinging upon them was the rapidly changing global situation.

The World Scene—Navigating Dangerous Waters

As the IMC considered its future relationship with the WCC, on the world stage seismic changes were occurring which would impinge upon their deliberations. At the end of the Second World War in 1945, the world changed forever when atomic bombs were dropped on Hiroshima and Nagasaki to end the war with Japan. The joy of Indian independence, in 1947, was soon superseded by its bloody partition polarizing religious communal identity in the sub-continent. And the Communist ascendancy in China in 1949 led rapidly to the expulsion of Protestant missionaries from this "showcase" of "mission fields."

Newbigin drew upon a maritime analogy to explain the changing situation in which missions found themselves at the middle of the twentieth century. "The winds of change no longer blow all in one direction"; the role of colonialism in assisting the missionary enterprise was rapidly diminishing. With Indian independence in 1947 and other countries demanding hasty decolonization there was the realization that such winds "are as likely as not to blow the other way, and the missionary has to learn the art of navigating against the prevailing wind."[3] Missions had been discredited because of their association with domineering cultural and political Western powers and needed to be rehabilitated. The church "faces a radically new situation, and nothing will suffice save radical rethinking of the nature of her mission."[4]

What were the factors which contributed to this "radically new situation" which demanded a fundamental reappraisal of the nature of mission? Besides the scourge of colonialism,[5] Newbigin recognized other forces: the resurgence of world religions.[6] The destruction of world faiths in their

3. Foreword in G. H. Anderson, *The Theology of the Christian Mission* (London: SCM, 1961) xii.

4. Ibid., xii–xiii.

5. For a study on the Protestant missionary movement's complex relationship with colonialism, see B. Stanley, *The Bible and the Flag: Protestant Missions and British Imperialism in the Nineteenth and Twentieth Centuries* (Leicester: Apollos, 1990).

6. Lesslie Newbigin, "The Summons to Christian Mission Today," *IRM* 48:190 (1959) 177.

encounter with Christianity had been rather naively and optimistically prophesied by some missionaries.[7] Instead, the consequence of missionary endeavor was often a reconstituted, resurgent, non-Christian faith, one better equipped to combat missionary advances.

Another factor was what Newbigin termed "the birth of a single world civilization." Newbigin interpreted the emergence of a common quest in "younger nations" for such things as technological advancement, universal human rights, and the development of a welfare state, as being evidence for the emergence of a single secular human civilization. Newbigin, with others, thought that all the discrete histories of the nations are being unified into a common, universal history: the "force which is drawing nations irresistibly out of their separate existence into a common world history, is a secularized and distorted form of the Christian eschatology."[8] These two factors—secularization displacing religion and the resurgence of world religions—are mutually exclusive. Only later did this become apparent to Newbigin when he realized that the latter prevailed over the former.

A further issue was, somewhat paradoxically, the harvest of the missionary enterprise, the growth of the church in what had been traditionally termed the "mission fields." With the emergence of Christianity for the first time as a truly worldwide faith, "the great new fact of our era."[9] Historical missions were now faced—to use Walter Freytag's term—with a perplexing loss of "directedness."[10] With the establishment of Christendom, Roman Catholic, and then Protestant missions had a geographic "directedness" from the West. This was no longer tenable, as now the "home base" was everywhere. The historical legacy which had given missions their direction and legitimacy was now discredited. With the loss of geographic legitimacy it was recognized that a new basis for missions was required. Concurrent with this was the realization that Western Christianity was in decline. It had lost ground in the West; mission needed to be to six continents not just three.

The breakdown of Christendom, the dissolution of the synthesis between the gospel and Western culture, according to Newbigin, could be attributed to three causes: first there was a failure of the Western church

7. Alexander Duff was perhaps the most famous missionary to advocate this view. G. Smith, *The Life of Alexander Duff* (London: Hodder & Stoughton, 1879) 57.

8. Newbigin, "Summons to Mission," 182. The force of secularization displacing religion was popularized in H. G. Cox, *The Secular City* (London: SCM, 1965). These issues will be examined in chs. 8 and 9.

9. W. Temple, *The Church Looks Forward* (London: Macmillan, 1944) 2.

10. Newbigin, "Summons to Mission," 178.

to be apostolic. "Missions were conceived of as the extension of the frontiers of Christendom and the conveyance of the blessings of Christian civilization to those who had hitherto been without them."[11] The church as chaplain to society was more concerned with maintenance and mortar rather than mission and lost its self-understanding of being a pilgrim people. With geographic isolation the church has lost sight of its apostolic calling, defining various factions of the church in distinction from each other rather than defining the church vis-à-vis other faiths. Second, having lost the theological apparatus to engage missiologically with society, the church had experienced anti-Christian forces "launching a full-scale attack upon the whole ethical tradition of western Europe and seeking to replace it by something totally different."[12] Third, Newbigin detected "a sort of atomizing process, in which the individual is more and more set free from his natural setting in family and neighborhood, and becomes a sort of replaceable unit in the social machine."[13] This was a consequence of the industrial revolution which has caused the mechanization and the division of labor.[14] When faced with such major theological challenges in its heartland, the inadequacy of the church's ecclesiology was exposed and it was forced it to re-examine its essential nature. The Western church was in decline and lacked the theological resources to counter new challenges.

Bringing this malaise into sharper focus was the situation in traditional "mission fields." There was "dismay" and "frustration" caused by the shrinking of geographic areas open to missions, the missionary *"debacle"* of China, the impact internationally of Islam, and the decline in number of recruits from mainline churches in contrast to the new Pentecostal mission agencies.[15]

Factors Internal to the IMC and WCC

Internally the two councils were affected by organizational, ecclesiological, and theological issues. At an organizational level there was a desire

11. Newbigin, *Household of God*, 12.

12. Ibid. Here Newbigin means the Enlightenment, which paved the way for totalitarian regimes. These ideas were further developed in his "retirement," where Newbigin is overcritical of the Enlightenment. E.g., see especially Lesslie Newbigin, *The Other Side of 1984: Questions for the Churches* (Geneva: WCC, 1983).

13. Newbigin, *Household of God*, 13.

14. Newbigin, *Foolishness*, 30–34.

15. Max A. C. Warren, "The Willingen Conference: a Report," September 1952, SOAS: IMC/264.011, 7.

to reunite the three streams which emanated from the Edinburgh World Missionary Conference of 1910. The IMC, as a continuation of the Edinburgh Conference, was formally constituted at a meeting at Lake Mohonk in 1921. Faith and Order and Life and Work had united to formally constitute the WCC in 1948. In continuity with Edinburgh John R Mott was appointed as chairman of the IMC, and JH Oldham as its secretary. Its constituency consisted of national missionary councils (not churches) which operated with a large degree of independence and autonomy. This regional emphasis allowed the IMC to function with a very small central staff who understood their role as that of a think-tank rather than a governing administration. This organizational structure continued throughout the life of the IMC. By the time of integration "The IMC had a very small staff divided between three offices in New York, London, and East Asia, made no attempt to create a public image of itself, and saw its role as that of a servant to the national councils which constituted its membership."[16] The leadership understood the role of the IMC to be mainly responsible for research rather than educating churches about mission. The regional ethos became very significant at the time of integration as the WCC was very much centralized, and centralizing, in its character.

"... in association with ..."

Since the inception of the WCC the IMC had been—at various levels—in association with it; this was evident in shared leadership, and an increasing overlap of operation. Oldham had first proposed the idea of a council of churches or *koinonia*. Similar ideas had also been proposed by Archbishop Söderblom, and the Ecumenical Patriarchate of Constantinople, but no concrete plans had emerged. Under the leadership of Oldham and Archbishop William Temple the crystallization of a blueprint to form the WCC took place at Westfield College, in London, in July 1937. That same year these plans were submitted and accepted by both Life and Work, convening in Oxford, and Faith and Order, meeting in Edinburgh.[17] The WCC "in the process of formation" had shared personnel with the IMC, Mott, the first IMC chairman being the first honorary president of the WCC,

16. Newbigin, *Unfinished Agenda*, 169.

17. Willem Adolph Visser 't Hooft, WCC Central Committee Minutes (hereafter cited as CCM), 1962, 77. For Visser 't Hooft own account of the formation of the WCC, see W. A. Visser 't Hooft, *The Genesis and Formation of the World Council of Churches* (Geneva: World Council of Churches, 1982).

and William Paton, Oldham's successor, being general secretary of IMC, concurrent with his service as associate general secretary of the WCC.[18] Paton was the most optimistic of the IMC leaders in anticipating integration of the two councils within a decade of the formation of the WCC. Oldham and Mott were more cautious. Oldham expressed the view that, after the formation of the WCC, the IMC might continue in independent service for as much as a further fifty years.[19]

At the conference in Tambaram (1938) the IMC had to face the question of how it would deal with the fledgling WCC. Whilst supporting the development of the WCC the IMC sought to maintain its separate identity. The reasons given by the IMC were: the problem of joining a well-established organization (the IMC) with an organization in the process of formation; special concern for the IMC constituency which would not be covered by the WCC, and radical organizational differences.[20] However, recognizing that the relationship between the two organizations needed to be clarified, the IMC, shortly after Tambaram, proposed the formation of a Joint Committee of the two councils.[21]

Delayed by World War II, the Joint Committee was not able to meet until 1946. The Committee proposed to the two councils that their official titles be changed to "The World Council of Churches in Association with the International Missionary Council" and "The International Missionary Council in Association with the World Council of Churches."[22] The proposal for "association" was accepted when the WCC was formally constituted at its first assembly in Amsterdam in 1948. This relationship of "association" was to dominate the inter-relatedness of the two councils during the 1950s.

The war years also marked significant changes in ecumenical leadership. Mott resigned as chairman of the IMC in 1942, and there were the untimely deaths of Paton (in 1943) and Archbishop William Temple (in 1944). Mott was succeeded first by Bishop James Baker, and then the IMC was chaired by John Mackay.[23]

18. Visser 't Hooft, CCM, 1956, 71.

19. Johannes Christiaan Hoekendijk to Norman Goodall, 23/1/1952, WCC: 27.0013.

20. Goodall, "WCC and IMC: Some Considerations Bearing on Their Relationships," February 1947, WCC: 27.0006, 2.

21. Van Dusen, *Minutes of the Assembly of the IMC, Ghana: December 28th, 1957 to January 8th, 1958,* (London: IMC, 1958) 126.

22. WCC Provisional Committee Minutes, Buck Hill Falls, April 1947, 67–69.

23. Scottish-born Mackay had served as a missionary in Latin America and was

For the next decade, the two councils continued to be "in association" with each other at an official level, but practically their relationship had become more intimate. The intermingling of the work of both councils, in study, international affairs and the work of the East Asia Secretariat,[24] "have since become so deeply interwoven as to go beyond what was described in 1948 as the 'inter-relatedness of two autonomous councils.'"[25] This was most clearly manifest with the integration of the study departments of the two councils which was ratified at the second assembly of the WCC.[26]

The Polarization between Mission and Church within the IMC

The IMC inherited an emphasis on mission and its independence from the institutional church from the *modus vivendi* of missionary societies and boards. This problematic legacy of separating "church" from "mission" was to become increasingly apparent during the history of the IMC. Whilst the original constituent members of the IMC represented Western missionary organizations, leaders from the "younger churches" were becoming progressively more prominent within the IMC and vocal at conferences. So, by Tambaram, the agenda of this *mission* council was centered upon the *church*. Yet the membership of the IMC remained polarized between those representing mission organizations and those representing the interests of the "younger church." The IMC thus embodied in its constituency a dichotomy between "church" and "mission." This polarization was to have at least three consequences. It led, first, to differing expectations between the Western mission society and the "younger church"; second, to an emphasis on the "thereness" of mission, an interest predominantly in the local rather than the universal; and third, the recognition that the missionary movement had horizons which always reached beyond the church. Although for the IMC the role of the "younger church" had become more central, the IMC continued to look beyond the church to the larger community, the interface between church and world being its primary focus. Fulfillment of

president of Princeton Theological Seminary when appointed as chairman. T. E. Yates, *Christian Mission in the Twentieth Century* (Cambridge: Cambridge University Press, 1994) 134.

24. The East Asia Christian Conference (EACC) first met in Bangkok in 1949 and was constituted in Kuala Lumpur in 1959.

25. Visser 't Hooft, CCM, 1956, 110.

26. W. A. Visser 't Hooft, ed., *The Evanston Report: The Second Assembly of the World Council of Churches 1954* (London: SCM, 1955) 221–22.

this goal required that "from time to time obedience in mission has been more apparent in movements structurally independent of the churches than in the churches themselves."[27] Thus, whilst missiological reflection became increasingly church-centric, the IMC constituency embodied the tension inherited between the institutions of church and missions.

Growth in the Church-Centric Mission Model—
From Tambaram to Willingen

At Tambaram the indissoluble relationship between church and mission was recognized, as was the universality of the church. Tambaram was the first IMC conference in which the majority of delegates were from the "younger churches" rather than being Western representatives of *missions*. Strong numerical representation by the church was also reflected in the centrality of "the church" to this *missionary* conference. The conference is remembered as marking the start of *church-centric* mission.[28] But gravitation towards the centrality of the church was already underway by the Jerusalem Conference (1928). Jerusalem called for a "church-centric" approach, in which "the indigenous church will become the centre from which the whole missionary enterprise of the area will be directed."[29] Brian Stanley notes that the impetus for devolving responsibility to the "younger church" may have been due more to financial necessity than any more noble motives.[30]

27. Goodall cited by J. V. Taylor, "Small Is Beautiful: Thoughts Arising from *Can Churches Be Compared?*" *IRM* 60:239 (1971) 334–35.

28. Even as this church-centric model was formulated at Tambaram it was critiqued by E. Stanley-Jones, who proposed that the Kingdom of God should be central. For further discussion, see S. Kim, "The Kingdom of God versus the Church: The Debate at the Conference of the International Missionary Council, Tambaram, 1938," in *Interpreting Contemporary Christianity: Global Processes and Local Identities*, ed. Ogbu U. Kalu and Alaine M. Low (Grand Rapids: Eerdmans, 2008) 131–47.

29. IMC, *Jerusalem Meeting Report: The Younger and Older Churches*, vol. 3 (London: Oxford University Press, 1928) 209.

30. B. Stanley, "Twentieth-Century World Christianity: A Perspective from the History of Missions," in *Christianity Reborn: The Global Expansion of Evangelicalism in the Twentieth Century*, ed. Donald M. Lewis (Grand Rapids: Eerdmans, 2004) 52–83. This was certainly the case for the Church of Scotland in South India. Despite Newbigin's pleas the Church of Scotland did not devolve its operations to the Indian church until forced to by financial crisis and impending independence. Correspondence concerning this, between Newbigin and the Rev. Dr. Alexander Kydd, secretary of the Foreign Mission Committee, can be found at: NLS:7548/130.

At Tambaram the centrality of the church was noted by the chairman, John R. Mott, when he addressed delegates in his opening address: "Notice it is the Church which is to be at the centre of our thinking and resolving these creative days. . . ."[31] Earlier at Jerusalem the "younger church" delegates had made the presence of the church felt in the domain of missions, now the church was very much central to the theological reflections on missions; at Tambaram: "*mission and the Church have now found one another.*"[32] With all the five main themes of the conference relating to the church this indicated a profound change in missionary reflection about the nature and role of the church in its relationship to mission. It contrast to earlier thinking it was now "recognized that mission and Church are indissolubly related to one another. . . . From now on it is impossible to speak of 'missions' without speaking simultaneously of the Church."[33]

The church-centered missiology which emanated from Tambaram raised questions about the forms of the church's life. If it was accepted that the church was missionary by nature, how should the church be structured to adequately embody this missionary ecclesiology? This question required answers at various levels, from the structure of the local congregation to relationship between international ecumenical bodies.

By the time of the Willingen Conference (1952) strident voices challenged the post-Tambaram church-centric model of mission. It was "an illegitimate centre" for mission which was thus "*bound to go astray.*"[34] Whilst Newbigin maintained his belief in the legitimacy of a church-centric model he later came to realize that there were considerable problems with the model which later opened new avenues of theological enquiry for him.

Factors within the WCC

Both Faith and Order and Life and Work had been dominated by Western leadership who had been shaped by Western ecclesiological assumptions and were naturally concerned with issues facing the Western—and latterly

31. IMC, *Addresses and Other Records: Tambaram, Madras, December 12th to 29th, 1938*, 4.

32. W. Andersen, *Towards a Theology of Mission: A Study of the Encounter between the Missionary Enterprise and the Church and Its Theology* (London: SCM, 1955) 20–21.

33. Ibid., 21.

34. Italics in original, J. C. Hoekendijk, "The Church in Missionary Thinking," *IRM* 41 (1952) 332.

the Orthodox—church. But a change was discernible within the WCC, a shift in balance away from the West "brought about by the growing participation by churches of the third world."[35] Although externally the WCC may have appeared as a unified council—the council was not as unified as it may have appeared to those unfamiliar with its internal organization.[36] The intimacy of relationship between "older" and "younger" churches was causing profound problems for the operation of the councils. The "younger churches," birthed by the Protestant missionary movement had historical ties to their respective mission organizations and related to the "older churches" through that conduit. Rather than paternalistic relationships being perpetuated they sought direct partnership with the "older churches" of the West. They faced the dilemma of relating to those "older churches" through two different organizations. There was also an overlap of remit and resources, this being most clearly concentrated in the relationship between the IMC and the Division of Inter-church Aid (DICA) after the mandate for the DICA was expanded beyond the reconstruction of post-war Europe, and put on a permanent footing.[37]

Another factor impacting integration was the prospect of Russian and other Orthodox Churches gaining full membership at the third assembly and thus profoundly changing the nature of the WCC.[38] Concern was raised that the Orthodox Church would then comprise the largest voting bloc of what had been predominately a *Protestant* Central Committee. Some were suspicious of these Eastern churches, many of which existed under Communist regimes, and were thus deemed to be tainted by Kremlin control. Orthodox ecclesiology on sacramental regeneration conflicted with prevailing Protestant theology. The more "fundamentalist" evangelicals rejected sacramental regeneration and viewed the sacramentalist churches as fair game for "evangelism." Thus, within the WCC

---

35. Lesslie Newbigin, "Faith and Faithfulness in the Ecumenical Movement," in *Faith and Faithfulness: Essays on Contemporary Ecumenical Themes*, ed. Pauline Webb (Geneva: WCC, 1984) 2.

36. Paul Löffler to Mark Laing, email, 17/08/2007.

37. The relationship between the IMC and the DICA will be considered in detail in ch. 6.

38. Russia was followed in succeeding years by all the other Orthodox Churches still outside membership, except for Albania, which only came into formal membership after the collapse of the Communist government. Martin Conway to Laing, email, 06/09/2008.

there were conflicts on the interpretation of the terms "evangelism" and "proselytism."[39]

Dr. John Mackay, the chairman of the IMC, highlighted two further factors affecting integration. The first he termed "psychological." Taking the example of the church in Communist China Mackay perceived that these churches sought to be free of "ecclesiastical colonialism" and to relate to other churches in a national council under a national umbrella, and directly to the WCC. Although Mackay interpreted the Chinese Church's response to colonial mission to be "both embittered and extremist" he anticipated similar nationalistic movements among the "younger churches" and a corresponding backlash against the missionary movement. The second factor which concerned Mackay was "conciliar." What was the future for IMC related national councils, some of which were deemed as "woefully weak," vis-à-vis the vitality and growth of church councils?[40] The main impetus for integration came from the "younger churches" who sought, indeed demanded, new relationships of partnership in place of colonial paternalism and its corresponding dependency.

Theological Factors

At a more fundamental level than that of practical organization or church relationships there were theological arguments proposed—and countered—for integration. There was a developing consensus that the twentieth century was witnessing a recovery in ecclesiology. Three factors were identified which facilitated this recovery: (as noted) the demise of Christendom, the missionary encounters of Western Christianity with the non-Western world, and the rise of the ecumenical movement.[41] In Newbigin's interpretation a recovered ecclesiology was expressed by the church's visible organic unity and its witness to the ends of the earth. These belonged to the true nature of the church, the demonstration of this unity being essential for the effective witness of the church. Newbigin understood the two as emanating from the heart of the gospel and as therefore essential to the dual calling of the church: "The connection between the movement for Christian reunion and the movement for world evangelization is of the deepest possible character. The two things are the two outward signs of a

39. C. F. H. Henry, "Report on New Delhi," *Christianity Today* 6:22 (1961) 3–7.

40. John A. Mackay, "Consideration on Integration," Herrenalb Joint Committee, July 1956, WCC: 27.0010, 2.

41. Newbigin, *Household of God*, 1–25.

return to the heart of the Gospel itself."[42] In Newbigin's recent experience these theological convictions had been embodied in the formation of the Church of South India (CSI).

In South India church reunion negotiations, which had run from the turn of the century, came to a successful conclusion with the formation of the CSI in 1947. For the first time full organic and visible church union of episcopal with non-episcopal churches was achieved. This demonstration that union was possible was inspirational for many, and generated international interest. Within the ecumenical movement there was tangible hope that many more union schemes would come to fruition. Newbigin, who entered the CSI negotiations near their completion, became instrumental in defending and promoting the CSI model internationally.[43] Newbigin, in entering IMC/WCC discussions, thus brought his experience of success in India, and the hope that this would serve as a catalyst to the ecumenical movement worldwide. Whilst many in the West understood church union to be desirable, for the "younger churches" it was essential: "We believe that unity of the churches is an essential condition of effective witness and advance. In the lands of the younger churches divided witness is a crippling handicap . . . While unity may be desirable in the lands of the older churches, it is *imperative* in those of the younger churches."[44] It was hoped that union of the two councils would be a powerful symbol to the churches of the inseparable relationship between mission and union.

In the case of the IMC/WCC how were these theological convictions to be structurally expressed? Two international (predominantly) Protestant organizations existing in parallel, one ostensibly for unity, the other for mission, created the erroneous impression that there could be two separate mandates. Both organizations had come to the realization that mission and unity must be pursued together, as both were understood to emanate from the heart of the gospel. Visser 't Hooft, as general secretary of the WCC, could identify those concerns of ecumenicity being evident from the origin of the WCC: "Ecumenicity—as we already saw in Oxford in 1937—means both the world-embracing character of the Church and its integrity, its wholeness . . . both aspects . . . point towards concern with mission. The witness to all nations is the primary *raison d'être* of the Church. How can it reach wholeness unless it fulfills the commandment

42. Lesslie Newbigin, *The Reunion of the Church: A Defence of the South India Scheme* (London: SCM, 1960) 19.

43. Laing, "Formation of the CSI."

44. "A Statement by Delegates from the Younger Churches," in *Missions under the Cross*, ed. Norman Goodall (London: Edinburgh House, 1953) 234.

to go forth and to witness? But it is equally true that the search for true universality demands expression in mission to the ends of the earth."[45]

These concerns served as a theological "ferment" which created pressure for integration from within the heart of the ecumenical movement, the main impetus coming from the "younger churches" which existed in a milieu in which "the missionary calling pervades the whole atmosphere."[46]

There were various approaches to the question of how to embody theological convictions. The question of how to express the relationship between mission and the church was equally applicable to the situation of local congregations involved in the ecumenical movement as it was to the international councils. There was a polarization between two main premises. On one hand there were those who argued that current structures should be reconstituted to reflect new theological insights. And on the other, were those who stated that historical realities rather than impractical theological ideals should determine organization. Others were dismissive of a particular emphasis on organic unity, arguing, from the example of history, that mission had been effectively pursued with little concern for unity. Could not a focus primarily on mission determine the proper type of unity, rather than the converse, a pre-occupation with unity determining the organization of mission? Newbigin insisted that the pursuit of mission *and* unity had to be maintained without detriment to the other.[47] Both emanated from the heart of the gospel, and pursuit of one alone, to the neglect of the other, was profoundly damaging both to the church, and its witness.

Evangelicals and the Prospect of Integration

Within both councils (and amongst those associated with them) there was growing enthusiasm about formalizing the increasing intimacy between the two councils. These warm sentiments contrasted starkly with evangelical views about the ecumenical movement. The role of conservative

45. Visser 't Hooft, CCM, 1957, 84.

46. Ibid.

47. Newbigin insisted in the essential inter-relatedness of mission and unity throughout his life. E.g., as the drafter of the report of the Anglican-Reformed International Commission, he used emotive words to describe unbridled, "urgent" evangelism, "The mere multiplication of cells, unrelated to the purpose of the body, is a sign not of life and health, but of cancer and death." "God's Reign and Our Unity: The Report of the Anglican-Reformed International Commission, 1981–1984," (http://warc.jalb.de/warcajsp/news_file/3.pdf, 1984), par. 31.

evangelicals in this process is most important as they were the most polemical in their opposition to integration and ultimately constituted a missionary movement which for decades perpetuated a stand-off between the two sides. Conservative evangelicals were alarmed about the perceived politicization of the WCC, disturbed by its seemingly "monolithic" organization, but, most crucially, opposed to theological liberalism and inclusivist, universalist tendencies.

The Importance of Conservative Evangelicals

At New Delhi in 1961, the IMC and the WCC "became one body"[48]—integration at the start of the sixties inaugurating ecumenical developments for that decade. But the sixties "ended up in a most violent polarization,"[49] when conservative evangelicals started a world missionary movement which was to have a polemical relationship with the WCC. It is ironic that those working for mission became estranged from those pursuing unity, as the terms "evangel" and "oikumene" are inextricably linked together. The Central Committee, in 1950, clearly understood the terms to be inseparable: "[ecumenical] is properly used to describe everything that relates to the whole task of the whole Church to bring the Gospel to the whole world." Therefore no person or group could properly claim to be "ecumenical" without being "evangelical," or vice versa.[50]

Various attempts have been made to define who exactly an "evangelical" is, and the various strands which comprise the evangelical movement. The movement is complex, ranging from individuals who remain members of non-evangelical "mainline" churches, to distinct congregations, through to national and international fellowships. Furthermore, the term "evangelical" is defined differently by evangelicals in different countries.

Bebbington identifies four characteristics which have defined the evangelical movement since its emergence in the 1730s: "*conversionism*, the belief that lives need to be changed; *activism*, the expression of the gospel in effort; *biblicism*, a particular regard for the Bible; and what may be called *crucicentrism*, a stress on the sacrifice of Christ on the cross. Together

---

48. J. Aagaard, "Trends in Missiological Thinking During the Sixties," *IRM* 62:245 (1973) 22.

49. Ibid.

50. Mackay, "What the Ecumenical Movement Can Learn from Conservative Evangelicals," 20. Cf. Newbigin, "Cross-Currents," 146.

they form a quadrilateral of priorities that is the basis of Evangelicalism."[51] Besides defining the common character of evangelicalism Bebbington also gives a helpful continuum of the spectrum of belief expressed within the movement. Again, as a historian, Bebbington describes how these expressions evolved within British evangelicalism during the twentieth century. The continuum ranges from liberal, to centrist, to conservative. Bebbington notes the ascendency of British conservative evangelicalism after the second world war and discerns a trend of increasing polarization within evangelicalism from the 1960s onwards: "In Britain as a whole, as the distance between the poles of theological opinion widened, the scope for centrist enterprise declined."[52]

Others, such David Bosch, have proposed alternative typologies.[53] Max Warren defined evangelicalism as "a particular balance" of seven "pillars," key emphases which, although each is not unique to evangelicalism, uniquely define the evangelical movement by their combined relationship.[54] Speaking of the North American context, Arthur Glasser would particularly highlight, "the obligation to evangelize non-Christians throughout the world."[55] The understanding and praxis of mission and evangelism have, in particular, polarized conciliar/evangelical relationships.[56] In examining evangelical influences and responses to integration three factors are important to keep in mind. Prior to integration some evangelicals, by way of membership of mission councils, related to the IMC. This made a "'relationship' with the WCC, whether positive or negative, superfluous."[57] Second, there are structural differences in the type of membership. The WCC is a council of member *churches*, whilst evan-

---

51. Bebbington, *Evangelicalism*, 2–3, 4–17.

52. Ibid., 253, 253–55.

53. D. J. Bosch, "'Ecumenicals' and 'Evangelicals': A Growing Relationship?" *ER* 40:3–4 (1988). J. M. Hitchen, "What It Means to Be an Evangelical Today—An Antipodean Perspective. Part One, Mapping Our Movement," *Evangelical Quarterly* 76:1 (2004).

54. Warren's seven pillars are: (1) an existential saving encounter with the Holy Spirit; (2) a right biblical perspective; (3) a concern for the proper, scriptural use of the sacraments, especially communion; (4) the essentiality of the atonement of Christ; (5) missionary vision; (6) a conviction about the priesthood of the laity; and (7) an understanding of the meaning of conversion. Max A. C. Warren, *The Sevenfold Secret* (London: SPCK, 1962) 2–23.

55. A. F. Glasser, "Mission in the 1990s: Two Views," *IBMR* 13:1 (1989) 2.

56. "Conciliar" is used with reference to Christians actively engaged in the ecumenical movement.

57. Bosch, "Ecumenicals and Evangelicals," 460.

gelical representation is not primarily through church membership but is more varied by way of associations, fellowships, federations and mission organizations. And third, the WCC enshrines inclusiveness; all churches that subscribe to its basis can join. Evangelicalism, on the other hand, is, by its very nature confessional and exclusive.[58]

During the 1950s and 1960s some evangelicals were constructively involved with the ecumenical movement. It is important to remember that evangelicals "constitute a large part of the membership of WCC churches."[59] For those who opposed integration, evangelical resistance to the ecumenical movement was mainly a "Western phenomenon"; with opposition mostly concentrated in North America and Scandinavia.[60] Because of their sheer numerical size the role of American "conservative evangelicals" was of particular concern. Speaking of the American situation Eugene Smith described "conservative evangelicals" (whom he equated with fundamentalists) as those who hold to "a conservative theology; a concern for 'purity' in the Church; a vivid missionary interest; and a profound distrust of the ecumenical movement." He suggests that the most valuable definition of this group was the last factor, that they are organizationally antagonistic, that is, they refused to be members of councils of churches, at whatever level, city, state, national or world.[61]

Not all American evangelicals should be tarnished with the same brush. After the modernist/fundamentalist crisis of the 1920s, those termed "neo-evangelicals" emerged, who sought to regain central ground and distance themselves from fundamentalism. Amongst the originators of this movement was Carl Hendry, who argued against the anti-intellectualism of fundamentalism in his book *The Uneasy Conscience of Modern Fundamentalism* and proposed that evangelicals re-enter the public arena of ideas.[62] Further influences were the founding of Fuller Theo-

58. Ibid., 461.

59. N. Goodall, "'Evangelicals' and WCC-IMC," *IRM* 47:186 (1958) 211.

60. Ibid., 210, 213. There was also a later German strand which understood itself as being in continuity with The Barmen Declaration of 1934. This will be considered later. For the Scandinavian response to integration, see K. Nissen, "Integration in Nordic Missions," in *Missions from the North: Nordic Missionary Council, 50 Years*, ed. Carl F. Hallencreutz, Johannes Aagaard, and Nils Bloch-Hoell (Oslo: Universitetsforlaget, 1974). See also K. Nissen, "Mission and Unity: A Look at the Integration of the IMC and the WCC," *IRM* 63 (1974).

61. E. L. Smith, "The Conservative Evangelicals and the WCC," *ER* 15:2 (1963) 182.

62. C. F. H. Henry, *The Uneasy Conscience of Modern Fundamentalism* (Grand Rapids: Eerdmans, 1947, reprinted 2003).

logical Seminary in 1947, and the founding of the Christian newspaper *Christianity Today* aided by Billy Graham. In seeking a centrist position neo-evangelicals were opposed to militant separatism and demonstrated a willingness to take at least some part in discussion with ecumenical bodies.

Carl Henry estimated that more than half of American Protestants were evangelical.[63] Although it is hard to be precise about how many of those would be militantly conservative or "fundamentalist," it is fair to say that they would represent a considerable proportion, exerted considerable influence, and, relative to other evangelicals, were growing in power and number.[64] From the 1950s they became a "problem" for the WCC, "a problem which has found a permanent place on the agendas of various WCC commissions ever since."[65]

Newbigin was fearful that integration could precipitate an evangelical schism with an enfeebled IMC integrating with the WCC—a view shared by other missionary statesmen such as Max Warren and Stephen Neill.[66] In the two decades before integration there were discernible trends that suggested that this fear would be realized. Norman Goodall estimated that in 1957, 70 percent of all foreign missionaries were American—more than doubling their numbers since the 1930s. Of those American missionaries only 42 percent were related to the National Christian Council of Churches (NCCCUSA). This meant that the other 58 percent worked with agencies which did not cooperate with either the IMC or the WCC.[67] Reflecting these trends was the fact that the circulation of *Christianity Today,* a periodical which was started in 1955 as a "voice for the conservative evangelicals," had, by the 1960s, eclipsed the circulation of *Christian Century,* a periodical sympathetic to the ecumenical movement.[68]

63. C. F. H. Henry, "Evangelicals and Ecumenism," *Christianity Today* 10 (1966) 11.

64. A poll (circa 1962) of American pastors recorded that 74 percent were "conservative" or "fundamentalist." Smith, "Conservative Evangelicals," 186–87.

65. H. Berkhof, "Berlin versus Geneva: Our Relationship with the 'Evangelicals,'" *ER* 28:1 (1976) 80.

66. Yates, *Christian Mission*, 155–56.

67. Goodall estimated there to be thirty-five thousand non-Roman Catholic missionaries, of which nearly twenty-four thousand were American and sixty-five hundred (16 percent) were British. Goodall, "Evangelicals," 214. C.f. Smith, "Conservative Evangelicals," 182.

68. Smith, "Conservative Evangelicals," 182–83.

The concern was that those not cooperating with the ecumenical movement were a growing majority, whilst the missionary task force from cooperating churches continued to dwindle.[69] Whilst the total number of American missionaries was growing the proportion of those cooperating with the WCC was dwindling dramatically. This growth was particularly pronounced amongst the most conservative of evangelicals, that is, those who would not even associate with conservative bodies such as the Interdenominational Foreign Mission Association (IFMA formed in 1917), and the Evangelical Foreign Missions Association (EFMA founded in 1945).[70]

W. R. Hogg, historian of the IMC,[71] gave a sober assessment of the impact of this growth, "one reports frankly and with sadness that some among these are parasitic. Some are contentiously divisive, and their appeals for support reflect an 'anti-this' or 'anti-that' spirit . . . They pose a problem."[72]

Conservative evangelicals saw themselves as being the true heirs of the IMC, maintaining its ethos and heritage beyond its "absorption" into the WCC. But to ecumenical critics, their alleged faithfulness to a now-discredited missionary ethos made them captive to a compromised mode of mission, which desperately needed liberation from its colonial heritage: "Conservative Evangelicals have failed to liberate themselves from the mentality of the nineteenth century western white Christian who conceived of the non-Christian world as a vast mass of black heathenism . . . their missionary enthusiasm is a form of ignorant spiritual imperialism."[73]

---

69. Primarily as a reflection of the general malaise and decline in the Western church, but also due to the belief that indigenous local churches should be free to run their own affairs. Decline continued such that by 1969 only 28 percent of American Protestant missionaries were related to the NCCCUSA, further dropping to only 14 percent by 1975. R. D. Winter, "Ghana: Preparation for Marriage," *IRM* 67:267 (1978) 349.

70. A wing of the National Association of Evangelicals, from the American neo-evangelical movement. Coote estimated that by 1980 conservative evangelical missionaries accounted for over 90 percent of the North American total, growth coming "almost entirely from non-EFMA/IFMA groups." R. Coote, "The Uneven Growth of Conservative Evangelical Missions," *IBMR* 6:3 (1982) 118–19.

71. Hogg, *Ecumenical Foundations*.

72. W. R. Hogg, "Role of American Protestantism in World Mission," in *American Missions in Bicentennial Perspective*, ed. R. Pierce Beaver (South Pasadena, CA: William Carey Library, 1977) 389.

73. Lesslie Newbigin, "The Call to Mission—A Call to Unity?" in *The Church Crossing Frontiers*, ed. Peter Beyerhaus and Carl F Hallencreutz (Lund: Gleerup, 1969) 257–58.

This was to be an ongoing concern. Conservative faithfulness to the Protestant missionary heritage was also manifest in an uncritical perpetuation of a discredited missiology. Newbigin would continue to raise concerns about the association between power and missionary progress in the strategizing of conservative evangelicals to evangelize unreached people groups. He recalled how, when Indian tanks invaded Bangladesh (in 1971), there was the suggestion by some in the CSI to follow the tanks with missionaries: "There seemed to be a strange inner compulsion which suggested that where our power goes, there is the place to send missionaries. To be frank, I am afraid of the strong stench of imperialism, which too often infects the call for world evangelization."[74]

Conservative Evangelical Concerns about Integration

The swing in emphasis in mission theology has often been referred to as a pendulum oscillating between extreme positions. Prior to the Tambaram conference (1938), especially in Anglo-Saxon circles, the emphasis was on the transformation of society. As noted, Tambaram placed the church at the centre of missionary thinking creating a germane culture for developments in thinking on mission and unity.[75] The church-centric model prevailed until Willingen (1952). From then on the pendulum swung again, with sustained attacks against church-centricism and calls that "the world must set the agenda." This swing away from the centrality of the redeemed community in mission provoked evangelical suspicion of "secularization" within the ecumenical movement.

Although the fundamentalist-modernist controversy occurred in the 1920s and 1930s many conservative evangelicals were, by the 1960s, still profoundly conditioned by this controversy. Conservative evangelicals were "haunted" by memories of the "social gospel movement" in which "a facile optimism about the course of human history, combined with a shallow theological mood, was equating the Kingdom of God with suburban comfort on earth."[76] One of the results of this conflict was "Protestant liberalism's rise to ecclesiastical power during the first third of this

---

74. Newbigin, "Cross-Currents," 150.

75. Newbigin, "Call to Mission," 255–56.

76. N. Goodall, "Evangelicalism and the Ecumenical Movement," *ER* 15:4 (1963) 407–8.

century . . . [which] removed evangelical emphases in denominational leadership, educational institutions, and religious publications."[77]

In reaction against the utopian promise of transformation of the "social gospel" many evangelicals, in what was largely a lay movement, turned for help to the Scofield Reference Bible, embracing dispensationalism with its "futuristic and millennial understanding of the Kingdom of God."[78] In their overreaction against the "social gospel," conservative evangelicals retreated from the public arena. Their understanding of the gospel became excessively pietistic, and individualistic, the gospel being merely the promise of *future*, eternal life. A major correction to this came through Carl Henry's critique of fundamentalism: "Whereas once the redemptive gospel was a world-changing message, now it was narrowed to a world-resisting message. . . . Fundamentalism, in revolting against the Social Gospel, seemed also to revolt against the Christian social imperative."[79] Henry's book contributed to the emergence of "neo-evangelicalism" which sought to recover the "social imperative" evidenced in the ministry of early pioneers of the evangelical movement. Evangelical protest against liberalism was crystallized with the formation, in 1941, of the National Association of Evangelicals and the militantly separatist American Council of Christian Churches.[80]

A generation on, both separatist fundamentalists and (to a lesser extent) the neo-evangelicals were still in "the trenches," the object of their ire now being the WCC.[81] As evangelicals looked on—sometimes profoundly ignorant of the ecumenical movement, yet critical nonetheless—they were thus tempted, by a sense of *déjà vu* from the fundamentalist-modernist controversy, to be suspicious or dismissive of the WCC. Their attack against the perceived liberalism within the WCC was typified by Carl McIntire, who founded the International Council of Christian Churches (in 1948), in opposition to the ecumenical alternative (the NCCCUSA). McIntire remained vehemently opposed to the ecumenical movement. The more moderate neo-evangelicals were antagonized by his extreme public vitriol.

77. Henry, "Evangelicals and Ecumenism," 10.

78. A. F. Glasser, "Reconciliation between Ecumenical and Evangelical Theologies and Theologians of Mission," *Missionalia* 7:3 (1979) 106.

79. Henry, *The Uneasy Conscience of Modern Fundamentalism*, 19, 22.

80. For a history of the National Association of Evangelicals, see J. A. Carpenter, *Revive Us Again: The Reawakening of American Fundamentalism* (New York: Oxford University Press, 1997) 141–60.

81. Glasser, "Mission in the 1990s," 4.

Yet, whilst abhorring his methods, many privately supported his critique against the WCC.[82]

The Politicization of the WCC

Of particular concern to many evangelicals was the perceived "politicization" of the gospel. At Willingen (1952) Paul Lehmann had sought to establish "a direct line between evangelism and politics"[83]—a position which was hotly contested at the IMC conference. The shift in the WCC's focus from the church to the world was confirmed in the eyes of many evangelical by various developments within the ecumenical movement. "The 'Christian Presence' school, Bonhoeffer's 'religionless Christianity,' and 'socio-political involvement' appeared to be replacing many classical approaches"; trends which, as they developed in the 1960s, were heralded "as proof of [the WCC's] apostasy."[84]

Was this "politicization" simply the WCC internalizing the struggles on the world stage between the first and third worlds, or was the WCC also initiating these changes?[85] Between internal and external factors which were most determinative for the WCC? Johannes Aagaard tracks the rise of MM Thomas' ecumenical career as a major vehicle for the politicization of the WCC. Thomas, through the 1950 World Student Christian Federation (WSCF) consultation in Paris, and its subsequent publication, introduced the word "revolution" as a theological concept. "What M. M. Thomas was able to say with a few friends in 1950, he expressed in 1966 as the chairman of the Geneva [Church and Society] Conference . . . [H] is political theology, which is through and through a missionary theology, was affirmed. It was then presented to the Uppsala Assembly in 1968, at which Thomas was elected the chairman of the Central Committee of the WCC."[86] Thomas' rise in prominence can thus be understood as a conduit for the increasing politicization of WCC theology. This is supported by Charles West who recalled that concepts introduced at the 1966 Geneva

82. This included such prominent evangelicals as Martyn Lloyd-Jones. Andrew Walls interview with Laing, 24/4/2009.

83. P. L. Lehmann, "Editorial: Willingen and Lund: The Church on the Way to Unity," *Theology Today* 9:4 (1953) 434–35.

84. Bosch, "Ecumenicals and Evangelicals," 458.

85. Berkhof thinks external factors were decisive in politicizing the WCC, *contra* Aagaard. Berkhof, "Berlin versus Geneva," 83.

86. Aagaard, "Trends in the Sixties," 23–24.

conference made it the "exploding point" between first and third worlds. He remembers how Thomas "was *always* asking revolutionary questions of the WCC."[87] Thomas, by his concerns and actions, was a pioneering representative for other ecumenical third-world leaders who emerged during this time.[88] Emilio Castro saw the 1966 conference as decisive, greatly influencing the agenda of the ecumenical movement for future decades.[89]

This process of theologizing on revolution naturally developed into action in the WCC's program to Combat Racism. During the 1970s this program took the significant step of moving beyond the WCC's remit of helping churches to instead be involved directly in political movements, some of which were violent in their protest.[90] Needless to say, these trends filled evangelical onlookers with alarm and suspicion as they saw "proclamation" being displaced by "political action," and the central role of the church being eclipsed by secular, militant groups.

Organizational Questions

Whilst evangelicals of various persuasions had been comfortable to have the freedom to associate with the IMC there was reticence, suspicion and fear of more formal membership of the WCC, which aroused connotations of a bureaucratic machine, and the ogre of a "super-church."

For many evangelicals organizational affiliation was much less of a priority than world evangelism. And many interpreted the trend of their growing missionary strength—which contrasted with declining numbers of missionaries and mission budgets in churches involved in the ecumenical movement—as confirmation that they held the right convictions.[91] The 1950s witnessed growing transdenominational cooperation for conservative evangelicals outside of the ecumenical movement. Why then risk their free association and emphasis on mission to be "imperilled by ecclesiasticism" within the WCC? This would dampen evangelical zeal, stifling the

87. Charles West, interview with Laing, 15/9/2008. Emphasis added.

88. Other notable leaders included Joshua Russell Chandran, president of the United Theological College, Bangalore, India; D. T. Niles, Methodist pastor and evangelist from Sri Lanka; and T. B. Simatupong, former commander of the Indonesian forces against the Dutch after World War II. Ibid.

89. E. Castro, "Ecumenical Social Thought in the Post-Cold War Period," *ER* 43:3 (1991) 305.

90. West, interview, 15/9/2008.

91. A. F. Glasser, "The Evolution of Evangelical Mission Theology since World War II," *IBMR* 9:1 (1985) 10.

voluntary spirit with "bureaucracy" and officialdom. Evangelicals were convinced that their particular concerns would be marginalized by the increasing politicization and secularization they perceived to be occurring within the WCC.

Integration of the IMC "caught many missionaries outside the conciliar movement in a double squeeze."[92] Evangelicals who sought, to whatever degree, to cooperate with the ecumenical movement found themselves subject to attack from two fronts. They exposed themselves to a "subtle" and sometimes "snide" "barrage" of criticism from the mainline churches. And, on the other front, for mere contact with ecumenicals, evangelicals also faced attack from "isolationist" fundamentalists such as Carl McIntire and Bob Jones, the latter of whom saw those evangelicals "as worse than theological liberals because they [were] harder to distinguish!"[93]

Membership of the IMC had been accepted by mission boards, but many would not tolerate *any* form of association with the WCC[94]—this was the case for boards which were members of the EFMA and IFMA. Even just to meet with persons involved in the conciliar movement was, for some evangelicals, to risk "loss of missionary money and candidates," "severe and scathing criticism," and the possibility of schism within their organization.[95]

The EFMA/IFMA sought to establish evangelical fellowships in other countries which would mirror the exclusive stance of the American National Association of Evangelicals. This contrasted with the more inclusive evangelical fellowships such as in the United Kingdom and India. In India membership in Evangelical Fellowship of India (EFI) was "open 'to Churches, missions, institutions, organizations, groups, or individuals." This meant that membership of the EFI did not adversely affect other affiliations.[96] However, for national evangelical fellowships established with EFMA /IFMA assistance, a condition of membership was exclusion from *any* form of association or membership with the WCC. Smith lamented the divisiveness this would cause, especially for Christian minorities in the majority world.[97]

92. Henry, "Evangelicals and Ecumenism," 12.

93. Ibid.

94. Through their membership of the DWME.

95. Smith, "Conservative Evangelicals," 185.

96. E. L. Smith, "Wheaton Congress in the Eyes of an Ecumenical Observer," *IRM* 55:220 (1966) 482.

97. Ibid.

Evangelicals were also concerned that their voice would be suppressed within the WCC. The charge was made that the WCC was neither representative of evangelicals, and, more seriously, was actively suppressing their concerns.[98] This charge has some credence. As noted, for a council of *churches*, it was organizationally difficult to relate to the multifarious forms of evangelicalism. The fact the WCC would not offer membership to individuals, independent congregations, or faith mission boards was evidence, to evangelicals, of its "monolithic character," and inflexible nature.[99] Donald Dayton demonstrated how "inadequately representative the WCC actually is of the worldwide Christian movement. Its ecclesiastical 'mainstream' represents barely half of all Protestants"[100]—that is, evangelicals were excluded. What is more significant is that Emilio Castro, in his editorial, endorsed Dayton's view that evangelicals "represent a layer of Christian truth . . . without which the ecumenical movement remains incomplete."[101]

Theological Opposition

Whilst evangelicals had happily associated with the IMC, which had no doctrinal basis, the broadening ecclesiological membership of the WCC made them critical of its "supposed latitudinarianism."[102] Suspicion in America and Britain of the WCC was exacerbated by the acceptance of several Orthodox Churches into membership and the warming of relationships with the Roman Catholics, culminating in the WCC being given official observer status at Vatican II.[103] To some fringe elements within British evangelicalism the WCC was thus to be interpreted as "a shadow of mystery Babylon, that great apostate body typified by the great whore of Revelation 17."[104] Such opinions racked Scottish Baptists in the 1950s and lead conservative elements within the English and Welsh Baptist Union, in the 1960s, to demand that the Union withdraws from membership of the

98. Henry, "Evangelicals and Ecumenism."

99. Smith, "Conservative Evangelicals," 189.

100. D. W. Dayton, "Yet Another Layer of the Onion: Or Opening the Ecumenical Door to Let the Riffraff In," *ER* 40:1 (1988) 87–110. Cf. Glasser, "Mission in the 1990s," 6.

101. E. Castro, "Editorial," *ER* 40:1 (1988) 3.

102. Goodall, "Ecumenical Movement," 404.

103. Ibid., 403.

104. Editorial in *The Advent Witness*, cited by Bebbington, *Evangelicalism*, 255.

WCC.[105] Yet, concurrent with this stance, other British evangelicals took a more positive view of the WCC accepting "that there was something for them to learn through ecumenism."[106] More centrist British evangelicals such as Stephen Neill and E. A. Payne were much more positively engaged with the WCC, accepting leadership roles within it.[107] And conservative British evangelicals, such as John Stott, whilst at times being highly critical of the WCC, did not remain isolated from it, but was consistently involved in its assemblies.[108]

American conservative evangelicals were, on the whole, more critical of the WCC (and more distant from it) than their British counterparts. They were critical of its inclusiveness, allowing membership of any and every church which accepted the WCC basis. Conservatives held to the concept of a "pure" church which consisted only of those who had a personal experience of conversion.[109] The "indifference" to this concern, exhibited by many "inclusivist" churches, repelled conservatives from association with the WCC. For conservative evangelicals there was the underlying fear that the WCC "cannot be trusted to preserve the faith-heritage" of the church.[110]

Conservatives held that personal rebirth was a requisite for true Christian unity; unity being primarily spiritual rather than organizational. They were thus dubious of "mechanical," "top-down" efforts from within

105. Ibid.

106. Ibid., 249.

107. From 1947 to 1951 Neill served as assistant bishop to the archbishop of Canterbury with the responsibility of liaising with the WCC; Dyron Daughrity, "Researching Bishop Stephen Neill: Engaging History, Methods, and the 'Reconstruction,'" Henry Martyn Paper, http://131.111.227.198/CDaurighty.htm. It was during this time that Neill wrote and edited several works on the ecumenical movement, such as R. Rouse, S. Neill, and H. E. Fey, *A History of the Ecumenical Movement, 1517–1968* (Geneva: World Council of Churches, 1993).

Payne was general secretary of the British Baptist Union from 1951 to 1967. For twenty-seven years Payne shared in the work of the WCC, serving on the Faith and Order commission and the central committee. "He was elected a president of the world council on his resignation from the central committee in 1968 and held that office until he retired from the council itself in 1975." W. M. S. West, "Payne, Ernest Alexander (1902–1980)," *Oxford Dictionary of National Biography*, Oxford University Press, Sept 2004; online ed., May 2006 [http://www.oxforddnb.com/view/article/40864].

108. For a biography, see T. Dudley-Smith, *John Stott: The Making of a Leader* (Leicester: InterVarsity, 1999).

109. Smith, "Conservative Evangelicals," 186.

110. G. C. Berkouwer, "What Conservative Evangelicals Can Learn from the Ecumenical Movement," *Christianity Today* 10 (1966) 17.

the WCC to impose unity with churches they understood to be "indifferent" to the need for personal conversion.[111] Furthermore, because of its inclusive, open basis, conservatives were critical of the "world council theology" for being "almost inescapably" universalist.[112] Conservative evangelicals accused the ecumenical movement of developing "an easygoing universalism that blunts the cutting edge of the gospel."[113]

The WCC operated on a provisional ecclesiological neutrality enshrined in the "Toronto statement" (1950).[114] Despite the insistence of the WCC that "no Church is obliged to change its ecclesiology as a consequence of membership," many evangelicals believed the WCC had an inherent ecclesiology, and that it could develop into a "super-church" which would rob evangelicals of their ecclesiological freedom.[115] The above factors meant that many conservative evangelicals, particularly in America, were profoundly wary of the growing intimacy between the IMC and the WCC.

Conclusion

By the middle of the twentieth century, the Protestant missionary movement interpreted the change in world events as the turning of the tide against Christian mission. Certainly the tide had turned against their antiquated definition of mission, historically tainted with colonialism. The hostility against the Protestant missionary movement, and the resultant introspection it produced, were to be creative rather than destructive forces, leading to a more adequate definition and foundation of mission.

Protestant missions, which had emerged from the West, faced a loss of confidence, not just in their own validity, but, more fundamentally, in the enduring validity of the gospel. The turmoil in the supposed "Christian" West undermined confidence in Christianity and the West's authority to propagate it. This loss of confidence was most critically felt by mission organizations through dwindling finances and declining numbers of missionaries. Missions had grown complacent from the benevolence furnished by colonialism. But now, in the traditional mission

111. Smith, "Conservative Evangelicals," 188.

112. Ibid., 189.

113. Newbigin, "Cross-Currents," 150.

114. This is discussed in ch. 5.

115. Smith, "Conservative Evangelicals," 189. A fear also shared by some Scandinavian evangelicals.

fields—especially the showcase, China—hostile forces were thwarting the advance of traditional Western missions. These factors led mission leaders to seek a more sure theological foundation for mission. They did so acknowledging the increasing overlap and growth in intimacy between the IMC and the WCC. Organizational and theological factors demanded that the "association" between the two world councils be clarified.

The exception to this was the conservative evangelicals. Perceiving the WCC to already be theologically compromised they eschewed ongoing association with the IMC as it became increasingly intimate with the WCC—why join a sinking ship? For conservative evangelicals increased numbers and revenue was interpreted as divine sanction for them to continue with business as usual. This resulted in a divisive pursuit of their missionary goals. The loose and broad-based association which the IMC had maintained for decades was fragmented with the relationship between evangelicals and ecumenicals becoming increasing polarized and antagonistic. Evangelical isolation delayed the reformation of their theology, and it was not until Lausanne (1974) that evangelicals began to make fundamental revisions to their missiology.

At least within the ecumenical movement it was acknowledged that the church was called both to mission *and* unity. This recovery of ecclesiology and the consensus that emerged on the missionary nature of the church led to the question: how then should the church be structured? What are the implications for the form of church and the ministry? For some each organization had an inherent ecclesiology which should therefore determine its organization. Others took a more pragmatic and functional approach, arguing that beyond the ecclesiology of the local congregation there was freedom to organize structures, the determining factor being their effectiveness.

As noted, the post-Tambaram, church-centric model of mission was not without its detractors. The ensuing debate between those who held to this model and those who rejected it facilitated fruitful enquiry on the relationship between the church and the world, and the relationship between salvation and secular history. For Newbigin, his critique of the inadequacies of the church-centric model would lead him to into more constructive theologizing on the trinitarian basis of mission; making the significant shift from addressing the *structures* of mission to exploring the *substance* of mission. The process of integration thus enabled Newbigin to move from reflecting upon the *reorganization and rehabilitation* of mission to more fundamental issues of how mission should be *redefined*. The acceptance of the *missio Dei* concept, which acknowledged that the church is missionary in its nature, led to an exploration of how this should be embodied in structures, ranging from the level of the local congregation to the international arena, the relationship between the IMC and the WCC.

In chapter 3 the focus now turns more directly to Newbigin, to examine his contribution to the process of integration. Newbigin, as a member of the Central Committee, drafted a document, "The Calling of the Church to Mission and to Unity" (Rolle, 1951) which provided an early theological foundation on which subsequent construction towards integration could be built. The following year, at the IMC conference at Willingen, Newbigin succeeded in having this document adopted by the IMC. But other factors ensured that Willingen was both a difficult and creative conference determining the theological agenda which would fully occupy Newbigin beyond his theologizing on integration.

3

Rolle and Willingen

A Theological Foundation for Integration (and Mission)

THE PURPOSE OF THIS chapter is to examine Newbigin's involvement in two meetings, at Rolle, Switzerland, in 1951 with the WCC and at Willingen, Germany, in 1952 with the IMC. These meetings, and Newbigin's contribution at them, were crucial to the process which would culminate in the integration of the two councils. Willingen in particular was turbulent but catalytic, first introducing Newbigin to questions which he would later return to. After his more immediate concerns about the *structure* of mission, Willingen enabled Newbigin to more fundamentally examine the *substance* of mission.

Newbigin's introduction to the ecumenical movement was not through the IMC but through involvement with the WCC. He attended the preparatory meeting and then the first assembly of the WCC as a delegate of the CSI (in 1948). A central and enduring conviction for Newbigin was that at the heart of the gospel, the church was called to mission, and to be one. This conviction had been strengthened during his career in India, first as a missionary and then as a bishop of the CSI. And this conviction was evident in his drafting of the statement "The Calling of the Church to Mission and to Unity,"[1] which, in many ways, became an early manifesto for integration and the theological foundation to enable its progression. This statement was drafted by Newbigin at the Central Committee meetings of the WCC in 1951 in Rolle. A year later, at Willingen, Newbigin

1. CC WCC, "The Calling of the Church to Mission and to Unity," *ER* 4:1 (1951) 66–71.

succeeded in having a revised version of the Rolle statement adopted by the IMC. At least on paper, there was an agreed theological foundation within the two councils on which further work towards integration could proceed.

Willingen, however, proved to be a very turbulent meeting. The main purpose of Willingen was to seek a renewed theological basis for the missionary obligation of the church. Consensus could not be achieved and the conference was polarized between what Paul Lehmann and Johannes C. (Hans) Hoekendijk advocated, and the majority of the delegates who rejected their report. To overcome the deadlock Newbigin was asked to draft a revised statement, which was accepted by the conference.

Although at the time the delegates felt they had failed at Willingen, with hindsight Willingen's importance is acknowledged for having identified the *missio Dei* concept as essential to theology of mission—although without having worked out clearly its full meaning. The tension between the differing interpretations of *missio Dei*, particularly concerning the relationship of the church vis-à-vis the world, was inaugurated at Willingen. Hoekendijk's position gained dominance a decade later. Newbigin's engagement with Hoekendijk enabled him to critique the church-centric mission model established at Tambaram. Besides providing the theological foundation for integration, Rolle and particularly Willingen set the agenda for missiology; the unresolved issues raised at Willingen providing fruitful avenues of enquiry for Newbigin and others.

The Rolle Statement: "The Calling of the Church to Mission and to Unity"

In the summer of 1951 Newbigin attended several meetings of the WCC; most significant was his input at Rolle.[2] He had been invited on to the "Committee of twenty-five," a steering committee whose remit was to develop the theme for the second assembly of the WCC (Evanston, 1954). Days after those meetings, Newbigin then attended the Central Committee, representing the CSI. Both meetings were characterized by heated debate and frank disagreements.

Before examining the statement which Newbigin drafted, "The Calling of the Church to Mission and to Unity," Newbigin's involvement in the drafting of other statements will be briefly reviewed, as they provide

2. For Newbigin's published account of the Rolle meetings, see Newbigin, *Unfinished Agenda*, 133–34.

important background to the climate of theological discussion within the WCC. Furthermore, they demonstrate Newbigin's concern to draft statements which would achieve broad theological consensus. For Evanston Newbigin was particularly keen that the preparatory documents would be acceptable to evangelicals and Pentecostals. In his preface to the draft on the Evanston theme of "Christian Hope," Newbigin recorded that "the discussion on this subject was often very difficult, both because of misunderstanding and defective insight and experience, and also because of unresolved differences of belief."[3] Newbigin reckoned that he had been given the daunting task of chairing the Committee of twenty-five as he was the only member from a pastoral background, all the other members were college professors. The major source of disagreement was between the Americans (and British) and the Continental group over their interpretation of eschatology. Newbigin's pastoral oversights were evident in letters to his wife, Helen; twice he mentioned that he felt the meetings needed more prayer if significant progress was to be made.[4] In bringing the report he drafted to an equally stormy Central Committee, Newbigin sought to get his report approved without it being toned down, with the hope that the report might heal the breach between the WCC and "radical sects."[5] Newbigin realized that there were profound suspicions within IMC circles about the "liberal theology" perceived to be emanating from the WCC. As a prerequisite to integration Newbigin sought to overcome those misgivings and build consensus with a mutually acceptable statement.

At the Central Committee Newbigin was asked to chair the section which dealt with mission and unity. To this end Newbigin drafted the report on "The Calling of the Church to Mission and to Unity." In contrast to the report on Christian Hope, it is significant that this statement was accepted by the Central Committee, although it too did not receive a smooth passage, "[t]he discussion in the section also came sharply up against the resistance of the dominant Anglo-Saxon theology to any serious

---

3. Lesslie Newbigin and W. A. Visser 't Hooft, "The First Report of the Advisory Commission on the Theme of the Second Assembly of the World Council of Churches," *ER* 4:1 (1951) 71.

4. Newbigin to Helen Newbigin, 21/7/1951, BUL: DA29/1/6/129 & 25/7/51, BUL: DA29/1/6/130.

5. By "radical sects" Newbigin meant conservative evangelicals. The report received a hostile reception from the Central Committee, with the result that "Visser 't Hooft thoroughly lost his rag about it." Instead of the report being sent by the Committee to the churches, the Committee decided "to take note of the fact that the General Secretary will send it to the Churches." Newbigin to Helen, 13/8/1951, BUL: DA29/1/6/137.

discussion of eschatology."[6] The Enlightenment concept of progress, the Kingdom of God coming by slow and steady evolutionary processes, undergirded Anglo-Saxon eschatology. In contrast, Continental Europeans, who had, at close quarters, experienced the apocalyptic events of World Wars I and II, held to a more literal interpretation of the biblical teaching of the *eschaton*.

The Rolle statement began by elucidating the current dichotomy between mission and church, this polarization being a consequence of the Protestant missionary movement. In the current confusion and crisis of relationship the danger continued of perpetuating this dichotomy in various ways. Some advocated a move from the age of mission to the age of ecumenism, discarding mission as a colonial relic; others were continuing with an exclusive concern for mission whilst distancing themselves from, or even denigrating the work of, the WCC.[7]

There was the danger of reductionism, understanding the role of the IMC to be missionary and that of the WCC to be for church unity. This did not reflect the reality that concerns for mission and unity were intermingled within both councils. As a consequence of the missionary movement there was a renewed quest for unity. "Younger churches" were locally seeking unity and calling others (especially Western Christians) to question their complacency about disunity. "Unity has been sought out of a deep conviction that only together can Christians give true witness and effective service to the world."[8] And those involved in the missionary movement had seen "a vision of unity which transcended those divisions within which Churches unmindful of their missionary calling had been so long content to live."[9] This section is almost autobiographical, Newbigin alluding to the recent formation of the CSI and the other union schemes in the subcontinent.

An enduring emphasis of Newbigin's was that the word "ecumenical" should maintain its full meaning and not be reduced to refer to the ecumenical movement (concerning only the church) in contradistinction to the missionary movement.[10] This concern was embodied in the text: "It is important to insist that this word [ecumenical], which comes from the

---

6. Newbigin, *Unfinished Agenda*, 133.

7. WCC, "Rolle: Mission and Unity," 67–68.

8. Ibid., 67.

9. Ibid.

10. Similar concerns are expressed in Newbigin, "Forms of Unity," 3. Lesslie Newbigin, "Ecumenical Amnesia," *IBMR* 18:1 (1994) 4.

Greek word for the whole inhabited earth, is properly used to describe everything that relates to the whole task of the whole Church to bring the Gospel to the whole world. . . . Both the IMC and the WCC, are thus properly to be described as organs of the Ecumenical Movement."[11]

The text argued from the theological premise that the church's call to mission and unity is central to the redemptive work of Christ: "the Church's unity and apostolicity rests upon the whole redeeming work of Christ—past, present and future." Concerning the past—"It rests upon His finished work upon the Cross." Christ's "atonement for the whole human race" brings reconciliation with God and with fellow humans; the church is thus constrained to proclaim that message of reconciliation. For the present—"It rests upon His continuing work as the risen Lord." "By His spirit we are joined as members in His body, committed to His redemptive mission." Abiding in Christ, the church is empowered as witness to the nations and as first fruit to gather the nations into Christ. And future—"It rests upon His promise that He will come again. In His final victory the kingdoms of the world will be His, there will be one flock as there is one Shepherd, and all things will be summed up in Him." "Thus the obligation to take the Gospel to the whole world, and the obligation to draw all Christ's people together both rest upon Christ's whole work, and are indissolubly connected"[12]—a repeated emphasis of Newbigin's.[13]

Based upon this theological premise questions were then raised: what are the implications for the life of the church, for the missionary task, and how can, or should, this theological premise be embodied in the organizational expression of the relationship between the two councils? Concerning the relationship between the councils, Rolle asked whether "'association' should now give way to a new and much closer relationship?" Both councils were asked to bring recommendations as to how they were to make "their relationship the most convincing instrument and best symbol possible of the unity affirmed throughout this statement."[14]

11. WCC, "Rolle: Mission and Unity," 68. Visser 't Hooft also expressed the same definition of "*Oikoumene*," CCM, 1962, 81.

12. Ibid., 69.

13. E.g., see Newbigin, "The Student Volunteer Missionary Union," 98; Newbigin, *Reunion*, 19.

14. The published version of the report in *Ecumenical Review* contained only sections 1 to 5, which the Central Committee recommended for discussion in the churches. The full version contained "Section 6: Implications for the future structure and relationship of the IMC and the WCC." Discussion on the text is recorded in CCM, 1951, 11–15. Response to the document, which includes discussion by the British National Council of Churches and the conference of British Missionary Societies,

A danger was that discussion would only take place at the organizational level. A more fundamental concern was the theological implication for the relationship between mission and the church. Newbigin continued to stress that the issues were greater than just organizational: "It cannot be emphasised too strongly that the real issues . . . have far wider and deeper implications that that of organization."[15]

Response to the Rolle Statement

The Rolle document, having been received and accepted by the Central Committee, was then distributed to the Joint Committee and constituent members of the WCC and IMC, elucidating much comment and discussion.[16] An illuminating response to the document was given by Hoekendijk (whose influential role at Willingen will be considered later in the chapter); although this was a personal response, it was based upon his discussion with European mission leaders and thus reflected their suspicion and disquiet at the prospect of integration.[17] European mission leaders accepted the theological argument of the Rolle statement but were profoundly skeptical of the theological direction they perceived the WCC to be taking. Hoekendijk was skeptical that, with just one document, this trend would be reversed:

> Everyone who has been through the recent discussions about "integration" will have been embarrassed and shocked by the fact that the pre-eminently "theological" section of the Ecumenical Movement, i.e. Faith and Order, has, in its preparatory material for the Lund Conference (NB centred round the Nature of the Church!) so largely ignored the missionary dimension of the Church. In the minds of many missionary people (on the European Continent at least!) this fact is held to be symptomatic of the thought-trends in the movement towards unity.[18]

including Max Warren's critique, can be found at: SOAS: IMC/27–00–01/7; 27–00–06/3–4; 264.007/1.

15. CCM, 1951, 11–15.

16. Ibid.

17. Hoekendijk to Goodall, 23/1/1952, WCC: 27.0013.

18. Ibid., 2. Hoekendijk was referring to O. S. Tomkins, *The Church in the Purpose of God: An Introduction to the Work of the Commission on Faith and Order of the World Council of Churches, in Preparation for the Third World Conference on Faith and Order to Be Held at Lund, Sweden, in 1952* (London: SCM, 1950).

The divide between mission and the church was the harvest of a long history of mutual isolation. For Hoekendijk, it was therefore premature, on the basis of one document, to propose discussion on the organizational relationship between the councils; much more foundational work was first required to deepen and clarify theological understandings and then disseminate those findings. Crucial to achieving that end was the function of the Joint Committee. Hoekendijk questioned how a committee that met only once a year, and did not have an executive, could facilitate adequate theological reflection on which consequent action might proceed. In Hoekendijk's opinion, in its existing guise the Joint Committee was far from being a convincing instrument and symbol for unity. To amend this Hoekendijk proposed that the role of the Joint Committee must be strengthened.[19] The Rolle statement had been accepted by the Central Committee and—as will be discussed later—by the enlarged body of the IMC (in 1952). There was therefore the danger that this rubber stamp of approval would result in further theological reflection being seen as unnecessary, and the next stage, organizational implementation would dominate discussion. In contrast to that possibility Hoekendijk contended that "We should not 'relax' theologically after Rolle, but rather give first priority to a further (and different!) theological re-thinking of the real issues."[20]

This was deemed necessary because of the profoundly different agendas held by leaders in the respective councils. Hoekendijk cited the opinion of mission leaders such as Charles Ranson, Max Warren, and Walter Freytag, who feared that "missions will be sold out to the WCC." Hoekendijk advocated that "we should try and understand the inarticulate, partly covert, and even almost instinctive resistance of these people to any form of further 'integration.'"[21]

A further concern Hoekendijk recognized was that mission leaders were conscious of the danger of a loss of support from evangelical groups by identifying with the WCC. Evangelicals were the growing majority in missions, their numerical strength growing particularly after the second world war. Whilst missionary leadership might unite with WCC, the rank-and-file majority shunned the ecumenical movement, and might instead

19. Ibid., 6. It is significant to note that at the Rolle Joint Committee meeting, Bishop Stephen Neill, who had resigned, was replaced by Hoekendijk, who at the time was Secretary for Evangelism of the WCC. Joint Committee, Rolle, 10/8/1951, SOAS: IMC/270002.

20. Hoekendijk to R. S. Bilheimer, 14/3/1952, WCC: 27.0013, 3.

21. Ibid., 1.

side with more conservative evangelicals, with a resultant rift emerging. There was thus the need to convince the grassroots of the need to create a truly effective ecumenical organization. "One of the weakest points in the present Ecumenical Movement is, I fear, that we have not yet succeeded in increasing in any significant way the ecumenical interest at the grassroots. It is still a rather 'aristocratic' movement." In order to do this Hoekendijk advocated the need to walk "the long and often wearisome road of cautiously explaining, patiently interpreting and . . . eventually convincing those groups which in fact carry the major responsibility for our present missionary work."[22]

But the leadership of both councils worked on the assumption that integration was the correct expression of their theological convictions. This focus, combined with the very limited resources of the IMC to engage in patient and protracted discussion with evangelicals prevented the IMC from adequately addressing Hoekendijk's plea. Others, such as Newbigin, however, shared Hoekendijk's concern. Newbigin's concern about evangelicals was strengthened the following year by his conversations with Pentecostal and Baptist representatives at Willingen. He anticipated that the acceptance of the doctrinal statement of the Commission of twenty-five, which he had fought to prevent being watered down, would be endorsed by the Evanston assembly. This would then bring the possibility of a new approach to evangelical groups.[23]

The Rolle statement, and the consensus it built at least within IMC/WCC circles, proved to be the theological foundation upon which progress towards integration could be built. What was the proper practical response to this theological foundation, how could the relationship between the IMC and the WCC be adequately embodied to reflect the sentiments of this statement? The following summer (1952) Newbigin again left India for meetings in Europe—to attend the IMC conference in Willingen. Despite opposition against the eschatology of the statement Newbigin prevailed in having the statement accepted at both Rolle (by the WCC) and at Willingen (by the IMC). The Willingen version of the text was much less discursive than the fuller Rolle statement. Nonetheless, the essential argument of both was the same—the church's calling to mission and unity are based on Christ's work, and are thus "indissolubly connected."[24] New-

22. Ibid., 2.

23. Newbigin to Goodall, 12/12/1953, SOAS: IMC/27–00–06/11.

24. Lesslie Newbigin, "A Statement on the Missionary Calling of the Church," in *Missions under the Cross*, ed. Norman Goodall (London: Edinburgh House Press, 1953) 193–94.

bigin recorded that "many of the [statement's] ideas were to be developed further at Willingen in the following year and they helped to create the theological climate for the later integration of the IMC and the WCC."[25]

The IMC Conference at Willingen (1952)

The IMC met at Willingen with the aim of restating the basis for the missionary obligation of the church. Although deemed a "failure" at the time because they could not establish consensus, with hindsight Willingen came to be recognized as one of the most important missionary conferences of the twentieth century.[26] At Willingen the *missio Dei* concept came to the fore.[27] This was evident in the statement, drafted by Newbigin, "A Statement on the Missionary Calling of the Church."[28] At Willingen a consensus was achieved which accepted the missionary nature of the church. This was to set the theological agenda for Newbigin and others to ask: how then should the church be structured to express its missionary nature? The scope of the answer to this question ranged from the level of the local congregation to the relationship between the two international councils. These councils, as agents of the church, expressed the church's ecumenical vision for the whole world.

Besides these important theological breakthroughs, Willingen also set the compass for future theological enquiry along another avenue. Although Newbigin did not appreciate it at the time,[29] Willingen first introduced him—particularly through the work of Hoekendijk and Lehmann—to questions concerning the relationship between sacred and secular history, between the church and the world, which would, a decade later, dominate his thinking as the first director of the Division for World Mission and Evangelism (DWME).

The Mood at Willingen

Willingen was characterized by dark foreboding: "At Willingen 'the shadow of things to come' was much more conspicuous [than at Whitby, in

25. Newbigin, *Unfinished Agenda*, 133.

26. Ibid., 138.

27. D. J. Bosch, *Transforming Mission: Paradigm Shifts in Theology of Mission* (Maryknoll: Orbis, 1991) 390.

28. Newbigin, "Missionary Calling."

29. Newbigin, *Unfinished Agenda*, 153.

1947] as the dominant influence in the mood of the conference."[30] During the conference Max Warren identified several reasons for malaise and a "loss of confidence" in missions. There was dismay: 1) at the shrinking of traditional mission fields; 2) that Christians were slow to recognize their international character; 3) at how Christian disunity was impairing and hampering witness; 4) at the development of worldwide denominationalism; 5) at the persistence of language barriers in mission; 6) by Americans that others perceived them as economic imperialists; 7) by "younger churches" that "older churches" were so slow to move out of old patterns of relationship.[31]

Minds were concentrated by what had transpired in China, which created a "peculiar precariousness" about the missionary task. There was the recognition that "[w]ork built up by the patient labour of generations may be swept away overnight." At Willingen they realized that they were on the brink: "We have come to the end of an age, perhaps to the end of the age."[32] On reflection there was the acknowledgment that the past missionary movement had not matched its activity with the "why" and "wherefore" of being active. Therefore, "No small part of our present embarrassment lies in the unwillingness of so many concerned with the missionary task of the Church to think theologically."[33] The mood of Willingen was symptomatic of a more general and pervasive malaise about missions. Willingen faced a fundamental loss of confidence in missions by churches in the West. This was exacerbated by the Cold War and by geopolitical upheavals and the emergence of new church movements such as Pentecostalism, Revivalism, and the African Independent Churches.[34] This forced Willingen to turn to fundamental theological reflection to seek an adequate basis for the continuing validity of mission.

30. Max A. C. Warren, "The Willingen Conference: A Report," September 1952, SOAS: IMC/264.011, 6.

31. Ibid., 7–13.

32. Goodall, *Minutes of the Enlarged Meeting and the Committee of the IMC: Willingen, Germany, July 5th to 21st, 1952,* (London; New York: IMC, 1952) 10.

33. Warren, "A Report," 14–15.

34. Max A. C. Warren, *Crowded Canvas: Some Experiences of a Life-Time* (London: Hodder & Stoughton, 1974) 154.

Theological Polarization

A Sense of Failure

At the conclusion of the conference Norman Goodall, the main organizer, acknowledged that faced with the need of the hour, Willingen had failed in its purpose.[35] Willingen had not provided a clear "message that would ring round the world and call the churches to a fresh dedication to their missionary task."[36] The failure was due to the lack of consensus concerning the report "The Missionary Obligation of the Church," the topic for the "Major Themes Group." In preparing for Willingen major work had been done in particular by Lehmann and Hoekendijk. But at Willingen the theological commission "refused to make up its mind," and after ten long days of wrestling the report was "received" rather than adopted.[37] For some the report acted as "little more than a paper-clip," holding together debating positions which were germane before the conference, evident during, and more fully articulated afterward.[38] Willingen was polarized between the strident voices of Hoekendijk and Lehmann, on the one hand, who sought a shift from a church-centric model of mission "to speak more of God's work in the secular world, in the political, cultural and scientific movements of the time," and, on the other hand, the majority of delegates, who still adhered to the model established at Tambaram.[39]

The rejected report was contentious because it sought "to explore a direct line between missions and history, between evangelism and politics" proposing that the "missionary obligation" was derived "from the judging and the redeeming activity" of God in the secular world.[40] Lehmann's account was that, at Willingen, this report was "torpedoed by the Anglo-Catholics and the German Lutherans." A small minority of Anglo-Catholics persisted in understanding the church "as the Body of Christ, is itself the mission, since it belongs to the outgoing activity of the Triune

35. Newbigin, *Unfinished Agenda*, 138. In 1944 Norman Goodall succeeded William Paton as London secretary of the IMC, becoming secretary of a joint committee in 1954. He retired from the WCC in 1963. P. R. Clifford, "Goodall, Norman (1896–1985)," rev., *Oxford Dictionary of National Biography*, Oxford University Press, 2004 [http://www.oxforddnb.com/view/article/31157].

36. F. Dearing to J. W. Decker, 29/8/1952, SOAS: IMC/264.012/4.

37. Lehmann, "Editorial," 434–35. N. Goodall, ed., *Missions under the Cross*, 187.

38. W. Richebächer, "Missio Dei: The Basis of Mission Theology or a Wrong Path?" *IRM* 92:367 (2003) 591.

39. Newbigin, *Unfinished Agenda*, 138.

40. Lehmann, "Editorial," 434–35.

God-head himself" and refused "to consider the instrumental character of the Christian mission." The German Lutherans, understandably cautious of equating divine activity with historical events due to the recent memory of Nazism, instead proposed that it was possible to discern God's *judgment* in historical events, but not God's *redemption*[41]—a distinction which was itself rather problematic.

Johannes (Hans) C. Hoekendijk

Hoekendijk was to be the most persistent critic of the post-Tambaram, church-centric model of mission. Prior to Willingen he had already articulated a strident critique of this model. Hoekendijk argued that the tendency towards "church-ism" was a consequence of the missionary theory first introduced by Henry Venn which, after years of implementation, was now harvesting the "missionary-doctrine-of-the-Church-in-reverse." Accepted mission theory advocated that "mission and Church are not conceived of as being coexistent, but rather as consecutive entities. The Church is the ultimate object of the Mission and takes its place."[42] The "younger church," having imbibed that theory—of *first* the mission, *then* the church—had taken it to its natural conclusion, "first the Mission, then the Church-free-from-the-Mission," "our missionary theory in reverse."[43] With missions obsessed with the church, "The world has almost ceased to be the world and is now conceived of as a sort of ecclesiastical training-ground. The kingdom is either confined within the bounds of the Church or else become something like an eschatological lightning on the far horizon," and missiological reflection is reduced to being a "veritable merry-go-round around the Church." [44] But "*Church-centric missionary thinking is bound to go astray, because it revolves around an illegitimate centre.*"[45]

Hoekendijk understood the church as "happening," as "event." "The nature of the Church can be sufficiently [and entirely] defined by its function, i.e. its participation in Christ's apostolic ministry."[46] The church, as apostolic event, functioned to establish *shalom* in the world.[47] The distinc-

41. Ibid., 435.

42. Hoekendijk, "Church in Missionary Thinking," 326.

43. Ibid., 329.

44. Ibid., 324.

45. Ibid., 333. Italics in original.

46. Ibid., 334.

47. J. C. Hoekendijk, *The Church Inside Out* (London: SCM, 1967) 19–20. This is a

tion between church and world was blurred as the church was envisaged as "the laboratory, the diakonia of a little group, living in a concrete situation, and serving each other and their environment by reforming the structure of a segment of society."[48]

With the church enmeshed in societal reform, mission cannot be equated merely with church planting, but must maintain its focus towards the "ends of the earth" and the "end of time." "The Church will then be the movement between kingdom and world, related to both; it is an apostolic event."[49] Although Hoekendijk had been advocating this interpretation of the church since 1950, it was to be another decade before his ideas gained wider acceptance, becoming "the overwhelmingly dominant ideas of the next decade."[50]

Newbigin recognized Hoekendijk as one of the chief critics of an "excessively Church-centric conception of the missionary task." In correcting against one danger Newbigin was right in his belief that Hoekendijk had fallen into another, that of "over-stressing" the missionary nature of the church "to the point of defining the Church *solely* in terms of its missionary function."[51] Newbigin is correct in his appraisal that Hoekendijk's purely functional interpretation of the church repudiated "completely the idea of the Church as an end in itself," and was thus an overstatement. This excessive "overemphasis" prompted Newbigin to respond that the "Church is both a means and an end, because it is a foretaste." The church is not merely instrumental and functional. "Precisely because the Church is here and now a real foretaste of heaven, she can be the witness and instrument of the kingdom of heaven." The church, correctly understood, does not simply point to the *eschaton* but embodies and expresses the community of the Holy Spirit in its worship and fellowship. "It is precisely because she is not *merely* instrumental that she can be instrumental."[52]

Newbigin later acknowledged that at Willingen, he had failed to understand the concerns of Hoekendijk and Lehmann.[53] But, five years later, his perspective shifted, and during his years in Geneva, he "flirted" with

---

reprint of an earlier article, J. C. Hoekendijk, "The Call to Evangelism," *IRM* 39 (1950).

48. Hoekendijk, *Church Inside Out*, 29.

49. Hoekendijk, "Church in Missionary Thinking," 336.

50. Newbigin, *Unfinished Agenda*, 138.

51. Newbigin, *Household of God*, 147. Emphasis added.

52. Ibid., 147–48. Italics in original.

53. Newbigin, *Unfinished Agenda*, 153.

the ideas of secular theology first proposed by Hoekendijk, engaging with them most extensively in *Honest Religion for Secular Man*.[54]

Newbigin's Contribution at Willingen

Coming from India to Willingen, Newbigin came "with the determination to challenge what [he] saw as the paralysis of missions, the practical exhaustion of the resources of the older churches in propping up relatively static churches in the old 'mission fields.'"[55] Although his theological convictions concerning the agency of the church in the world were at odds with Hoekendijk, Newbigin shared with Hoekendijk a similar assessment of the outcome of missionary enterprise in which the "younger church" was obscuring the horizon of the world beyond. At one of the plenary sessions Newbigin provoked "one of the most" lively debates when he stated that "the greater part of the contribution of the western churches towards the world mission of the Church, in service and money, was no longer employed on the frontier between the Church and the world." This debate concluded by rejecting this "too sweeping generalization."[56] Yet statistically Newbigin was entirely correct in his assertion.

Besides the acceptance of the Rolle statement drafted by Newbigin, "The Calling of the Church to Mission and to Unity," Newbigin also presented a paper at Willingen titled "The Christian Hope."[57] As already noted, his reflection on this theme would have no doubt been galvanized by the turbulent meetings he had already chaired of the "Committee of twenty-five" which wrestled with this theme in preparation for the second assembly at Evanston.

In this paper Newbigin noted that Christians do not hope in the debased way that the world does. Christian hope is rooted in the historical events of Christ's death and resurrection and consummated when Christ shall return as savior and judge. Christian hope is therefore not to be reduced to be merely the personal assurance of salvation of individuals. Rather, Christians hope in Christ, "who will visibly terminate and

---

54. Newbigin, *Honest Religion*. Wainwright uses this term of enamourement. Wainwright, *Newbigin*, 341–54. This topic will be explored in chs. 8 and 9.

55. Newbigin, *Unfinished Agenda*, 137.

56. Goodall, ed., *Missions under the Cross*, 18. Cf. Newbigin's original statement which was accepted by Rolle, WCC, "Rolle: Mission and Unity," 71.

57. Lesslie Newbigin, "The Christian Hope," in *Missions under the Cross*, ed. Norman Goodall (London: Edinburgh House, 1953).

consummate the world history in which He is now at work hiddenly," in bringing his kingdom. The church, living between the times has been entrusted as ambassadors of reconciliation, constrained to "press on to every nation and into every human situation" as ministers of its hope in Christ as savior and judge of the world.[58] Besides these more minor contributions Newbigin's most significant contribution at Willingen was his drafting of a fresh statement on "The Missionary Calling of the Church."

"A Statement on the Missionary Calling of the Church"[59]

After extended days of wrangling the theological group had failed to reach a consensus but had become "polarized between Hoekendijk, Lehmann and others on the one side with their radical 'worldly' concept of mission, and the more traditional people on the other side."[60] This resulted in a stalemate, with the conference unwilling to endorse the original report.[61] This report "spoke of discerning by faith God's action of judgment and redemption in the revolutionary movements of our time."[62] As mentioned, this report was only "received" "not formally adopted" due to the divergence of opinion over key issues.[63] In the concluding section, "VI Problems for Further Study and Discussion," it was significant that consensus was reached: "*All* were agreed that 'mission' is essential to the nature of the Church and not something super-added to it."[64] However, lack of clarity or consensus remained concerning several issues:

1) Is the missionary obligation of the church to be understood primarily as derived from the redemptive purpose and acts of God or as derived from the nature of God Himself?

2) What is the precise relation of the church to its mission?

3) What is the relation of the church's mission to the Kingdom of God?

4) What is the significance of eschatology for the church's mission?[65]

58. Ibid., 115–16.

59. Newbigin, "Missionary Calling," 188–92.

60. Newbigin to Bosch, 7/9/1990, BUL: DA29/2/3/148.

61. "The Theological Basis of the Missionary Obligation (an Interim Report)," in *Missions under the Cross*, ed. N. Goodall, 238–45.

62. *Willingen Minutes*, 18; Newbigin, *Unfinished Agenda*, 138.

63. Goodall, ed., *Missions under the Cross*, 187, 238.

64. Ibid., 244. Emphasis added.

65. "Missionary Obligation (Original)," 244–45.

In an attempt to resolve this conflict Newbigin, as a member of the editorial committee, was asked to draft a statement as a last-minute attempt to achieve general consent, albeit bypassing the more thorny issues. Quoting from his diary, Newbigin recalled: "I wrote the new document from 8:45 to 10:45 in the morning, and I well remember that I felt it had to be a very traditional sort of statement which could be accepted by everyone and which (admittedly) by-passed the issues raised by Hoekendijk etc. (I only came to see these issues later)."[66]

Newbigin's redrafting was successful and his statement was adopted by the enlarged meeting of the IMC. However, it should be noted that even then the adoption of his statement was not unconditional. There was the insistence on further qualification: that Newbigin's statement "*arose out of the report of Group I*" rather than being the report of the discussions.[67] Newbigin, in his redrafting of the original (rejected) report, preserved four of the headings and much of the original text.[68] In the following section the two documents are compared to gain an understanding of Newbigin's redaction of the original, rejected, report, and thus the emphasis he brought.

The Context of Mission

Regarding the world situation, in Newbigin's statement he was conscious of the context of the cold war and the rise and triumph of communism: "other faiths of revolutionary power confront us in the full tide of victory"—although neither Russia nor China was directly mentioned. The tide has turned against the propagation of Christianity associated with colonialism and Newbigin acknowledged that the church has not faced such a hostile environment since the rise of Islam. However, in such a hostile and seemingly hopeless climate, the church must go forward into the world, assured of its hope in Christ and in the knowledge that "we know that God rules the revolutionary forces of history and works out His

66. Newbigin to Bosch, 7/9/1990, BUL: DA29/2/3/148.

67. "The feeling of the meeting was that while Bishop Newbigin's revision might be regarded as a statement arising out of the work of Group I, it could not legitimately be described as a report of the discussions of the Group." Goodall, ed., *Missions under the Cross*, 188; *Willingen Minutes*, 19. This was at the insistence of Hoekendijk, Warren, and Goodall; Newbigin, *Unfinished Agenda*, 138. Contra Wainwright, *Newbigin*, 165.

68. Newbigin made a minor change to the wording of heading I; he preserved headings II–IV. Goodall, ed., *Missions under the Cross*, 188–92, cf. 238–45.

purpose by the hidden power of the Cross."[69] The church faced a hostile climate, and yet maintained the persistent conviction that it must advance the gospel.

In Newbigin's statement the triumphalistic language which characterized earlier conferences (especially Edinburgh) was absent. However, Newbigin retained militaristic metaphors, understanding mission as "warfare" engaged in by the church: "The battle is set between His hidden Kingdom and those evil spiritual forces," and "[t]here is no room for neutrality in this conflict." The church is God's pilgrim people sent forth into the world, but sent as a military force: "The Church is like an army living in tents. God calls His people to strike their tents and go forward."[70]

For Newbigin the church in this hostile context must "discern the signs of the times" and "proclaim anew the hidden reign of our crucified and ascended Lord."[71] "We believe that the sovereign rule of Him who is Saviour and Judge of all men is no less to be discerned by eyes of faith in the great events of our day, in the vast enlargements of human knowledge and power . . . [and] in the mighty political and social movements . . ."[72] In contrast, the rejected report was more forthright, and interpreted these signs as God's judgment: "In this situation, the missionary movement is being judged for its failures and called to repent."[73]

The Trinitarian Basis for Mission

The most significant theological breakthrough in Newbigin's statement was to base the missionary calling of the church on the doctrine of the Trinity. "The missionary movement of which we are a part has its source in the Triune God Himself. Out of the depths of His love for us, the Father has sent forth His own beloved Son to reconcile all things to Himself . . ."[74] Newbigin's change to the original, anchoring the source of mission to the Trinity, is a considerable advance from the original report.[75] David

69. Newbigin, "Missionary Calling," 188.

70. Newbigin retained these military metaphors and added "warfare." Ibid., 189, 190. Cf. "Missionary Obligation (Original)," 238, 242–43.

71. Newbigin, "Missionary Calling," 192.

72. Ibid.

73. "Missionary Obligation (Original)," 239. An assertion that, as noted earlier, was not palatable to the Germans.

74. Newbigin, "Missionary Calling," 189.

75. Cf.: "The missionary obligation of the Church comes from the love of God in

Bosch, writing personally to Newbigin in 1990, interpreted this as a major theological advancement: "To see mission primarily as flowing from the missionary heart of God is certainly an improvement over defining mission as the 'obligation' of the church."[76] The source of mission is located as proceeding from the Trinity rather than being located, as it has traditionally been, within ecclesiology or soteriology. Mission is thus not seen as originating out of the church or from any other human agency, but as an attribute of the Triune God himself. Therefore, mission is the participation in the divine movement of God's love toward people, the church being the central channel through which God continues to pour out his love to the world.[77]

With hindsight Willingen is recognized for the emergence of the *missio Dei* concept. On preparing an endorsement of David Bosch's book *Transforming Mission*, Newbigin expressed surprise at the weight Bosch gave to the emergence of *missio Dei* at Willingen.[78] When called upon to draft a statement which would meet with general approval, Newbigin recorded that "I certainly had no idea that I was making anything like a fresh or original statement." Instead, at the time he accepted Goodall's analysis that Willingen had failed: "I vividly remember how Norman Goodall, at the end of the conference, told us that the conference had failed in its main purpose—namely to achieve a consensus on 'The Missionary Obligation of the Church.' In a sense he was right, and yet it proved to be a very creative meeting in many respects."[79]

Although the *missio Dei* concept was a major theological advance, questions persisted concerning its origins and, more importantly, its ambiguous content. Whilst the origin of the actual term is easily established,[80] determining the origin of the concept proved to be more problematic.[81] The received history traced a trajectory from a lecture delivered by Karl Barth

His active relationship with men." "Missionary Obligation (Original)," 241.

76. Bosch to Newbigin, 21/9/1990, BUL: DA29/2/3/139.

77. Bosch, *Transforming Mission*, 392.

78. Ibid., 389–93.

79. Newbigin to Bosch, 7/9/1990, BUL: DA29/2/3/148.

80. Karl Hartenstein, in 1934, is attributed with the first contemporary usage of *missio Dei*. J. G. Flett, "God Is a Missionary God: Missio Dei, Karl Barth, and the Doctrine of the Trinity" (PhD thesis, Princeton Theological Seminary, 2007) 188.

81. See the study by H. H. Rosin, *"Missio Dei": An Examination of the Origin, Contents and Function of the Term in Protestant Missiological Discussion* (Leiden: Interuniversity Institute for Missiological and Ecumenical Research, Department of Missiology, 1972).

(in 1932), to Willingen, which was supposedly mediated by Hartenstein.[82] However, in a recent thesis by John Flett, the historicity of this transmission has been convincingly refuted. Flett demonstrates that "not a single fragment of textual evidence supports the connection between Barth's 1932 lecture and Willingen's trinitarian developments."[83]

So what then is the source of the *missio Dei* concept which emerged at Willingen? Flett argues that its origins can be traced to the American report prepared for the conference. This report, "Why Missions?" which was chaired by Paul Lehmann, was "responsible for locating missions within the doctrine of the Trinity."[84] With the link to Barth discredited, Flett can then make the assertion that "the trinitarianism of *missio Dei* theology developed, not in continuity with, but in direct opposition to Barth."[85]

In the Willingen text drafted by Newbigin, "The Missionary Calling of the Church," Newbigin maintained the trinitarian position first articulated by Hoekendijk and Lehmann. But in order to achieve consensus, Newbigin resorted to ambiguity so that "the trinitarian approach advocated in the text must be understood as a modification and reduction of the rejected approaches,"[86] which concealed "a contrast between the American preparatory report . . . and the more classic salvation-historical approaches."[87] The general endorsement of this ambiguity meant that Willingen "wavered uncertainly between Trinitarianism, Christocentrism, and church-centrism. It appeared mostly to reject any criticism of church-centered missionary thinking."[88] This lack of theological precision

---

82. Bosch, *Transforming Mission*, 389. Following the Willingen conference the concept was popularized by the book G. F. Vicedom, *Missio Dei: Einfuhrung in Eine Theologie Der Mission* (Munich: Chr. Kaiser, 1958) and its English translation, *The Mission of God*, trans. Gilbert A. Thiele and Dennis Hilgendorf (St. Louis: Concordia, 1965).

83. Flett, "God Is a Missionary God," 16–17, 174–253.

84. Ibid., 201. This is supported by R. C. Bassham, "Seeking a Deeper Theological Basis for Mission," *IRM* 67:267 (1978): 330.

85. Flett, "God Is a Missionary God," 210.

86. L. A. Hoedemaker, "Mission and Unity: The Relevance of Hoekendijk's Vision," in *Changing Partnership of Missionary and Ecumenical Movements: Essays in Honour of Marc Spindler*, ed. Leny Lagerwerf, Karel Steenbrink, and F. J. Verstraelen (Leiden-Utrecht: Interuniversity Institute for Missiological and Ecumenical Research, 1995) 29.

87. L. A. Hoedemaker, "The People of God and the Ends of the Earth," in *Missiology: An Ecumenical Introduction*, ed. Frans J. Verstraelen et al. (Grand Rapids: Eerdmans, 1995) 165.

88. Scherer cited in Flett, "God Is a Missionary God," 234.

prompted H. H. Rosin to describe *missio Dei* theology as "the Trojan horse through which the (unassimilated) 'American' vision was fetched into the well-guarded walls of the ecumenical theology of mission."[89]

This Trojan invasion has not been without consequence. Newbigin's compromise document was pioneering in being trinitarian, but it failed in not being *sufficiently* trinitarian. Instead, its "trinitarianism [was] a concession—ecumenical damage control": "However, despite the burden of received history, *missio Dei* is insufficiently trinitarian, and its contemporary problems, especially the dichotomy of mission from church, constitute a faithful maturation of its historical origins."[90] In juxtaposing christology and trinitarianism, as the compromise report sought to do, Flett identified the incorporation into the *missio Dei* concept of an enduring dichotomy, "between God's act and being."[91] Flett disproved the Barthian origins of the *missio Dei* concept. However, to resolve the dichotomy between God's act and being, Flett again turned to Barth. Barth cannot be credited with the origin of *missio Dei*, but is necessary for understanding it, in that he gives the concept adequate trinitarian grounding: "Barth's method of thinking from God's act of self-revelation in Christ to God's triune being—God as being-in-act—proffers a suggestive solution."[92]

One of the aims of Willingen was to stimulate ongoing reflection on the new consensus achieved on the trinitarian source and foundation for mission.[93] Whilst this did not transpire at an official level within the IMC/WCC, Flett is too categorical in his statement that "the Willingen statement remains close to a complete definition of *missio Dei*: beyond Willingen, it receives no substantial theological development."[94] Willingen was the catalyst which inspired Newbigin's theological journey to resolve the tensions which the conference had failed to, although Newbigin's initial tentative efforts neither fully satisfied himself, nor convinced others.[95]

89. Rosin, *Missio Dei*, 26.

90. Flett, "God Is a Missionary God," 235, 26.

91. Ibid., 236.

92. Ibid.

93. Andersen, *Towards a Theology of Mission: A Study of the Encounter between the Missionary Enterprise and the Church and Its Theology*, 53.

94. Flett, "God Is a Missionary God," 238.

95. This is considered in ch. 7.

The Missionary Nature of the Church

The divine movement within the Godhead was expanded to include yet another "movement," the sending of the church into the world: "We who have been chosen in Christ . . . are . . . committed to full participation in His redeeming mission. There is no participation in Christ without participation in His mission to the world. That by which the Church receives its existence is that by which it is also given its world-mission. 'As the Father hath sent Me, even so send I you.'"[96]

The church is missional, being constituted by being sent into the world by Christ, in continuity with Christ's own sending. Mission is therefore not to be understood as an additional activity of the church, but as inherent to its very nature. "God sends forth the Church to carry out His work to the ends of the earth, to all nations, and to the end of time."

At this point the original report was silent on the agency of the church in particular situations. Instead it was "necessary" to discern God's sovereign action, irrespective of the church, in the world at large: in personal life, in the movements of political and social life, and in the processes of scientific discovery.[97] Here Newbigin made a critical change to the original report. He maintained the centrality of the agency of the church, being sent into each of the above locations.

Newbigin's amendment has several implications for the church. First, "[t]he Church is sent to every inhabited area of the world." The church is God's mission to the world. Wherever the church is, it is called to transcend geographic boundaries. As the church itself is missionary and each location is a missionary situation, the historical "directedness" of mission from so-called Christian West to non-Christian lands is no longer tenable. Second, the sending of the church "involves both geographical extension and also intensive penetration of all spheres of life." Thus the church is also sent to "every social, political and religious community of mankind" and "to proclaim Christ's reign in every moment and every situation."[98]

The third major implication which emerges from Newbigin's statement was that mission is incarnational—"*As* the Father hath sent Me."[99] The church is missionary by nature and its manner of mission must be characterized by the same manner that characterized Christ during his

---

96. Newbigin, "Missionary Calling," 190.

97. "Missionary Obligation (Original)," 240.

98. Newbigin, "Missionary Calling," 190–91.

99. This quotation from John 20:21 is absent from the original report.

incarnation. Newbigin in his statement particularly emphasized Christ's identification with the world: "The Church is in the world, and as the Lord of the Church identified Himself wholly with mankind, so must the Church also do. The nearer the Church draws to its Lord the nearer it draws to the world. Christians do not live in an enclave separated from the world; they are God's people in the world."[100]

Compared with Newbigin's statement the rejected report was more explicit in recording that the church is missionary. The very existence of the church springs from "God's sending forth of His son," and the repeated refrain was that mission belonged to every aspect of the Church. "Whatever else ought to be said about the structure, life, and purpose of the Church, this one thing must be said: that 'mission' is woven into all three and cannot be separated out from any one without destroying it." Mission is thus not an option which can be appended to other "duties" the church must fulfill, rather the church's commission "belongs to its royal charter (covenant) to be the Church."[101]

With consensus achieved that the church is missionary in nature, that then raised the question, how then should that be expressed, how should the church be structured? This question, on the missionary structure of the congregation, became the focus of formal research within the WCC and personal reflection for Newbigin. But it was not until the 1960s that the question received its deserved attention. After Willingen, Newbigin recorded frustration that the debate "has centred on the question of the place of institutions such as schools and hospitals, but did not go further and deal with the questions of the forms of Church life itself. There is still a need for debate on fundamental questions regarding the visible forms of Church life and ministry . . ."[102] Newbigin recognized that congregational forms and ministry needed, simultaneously, to "be authentically one with the whole family of God and yet on the other hand genuinely relevant to the situation." He was concerned that whilst the former might be true, there was the danger with the latter, of simply replicating forms faithful to historical patterns but regardless of a rapidly changing context.[103]

---

100. Newbigin, "Missionary Calling," 191.

101. "Missionary Obligation (Original)," 241.

102. Lesslie Newbigin, "The Gathering Up of History into Christ," in *The Missionary Church in East and West*, ed. Charles C. West and David M. Paton (London: SCM, 1959) 90.

103. Ibid.

Conclusion: The Outcome of Rolle and Willingen

The Broadening Theological Discussion

At Willingen the missionary nature of the church and the trinitarian basis for mission were established. This chapter has shown how Newbigin's role was critical in establishing this theological breakthrough, overcoming the deadlock, to produce a statement the assembly could endorse. Willingen was a catalyst which started a consultative process for ongoing discussions to explore these developments. Follow-up was formalized at the next IMC assembly, in Ghana (1957/8), when "the decision to have these issues systematically discussed" was taken.[104]

The fruit of this research resulted in three publications, one of which, Johannes Blauw's *The Missionary Nature of the Church*, sought, by way of biblical study, to provide a foundation for the missiological developments in the 1950s.[105] Whilst Blauw was retrospective, D. T. Niles's book *Upon the Earth* was prospective, written to meet the demand for "a major re-appraisal of the 'foreign' missionary enterprise of the Churches, if not of the Church's evangelistic mission itself."[106] The third publication arose out of a consultation of theologians convened by the WCC and the IMC. The consultation met to address the question, "What does it mean in theological terms and in practice in this ecumenical era for the Church to discharge its mission to all the nations?"[107]

Willingen first introduced Newbigin to the concerns of Hoekendijk and Lehmann with their critique of church-centric missiology. Later Newbigin too became critical of the post-Tambaram church-centric model and his theological enquiry returned to the unresolved questions he was first introduced to at Willingen. Although he did not initially appreciate Hoekendijk and Lehmann's concerns, when Newbigin later returned to the questions of the relationship of the church vis-à-vis the world, and the relationship between sacred and secular history, Hoekendijk's critique provided him with a theological signpost which would direct him in his

104. D. T. Niles, *Upon the Earth: The Mission of God and the Missionary Enterprise of the Churches* (London: Lutterworth, 1962) 21.

105. J. Blauw, *The Missionary Nature of the Church: A Survey of the Biblical Theology of Mission* (London: Lutterworth, 1962).

106. Niles, *Upon the Earth*, 9.

107. Ibid., 21. The consultation used a draft of Niles's book as the basis for their discussion. It was held in Bossey, Switzerland, July, 1961, and the report was published as: "The Missionary Task of the Church: Theological Reflections, Report of Meeting in Bossey, July 1961," *Bulletin of the Division of Studies, WCC* 7:2 (1961).

future journey, as he engaged with these issues. This enabled Newbigin, after integration, to shift his theological focus from questions on the *structure* of mission to more penetrating questions on the *substance* of mission.

It was the World Student Christian Federation Conference on "The Life and Mission of the Church" (in Strasbourg in 1960) that marked the coming of age of Hoekendijk's secular missiology. The call was given to "move out of the traditional Church structures in open, flexible and mobile groups," and to "'begin radically to desacralize the Church' and to recognize that 'Christianity is a secular movement—this is basic for an understanding of it.'"[108] At Strasbourg the consensus on *missio Dei* was not questioned; "what was attacked was its imprisonment in the institutions of the Church."[109] As at Willingen, the central issue was the relationship "between 'salvation history' and world history," the emphasis during the 1960s being on the latter.[110]

At Willingen Hoekendijk had tried, and failed, to dislodge the church from its central position in missiology. His success at Strasbourg marked a decisive shift of focus from the church to the world, a shift which would dominate missiological reflection throughout the 1960s.[111] From Willingen the church was defined in terms of its participation in the *missio Dei*. But the ideas first proposed by Hoekendijk clashed with the previously accepted ecclesiology which was ordered: God → church → world, and which sought to maintain the church as the central agent of God's mission. As their former secretary, Hoekendijk exerted influence on the study commissioned by the WCC Department of Evangelism, "The study of the missionary structure of the congregation," which culminated in the European and North American reports being adopted by the Uppsala assembly in 1968.[112] Within both groups Hoekendijk was influential in steering the groups in a secular direction, in which the goal of mission was

108. J. C. Hoekendijk, "Christ and the World in the Modern Age: Strasbourg 1960," *Student World* 54:1–2 (1961) 81–82.Cf. Lesslie Newbigin, "Recent Thinking on Christian Beliefs: VIII Mission and Missions," *Expository Times* 88:9 (1977) 261.

109. Newbigin, "Recent Thinking," 260.

110. Ibid., 261.

111. R. C. Bassham, *Mission Theology, 1948–1975: Years of Worldwide Creative Tension—Ecumenical, Evangelical, and Roman Catholic* (South Pasadena, CA: William Carey Library, 1979) 47.

112. WCC, *The Church for Others; and, the Church for the World: A Quest for Structures for Missionary Congregations* (Geneva: WCC, 1967).

identified as *shalom,* by the European team, and as *humanization,* by the North Americans.[113]

A reordering was proposed of: God → world → shalom (or humanization); in which "[t]he world provides the agenda," and the distinction between church and world has collapsed.[114] From the 1960s this unresolved tension, between two conflicting ecclesiologies, between "salvation" and "humanization," between the camps of those rather clumsily referred to as "evangelical" versus "ecumenicals," remained.[115] The nuanced position that Newbigin strove to maintain between the polarities of "salvation" and "humanization" will be considered in chapters 7 and 8.

The Theological Foundation for Integration

The meetings at Rolle and Willingen proved to be foundational to the missiological agenda for at least the next decade. At Willingen the stark polarization in theological position provided Newbigin (and others) with an agenda to seek resolution of this dichotomy. Willingen was catalytic whereas Rolle was constructive. The theological foundation for integration was provided by Newbigin's Rolle statement which he also succeeded in getting accepted at the turbulent Willingen conference. This foundation, coupled with the growing closeness of "association" between the two councils, gave new impetus to the Joint Committee.[116] The Joint Committee requested that its mandate be strengthened and extended, and for permission to study "the advantages, disadvantages and implications of a full integration of the IMC and the WCC."[117] By 1956 the "reconstituted" Joint Committee "believed the time had come to consider afresh the possibility of integration." To this end the 1956 Joint Committee commissioned a "Draft Plan of Integration" with Newbigin chairing the committee charged with preparing the "Draft Plan." This was presented to the 1957 Central Committee meeting, at New Haven, and to the IMC, at the assembly in

---

113. Ibid., 15, 78. Wilbert Shenk commented on how Hoekendijk influenced both groups as he moved from involvement with the European group to then join the North American group, unifying and directing the findings in a secular direction. Shenk, interview with Mark Laing, 1/11/2006.

114. WCC, *Church for Others,* 16–17, 20.

115. Goheen, *As the Father,* 5. Cf. Bosch, *Transforming Mission,* 381–89.

116. "Report of the Joint Committee," in *The Evanston Report,* ed. W. A. Visser 't Hooft (London: SCM, 1955) 322–23.

117. Ibid., 324.

Ghana 1957–58.[118] The Central Committee at New Haven "decided to send the [draft] plan to all its member churches for their consideration."[119] The response of the churches was to approve the essence of the plan.[120]

By contrast, the IMC response at Ghana resulted in extensive debate over the possible merits of integration. Hoekendijk had alluded to the disquiet concerning integration prevalent amongst European mission leaders. At Ghana their protest was most clearly vocalized. Newbigin had provided an early theological foundation for integration. Who better then, to lead the councils to unity, than the one who had voiced those convictions and who sought to embody them.

---

118. This draft was published as a pamphlet: E. A. Payne and D. G. Moses, *Why Integration?* (London: Edinburgh House Press for the Joint Committee, 1957) 19.

119. Ibid., 20.

120. Nissen, "Nordic Missions," 129.

4

The IMC at Ghana

Debating Integration and Calling Newbigin

THIS CHAPTER FOCUSES ON the Ghana Assembly of the IMC, which
was dominated by the issue of integration. Whereas the WCC approved integration with little discussion, Ghana demonstrated the width
and depth of conviction held within the IMC on integration. At the Ghana
assembly the IMC made two important decisions, to approve of the plan
to integrate and second, to call Newbigin to facilitate integration, inviting
Newbigin to become the next general secretary of the IMC.

In response to the deepening association between the IMC and the
WCC, and to address pressing practical problems, the Executive Committee of the WCC authorized the Joint Committee to prepare a draft plan of
integration, appointing Newbigin as the chair of this drafting committee.
The draft was to incorporate amendments from the respective constituencies of both councils before it was presented for approval to the Central
Committee of the WCC in 1957, and the Ghana assembly of the IMC,
meeting in 1957/8.[1] The final approved plan of integration was then to be
acted upon at the third assembly of the WCC, which had been planned for
1960, but was delayed until 1961 to allow time for a consensus on integration to be reached.

When the Joint Committee reported to the Central Committee at
New Haven, Connecticut, in 1957 their recommendation was that integration should be pursued as it was the "preponderant although not

---

1. Visser 't Hooft, CCM, 1956, 74.

unanimous judgment of the [Joint] Committee."[2] The aim of integration was twofold: "the permeation of the life of the integrated Council with missionary conviction and commitment, and the continuation of the life and programme of the IMC in its full scope and strength."[3] Newbigin, whilst he endorsed the draft plan of integration, also hoped that integration would go even further than what was now being proposed, as the solution to problems between "younger" and "older" churches required a single ecumenical body, which was "profoundly churchly and profoundly missionary."[4] Without much dissent or discussion the WCC Central Committee meetings in New Haven had given their approval to integrate, the Draft Plan for integration being forwarded to member churches for their approval.

Events at (Accra) Ghana were of a different nature. The question of integration was not the only item to be discussed at the Ghana assembly of the IMC,[5] but it became the predominant one requiring extended plenary discussion. The main argument for integration, proposed by both IMC officers and WCC representatives, was on theological grounds. Integration of the two councils would reflect a recovered ecclesiology which emphasized the church's dual calling to mission and to unity.

Opponents to integration were fearful of an evangelical schism within the IMC and argued that integration would detract from what they maintained should be the central concern of the IMC, to facilitate foreign missions. They argued less from a theological premise, but more pragmatically about the actual historical situation, and the need to address those realities. The most eloquent opponent to integration was Canon Max Warren.[6] Despite opposition the conference voted overwhelmingly in favor of integration.

Ghana also marked an important transition for the IMC with John Mackay and Charles Ranson stepping down as chairman and general secretary respectively. Coupled with the vote for integration the IMC recognized the need to appoint new leaders who would enable integration. The second major decision at Ghana was to call Newbigin to lead the IMC at this critical juncture. Newbigin was *the* candidate of choice to lead the

2. Joint Committee Report, CCM, 1957, 44.

3. Ibid.

4. Ibid., 44–45.

5. Held from 28/12/1957 to 8/1/1958.

6. Warren was general secretary of the Church Missionary Society from 1942 to 63. For details of his life, see his autobiography, *Crowded Canvas*.

IMC. This choice reflected Newbigin's earlier contributions, in providing a theological foundation for integration which was acceptable to both the WCC (at Rolle) and the IMC (at Willingen), and practically, in chairing the committee responsible for devising the "Draft Plan" for integration.

The Ghana Debate on Integration

The Theological Case for Integration

By the time of the Ghana assembly the leadership of the IMC (and WCC representatives in attendance) considered integration of the two councils an inevitability. From the perspective of both IMC and WCC leadership, the process of integration was understood as the "consummation" of a deepening intimacy between the two councils. John Mackay, the IMC chairman, in his address to the assembly, perceived that underlying their growing together was "a certain logic of events under what we believed was the guidance of the Holy Spirit."[7] The impetus for integration was understood as divine initiative and the answer to the question "why" was theological: "A basic and long-forgotten truth is being rediscovered in our time, which might be stated thus: the unity of the Church and the mission of the Church both belong, in equal degree, to the essence of the Church."[8] The fundamental justification for integration was based upon the rationale that the recovery of a missionary ecclesiology, which restored the problematic relationship between mission and church, should be embodied internationally in the integration of the councils.

This view, that the WCC had an inherent ecclesiology to which mission rightly belonged, was shared by WCC leadership. Dr. Franklin Fry, chairman of the Central Committee of the WCC, stated that "we are overwhelmingly convinced that the proposed integration, quite apart from its mechanics, is theologically correct," and "[w]e believe . . . that mission as well as unity, belongs to the esse of the Church." Fry's interpretation (for the WCC), corroborated Mackay's of the historical process of growing association. The chief architect lay beyond human agency: "we believe we have been carried along, not only by the Nemesis of inexorable logic,

---

7. Mackay, *Ghana Minutes*, 124. Dr. H. P. Van Dusen, chairman of the Joint Committee, spoke of the impetus towards integration as "the providential pressure, the living direction of the Divine Spirit," *Ghana Minutes*, 126.

8. *Ghana Minutes*, 124. Mackay quoting from Payne and Moses, *Why Integration?*, 29.

but much more by the Will of God."[9] Under providential guidance, the plan before the assembly was thus not to be understood as "some new unprecedented and radical proposal." Instead, it was the culmination of a twenty-year process, the "placing of a coping-stone in the structure of co-operation which is already largely built." Dr. H. P. Van Dusen, chairman of the Joint Committee, was one of the few who had been present "when the first stone in the structure was placed, at the Tambaram Assembly in 1938, when the Joint Committee was authorized."[10] Thus, for Van Dusen, integration was not a future possibility, but already an established reality, the two councils growing "far beyond" mere association in their "step-by-step development" such "that actual integration in their work is today already a fact" in much of the common activities of the councils.[11]

Integration was commended on several grounds. First, historically, it was seen as the fitting conclusion to a twenty-year process, the "appropriate outcome of the trends of development which have brought the two bodies to their present situations."[12] Second, theologically, integration expressed the belief that mission and unity were of the *esse* of the church. Third, integration was commended for its potential outcome in putting "mission at the heart of the ecumenical movement." Fourth, was the argument of necessity, if not integration then what? Many saw that "there was no justification for the continued existence of two separate world bodies"; and "[t]he continued separation of what belongs together leads to tension and embarrassment in the work of the two bodies themselves." And fifth, the argument of preservation, integration "would conserve in the new body all that was represented by the IMC Assembly."[13]

It was acknowledged that amongst some national councils there were misgivings about integrating with the WCC, with fear that the council might become a "super church"; was doctrinally liberal; and lacked evangelical concern.[14] However, it was "widely felt" that those concerns "arose from ignorance of or misunderstandings" rather than being substantive;

---

9. Fry, *Ghana Minutes*, 128.

10. Van Dusen, ibid., 126.

11. Ibid.

12. R. K. Orchard, ed., *The Ghana Assembly of the International Missionary Council* (London: IMC/Edinburgh House, 1958) 157.

13. Ibid., 157–60.

14. Opinions that Rev. R. V. de Cane Thompson, as representative of the Congo Protestant Council, had expressed in writing, and aired at Ghana, *Ghana Minutes*, 134. The Congo Council was dominated by American conservative evangelicals.

the solution thus being to disseminate a better understanding of the WCC.[15]

Opposition to Integration

However, at Ghana, the assumption that integration was an inevitability, to be endorsed by the assembly, resulted in considerable "anger" and a "wide measure of resentment" that the decision to integrate was *"chose jugé."*[16] Expression of this "resentment" resulted in the issue of integration dominating the agenda, necessitating extensive extra plenary discussion. Beyond the unanimity that the respective chairmen presented there were substantive voices of dissent and disquiet. Max Warren failed to see divine providence leading inexorably to integration: "I cannot see clearly that this is the leading of the Holy Spirit."[17] Warren later made the important observation that "despite strenuous efforts to affirm that the integration . . . was manifestly a response to the Holy Spirit, this note was significantly omitted from the statement received by the assembly and commended to the member organizations . . ."[18]

Some from IMC circles took a more functional approach to the roles of the councils and thus dismissed the premise that the councils should reflect ecclesiological understanding. "We think that the whole question is a question mainly of organization, and fear that sometimes this question is obscured from both sides by taking it into theological reasoning, especially if we do it in analogy to the relation of missionary society and church. There is no such analogy here because the WCC is no church and the IMC is not a missionary society."[19]

The Danger of the IMC Losing Its Primary Focus

For others there was concern that the particular focus of the IMC upon foreign missions would be dissipated by integration. In comparing the WCC with the IMC Ralph Winter noted three main tasks which characterize their function: "the work of the Church," "evangelism," and "frontier

15. Orchard, ed., *Ghana Assembly*, 162.

16. Warren, *Crowded Canvas*, 159.

17. Warren, *Ghana Minutes*, 132.

18. Max A. C. Warren, "The Fusion of IMC and WCC at New Delhi: Retrospective Thoughts after a Decade and a Half," *OBMR* 3:3 (1979) 106.

19. W. Freytag, *Ghana Minutes*, 138.

evangelism." "[W]hile *mission* organizations commonly labour in all three tasks, *churches* as such are not often involved effectively in the third."[20] Winter's argument was a pragmatic one; he was concerned that the focus on "frontier evangelism" (what he understood rather narrowly as cross-cultural missions) be maintained. He did not engage with the theological arguments proposed for integration but maintained that, since the first missionary journey of Paul and Barnabas, the church and its mission, has depended upon these two structures, the stationary church and the "travelling missionary team," and that both are "contrasting manifestations of the church."[21]

This loss of focus on "frontier evangelism" was a process some discerned as already being inherent within the development of the IMC. The mission organizations constituted national *missionary* councils which were gradually reconstituted as national *Christian* councils (i.e., councils of *churches*). This reflected the central concern that the "younger church" came to occupy within the IMC. One consequence of this increasing church-centricism was the concerns of the church dominating the IMC with a loss of focus on the horizon beyond the church. Instead of the IMC facilitating the establishment of indigenous missionary agencies it became embroiled in the affairs of the *church*. "The cultivation of these tender plants became the major focus of Western mission energies (less and less the penetration of new frontiers)." With the "euthanasia of the missions," the establishment of the church became the goal of mission strategy. The consequence of this strategy being that "it is difficult to find much more than a trace of thinking [in the IMC] about the need to found indigenous mission societies. . . . The non-Western churches certainly did not move decisively forward to create their own mission structures."[22] So, for some, the timing for integration was "unfortunate" because it took place when the IMC had become increasingly church-centric, but *before* non-Western churches had been able to develop viable mission organizations of their own.[23] With missionary councils becoming church councils the "younger churches" therefore lacked the organizational provision to develop mission

20. Winter, "Ghana," 340. Italics in original.

21. Ibid., 339–40.

22. Ibid., 344, 346. Earlier, at Willingen, Hoekendijk and Newbigin had raised similar concerns.

23. Ibid.

structures, these "organizational anomalies" being symptomatic of more fundamental realities of "spiritual confusion and inhibition."[24]

Warren was more harsh and held the "younger churches" accountable for thwarting the ambitions of mission agencies and deflecting them from their central focus: "Today the gravest embarrassment of the mission societies lies in the actual unwillingness of the younger churches to set them free to perform the tasks for which they properly exist—the pioneering of those new frontiers, not necessarily geographical, which have not yet been marked with a cross."[25]

Some felt that through this process the IMC at Ghana was now but a shadow of its former self, characterized by "confusion of our minds, lack of definition in our vocabulary, [and] hesitancy of action."[26] Ghana had become, in effect, the "funeral" of the IMC.[27] A view that Stephen Neill expressed privately to Newbigin, suggesting that, had Newbigin been at Ghana, "perhaps we should not have come to so lamentable an end." [28] Neill too was of the opinion that integration would result in a loss of focus. The WCC was by its nature "concerned with that third of the world's population which is nominally Christian . . . whereas the IMC is concerned with the two-thirds of the world's population which is not and has never been Christian."[29] It is surprising that Neill,[30] after years of missionary experience in South India, expressed such a Eurocentric view, which neglected both the growing post-Christian situation in Europe and the growth of the church in the majority world. Neill anticipated that with integration "the IMC would become simply one department of the WCC among ten or twelve, and by no means one of the most important."[31] Reflecting just after Ghana Neill anticipated that as a consequence of integration a rival "evangelical IMC" would emerge which would maintain this focus on foreign mission.[32]

24. J. V. Taylor, *Ghana Minutes*, 147.

25. Warren cited by S. C. Graaf Van Randwijk, in Orchard, ed., *Ghana Assembly*, 94.

26. Taylor, *Ghana Minutes*, 147.

27. F. Birkeli, ibid., 133.

28. Stephen Neill to Newbigin, 10/4/1958, BUL: DA29/1/7/159.

29. Neill cited by Nissen, "Mission and Unity," 546.

30. For a recent biography on Neill, see D. B. Daughrity, *Bishop Stephen Neill: From Edinburgh to South India* (Oxford: Peter Lang, 2008).

31. Nissen, "Mission and Unity."

32. Neill to Newbigin, 10/4/1958, BUL: DA29/1/7/159.

The foundational conference at Edinburgh (1910), through which the IMC was birthed, had been described as a lens—"a lens catching diffused beams of light from a century's attempt at missionary cooperation, focusing them and projecting them for the future in a unified, meaningful and determinative pattern."[33] Winter suggested that by Ghana it had become apparent that the metaphor should be changed from lens to prism: "[Edinburgh] projected a spectrum of interests which in fact do not now converge and may never do so."[34] With the benefit of hindsight Winter realized that an evangelical missionary movement had emerged to sustain the ethos of the IMC rather than allowing it to be subsumed within the WCC—this has existed, at times, in antithesis to the Commission for World Mission and Evangelism (CWME),[35] and, as we approach the centenary of 1910, shows no sign of convergence.

Canon Max Warren's Opposition

One of the most well-known evangelical opponents of integration was Canon Max Warren, who spoke against it at the assembly. Warren has been caricatured as a "violent opponent" to integration, but his opposition, the reasons for it, and his subsequent pragmatism faced with the inevitability of integration, demonstrate a more nuanced response than other evangelical responses, moreover Warren was very well acquainted with the process of integration. Throughout this time Warren remained "as opposed as ever to . . . integration."[36]

Prior to the Ghana assembly, at the 1956 meeting of the Joint Committee (Herrnalb), Warren was given opportunity to express his concerns on integration. He believed that the "administrative marriage" would undermine the dynamic character of the missionary enterprise. He noted that any organization (including the church) has a provision for coordination of activity and for diffusion of power; a creative tension existing

---

33. Hogg, *Ecumenical Foundations*, 98.

34. Winter, "Ghana," 338.

35. At integration the Division of World Mission and Evangelism (DWME) was created. This existed until the 1971 restructuring of the WCC, when it became a commission (CWME). P. A. Potter and J. Matthey, "Mission," in *Dictionary of the Ecumenical Movement*, ed. N. Lossky et al. (Geneva: WCC, 1991) 787.

36. Warren was a member of the Ad-Interim Committee of the IMC from 1943 to 1958, and also, for a number of years, a member of the Joint Committee. Throughout that time he kept detailed diaries. Warren, *Crowded Canvas*, 157; Warren, "Retrospective Thoughts," 105.

between the two. As with the missionary movement, organs of voluntary action must exist if there is to be spiritual experimentation and initiative. In the creative tension between control and freedom Warren maintained that the missionary movement must be allowed to continue with "maximum flexibility," by allowing a "vanguard" of the those particularly committed to mission; rather than it being stifled through centralization and control—an outcome he anticipated with integration.[37]

By the time of Ghana Warren could identify four grounds for "serious doubts" about the desirability of integration: 1) "there were strong grounds for believing that it was premature"; 2) "there was a widespread fear that there was a great danger in centralizing the direction of missionary strategy"; 3) the IMC had fostered "mutual respect and trust" between "an extremely wide section of Christian thinking," and this would be endangered; 4) concurrent with 3), there was a polarization between the theologically "conservative" and "liberal." There was the danger that integration would fracture a fragile coalition along those fault lines.[38]

Reflecting upon his own diary accounts of the discussion prior to Ghana, Warren noted how a postwar "preoccupation" with organizational structures had become obsessive and "dangerously neurotic" to the extent that "organizational tidiness is to have priority in regard to mission."[39] Warren identified the "exclusively theological" presupposition that mission and unity belong together, as the impetus for this organizational obsessiveness. Yet this "exclusive" theological focus failed to recognize the reality that "in terms of history, there had . . . been very little symbiosis of these two aspects of Christian obedience." Instead, "[m]any mission groups . . . are almost dedicated to non-cooperation on the ground that he travels the fastest who travels alone."[40]

Warren's Speech at Ghana

As a member of the Joint Committee Warren was unhappy about decisions taken by the Committee on integration, but since the decision favoring integration had been made, Warren had decided not to speak against it at Ghana.[41] However, Mackay, learning of the "wide measure of

37. Warren, *Crowded Canvas*, 157–59.
38. Warren, "Retrospective Thoughts," 105–6.
39. Ibid., 104.
40. Ibid., 104–5.
41. Warren, *Crowded Canvas*, 159. Cf. Newbigin, *Unfinished Agenda*, 151.

resentment" and anger at how the case for integration had been presented, allowed Warren to redress this imbalance. Warren was asked in particular by German and Scandinavian delegates to speak against integration. So, as their representative, he did so, although he maintained that he would vote for it, because "things have gone too far for us to avoid the decision in favour." This was partly due to "an error in tactics" with the IMC officers presenting a "wholly" one-sided case for integration.[42] The key IMC and WCC chairmen had invoked divine providence as the ultimate rationale for integration, thus creating a difficult platform for Warren to then counter their argument.

Warren opposed integration for several reasons. He was concerned that the IMC would become just a division or department of WCC. There was the danger of dampening, if not extinguishing, the voluntary spirit which was the vanguard of the modern missionary movement. Warren feared that the great and free fellowship of missionary societies within the IMC could easily lose its drive and enthusiasm if regarded as simply a department of WCC. He thought that integration would be premature and would lead to the withdrawal of certain (evangelical) mission societies. And he was concerned about the centralizing tendency of the WCC and the consequent danger of stifling structures.[43]

Besides those pragmatic reasons against integration Warren spoke in Ghana to counter the prevailing theological arguments for integration, that mission and unity belong together to the esse of the church, and this truth should be administratively expressed. Warren presented two counterarguments. First, "In the fullness of God's purpose the *anakephaliosis* will indeed see unity complete and mission fulfilled, but it is, I insisted, a serious nonsequitur to suggest that 'without unity mission cannot be pursued.'" The "facts of the human situation" demonstrate "that mission can be prosecuted without unity."[44] Warren then gave various historical and contemporary examples as support to his case, in particular the Pentecostals and Roman Catholics, who demonstrate little concern for discussing mission or pursuing unity, but instead "get on with it." In contrast, and rather wearily, Warren reflected that those connected with the IMC "spend conference after

42. Warren, *Crowded Canvas*, 159. Warren to Bishop of Chelmsford (Falkner), draft letter, June 1960, BUL: DA29/1/8/76. Warren was referring to the Draft Plan of Integration. Warren's speech is recorded in the *Ghana Minutes*, 129–32.

43. Max Warren, "Plenary Session—Under pressure from many I express misgivings on integration issue," Travel Diaries, West Africa, vol. 3, 1957–58, BUL: CMS/ Unofficial papers Acc 882, 615–24.

44. Warren, *Ghana Minutes*, 131.

conference asking what it [mission] is, and setting up committees . . . we are paralysed while they go from strength to strength."[45]

Warren's second point was that *mission*, not unity, should be the first priority: "in pursuing mission we are more likely to discover what is the right kind of unity."[46] "Preoccupied with unity, you are preoccupied with the nature of the Church; preoccupied with mission, you leave the nature of the Church in the final out-working of the Will of God."[47] Warren railed against the fixation in the ecumenical movement on "organic union" as the first principle against which other concerns could be prioritized; why not consider the reverse: "a preoccupation with mission would lead to a reconsideration of what we mean by organic unity."[48] "I felt it quite vital to take this opportunity . . . to challenge publicly the whole approach of those concerned with integration who insist on basing it upon theological premises which are at one and the same time *a priori* hypotheses and also do not correspond with the realities of history and experience. It is a fallacy to start from what you think ought to be and then to force the facts to fit that premise and demand that action be determined by it."[49]

Warren was "exasperated" by the repetition of the assumption that there was only one form of unity possible and only one desirable ecumenical model. In his recollection of his speech he believed that he had "explicitly denied that there was any theological justification for administrative unification of the IMC and the WCC."[50] He had profound "misgivings" that integration would squander a "priceless asset" only for mission to be "imperilled by fresh organizational developments which will waste manpower."[51]

The Decision in Favor of Integration

After extended plenary sessions the IMC voted in favor of integration, with fifty-eight voting for and seven against.[52] Visser 't Hooft had consid-

---

45. Ibid.

46. Warren, Travel Diaries, 618–19.

47. Warren, *Ghana Minutes*, 131.

48. Ibid. This would set Warren on a collision course with Newbigin, whose experience of organic union in South India informed his approach to integration.

49. Warren, Travel Diaries, 620.

50. Ibid., 621.

51. Warren, *Ghana Minutes*, 132.

52. Mackay to Newbigin, 21/1/1958, BUL: DA29/1/7/128.

ered Mackay to be a "Platonist" with his "head too much in the clouds," but at Ghana he proved "to be the man that saved the situation." Mackay ensured a definite proposal which received an overwhelming vote in favor of integration.[53] This was not the definitive IMC vote for integration, only approval of the "Draft Plan." The most significant amendment to the plan was the resolution to enable various levels of affiliation: "It should also provide for other links with the Commission by some other form of mutually satisfactory relationship."[54] The amended draft plan for integration was then circulated to IMC member councils for their final approval. All the member councils, apart from two exceptions, approved integration.[55]

Although the mandate was given to proceed, personal recollections of the assembly were of chaos and turbulence: with the IMC losing heart, losing morale, being uncertain of its future and unable to give a clear lead on the future of missions, and facing a crisis of leadership. Visser 't Hooft's recollection was that "in many ways the Ghana Assembly was the most chaotic ecumenical meeting that I have attended for many years."[56]

Warren's Position: An Evaluation

Warren would not deny the necessity for human agency for the fulfillment of mission. But placing the fulfillment of unity at the *eschaton*, as God's "recapitulation," belittles human agency in the process of that recovery, and denies the theological connection between mission and unity—a connection which has developed theologically as a consequence of the historical process of the missionary movement. Despite purporting to present theological arguments, Warren's propensity was to argue from the pragmatics created by historical processes. Yet it was as a product of these processes that the question was raised of the relationship between mission and unity, and the proper embodiment of that relationship. To ignore those questions and continue to prosecute mission divorced from concerns for unity—as Warren advocated—was a denial not just of theology, but also of the historical process which had enabled those questions.

53. Visser 't Hooft to Newbigin, 27/1/1958, BUL: DA29/1/7/131.

54. Orchard, ed., *Ghana Assembly*, 168.

55. No reply was received from the NCC of China, the Norwegian Missionary Council voted against, and the Protestant Council in Congo had already withdrawn their membership from the IMC. IMC, *IMC Minutes, November 17–18, 1961 at New Delhi* (London: 1962) 9, 11.

56. Visser 't Hooft to Newbigin, 27/1/1958, BUL: DA29/1/7/131.

The position for or against integration was personified by Warren, who allowed the historical realities priority over theological ideas. Warren had read history at Cambridge, and was general secretary of the Church Missionary Society which symbolized the voluntary ideal. In contrast Newbigin, who was theologically trained, could at times be rather dismissive of an historical approach.[57] Newbigin allowed a theological perspective to determine his response; with the understanding that historical processes had established the theological agenda.

As a generalization those approaching integration from a WCC background (including Newbigin) argued from a theological premise to the organizational outcome. Perhaps they had been conditioned by their concern, especially through the Faith and Order movement, over the minutiae of church government and structure which led them, on theological grounds, to pursue "organizational tidiness"; combined with a centralizing tendency inherent within the ethos of the WCC. This approach was shared by the IMC leadership, but not the rank and file membership. Instead their ethos was shaped by the free and loose association engendered by the IMC, which was locally orientated towards a particular task rather than be concerned about structures, and eschewed centralizing tendencies.

By Ghana it was recognized that mission was at a crossroads and needed radical re-evaluation. Newbigin recognized the contradiction between missionary language and mission structures. Warren had complained that, on the issue of integration, the IMC was obsessed with questions of structure and organization. Newbigin responded: "However, I think it must also be emphatically said that questions of structure have profound theological implications, more particularly when, as at present, our missionary structure flatly contradicts our theological language, the latter becomes sour and meaningless."[58] There would always be a time-lag between theological development and the adequate embodiment of it. For Newbigin, as he accepted leadership responsibility within the IMC, recognized that there must be the corresponding attempt to express the growing theological consensus of the missional church.

---

57. For example, in writing to advise David Bosch on his manuscript *Transforming Mission*, Newbigin commented on the work of his contemporary, Stephen Neill: "The only other person in the field of missiology known to me who had a comparable sweep was Stephen Neill, but I always felt that in the end he sat on the fence and did not express his own judgment. He was much more a historian than a theologian." Newbigin to Bosch, 7/9/1990, BUL: DA29/2/3/148.

58. Newbigin to Warren, 10/6/1958, BUL: DA29/1/7/165.

At a time when the Protestant missionary movement was becoming polarized between "evangelicals" and "ecumenicals" Warren, despite his opposition to integration continued to be supportive of the IMC and Newbigin's leadership. Warren, the pragmatic mission administrator, provided Newbigin with an agenda of proposals the IMC should consider developing.[59] When the DWME (Division of World Mission and Evangelism) became a reality there was strong pressure upon Newbigin from the WCC secretariat for him to be based in Geneva.[60] Warren sought to counter this pressure upon Newbigin. For Warren the maintenance of the London office was essential to strengthen links with mission societies and overcome the perception that the IMC was "sunk without a trace" by integration. He did so by appealing to the Bishop of Chelmsford who could influence decisions made at the St Andrews Central Committee meetings.[61] Warren's intercession allowed Newbigin to commute to Geneva whilst maintaining the London and New York offices of the IMC. However, in Warren's subsequent assessment on integration he felt that his original opposition to integration had been ultimately vindicated. [62]

Ghana's Invitation to Newbigin

Two major decisions on integration were taken by the IMC at Ghana. The first was to approve the Draft Plan for integration. The second major decision was to choose a leader to facilitate integration. It is no exaggeration to say that Newbigin's appointment as chairman and then general secretary of the IMC was crucial to the whole process and outcome of integration. This section explores why Newbigin was chosen for those posts, his understanding of his responsibilities, and the issues at stake.

The IMC officers knew that Ghana would be a milestone with Dr John Mackay stepping down as chairman, and the general secretary's post becoming vacant as Dr Charles Ranson would move to take up a new post as executive director of the Theological Education Fund. Before Ghana

59. This being in response to Newbigin's request to Warren; Warren to Newbigin, 11/3/1958, BUL: DA29/1/7/153.

60. It was mainly for family reasons that Newbigin sought to maintain his base in London, working out of the IMC office.

61. Warren to Falkner, June 1960, BUL: DA29/1/8/76. Warren sought approval from Newbigin before he sent his letter to the bishop. Newbigin did not want to pressurize the bishop and would accept the decision of the Central Committee, Newbigin to Warren, 30/6/1960, BUL: DA29/1/8/73.

62. Warren, "Retrospective Thoughts," 104–8.

Alfred Carleton wrote confidentially to Newbigin to ascertain his response to the possibility that Newbigin's name would be suggested for the post of general secretary; "the man chosen now must be suited for that high and delicate post—one of the most significant in the whole Christian world."[63] Newbigin's initial response to this strictly unofficial enquiry was quite negative, he had many reservations, and practically, his commitment as bishop meant he would be unable to accept the position until 1960 at the earliest, which would necessitate an interim secretary at a critical juncture. Furthermore, "[o]ne has to be on one's guard against self-deception here, and the general human tendency is to exaggerate one's own importance in a situation."[64]

Ghana gave a unanimous (official) call for Newbigin to succeed Mackay as chairman of the IMC. Newbigin accepted this call, but privately acknowledged that he felt rather daunted by this "complete surprise," the prospect of succeeding both Mott and Mackay: "So far there have been only two Chairmen . . . Mott and . . . Mackay, both of them Americans. I shall feel very strange rattling about in the place of those two giants."[65]

In appraising the work of the previous chairmen, Norman Goodall requested that Newbigin should emulate the chairmanship of Mott rather than of Mackay. The chairman needed to be good both administratively, and in representing the council to the public. In Goodall's estimation Mackay had been good in his public function but not at leading the organization, both abilities were now critical as the IMC moved towards integration.[66] Visser 't Hooft hoped that Newbigin would give a clear lead to the IMC, oversee integration and become first head of DWME, thus enabling Newbigin to bring the needed radical changes to missions.[67] Interestingly, Visser 't Hooft recognized the need for mission structures to be overhauled, but did not recognize a corresponding need to restructure the WCC to reflect the church's missionary nature.

63. Alfred Carleton to Newbigin, 6/12/1957, BUL: DA29/2/1/573.
64. Newbigin to Carleton, 18/12/1957, BUL: DA29/1/7/48.
65. Newbigin to his mother, 27/1/1958, BUL: DA29/1/7/56.
66. Goodall to Newbigin, 10/2/1958, BUL: DA29/1/7/138.
67. Visser 't Hooft to Newbigin, 27/1/1958, BUL: DA29/1/7/131.

Invitation to Become General Secretary
and Newbigin's Response

Prior to Ghana, as noted, Carleton had privately approached Newbigin about him becoming general secretary. At Ghana there was then the official call for Newbigin to become the new chairman of the IMC. These private and public invitations were quickly superseded by the official call for Newbigin to become their general secretary, with Newbigin receiving this invitation on the 4th of January 1958.

As with the prior invitation from Carleton, Newbigin's response was again to decline, citing the fact that he would not become available until 1960. But, in a letter to Visser 't Hooft, he explained the process by which he changed his mind and was ready to accept appointment as general secretary with the plan to leave his diocese in south India in June 1959 to commence this role.[68] Newbigin's change of heart was as a consequence of a conversation with Bishop Michael Hollis and correspondence with William Greer, Bishop of Manchester. Hollis's interpretation of the invitation to Newbigin was that this was a summons (by God) which therefore ought to be obeyed. Greer made Newbigin see that it would be "uncomfortable to be a Bishop under notice for too long."[69]

After five months of reflection, in a more intimate letter, Newbigin explained his reason for accepting the position of general secretary to his friend Sabapathy Kulandran: "I do not think that I am a particularly suitable person for the job, but those responsible seem to think that I'm the most likely available candidate. I have not in any way sought the post, nor do my natural desires lead me that way. . . . [T]his has come with the accents of a call from God to do a necessary duty, and I have come to feel that I could not refuse."[70]

For many, Newbigin was not only the best choice but the *only* suitable choice of candidate. In contrast to Mackay, whom Goodall deemed to be weak administratively, the IMC sought a leader who had a firm hand and a sound mind—who was "authoritative."[71] Newbigin was also considered the essential candidate because of the respect he commanded

68. George Carpenter served as interim general secretary. Newbigin to IMC staff, 1/12/1958, SOAS: IMC/26–11–25/7. Newbigin to Visser 't Hooft, 16/1/1958, SOAS: IMC/26–11–25/3.

69. Ibid. W. Greer to Newbigin, 18/1/1958, BUL: DA29/1/7/126.

70. Kulandran was Bishop in Jaffna; Newbigin to Kulandran, 26/5/1958, WCC: D. T. Niles letters, #39–41.

71. Alford Carleton to Newbigin, 15/1/1958, BUL: DA29/1/7/125.

across the ecclesiological spectrum; crucially he had the confidence of both evangelicals and Orthodox leaders: "There simply is no one in this field who possesses the range of confidence which you enjoy."[72] Such sentiments were verified by "fundamental" leaders, such as David du Plessis, whom Newbigin had first met at the Willingen conference.[73]

David du Plessis, as secretary for the fifth "World Conference of Pentecostal Churches,"[74] reported to Newbigin his concern about the negative response of the Pentecostal movement to the prospect of the IMC integrating with the WCC. Specifically, Du Plessis had received reports from various Pentecostal mission agencies that they had withdrawn, or would imminently withdraw, from the IMC in response to integration: "This will mean that no Pentecostal missionary society will be even indirectly associated with the IMC or the WCC."[75] Despite a largely negative response, du Plessis wrote to Newbigin on hearing the news that he would become chairman of the IMC, "There was no one in the entire IMC community for whom I could have voted more wholeheartedly, for that position." And he congratulated Newbigin on taking the position of general secretary.[76]

For Visser 't Hooft the key quality which made Newbigin ideal for the position of general secretary was that Newbigin "embodied" concerns for mission and unity. The two key decisions of the Ghana assembly were thus interrelated: "There was a deep connection between these two decisions. The man who was to be the leader in the years leading up to integration and in the period of making it a reality had to be a man in whose thought and teaching integration between 'mission' and 'unity' had already taken place. And this was especially true of Newbigin. For he had been the advocate of the missionary cause among ecumenists and the advocate of the cause of unity among the missionaries."[77]

72. Goodall to Newbigin, 15/1/1958, BUL: DA29/1/7/124.

73. David du Plessis was secretary for the fifth world conference of Pentecostal Churches. Through personal invitation du Plessis attended the second and third assemblies of the WCC. C. Robeck and J. Sandidge, "The World Council of Churches," in *The New International Dictionary of Pentecostal and Charismatic Movements*, ed. Stanley M. Burgess and E. M. Van der Maas (Grand Rapids: Zondervan, 2002) 1214.

74. The fifth World Conference of Pentecostal Churches was held in Toronto in September 1958.

75. Du Plessis to Newbigin, 8/10/1958, BUL: DA29/1/7/71. In contrast to the overwhelming negative response of Pentecostals to the WCC, two independent Chilean Pentecostal churches joined the WCC at the third assembly. W. J. Hollenweger, *The Pentecostals* (London: SCM, 1972) 439–41.

76. Ibid.

77. Visser 't Hooft, "Statement on Newbigin's Role in Integration," 25/10/1965,

Mackay was pleased to know that Newbigin would become the next general secretary, because in Newbigin he saw someone who would perpetuate his belief in the place of mission within the ecumenical movement: "My hope is, and I know it is yours, that in God's gracious providence the missionary movement will take the place that belongs to it at the heart of the ecumenical movement and fulfil what you and I stood for at Rolle in 1951, that the term 'ecumenical' has no meaning unless it stands equally for the mission of the Church and the unity of the Church."[78]

Issues Concerning Integration as Perceived by Newbigin

Newbigin was respected as one able to build bridges across theological chasms. He was also respected for his ability to consolidate consensus and provide a theological foundation for integration. Newbigin was chosen to steer the IMC on this difficult course as he could see beyond the merely organizational aspects of integration. Newbigin recognized that not only was the redefinition of mission critical, he also needed to provide direction for the uncharted course that lay ahead. Leading the IMC at a time of loss of confidence, direction, and morale, as an apologist for integration, he was able to challenge opponents and encourage the weak and doubting.

With integration accepted, in principle, by both the IMC and the WCC, there was a danger that discussion would proceed merely on organizational terms without getting to the heart of the theological issues at stake. Visser 't Hooft was critical of discussion by both the IMC at Ghana, and the previous WCC Central Committee at New Haven (1957), for being "superficial" in their approach to integration. "The number of people who understand that integration has a theological dimension and that it raises fundamental issues about the whole concept of mission in relation to church as well as fundamental issues for the churches themselves is still exceedingly small."[79] Newbigin had been chosen as general secretary as some perceived him to be the *only* person who could get discussion beyond the mere organizational level. In pleading with Newbigin to do just that EW Nielsen noted how the IMC itself now reflected and embodied all the problems that the Western missionary movement faced, with its loss of confidence and lack of a clear forward direction.[80]

WCC: 421.050.

78. Mackay to Newbigin, 21/1/1958, BUL: DA29/1/7/128.

79. Visser 't Hooft to Newbigin, 30/6/1958, SOAS: IMC/ 26–11–25/2.

80. Nielsen to Newbigin, 20/1/1958, BUL: DA29/1/7/139.

For Newbigin integration had always meant more than just an organizational merger, and his vision of what could be achieved far exceeded mere union of the IMC with the WCC. At the New Haven Central Committee meeting (1957) Newbigin gave support to integration as but the preliminary stage to much more radical changes that he hoped for—accepting that such changes could be pursued after integration.[81]

In planning for integration Newbigin identified several problems within the Protestant missionary movement which needed to be addressed. Within the movement theological developments, namely the recovery of a missionary ecclesiology exceeded the pace of adequate embodiment and organization. That created a dichotomy in mission between what was being said and what was done, whilst saying that the church was living with the model of a global fellowship facing a global task, the reality was that " the actual structure of our Churches (younger as well as older) does not reflect that theology. On the contrary it continues placidly to reflect the static 'christendom' theology of the 18th century."[82] A major concern for Newbigin was that integration might revive the failing Western church. Newbigin was skeptical that Western churches could change adequately or swiftly enough to effectively embody a recovered ecclesiology. It is important to remember that the factors promoting a recovery of ecclesiology were external to the Western church. And the demise of Christendom exposed the church's inadequate ecclesiology without itself providing an alternative model. Instead—no doubt inspired by his own student experience of the SCM and his direct knowledge of the dynamic non-Western church—Newbigin encouraged student leaders to be the theological catalysts to enable such changes, to be the "church ahead of the church."[83] In correspondence Newbigin recorded how he had pleaded at a WSCF (World Student Christian Fellowship) conference to "do the pioneer thinking needed for such radical changes."[84] The churches were

81. Newbigin to Carleton, 18/12/1957, BUL: DA29/1/7/48. But, as general secretary, Newbigin had a change of mind, that the structure of the IMC and the WCC should be examined "whilst fluid": "I have now come to feel that it will be a mistake to postpone thinking about these changes until after integration." Newbigin to Visser 't Hooft, 3/7/1958, SOAS: IMC/ 26–11–25/2. This will be considered in ch. 6.

82. Newbigin to Carleton, 18/12/1957, BUL: DA29/1/7/48.

83. It is significant to remember just how many ecumenical leaders of Newbigin's generation were trained and envisioned through the SCM and the WSCF. See Boyd, *The Witness of the Student Christian Movement: "Church Ahead of the Church."*

84. Ibid.

"static" and mission needed to be rid "of the taint of colonialism which still hangs so heavily over it."[85]

Newbigin accepted Walter Freytag's analysis of the potential future of missions at this "critical time." Freytag foresaw three possible outcomes: first, death—that missions would "peter out through lack of conviction." The first erroneous alternative was to abandon mission, as it was inextricably bound up with and tainted by colonialism, to proclaim that the age of missions was dead and that this was now the age of inter-church aid. Second, that rather than mission being redefined, old paternalistic patterns could be perpetuated in "backward" regions as was being done by "fundamentalist" missions. This could result in the danger of an evangelical schism from the IMC, continuing to perpetuate colonial patterns of relationship, and leaving an enfeebled IMC to integrate with the WCC. The third alternative was "that there should be a real creative re-thinking and re-statement of what mission means in the new context of the world and the Church." In applying these scenarios to the integration of the IMC, Newbigin interpreted the possibility of the first and second outcomes occurring together, "an enfeebled missionary movement tacked on to the WCC as an appendage and a reactionary fundamentalist 'IMC Continuing' trying to enlist the support of the western churches. Our first priority must be Freytag's number 3," which required an adequate theological foundation for integration.[86] Newbigin was aware that the cohesiveness of the IMC constituency was fragile and would be tested by the process of integration, there was the "very real danger that the IMC, in the process of trying to integrate with the WCC, will itself disintegrate." This danger was accentuated after Ghana by a "loss of morale in IMC quarters":[87] "There is a real danger that what goes into the WCC may be a somewhat weakened and reduced IMC, and that there may be set up a new IMC of a reactionary and fundamentalist character which would try to carry forward the nineteenth century pattern of mission and claim to be the true inheritor of the tradition of the IMC. This would be in every way deplorable."[88]

Newbigin felt that this would be the likely outcome if IMC was left without definite leadership for the next three years. Critical to such leadership was the understanding that "mission" carried "such different

---

85. Newbigin to D. T. Niles, 26/5/1958, WCC: D. T. Niles letters, #39–41.
86. Ibid.
87. Newbigin to Visser 't Hooft, 3/7/1958, SOAS: IMC/ 26–11–25/2.
88. Newbigin to Kulandran, 26/5/1958, WCC: D. T. Niles letters, #39–41.

overtones of meaning" between the West and the non-West.[89] Newbigin, with his cross-cultural missionary experience in South India, was aware of such overtones. The repeated crossing of those cultural barriers as Newbigin attended Central Committee meetings highlighted to him the very different worlds that existed between Geneva and the local parish in south India. "I have felt acutely conscious of it, every time I have come from India to attend Central Committee meetings. . . . One feels that one has moved into a completely different world, and that it is very hard to relate the thinking going on in 'ecumenical circles' to the ordinary problems of parish . . . that one left behind."[90]

Experience of these two worlds made Newbigin aware of the problems inherent in integrating the IMC, which was regionally based and had strong representation from the "younger churches," with the centralized and Western dominated WCC.[91] There were problems of disparity in theological understanding between WCC in Geneva and ordinary church members; with the WCC centered in Geneva it therefore had the Western agenda at heart, and the historical legacy, particularly in the Faith and Order movement, of a bias towards Western ecclesiological concerns. Theologizing would be done in the context of the West, and might therefore be dominated by the West's agenda.[92] With the disparity between the West and developing world, integral to integration was the desire on both sides—"older" and "younger" churches—to move from relationships of paternalism and dependency to that of true partnership. To guard against Western domination, and reflect in the WCC a model for the global church, Newbigin contended that the integrated council needed to be decentralized so that what was created in Geneva would serve as an ecumenical model for other such study centers in Asia and Africa: "I think it is quite vital that we should take seriously the necessity for more decentralisation in the structure of the integrated Council."[93]

89. Ibid.

90. Newbigin to Visser 't Hooft, 29/11/1958, SOAS: IMC/ 26–11–25/2.

91. Although, as noted, this bias was being diluted by leaders such as M. M. Thomas.

92. Despite the international impact of the formation of the CSI discussion on united churches was kept off the agenda of the 1952 Faith and Order conference in Lund. Newbigin, *Unfinished Agenda*, 139.

93. Ibid.

Conclusion

The IMC officers and WCC representatives, in their presentations at Ghana, all commented on the growing intimacy between the two councils and their overlapping remit. Integration was already a process which merely required final consummation. The leaders of each council had, since Tambaram, been discussing future relationships with their respective partner. At Ghana it became apparent that whilst the IMC officers had reached the conclusion that integration was a necessary inevitability, they had failed to facilitate a similar discussion within the national councils. By nature the IMC was a consultative body, a think tank, which was decentralized and non-executive, with the national councils being locally autonomous and preoccupied with their concerns. The discordant voices which emerged at Ghana reflected the IMC structure; the leaders, who for years had engaged in discussion on integration, were in favor, whilst the grassroots were resentful that they had not had a similar process for discussion or opportunity to voice their opinions.

Ghana was the first time opposition to integration could be clearly aired. Opposition to integration came as a surprise for IMC leadership, who had not anticipated the strength of resentment and anger against it. Feelings ran high because integration was presented as a *fait accompli*. The process of growing administrative association supported by IMC and WCC leaders meant integration had gone too far to prejudice a fair discussion. The leadership had already decided in favor, even evoking divine sanction as their ultimate seal of approval.

Responding to the resentment and anger John Mackay allowed time for discussion in extra plenary sessions and the issue of integration came to dominate the agenda. Max Warren, who had been a lone voice against integration within the joint committee, was called upon to represent opponents to integration. It was significant that the Ghana Report did not record integration as the obedient response to the move of the Holy Spirit, even though that was the unanimous interpretation of IMC and WCC leadership. Due to the obsession with structures, and growing association between the two councils there was the danger of interpreting integration only at a structural level. Whereas the WCC representatives consistently argued theologically, many with the IMC saw integration in mere administrative terms, with organizations being freely structured to facilitate the common goal. After prolonged discussion Ghana voted overwhelmingly in favor of integration.

The second major decision at Ghana was the unanimous call for Newbigin to lead the IMC into integration. Newbigin's ecumenical experience had not been through the IMC but the WCC. He was thus well acquainted with WCC and had already won broad respect, ranging from Pentecostals and "fundamentalist" evangelicals to Orthodox representatives. Newbigin demonstrated a clear understanding of the issues of integration and a persistent desire to move the focus of discussion from the organizational to more fundamental theological concerns. Showing acumen for the issues at stake, what then were the practical steps Newbigin took to ensure a good integration? How effective was he in facilitating adequate discussion within the IMC (and the WCC)? Newbigin's tenure as general secretary is discussed and assessed in the next chapter.

5

Newbigin's Tenure as General Secretary of the International Missionary Council

WHAT WERE THE KEY issues for Newbigin in integration, what agenda did he pursue as general secretary, and how effective was he in implementing his goals—particularly vis-à-vis evangelical opinion and response on integration? This chapter seeks to answer these questions. Newbigin was indefatigable in his quest to present the case for integration. As general secretary it was natural that most of the focus of his energy was within the IMC. Newbigin undertook extensive travel to acquaint himself with the IMC in Africa and Latin America and thus give him a more rounded picture of world missions, as his prior knowledge had been dominated by Asian concerns. He was also aware of the need to communicate his agenda for integration to the wider remit of the ecumenical movement; his prior links with the WCC gave him obvious openings within those circles. Then there was the difficult diplomatic task of persuading those unconvinced or suspicious of integration. One of the reasons for the choice of Newbigin, as *the* candidate for general secretary, was the respect he commanded across a wide Christian spectrum. The chapter concludes with an assessment of the consequences of integration, particularly evangelical responses, and an evaluation of Newbigin's tenure as general secretary.

Setting the Agenda for Integration

Critical to Newbigin's thinking to avert disaster and steer towards a successful integration was the need to shift discussion from a merely organizational level to examine the fundamental theological issues. Simply to answer the question of how the IMC could be made to fit within the existing structure of the WCC was to forestall a more searching theological enquiry. For Newbigin, integration raised questions about the very nature of the church; if the "church *is* the mission," how was that to be expressed, and what changes were needed within the WCC to embody mission? Newbigin received a positive response from the IMC on his desire to shift discussion from the "obsession" with organization to a theological level. As general secretary Newbigin had a very clear agenda for the IMC:

> [W]e must put into the very centre of the IMC's task for the next two years the task of adumbrating a theology, and still more a picture, of what the Christian world mission means in this mid 20th century, and a type of structure which will correspond to that picture. I personally believe that this means (slowly or quickly) the ending of the present mission-board/ younger Church relationship, within which I do not believe that the younger churches (so-called) can develop real freedom and self-hood, and the development of a pattern which expresses real ecumenical partnership in the one task of mission.[1]

To achieve these ends he realized that his role must be to promote study at all levels: "All this means that the IMC study will have to be shifted to a different gear. So far I think it has been rather leisurely."[2] On making the move from India to the international arena Newbigin's reflection on his praxis of mission led him to renewed study of the New Testament, a practice which he sought to inculcate in his staff at the IMC—making bible study central to his leadership of the IMC staff, and a determinative feature of his extensive tours of IMC constituencies. Paul Löffler's recollection, as a staff member under Newbigin's leadership, was that this "was almost an obsession for him, to study and discuss the burning issue . . . the 'proper concentration on the specifically missionary task' . . . It was his practical experience . . . which he relayed to us on the staff again and again, which led him to renewed biblical study." Newbigin's modus operandi was "always from the conceptual to the organizational, conceiving [the]

---

1. Newbigin to Niles, 26/5/1958, WCC: D. T. Niles letters, #39–41.
2. Ibid.

IMC/DWME as a think tank rather than an operational unit."[3] Newbigin's agenda was not just the integration of the IMC with the WCC—the *reorganization* of mission; more fundamentally, he sought the *redefinition* of mission—mission free of colonial connotations and centered in the local church.[4]

Based upon his "fundamentals" of the integral relationship between mission and unity, for Newbigin integration was "inevitable"; he could see "no other future for IMC except as an integrated part of the World Council." Knowing that the IMC was a fragile coalition Newbigin also took on the role of an apologist within IMC circles, with the strategy of "convincing the doubting and opposing elements about integration."[5]

The Ghana Assembly, whilst endorsing the "Draft Plan" on integration also "expressed the conviction that this required 'a much wider growth of understanding, mutual confidence and co-operation at local levels.'"[6] To this end Newbigin embarked upon several extensive tours to meet the grassroots IMC constituency, to convince them about integration, and discuss the proper expressions of missionary ecclesiology, calling people to think beyond organization to the matter of "the missionary calling of the whole Church." Newbigin did an "enormous" amount of traveling, mainly to Africa and Latin America, being "on the road" for eighteen months in his initial two years with the IMC. "The purpose of these travels was to help churches and missionaries to 'take on board' a new vision of the missionary task as that of the whole church in every continent to the world."[7]

Newbigin's Endeavors to Ensure a "Good" Integration

As early as the Rolle meetings of 1951 Newbigin was convinced, from his theological premise, that the IMC had no other future but to integrate with the WCC, that mission and unity belonged together. He was chosen as general secretary because he held and articulated those convictions. Yet, within the wide constituency of both councils, there were skeptics

3. Löffler to Laing, email, 17/08/2007.

4. In this Newbigin was not adhering to the church-centric model established at Tambaram, but was acknowledging the trinitarian source of mission, the church being the chief agency of the *missio Dei*. This will be considered in chs. 7 and 8.

5. Newbigin to Visser 't Hooft, 15/2/1958, SOAS: IMC/26–11–25/2.

6. IMC Ghana minutes cited by Newbigin to IMC staff, 1/12/1958, SOAS: IMC/26–11–25/7.

7. Newbigin, Curriculum Vitae, 20/2/1977 and 1988, BUL: DA29/1/14/147, BUL: DA29/1/14/1.

and opponents to integration. The path towards a successful integration entailed that Newbigin muster all his diplomatic skills to keep those favorable to integration onboard, whilst seeking to win over the skeptics and potential schismatics. Within the wider remit of each council were those concerned about what mission would do to the church, and what the church would do to mission. Threatening a successful integration on the WCC side was the inertia of the Western churches, the historical legacy pervading the Western bias of the WCC. At the time of integration the Orthodox Churches were assuming a more dominant role within the WCC. Their concerns about proselytism by Western mission organizations, and the daunting prospect of the proselytizers being brought into the heart of the ecumenical movement, threatened to undermine the outcome. On the IMC side, there were various evangelicals opposed to integration, as had been expressed at Ghana.

Within WCC Circles

Although, as general secretary of the IMC, Newbigin's remit naturally lay with that constituency, his previous membership of the Central Committee and Joint Committee gave him a natural avenue for influence within WCC circles. Indeed, the fact that Newbigin was already well tested and trusted within WCC circles boded well for a genuine integration. If a general secretary, who knew only the mission world, had been appointed, the process of integration would have been more fraught.[8]

Newbigin and Visser 't Hooft were aware that whilst Newbigin was driving a theologically based discussion of integration within the IMC, there was the danger that the necessary parallel process of discussion within the WCC might be, in contrast, somewhat stymied. To ameliorate against this Newbigin, perhaps somewhat naively, also sought to initiate a similar discussion within the WCC. Recognizing that questions of structure have profound theological significance he sought discussion on how to resolve the contradiction between missionary language and existing mission structures; that is, how could mission ecclesiology be embodied in the church and in the WCC as a servant of the church.[9] Visser 't Hooft invited Newbigin to present four bible studies on the mission of the church for discussion by the Central Committee. The Executive Committee proposed bible studies rather than allowing Newbigin to give an address on

8. Martin Conway, interview with Laing, 17/8/2008.
9. Newbigin to Max Warren, 10/6/1958, BUL: DA29/1/14/165.

mission to the Central Committee: "We came to the conclusion that we should not have a formal address on some missionary subject since this might give the impression of propaganda."[10] The chairman of the Joint Committee, Dr. Van Dusen, in his report to the Central Committee, also raised similar concerns to Visser 't Hooft. Van Dusen "pleaded" that the self-scrutiny initiated within the IMC by Newbigin, "was no less imperative for the WCC," and should begin with the Central Committee.[11]

On his tours of the IMC constituency Newbigin encountered, at the grassroots level, the understanding of the WCC council members about integration and the role of mission within the ecumenical movement. The case of the WCC council in Australia is taken as a representative example. Reporting, confidentially, to the IMC staff of his Australian tour Newbigin recorded: "'The missionary era is over.' I don't know how often I encountered this phrase." The WCC in Australia had no concern for mission, their understanding was, that the age of mission had given way to the age of inter-church aid. For this perception Newbigin laid blame, not upon the WCC, but on the National Missionary Council (NMC) of Australia, and the inadequate resources the IMC had for educating the churches in contrast to the organization of the WCC. "[T]he AC/WCC [Australian Council] has a considerable paid staff of very awake and energetic people; it is precluded from taking missions into its thinking because that is the job of the NMC; and the NMC has no paid staff."[12] In places where the two councils co-existed, it can be surmised that this picture was fairly representative; that a low profile and low budget council—reflecting the organizational ethos of the IMC—was failing to communicate the message regarding the redefinition of post-colonial mission to the churches.

With the Orthodox Churches

Much of Newbigin's influence on the Orthodox Churches' representatives to the WCC, in which he sought to persuade them to support integration, was through personal contact with delegates. As the CSI representative to the Central Committee at New Haven (1957) Newbigin was appointed to chair the committee preparing a draft for integration. In letters to his wife, Helen, he recorded how the committee had grown in mutual trust to the

10. Visser 't Hooft to Newbigin, 24/2/1958, SOAS: IMC/26–11–25/3.

11. CCM, 1958, 17.

12. Newbigin, "Confidential notes for IMC Staff on Australian tour," 2/3/1960, SOAS: IMC/26–11–25/14.

extent that the Orthodox representatives seemed pleased with the draft statement—an outcome he could not have envisaged as possible before.[13]

When Newbigin left India (in 1958) to take up his responsibilities with the IMC, the family travelled back to the United Kingdom overland. Knowing of that intended journey Visser 't Hooft requested that Newbigin visit the Orthodox Patriarch in Istanbul to help intercede in the process of integration. Visser 't Hooft thought it would be helpful if Newbigin, as the chairman of IMC, could meet with the Patriarch and Synod, with the hope that this would help to remove misunderstandings about integration.[14] No doubt the warmth from this initial personal contact in these meetings facilitated a conducive atmosphere for the more formal meetings which occurred later.[15]

A major concern of the Orthodox Churches was on the issue of proselytism, with zealous missionary agencies proselytizing members from Orthodox Churches. Although hesitant about integration the Orthodox Churches hoped that integration would bring such missionary agencies under the control of the WCC.[16] Such a reassurance could not be given,[17] but through their engagement with the WCC, the Orthodox representatives came to realize that WCC representatives were most sympathetic to their concerns; and that they were more able to bring their concerns to the WCC than directly to the IMC.[18]

At the Nyborg meetings of the Central Committee (1958) the Orthodox representative Metropolitan James agreed with the theological basis for integration presented by Newbigin; that mission and unity belong equally to the essence of the church. Consequently, the historical anomaly of the dichotomy between church and mission should be healed by integration.[19] A year later, at the Rhodes meetings Newbigin sought the support of the Orthodox Churches for integration and again sought to allay any fears which they might have regarding integration. In discussion with Orthodox representatives Newbigin agreed theologically with them, that

13. Newbigin to Helen, 4/8/1957, BUL: DA29/1/7/38; 8/8/1957, BUL: DA29/1/7/39.

14. Visser 't Hooft to Newbigin, 24/2/1958, SOAS: IMC/26–11–25/3.

15. For Newbigin's account, see his *Unfinished Agenda*, 159.

16. CCM, 1958, 18.

17. As some of the most zealous evangelical missions eschewed relationship with the IMC.

18. Carleton to Newbigin, 7/2/1958, BUL: DA29/1/7/136.

19. Metropolitan James, "Orthodox View on Integration: A Confidential Personal Statement Made in the Course of an Informal Discussion at Nyborg Meetings," August 1958, WCC: 27.0003.

mission must be mission *of* the church, but he emphasized the need to approach the question of integration from a historical perspective. There is only one church, but the ecumenical movement has founded the World Council of *Churches*, which although theologically a "monstrosity," was God's given means for the church to recover its unity. Newbigin perceived a similar historical process with mission agencies, which formed councils in which their "Only purpose was to bring together the missions so that disunity would not spoil their witness."[20] Originally these were councils of mission agencies which over time became church councils. Newbigin thus maintained that integration was a continuation of that historical process of recovery, bringing mission to its rightful place at the heart of the church. This required commitment to work with the structures for mission and unity as they currently existed. In allaying Orthodox fears on proselytism Newbigin commented on how most of the IMC members were as much victims of freelance activity as the Orthodox Churches were.[21]

At Ghana the Orthodox representative, Metropolitan James of Melita, read a statement on the Orthodox view of integration. The Orthodox Churches insisted that the WCC preserve its ecclesiological neutrality enshrined in the "Toronto statement."[22] And again they reiterated their concern about proselytism: "the sole aim of 'missions' should be to reach peoples yet unconverted to Christ and never to proselytize among the members of other Christian churches."[23]

The St Andrews' Central Committee in 1960 marked the last round of meetings before integration at the 3rd assembly in 1961. The response of member councils of the IMC and the WCC to integration was presented to the Central Committee. Of the IMC councils, twenty-five approved,

20. R. E. Maxwell, "Report of Reference Committee II of Rhodos on Orthodox Church," 24/8/1959, WCC: 27.0016.

21. CCM, 1959, 26.

22. The "Toronto statement" allowed for a provisional neutrality of churches joining the WCC: "no Church is obliged to change its ecclesiology as a consequence of membership in the World Council." Central Committee, "The Church, the Churches and the World Council of Churches: The Ecclesiological Significance of the World Council of Churches," ER 3:1 (1950) 49. Newbigin recognized the need for this temporary neutrality but was critical of its becoming permanent. Through the Faith and Order movement, Newbigin urged the WCC to examine its own ecclesiology and move beyond provisional neutrality to seek a "churchly unity." For Newbigin's comments, see Lesslie Newbigin, "Comments on 'the Church, the Churches and the World Council of Churches,'" ER 3:3 (1951) 252–54; Newbigin, *Household of God*, xi–xii; Newbigin, *Reunion*, x–xvii.

23. Orchard, ed., *Ghana Assembly*, 163.

seven were still considering, six had still not replied; of the WCC, there were sixty-seven affirmative replies and four dissents.[24] Partly due to the ongoing discussion between Newbigin and Orthodox representatives he was able to record that, at the Central Committee, Orthodox anxieties had been allayed and that the Orthodox Churches were "in a state of brotherly favourable abstention" towards integration.[25]

As with his initiatives with member churches, Newbigin again sought, both centrally (at the Central Committee) and regionally, to persuade Orthodox representatives of the case for integration; in his argument moving from the theological premise to the need for action within the councils which had historically evolved. An example of his regional endeavors were the various initiatives he proposed to foster improved mutual understanding between the Western churches and the Eastern Orthodox Churches through initiatives in the Near East Christian Council.[26]

With Evangelicals

Amongst the mission councils that constituted the IMC there was a general consensus for integration, the vast majority of the 38 IMC councils favored integration, and some, such as the Asian churches—especially through the East Asian Christian Council (EACC)—were pressurizing the IMC to hasten integration. This contrasted with various evangelicals, some of whom, whilst cooperating with the IMC, were nonetheless resistant to integration. Strong minority voices in opposition came from Norway, the Congo, Brazil and Belgium. Newbigin's view was that it would be "unchristian" to disregard the minority view, forcing the majority opinion upon the opposing minority. Above all Newbigin sought to maintain communication and fellowship: "Even when we have done our best to understand one another, differences will remain. But I do not believe that it is necessary for these to break our fellowship."[27]

The most vitriolic opposition to integration came from the Conseil Protestant du Congo (Congo Protestant Council).[28] They were very nega-

---

24. CCM, 1960, 14.

25. Newbigin, *Unfinished Agenda*, 177. The CCM voted as follows on integration: sixty-three in favor, one against, three abstentions; CCM, 1960, 72.

26. Newbigin proposed various joint study and exchange programs. Newbigin to Visser 't Hooft, 11/10/1960, SOAS: IMC/26–11–25/3.

27. Newbigin cited in Carpenter to John H. Yoder, 17/11/1959, WCC: 27.0015, 3.

28. As noted, this council was largely controlled by American missionaries.

tive about WCC leaders and members who they perceived as "flirting" with the Roman Catholic Church; were "supporters of Communism"; responsible for spreading "propaganda" about integration, and using invidious methods, such as saying integration was inevitable to wear down opposition: "[W]e are persuaded that there are many, like ourselves, who view the whole ecumenical movement with profound distrust, and who would shun to be associated with the liberal theology and doctrinal laxity of many of its leaders and members. . . . With liberals, orthodox and state church officials in control of the WCC, what is the future of evangelical missions within the body of the ecumenical church?"[29]

The members of the Congo Protestant Council viewed integration with the WCC as a *fait accompli* which was being forced upon them despite their opposition. They claimed that their local unity was of higher value than relationships between the IMC and the WCC. In order to preserve their local unity they therefore withdrew their membership from the IMC before councils were called to vote on integration.[30]

Whilst Congo withdrew, the Evangelical Confederation in Brazil voted against integration. In the case of Brazil, Newbigin's response was to personally meet with the secretary to facilitate discussion about future relationships between the DWME and the Confederation: "I continue to hope that it may be possible to us to have fraternal relationships."[31]

After the Ghana Assembly it was clear that missionary councils which opposed integration would choose not to remain as members of the IMC and thus not become officially "affiliated" to the WCC through the DWME. At the Oxford IMC Staff Consultation (16–18/9/58), a "device" was established which would allow those councils, such as Norway, to be "councils in consultation."[32] In the case of the Conference of British Missionary Societies the consensus supported integration, but some missionary societies opposed being linked with the WCC. The British Conference would become affiliated with the DWME of the WCC, but in order to give a nuanced statement of their relationship, a special minute was adopted: "Affiliation, however, does not necessarily imply that every member is in

29. P. J. Brashler, Secretary of Africa Inland Mission, to Councillors of Congo Protestant Council, 27/1/1958, WCC: 27.0016.

30. For the discussion on this between R. V. de Carle Thompson, Secretary of the Conseil Protestant du Congo, with various IMC officers, see WCC: 27.0011; 27.0015.

31. Newbigin to Rodolfo Anders, Confederacao Evangelica do Brasil, 3/3/1961, WCC: 27.0008.

32. IMC Record of Staff Consultation, Oxford, 13–16/9/1958, WCC: 26.0042/2, 5.

favour of such relationship to the Commission."[33] The constituent councils of the IMC had existed in loose cordial fellowship without any centralized dominance by the IMC. Official membership of the WCC, as a council of *churches* was only open to churches who agreed with the WCC basis. In allowing "affiliation" of the former members of the IMC with the DWME Newbigin was keen to maintain a similar pattern of relationship as had existed before integration, entertaining discussion of various forms of association in his endeavor to maintain fellowship.

Norwegian objection to integration was focused on the perceived "liberal theology" emanating from WCC circles, and concerns that the WCC might try to constitute a "super-church."[34] Newbigin kept abreast of the debates within the Norwegian Missionary Council reading translations of Norwegian objections to integration. At the Rhodes Central Committee Newbigin also raised the possibility of visiting Scandinavia (which he subsequently did). The Norwegian response to his proposed visit was that it would help to improve relationships, attitudes and the atmosphere, but that it would not ensure a vote for integration.[35]

After the Ghana Assembly the constitution of the IMC stated integration would proceed unless Newbigin received, by an agreed deadline, written disapproval from six or more councils. By the deadline the only official disapproval received was from Brazil—although it was known that the Norwegian councils disapproved of integration no official word had been received by the deadline. Later the Norwegian missionary council voted on and rejected "consultative membership" placing them outside of the IMC and the WCC.[36] The IMC officers were thus to proceed as instructed by the Administrative Committee to effect integration at the New Delhi assembly.[37]

33. Newbigin to Jan Hermelink, 17/3/1961, SOAS: IMC/26–11–25/12.

34. Olav G. Myklebust to Goodall, 6/1/1960, SOAS: IMC/27–00–06/13.

35. Henrik Hauge to Newbigin, 6/1/1960, SOAS: IMC/27–00–06/13. The debate in the Norwegian mission council was mainly between Vagen and Myklebust. For details of this, see Nissen, "Nordic Missions."

36. On 19/5/61, nine voted for, fourteen against. Newbigin to IMC officers and staff, 28/6/1961, WCC: 27.0009.

37. Newbigin to IMC Member Councils, 2/3/1961, WCC: 27.0008

The Third Assembly: New Delhi 1961

With integration the DWME could not function simply as a perpetuation of the IMC, now within the WCC. The expectation was that the WCC would be imbued with missionary concern by integration. There was also the realization that ecumenical concerns would redefine mission. This was evidenced in the actual change of the WCC "Basis" at New Delhi. Originally, the WCC had identified itself as "a fellowship of churches which *accept* our Lord Jesus Christ as God and Saviour." At New Delhi, "accept" was replaced with "confess" and the words "and therefore seek to fulfill together their common calling to the glory of one God, Father, Son and Spirit" were added. "The 'common calling' was understood to refer to 'confess' and thus had a clear missionary thrust, something that was absent in the original basis."[38]

There was the reciprocal expectation that new insights would be brought to mission and the church as both councils now operated in a united ecumenical perspective. This reciprocity was expressed between the reports on "Witness" and "Unity" in the New Delhi Report. For example, the report on "Witness" stressed the necessity of unity: "The question of the Church's unity is of vital importance, since the Bible teaches us that the Gospel cannot be authoritatively proclaimed to the world by a disunited Church."[39] Similarly, the report on "Unity" stressed the relationship between unity and mission: "In the fulfilment of our missionary obedience the call to unity is seen to be imperative. . . . There is an inescapable relation between the fulfilment of the Church's missionary obligation and the recovery of her visible unity."[40]

In his sermon, during the service of integration, Newbigin reminded the assembly of the theological foundation for integration, the Rolle statement, which had paved the way for integration ten years earlier: "The obligation to take the Gospel to the whole world, and the obligation to draw all Christ's people together, both rest upon Christ's whole work and are indissolubly connected. Every attempt to separate these tasks violates the wholeness of Christ's ministry to the world." The fundamental justification for union lay "in the nature of the Gospel itself."[41] Beyond the

---

38. WCC, *The New Delhi Report: The Third Assembly of the World Council of Churches, 1961* (London: SCM, 1962) 152–59. Cf. Bosch, *Transforming Mission*, 460.

39. WCC, *New Delhi Report*, 78.

40. Ibid., 121.

41. Lesslie Newbigin, "The Missionary Dimension of the Ecumenical Movement," *ER* 14:2 (1962) 208. It was fitting that Newbigin, as the preacher, could remind the

administrative union being enacted Newbigin again called for a deeper spiritual union of those two concerns which had been the respective focus of the two councils, "For the churches which constitute the World Council this means the acknowledgment that the missionary task is no less central to the life of the Church than the pursuit of renewal and unity."[42] It was acknowledged, in the post-colonial situation, that the church everywhere was in a missionary situation. Mission, at a historical crossroad between the past and the future, was to six, not just three continents.[43] Newbigin anticipated that one practical consequence would be the sending of missionaries from the majority world to the West, "to make the Gospel credible to the pagan masses of those continents."[44]

As the author of the report from the DWME, Newbigin was anxious that the concerns and expectations of the missionary movement be maintained in integration: "This spiritual heritage must not be dissipated; it must remain . . . at the heart of the WCC. Without it the ecumenical movement would petrify. Integration must mean that the WCC takes the missionary task into the very heart of its life."[45] This was made explicit in a resolution to the Central Committee which requested that "high priority should be given to the task of helping the churches to fulfil their common calling to mission and evangelism."[46]

To symbolize the act of integration Visser 't Hooft, as general secretary of the WCC, walked in procession with Newbigin, the general secretary of the IMC.[47] The New Delhi Assembly stands as a major milestone in embodying an ecclesiological recovery of the relationship between mission and unity. And the formation of the C/DWME was interpreted by some as the "IMC reborn."[48] Stephen Neill stated that "if the theological significance of the action was realized, this was indeed a revolutionary

---

assembly of this text, which he had drafted for the Central Committee in 1951.

42. Ibid., 214.

43. Lesslie Newbigin, "Report of the Division of World Mission and Evangelism to the Central Committee," *ER* 15:1 (1962) 89.

44. Newbigin, "Missionary Dimension," 211. After his address Newbigin was surprised to learn that some people thought he was making a joke at this point.

45. WCC, *New Dehli Report*, 249–50.

46. CWME Report, in ibid., 257.

47. Despite their close working relationship over decades, Visser 't Hooft only makes two brief mentions of Newbigin in his autobiography. W. A. Visser 't Hooft, *Memoirs* (London: SCM, 1973) 311.

48. Hogg cited by T. E. Yates, "Edinburgh Revisited: Edinburgh 1910 to Melbourne 1980," *Churchman* 94:2 (1980) 145.

moment in church history . . ." Neill, perhaps exaggerating, added that "such an event had never taken place in the history of the Church since Pentecost."[49]

The Impact of Integration upon Understandings of Mission

Membership of Eastern Orthodox Churches at New Delhi profoundly changed the constituency of the WCC. But of the twenty-three churches applying for membership it is important to remember that eleven were African and two were Pentecostal churches. New Delhi was thus a significant milestone, with the induction of so many non-Western churches, and the holding of the assembly for the first time outside of the West, this demonstrated that the WCC was entering into "a more truly world-wide period in [its] life . . . [and was] forced to think henceforth in terms of the whole world."[50]

With the broadening ecclesiastical membership of the WCC, one of the consequences of integration was to broaden the missiological discussion, with an increase in number and varieties of churches participating in the missionary forum. The IMC had been confined to Protestants. Post-integration discussion now included the Orthodox Churches, and those churches from the majority world which had distanced themselves from the Protestant denominations, the various independent churches.[51] As a consequence of Vatican II, relationships were thawing with the Roman Catholic Church and they too became reciprocally involved in missiological discussion. During the tenure of subsequent directors of the CWME, integration "was taken for granted," the administrative consequence of the theological understanding that mission and unity belonged together. The question of integration was "never re-opened," instead the issue was how the WCC could be mobilized into the direction of a missionary standing in the world.[52]

Mission had been the central concern of the IMC. After integration mission was now just one of many concerns within the WCC. A plethora

---

49. Neill, *Church and Christian Union*, 108–9. Similarly, Cavert said that the integration "marks a new stage in the Christian world mission." WCC, *New Delhi Report*, 55.

50. Visser 't Hooft, *Memoirs*, 317. Visser 't Hooft declined the opportunity, with the benefit of hindsight, to assess integration.

51. E. Castro, "Editorial," *IRM* 70:280 (1981) 238.

52. Castro, interview, 10/9/2008.

of small units, each with a commission and budget, were competing for attention by appealing directly to churches, and thus diluting the effectiveness of the CWME in its communication with the churches. By the early 1970s Emilio Castro estimated that there were as many as seventeen of these distinct small units within the WCC, each anxious to ensure its concerns received adequate attention.[53] One of the most successful was the Program to Combat Racism, which established a clear link between mission and political action.

As had happened with the IMC earlier at Ghana, the New Delhi assembly also signaled the passing of the old generation, with the quest initiated for a new generation of leaders.[54] Other important factors which impacted the outcome of integration were the theological tensions within the life of the WCC and the political divisions external to it—the dominance of the Cold War and the East-West polarization.[55] This raised the question, could the WCC maintain its cohesion and integrity in spite of these threats?[56]

Already inherent in the New Delhi report was evidence of more fundamental changes in the understanding of mission. Newbigin noted how the church-centric model of mission, which had dominated since Tambaram, was breaking down and that, "The report contained many signals pointing the way. It spoke of God's rule over the whole created world and said, 'We have but little understanding of the wisdom, love and power which God has given to men of other faiths and of no faiths.'"[57] These changes, inaugurated at New Delhi, were to pave the way for an ecumenical discussion on cosmic christology. Joseph Sittler is attributed with explicitly starting the discussion at the Assembly with his paper entitled "Called to Unity."[58] This cosmic christology, with its emphasis more on creation than on redemption, imported new meanings to the concepts of "mission" and "unity": (1) a "cosmic redemption" leading to a "fuller

53. Castro, interview, 10/9/2008.

54. Visser 't Hooft, *Memoirs*, 309–10. This was Visser 't Hooft's last assembly as general secretary.

55. This of course became internalized within the WCC. E.g., the nomination of a candidate to a particular committee by the Russian Orthodox Church was apparently influenced by Russia's political interests in the Middle East. Newbigin, *Unfinished Agenda*, 192.

56. Visser 't Hooft, *Memoirs*, 309.

57. Newbigin, *Unfinished Agenda*, 192.

58. His paper is based on the text Colossians 1:15–20. J. A. Sittler, "Called to Unity," *ER* 14 (1962) 177–87.

unity"; (2) that unity is grounded primarily in creation, rather than in re-creation; (3) the apparent antithesis between church and world is overcome as they become part of the larger synthesis, thus breaking down the boundary between Christianity and other faiths; and (4) that "unity in Christ" requires a broader definition than the classical understanding of the term.[59] This early signpost signaled a broadening of the basis of the ecumenical movement which would become more apparent during Konrad Raiser's tenure as general secretary (1993–2003).[60]

DWME Mexico (1963)

Willingen and Ghana had been characterized by their lack of confidence. By as early as 1963, Newbigin's reflections on the first conference of the DWME, was that confidence had been restored. "The word most often used in describing it [Mexico] has been the word 'confidence.' There was, indeed, a sense of assurance and of direction—due fundamentally, I am persuaded, to the fact that the exposition of Scripture was the foundation of all else in the programme."[61] Newbigin attributed the restoration of confidence to the practice of bible study, a practice he had made central to his directorship of the IMC. By Mexico Newbigin was assured that, at least at the administrative ecumenical level of the two councils, integration had been highly successful.[62]

In a broader sense Newbigin always hoped that the integration of the IMC, at an international level, would be a catalyst for the recovery of the proper relationship between mission and church at the local level: "What is said about the mission of the church must apply in the first instance to the local congregation."[63] On this Newbigin was much more cautious in his appraisal. In the West, in what had been a Christianized society,

---

59. Saayman, *Unity and Mission*, 23–24.

60. Newbigin expressed his disquiet about the place of mission in the WCC whilst in office as the first director of DWME. Later, he entered into a more strident debate with Raiser. Newbigin, *Unfinished Agenda*, 197. M. W. Goheen, "The Future of Mission in the World Council of Churches: The Dialogue between Lesslie Newbigin and Konrad Raiser," *Mission Studies* 21:1 (2004) 97–111.

61. Lesslie Newbigin, "Editor's Notes," *IRM* 53 (1964) 248.

62. Newbigin detailed the impact of integration upon various programs. Lesslie Newbigin, "Director's Report," in *Minutes of the Second Meeting of the CWME, Mexico City, December 8th–19th, 1963*, ed. WCC (London, New York: The Commission, 1963) 76.

63. Newbigin, "Reflections upon CWME Mexico," 1964, BUL: DA29/5/3/27.

Newbigin acknowledged that "the local congregation provided the place where one withdrew for . . . specifically religious activities. . . . The process of secularization threatens it with the fate of becoming completely irrelevant." Moreover, the historical process in the West, of privatized denominationalism, through the missionary movement, had become the West's legacy to the world. Confessional boundaries were exported and then perpetuated by the "younger church" birthed as a result of this process. "In spite of all that the ecumenical movement has achieved, the disunity of our missionary work is still a scandal."[64]

For others, in their assessment of integration, what happened *outside* the WCC was much more significant that what occurred within the council. It is telling that Warren does not equate the integration of the IMC with its continuance within the WCC. Instead, he refers to its "disappearance" which resulted in the continuity of mission concerns through a variety of avenues *outwith* the WCC: "Insofar as the disappearance of the IMC created a vacuum, that vacuum is being filled with unforeseeable consequences for the ecumenical and missionary movements of the future."[65] Whilst remaining (diplomatically) mute on the D/CWME, Warren was positive on the preservation of missionary concern which the IMC had previously embodied developing independent of the WCC. This, the non-cooperating evangelical response to integration, is now considered.

Evangelical Responses to Integration

The demands of integration, with the questions of how to resolve the numerous structural issues fully occupied the energies of the leadership. Beyond their immediate concerns, what was less apparent to the IMC leadership was the extent to which evangelical support for the IMC had eroded. The numerical trends were alarming: by 1957 almost 60 percent of American missionaries were not cooperating with the IMC—and 70 percent of all foreign missionaries were American. Sterling efforts were made to retain the loyalty of evangelicals within IMC councils. But, considering the "barrage" of anti-ecumenical "propaganda," the facilities did not exist to effectively communicate the IMC message on integration to the growing majority outwith the remit of the IMC. Instead, those missions continued their isolation from the ecumenical movement with growing

64. Ibid.

65. Warren identified six channels through which the IMC's concerns were being fulfilled. Warren, "Retrospective Thoughts," 108.

suspicion about liberal theological developments within the WCC. With most missions already not cooperating with the IMC it was inevitable that, from their perspective, faced with the specter of the IMC being compromised by integration, an evangelical schism would occur, as had first been predicted by Walter Freytag.

Both Winter and Warren interpreted the evangelical separation and isolation from the IMC positively, as a continuation of the key concerns which the IMC had embodied.[66] And one can draw parallels between the IMC emerging as a continuation committee from Edinburgh, and the Lausanne movement continuing in the spirit of the IMC. The American origins of the evangelical schism within the Protestant missionary movement can be dated to the conference held in Chicago in 1960 of the Interdenominational Foreign Mission Association (IFMA).[67] John F. Walvoord, President of Dallas Theological Seminary (which was famous for advocating a dispensationalist view), gave an address, "The Theological Basis for Foreign Mission." Walvoord was not seeking to innovate but to be true to his understanding of evangelical tradition. As a theological basis for mission he thus emphasized the need for commitment to Jesus; God's commissioning of individuals (as derived from the Apostle Paul's theological conviction [Rom 1:14–18]); and condemnation as a consequence of rejecting Christ. Walvoord by-passed the issues on *missio Dei* which were first raised at Willingen, and thus entirely ignored current developments in missionary ecclesiology. Whereas the IMC at Willingen acknowledged their need of a new theological basis, Walvoord's theological basis was a re-statement of fundamentalist convictions—which had already been acknowledged as inadequate within IMC circles.[68]

Wheaton and Berlin 1966

By 1966 a broader conservative evangelical consensus allowed for the cooperation between the IFMA and the EFMA, who co-sponsored a conference, in April, at Wheaton College. Meeting soon after the Second Vatican Council, Wheaton sought to "refute" and "rebut" perceived tendencies and

66. Warren, "Retrospective Thoughts"; Winter, "Ghana."

67. Germination of the much earlier American schism on fundamentalism in the mid-1920s.

68. J. F. Walvoord, "The Theological Basis for Foreign Missions," in *Facing the Unfinished Task: Messages Delivered at the Congress on World Missions*, ed. Mary Bennett and J. O. Percy, compiler (Zondervan, 1961) 245–49.

errors amongst Roman Catholics and conciliar Protestants. Dangerous issues and tendencies were identified, particularly that of syncretism and neo-universalism.[69]

Eugene Smith, as the WCC observer at Wheaton, was surprised at how deep their hostility was. "The distrust of the ecumenical movement within this group has to be experienced to be believed"; with nine of the fifteen major papers publically attacking the movement.[70] Conservatives continued to charge the WCC with "theological liberalism, loss of evangelical conviction, universalism in theology, substitution of social action for evangelism, and the search for unity at the expense of biblical truth."[71] For all the passion expressed in these attacks, and "the deep intensity of conviction underlying them," the battle-hardened Smith came to a surprisingly positive conclusion: "We must remember that the attacks were probably much less extreme than they would have been five years ago."[72]

Wheaton also marked a considerable advance for evangelical missiology. Besides their critique of others, perhaps for the first time evangelicals were also self-critical of their own missiology, recognizing the neglect of social responsibility in past formulations of evangelicalism.[73]

Six months after Wheaton, in October 1966, twelve hundred evangelicals met in Berlin for a World Congress on Evangelism.[74] Whilst Wheaton had attacked the ecumenical movement, Berlin—if only in its official publication—ignored it, with virtually no reference to the WCC in its reports.[75] However, Walter Hollenweger, the WCC observer, recalled "the repetitive, almost liturgically polemical remarks against the WCC"

---

69. "Wheaton Declaration," in *The Church's Worldwide Mission: Proceedings of the Congress, Wheaton, April 9–16*, ed. Harold Lindsell (Waco, TX: Word, 1966) 222–25.

70. Smith, "Wheaton Congress," 480–81.

71. Ibid., 481.

72. Ibid., 481–82.

73. This was evident in the paper by H. Fenton, "Mission and Social Concern," in *The Church's Worldwide Mission*. Fenton's appraisal came from his experience as a missionary in Latin America. It is interesting to note that the later social correction to evangelicalism at Lausanne (1974) also came from Latin America, in this instance from Rene Padilla and Samuel Escobar. For a study on this theme, see J. Thomas, *From Lausanne to Manila: Evangelical Social Thought* (Delhi: ISPCK, 2003).

74. The conference was sponsored by the Billy Graham Evangelistic Association and *Christianity Today*. Although hosted in Berlin, it too was dominated by American leadership and conservative evangelical presuppositions.

75. Bosch, "Ecumenicals and Evangelicals," 463. C. Henry and S. Mooneyham, eds., *One Race, One Gospel, One Task*, 2 vols. (Minneapolis: World Wide Publications, 1967).

made at Berlin. In response Hollenweger raised his concerns personally with Billy Graham. He was assured that Berlin was not in "opposition" to the WCC, but sought instead to "complement" its work.[76]

The radicalization on the WCC was confirming "the darkest thoughts" evangelicals had of its future. Yet, during the 1960s, evangelicals were showing more openness to at least read beyond the confines of conservative theology.[77] Some conservatives were questioning whether "they [had] been preoccupied with an 'evangelical canon.'" As a corrective against this they realized the need "to enter the arena of public debate," and to "listen as well as speak."[78]

Uppsala 1968: The 4th Assembly of the WCC

The year 1968 is remembered for marking a decisive shift in attitudes: "A radical change in the general attitude to political, social, cultural, philosophical and theological matters came into existence in 1968 and onward."[79] Events which contributed to this radical change include the student riots in Paris, the communist invasion of Prague, developments in Vietnam and in Latin America, and concerns about the continued validity, and underlying ethos, of Western development programs. The world impinged upon Uppsala in ways that could not have been foreseen.[80]

Prior to the assembly Donald McGavran embarked upon a "propaganda barrage,"[81] asking pointedly, "Will Uppsala Betray the Two Billion?"—that is, those who have yet to be evangelized.[82]

At Uppsala attempts were made to hold together the "Gospel of personal conversion and the Gospel of social responsibility."[83] But John Stott recalled the polarization in the discussion between evangelicals and ecumenicals in Section II of the Report ("Renewal in Mission") as a "fruitless

---

76. "World Council Diary," *ER* 19:1 (1967) 89.

77. Glasser, "Evolution," 10.

78. Ibid., 11–2.

79. J. Aagaard, "Mission after Uppsala," in *Crucial Issues in Mission Today*, ed. Thomas F. Stransky and Gerald H. Anderson (New York: Paulist, 1974) 13.

80. Ibid., 14.

81. Newbigin, "Cross-Currents," 150.

82. D. A. McGavran, *Conciliar-Evangelical Debate: The Crucial Documents, 1964–1976* (South Pasadena, CA: William Carey Library, 1977) 233–41.

83. J. V. Taylor, in *The Uppsala Report, 1968: Official Report of the Fourth Assembly of the WCC, Uppsala July 4–20, 1968*, ed. N. Goodall (Geneva: WCC, 1968) 24.

confrontation" which resulted in neither the "true meeting of minds [n] or clarification of issues."[84] McGavran's (and Stott's) conclusion was that Uppsala had indeed betrayed the two billion.[85] Despite their efforts, from an evangelical perspective, the Section II report "remained manifestly unsatisfactory."[86]

Uppsala thus marked a decisive watershed between evangelical and ecumenical understandings of mission. From Uppsala, "Not Christianization and Church planting but humanization and radical change of the structures of society seem to be the new ecumenical missionary strategy."[87] Peter Beyerhaus traced the origin of these trends to the American study group on the Study of the Missionary Structure of the Congregation which presented their report at the assembly: "We have lifted up humanization as the goal of mission because we believe that more than others it communicates in our period of history the meaning of the messianic goal. In another time the goal of God's redemptive work might best have been described in terms of man turning toward God. . . . Today the fundamental question is much more that of true man, and the dominant concern of the missionary congregation must therefore be to point to the humanity in Christ as the goal of mission."[88]

Beyerhaus' response was to lead a polemical attack against this understanding of mission as humanization. His assessment was that Uppsala amounted to much more than "surface ripple[s]." Instead it heralded a "profound change of direction," a "fundamental crisis" in the definition of mission.[89] In response Beyerhaus, in 1970, drafted "The Frankfurt Declaration on the Fundamental Crisis in Christian Mission." The Declaration evoked the memory of the 1934, Barmen Declaration, with its seven declarations. The Frankfurt Declaration sought to "oppose," "reject" and "refute" the WCC's perceived deviation from a biblical definition of mission.[90]

---

84. Cf. Newbigin, "Call to Mission," J. R. W. Stott, "Significance of Lausanne," *IRM* 64:255 (1975) 291. Stott, in *Uppsala Report*, ed. N. Goodall, 26.

85. Their reflections were reprinted in McGavran, *Conciliar-Evangelical Debate*, 233–41, 266–68, and 273–79. For McGavran's comments on the debate, see D. A. McGavran, "My Pilgrimage in Mission," *IBMR* 10:2 (1986) 54.

86. Yates, *Christian Mission*, 198.

87. P. Beyerhaus, "Mission and Humanization," in *Crucial Issues in Mission Today*, 234.

88. Cited in ibid., 242. Original source: WCC, *Church for Others*, 78.

89. "The Frankfurt Declaration," in *Missions: Which Way? Humanization or Redemption*, ed. Peter Beyerhaus (Grand Rapids: Zondervan, 1974) 107–8.

90. W. Künneth and P. Beyerhaus, eds., *Reich Gottes Oder Weltgemeinschaft? Die*

The Declaration received numerous signatures in Germany. McGavran, through *Christianity Today*, disseminated the Declaration to the English-speaking world, particularly amongst American conservative evangelicals, and encouraged Beyerhaus to translate his critical study of the WCC into English.[91] The polarization continued such that after the second meeting of CWME (in Bangkok, 1973), "[t]he split in Germany between conciliar and evangelical missionary agencies had become final."[92]

Lausanne 1974

With the recognition that relations had "hardened" and become confrontational, other evangelicals, such as John Stott, chose a more constructive engagement with ecumenicals. At Lausanne (1974),[93] Stott wished to "strike a note of evangelical repentance . . . We have some important lessons to learn from our ecumenical critics. Some of their rejection of our position is not a repudiation of biblical truth, but rather of our evangelical caricatures of it."[94] Rather than earlier confrontations Lausanne was characterized by a spirit of humility with divergent evangelical voices being heard, and the evidence of self-criticism in response to genuine dialogue.[95] But strident voices continued, with some hoping Lausanne "might usher in a global organization in opposition to the WCC." This did not transpire, one reason being that as many as 60 percent of evangelicals gathered were estimated to be from member churches of the WCC.[96] But some of the Lausanne leadership understood themselves, in contrast to the WCC, as "the legitimate heirs of Edinburgh 1910."[97]

Berliner Ökumene-Erklärung Zur Utopischen Vision Des Weltkirchenrates [Kingdom of God or World Community? The Berlin Ecumenical Manifesto on the Utopian Vision of the WCC] (Bad Liebenzell: Liebenzeller Mission, 1975).

91. "Frankfurt Declaration," 107–11. See also P. Beyerhaus, "Mission and Humanization," *IRM* 60:237 (1971).

92. Yates, *Christian Mission*, 199.

93. The "International Congress on World Evangelization" marked the inauguration of the Lausanne movement. Conference report: J. D. Douglas, ed., *Let the Earth Hear His Voice* (Minneapolis: World Wide Publications, 1975).

94. J. R. W. Stott, "The Biblical Basis of Evangelism," in *Let the Earth Hear His Voice*, 65.

95. Stott, "Significance of Lausanne," 288.

96. Bosch, "Ecumenicals and Evangelicals," 464.

97. Gerald Anderson, interview with Laing, 21/8/2008.

A significant legacy of Lausanne is the Covenant,[98] a document defining evangelicalism in a "comprehensive and unpolemical nature."[99] As such it thus differed markedly from the Frankfurt Declaration. Crucial to the debate between evangelical and ecumenical streams was the question of whether socio-politico-economic liberation is, in biblical terms, "salvation." The Covenant denied that liberation could be equated with salvation.[100] Stott, drafter of the Covenant, noted that, "The confusion of creation and redemption, common grace and saving grace, the reformation of structures and the regeneration of persons seems to lie at the heart of current ecumenical-evangelical tensions."[101]

Despite the more conciliatory nature of Lausanne Stott was aware of "the wide gap of confidence and credibility which exists today between ecumenical leaders and evangelicals, between Geneva and Lausanne."[102] This was exemplified in the numerous studies published around this time which contrasted the two streams of mission theology. Most, written by evangelicals, were naturally critical of perceived erroneous tendencies within the WCC.[103] Further evidence of continued polarization was the hosting of separate mission conferences which gave the impression of an ongoing competitiveness, reflecting unresolved differences. Thus, in 1980, CWME (Melbourne) and Lausanne (Pattaya) held conferences within five weeks of each other. The Roman Catholic missiologist, Thomas Stransky, saw this schism as "the most ominous and depressing negative sign on the mission horizon of the next decade," which would institutionalize differences and force many to "take artificial sides."[104]

Despite Stransky's plea almost a decade on the trend continued with, in 1989, the CWME meeting in San Antonio and the Lausanne II Conference convening at Manila. The two camps were still too estranged

---

98. "The Lausanne Covenant," in *Let the Earth Hear His Voice*, ed. J. D. Douglas.

99. Bosch, "Ecumenicals and Evangelicals," 465.

100. "Lausanne Covenant," par. 5.

101. Stott, "Significance of Lausanne," 289.

102. J. R. W. Stott, "Response to Bishop Mortimer Arias," *IRM* 65:257 (1976) 33.

103. For example: Bassham, *Mission Theology*; D. J. Bosch, *Witness to the World: The Christian Mission in Theological Perspective* (London: Marshall Morgan & Scott, 1980); A. F. Glasser and D. A. McGavran, *Contemporary Theologies of Mission* (Grand Rapids: Baker, 1983); R. E. Hedlund, *Roots of the Great Debate in Mission* (Madras: Evangelical Literature Service for Church Growth Research Centre, 1981); H. T. Hoekstra, *The World Council of Churches and the Demise of Evangelism* (Wheaton: Tyndale House, 1979).

104. T. F. Stransky, "Mission Power in the 1980s," *IRM* 69:273 (1980) 48.

from each other for a future unified conference to be conceivable. But, after years of polarization, the suggestion of an overlapping conference was proffered, to "be held simultaneously, on the same site and share a number of sessions."[105]

In spite of the institutionalization of missiological differences there has been some past evidence of reconciliation. Notable leaders, such as Newbigin, Stott, David Bosch, Emilio Castro and Bishop Mortimer Arias have been able to bridge the gap between the two sides. An early attempt to build a bridge between ecumenicals and evangelicals was in joint publications, such as *The Church Local and Universal*, the book being co-edited by Newbigin, of the WCC, and Leslie Lyall from the Overseas Missionary Fellowship (formerly the China Inland Mission).[106] Castro[107] held together an insistence on mission as proclamation with his Latin American concerns for social justice.[108] Arias, in his address to the WCC meeting at Nairobi (1975), demonstrated a desire for reconciliation by drawing "equally on the Lausanne Congress and the Roman Catholic Synod of Bishops."[109] He stressed that evangelism was an "essential," "primary," "normal," "permanent," and "costly" task of the churches—an emphasis which was "warmly welcome" by evangelicals such as Stott.[110] A further significant step in helping to heal the rift between the two sides was the publication of the ecumenical affirmation of "Mission and Evangelism,"[111] which became "a kind of catechism" with many churches adopting it as their own position on mission and evangelism.[112]

The personal endeavor of CWME directors, such as Jacques Matthey, has also helped to build bridges with evangelicals in the Lausanne movement and the World Evangelical Alliance; the CWME and Lausanne

---

105. "Those with Evangelical Concerns at the World Council of Churches' Conference at San Antonio to the Lausanne II Conference at Manila," *IBMR* 13:3 (1989) 134.

106. L. T. Lyall and L. Newbigin, *The Church Local and Universal* (London: World Dominion, 1962).

107. Castro was director of CWME from 1973 to 1983, and general secretary of the WCC from 1985 to 1992.

108. Castro, telephone interview with Laing, 10/9/2008. Yates, *Christian Mission*, 219.

109. Yates, *Christian Mission*, 219.

110. M. Arias, "That the World May Believe," *IRM* 65:257 (1976) 13–26; Stott, "Response to Arias," 30–34.

111. WCC, "Mission and Evangelism: An Ecumenical Affirmation," *IBMR* 7:2 (1983).

112. Castro interview, 10/9/2008.

collaborating on evangelism, and producing a common text, the Stuttgart Declaration (1987).[113]

The CWME and Lausanne have continued their own agendas through separate conferences and consultations. A major step of reconciliation, such as a joint conference, has yet to materialize. It would have been fitting if the conferences planned to celebrate the centenary of Edinburgh 1910, the source of the modern ecumenical movement, could have brought some resolution, although prospects of this were rather bleak. Whereas CWME were "fully involved" in the main celebration and conference in Edinburgh in 2010 (and the ongoing consultations elsewhere), the Lausanne movement convened a separate conference, "Lausanne III," in Cape Town in October, 2010.[114]

Conclusion

Newbigin's Tenure as General Secretary: An Evaluation

Reflecting upon Newbigin's tenure in the IMC and DWME, and his contribution to the ecumenical movement at large, Visser 't Hooft recorded that, "It was in no small measure due to his [Newbigin's] vision that integration took place. . . . For he believed deeply that the missionary-evangelistic concern and the concern for church-unity are both rooted in the same mandate. . . . He wanted unity for the sake of mission. He wanted mission to proclaim the message of reconciliation between all who believed in Christ."[115]

Newbigin was ideally suited to lead the IMC into integration. Through reflection upon his missionary career he had inculcated the theological integration between mission and church, and was adept at articulating his developing missionary ecclesiology to others, as apologist and defender of it.

The IMC, throughout its history, had existed as a think tank rather than as an organ for dissemination and education of the church and mission societies. Newbigin was more effective than most in disseminating a rethinking on mission, particularly through his personal "manifesto" *One*

---

113. Jacques Matthey, interview with Laing, 20/8/2008.

114. http://www.oikoumene.org/en/who-are-we/organization-structure/consultative-bodies/world-mission-and-evangelism/history.html#c16564, 21/5/2009; http://www.lausanne.org/cape-town-2010.

115. Visser 't Hooft, "Statement on Newbigin," February 1974, WCC: 994.1.09/10.

Body.[116] However, the small administrative structure of the IMC meant that this rethinking, initiated by Newbigin, was limited to only a few of the IMC staff.[117] The limited infrastructure curtailed their ability to re-educate the grassroots constituency of the necessary changes in mission structures.

A principle that Newbigin had learned as a student in the Cambridge SCM was "that the health of the whole depends upon the health of the smallest unit."[118] His approach to integration was to emphasize the regional and local expressions of new relationships between church and mission, rather than allow a centralized hierarchy to be determinative. For this to become a reality he pleaded that each area and region would have to look at the unfinished task of evangelism "so that the proposed new Division . . . would start its work with the confidence that the whole constituency was ready for a fresh and vigorous advance in the world mission of the Church . . ."[119] Rather than abstract theological discussion Newbigin advocated that the IMC develop local experiments on the relationship between mission and the church; he proposed a shift from bilateral relationships between individual mission boards and "younger churches" to multilateral experiments in mission.[120] However, his call was met with little response, his repeated pleas for action going unheeded.[121]

Although failing to promote action, Newbigin was successful in initiating a wide-ranging rethinking of mission within the IMC; but discussion was largely limited to IMC circles. It was recognized that similar analysis was required within WCC circles. The plea was made that similar self-scrutiny "was no less imperative for the WCC," and should begin with the Central Committee.[122] At the invitation of Visser 't Hooft, who recognized that danger, Newbigin had been able to initiate some discussion within the Central Committee, but his remit was largely confined to IMC circles, and the demands of his job ensured that he was fully engaged, and travelling extensively, as general secretary. Integration failed to achieve all

---

116. Newbigin, *One Body*.

117. For example, in their staff gathering in Oxford (16–18/9/58) to discuss Newbigin's draft paper, "The Organization of the Church, Mission to the World," June 1958, BUL: DA29/2/9/2.

118. Newbigin, *Unfinished Agenda*, 68.

119. Newbigin to the Secretaries of IMC Member Councils, Covering letter to introduce the aim of *One Body*, 1/12/1958, WCC: 26.0042/4.

120. Ibid.

121. E.g., at the Paris Central Committee, CCM, 1962, 103.

122. CCM, 1958, 17.

that Newbigin hoped for within the WCC as there was no person within WCC circles who was like him in ensuring adequate discussion on integration. IMC discussion on integration, with the rethinking and change to a post-colonial model of mission, was partly in response to criticism from "younger church" leaders who had arisen as the fruit of Protestant mission, and were now influential in IMC national councils.

In contrast, the Western church continued to dominate the WCC offices, WCC funding and thus its agenda.[123] Corresponding critics of Western Christianity, who could raise the issues of denominationalism, and the divorce of mission from the Western church, were not as prevalent or vocal. Whilst missions went through cathartic changes the Western church continued life largely unscathed and unreformed. Although changes were afoot within the WCC, theologians such as M. M. Thomas were effective in vocalizing the concerns of the majority world. By the middle of the 1960s the WCC was engaging with the concerns of those in the second world—behind the iron curtain, and the third world, particularly in programs such as "Church and Society."[124]

The need to restructure mission was not initially matched by a corresponding recognition that the church itself needed to change in its relationship to mission.[125] This oversight enabled the WCC executive to accept the integration of the IMC without an analogous reformation of the structure of the WCC, perpetuating the dichotomy between theological formulation and embodiment.[126]

The pressure to bring such changes were absent because the IMC's ethos of regionalization limited its ability to impact the centralizing tendency of the WCC in Geneva at this time. This was compounded by Newbigin's methods of administration. Throughout the process of integration

123. Conway estimated that, before the change in tax legislation introduced by Chancellor Kohl, as much as 80 percent of total WCC funding was coming from the German churches. Conway, interview, 17/8/2008.

124. Charles West recalls M. M. Thomas's influence at the 1952 Church and Society conference in Lucknow, and in the Church and Society report for the second assembly, structuring it such that it recognized three areas of the world and made recommendations for each. "Social Questions: The Responsible Society in a World Perspective," in *The Evanston Report*, ed. W. A. Visser 't Hooft (London: SCM, 1955) 112–30. By the 1966 Church and Society conference (Geneva), tensions between representatives from the West and the majority world had reached an "exploding point." West, phone interview with Laing, 15/9/2008.

125. Hoekendijk's early pleas (from 1952) were being heeded by the Uppsala Assembly (1968).

126. This will be examined in ch. 6.

Newbigin sought to maintain the regional emphasis of the IMC and use that as a means to then steer the WCC to also imbibe this regional emphasis. Yet concurrently, he sought to impart to the WCC the concept of "church as mission."

It is questionable whether he was not rather naive in his objective. At the time of integration the WCC "was rapidly building up a very large staff in Geneva, which necessarily became a centre of initiatives for action and study of all kinds. [In contrast] [t]he IMC had a very small staff divided between three offices in New York, London and East Asia."[127] Throughout Newbigin's tenure as general secretary—of the IMC and then the DWME—he maintained this decentralized structure. And yet, concurrently, he sought to impart the concept of church as mission to every aspect of church life, and hence to permeate all of the WCC with this concern. Löffler asks the obvious question, "how could a group of around ten executive staff [of the IMC] achieve that among a WCC operation 20 times that size?"[128] Yet Newbigin even thought he could achieve this single-handedly, as in Geneva, the centre of WCC operations, "he operated largely alone."[129] Newbigin conceded that his attempt at "bogus omniscience," spreading himself very thinly, was "a strain." "It was very tough work, because—to begin with—I was the sole representative of the new Division in Geneva, and 'Mission is Everything' was the slogan. There was nothing from which I could opt out with a good conscience."[130]

Later, Newbigin conceded, that this administrative failure had impacted the effectiveness of bringing the concern of mission into the centre of the WCC's agenda: "I have to confess that my own leadership as the first director of the new Division was defective. I was concerned about maintaining the continuity of relationships centered in the London and New York office of the IMC. Consequently for several years the staff of the new Division was divided and the presence in Geneva was not strong enough to make the needed impact there."[131] The impossible task of trying to do two jobs with barely the staff for one should have forced Newbigin to centre his

---

127. Newbigin, *Unfinished Agenda*, 169.

128. Löffler to Laing, email, 17/08/2007.

129. I.e., without other IMC officers, Löffler to Laing, email, 17/08/2007. After integration Newbigin established a permanent office in Geneva whilst still maintaining the London and New York offices. Newbigin to DWME staff, 21/2/1962, WCC: 421.051.

130. Newbigin, CV, 20/2/1977, BUL: DA29/1/14/1.

131. Lesslie Newbigin, "Integration—Some Personal Reflections 1981," *IRM* 70:280 (1981) 250.

efforts on Geneva. But this lack of a clear single-minded administrative focus characterized Newbigin's directorship, as he acknowledged at Mexico
(1963).[132] At heart Newbigin was a pastor rather than an "office-wallah." In
his earlier missionary career he had often been critical of mission becoming embroiled in administration.[133] It is telling that Newbigin's successor,
Philip Potter, in contrast, insisted upon closing down the London office of
the IMC for the sake of a stronger presence in Geneva.[134]

An early fear of Newbigin's was than an enfeebled, emaciated IMC
would integrate, with the majority of Western evangelicals seeking alternative structures for their missionary concerns. That fear materialized and
the schism that opened in the 1960s still continues.

For Newbigin structures should be shaped to embody theological
convictions. This led him to make bold demands, to avoid the mere incorporation of the IMC into the accepted structure of the WCC. Instead,
he demanded an equally radical restructuring of the WCC to embody
theological convictions on the missionary nature of the church. The next
chapter, on the debate on the structural expression of integration, focuses
on the increasingly problematic relationship between the IMC and Inter-
Church Aid, between mission and service.

132. Newbigin, "Director's Report," 88.

133. See, for instance, Lesslie Newbigin, "Ordained Foreign Missionary in the Indian Church," *IRM* 34 (1945) 86–94.

134. Löffler to Laing, email, 17/08/2007. The London office closed in March 1967.
WCC, *New Delhi to Uppsala 1961–1968: Report of the Central Committee to the 4th
Assembly of the WCC* (Geneva: WCC, 1968) 24.

6

Mission and Service

The Relationship between the IMC and
the Division of Inter-Church Aid

Tʜᴇ Pʀᴏᴛᴇsᴛᴀɴᴛ ᴍɪssɪᴏɴᴀʀʏ ᴍᴏᴠᴇᴍᴇɴᴛ had historically understood their mandate to include both proclamation and service. Although service, which included education, health care, and agriculture, was interpreted as integral to mission, in practice the relationship between word and deed had at times been problematic.

The Division of Inter-Church Aid (DICA) of the WCC had been created to respond to the need for post-war reconstruction in continental Europe. As such its mandate was understood as being to provide temporary, emergency aid. However, at the second assembly of the WCC, in 1954, its mandate was expanded beyond Europe. The terms of that expansion were clarified at the 1955 Davos meeting of the Central Committee which gave the DICA a "worldwide" and "permanent" mandate.[1] So, at the time when the Western mission boards were withdrawing from relationships with, and rescinding their support of "younger churches," powerful Western *service* agencies were replacing mission boards in their involvement with the "younger church."[2]

---

1. WCC Central Committee Minutes (hereafter cited as CCM), 1955, 31, 33. For an introduction to the history of the DICA, see G. Murray, "Joint Service as an Instrument of Renewal," in *The Ecumenical Advance*, vol. 2, *1948–1968*, ed. Harold E. Fey (Geneva: WCC, 1986).

2. However, service agencies were not replicating past paternalistic relationships. The withdrawal of Western mission agencies was to honor the requests of post-colonial

Previously, the Joint Committee of the IMC and the WCC had been satisfied with the two councils being "in association" with each other. But the overlap in operation in what had traditionally been *"mission* fields" brought conflict and forced the issue of the relationship between the DICA and the IMC. How were mission agencies to relate to service agencies, what was the best way to express that relationship in the structures of the two councils, and in an integrated council? The impetus for integration was the attempt to resolve this critical issue.

As General Secretary, Newbigin argued, on theological and practical grounds, that as mission and church belong together so too do mission and service. The logical expression of that relationship was to unite the DICA with the IMC into one division in the integrated council, the Division of World Mission and Evangelism (DWME). The quest to settle this central issue, which had first prompted calls for integration, and the debate it provoked, was a crucial test of just how thorough and far reaching integration would be. It was acknowledged that missions needed to be reorganized and redefined. Would theological reflection on the role of service and the missionary nature of the church result in an equally thorough-going reorganization and transformation of the WCC as it incorporated the IMC? Or would the WCC simply absorb the IMC into its existing structure without radically re-evaluating its role and function as the ecumenical expression of the universal church? This chapter seeks to address these questions. Critical to what kind of integration would transpire were the decisions of Visser 't Hooft, General Secretary of the WCC, Leslie E. Cooke, director of DICA,[3] and Newbigin as General Secretary of the IMC, and first director of the DWME.

The History and Background of Inter-Church Aid

The Enlarged Mandate of the Division of Inter-Church Aid

Inter-church aid officially began in 1942, several years before the founding of the WCC, when Visser 't Hooft drafted a memorandum calling for churches to help with the post-war reconstruction of Europe. Inter-church aid was envisaged as a temporary enterprise and limited to the confines of

---

"younger churches," and in part due to financial duress.

3. Cooke served as the director of DICA from the summer of 1955 until his death in February 1967.

continental Europe.[4] By the WCC's second assembly in Evanston (1954), an enlarged mandate was given, allowing the DICA to operate beyond the confines of Europe.

This expansion in mandate was later reflected in the inclusion of "world" in the title of the Division at the third assembly of the WCC (1961);[5] and the recognition that inter-church aid was "a permanent obligation" of the WCC.[6]

What were the reasons contributing to this expansion of mandate? In part the answer is because the refugee problem in Europe, especially Germany, was much reduced by 1954. The Marshall Plan to reconstruct war-torn Europe had been remarkably successful. Churches which had raised and channeled resources to aid postwar reconstruction now sought other potential beneficiaries beyond the confines of Europe. At this time other factors also contributed to a rising interest in development within the ecumenical movement. Starting with India in 1947, approximately fifty nations gained independence. Nationhood was coupled with a "revolution of rising expectations," with the expectation that advances in political freedom would be mirrored by technological and scientific advances. As nations gained freedom the civil rights movement fought for the liberation of those oppressed *within* nations.[7] Changes in personal aspirations were encapsulated in the United Nations Universal Declaration of Human Rights in 1948.[8] And development also gained prominence as an ideological tool as superpowers sought to extend their global influence, the Cold War polarizing the world into Eastern and Western blocs.[9]

The enlarged mandate meant that DICA was given sanction to operate in territory which had historically been the domain of mission organizations. Despite very different origins and ethos, Protestant mission and service agencies were now, potentially, in competition with each other:

---

4. W. A. Visser 't Hooft, "Inter-Church Aid: How It All Began," in *Hope in the Desert*, ed. Kenneth Slack (Geneva: WCC, 1986) 9.

5. DICASR (the Division of Inter-Church Aid and Service to Refugees) became DICARWS (the Division of Inter-Church Aid, Refugee and World Service), CCM, 1962, 118. Throughout this chapter, DICA will be used specifically for the Division of Inter-Church Aid, and "inter-church aid" as a general term.

6. CCM, 1960, 128.

7. R. D. N. Dickinson, "Development," in *Dictionary of the Ecumenical Movement*, ed. N. Lossky et al. (Geneva: WCC, 2002) 298.

8. http://www.un.org/en/documents/udhr/.

9. Dickinson, "Development," 298.

Missions beginning with the simple obligation to make Christ known to the non-Christian nations, have been led to a point where they can conceive of their task only as the task of the whole Church to make the Gospel known to the whole world by a witness which includes both word and deed. Inter-church aid, beginning with the needs of stricken churches in Europe, has been led to a point where it defines its task as nothing less than the strengthening and renewal of all church life in all continents and a ministry to human need throughout the world.[10]

The overlap in remit between inter-church aid and missions belied their very different natures. Inter-church aid was centralized within the WCC; the service it provided was contingent and based upon short-term projects. Being strongly centralized and short-term there was the danger of improvisation and discontinuity, with no long-term commitment to local congregations and the cultures in which they were operating. In contrast Protestant missions were decentralized and fragmented. Historically they had developed strong links with local churches, with deep engagement with local cultures to the extent of becoming embroiled in the affairs of the "younger churches."[11]

The overlap of remit, with the potential for confusion, and duplication of service, forced the two councils to clarify the relationship between the DICA and the IMC. The enlarged mandate of the DICA also made the councils aware that their relationship of mutual co-existence in "association" with each other had become inadequate, leading to the call for full integration of the IMC and the WCC. "The dramatic change in direction between 1955 and 1956 [to seek to unite the IMC with the WCC] was made possible . . . *only* by developments in the activities of the Inter-Church Aid division."[12] The overlap of operation in traditional "mission fields" "forced" the issue of relationship and brought "tension and conflict" between the DICA and mission boards.[13]

Tension was created between the Western mission boards, which "had been struggling for decades to wean the 'younger churches' away from financial dependence on the West," and the agents of Western service agencies, who were seemingly doing the opposite. In Newbigin's opinion, they were "offering apparently unlimited largesse to these same churches

---

10. Newbigin, *One Body*, 40.

11. H. Witschi to Newbigin, 10/3/1960, WCC: 27.0012.

12. Ranson to Carpenter, 6/8/1958, WCC: 27.0015. Emphasis added.

13. Ibid.

in order that they might become constructively involved in . . . develop-ment programmes."[14] In Newbigin's perception traditional missions had been distracted from their crucial task of sharing the gospel to instead serving and "propping up" churches which had become dependent upon them.[15] Of course the policies of mission agencies had often created this very dependency, with the devolution of large institutions, which were already financially crippling to Western missionary societies, let alone the "younger church." The overlap of engagement with the "younger church," with new initiatives and resources from the DICA, was perceived as a threat by mission boards. Newbigin recorded that, "*No other issue loomed as large as this* in the discussions leading to the integration of the two councils. It was always apparent that one test of the effectiveness of the integration would be at this point."[16]

As mission boards retracted and were replaced by Western service agencies, some interpreted this as the move from the age of mission to that of ecumenical partnership between churches. Inter-church aid was under-stood as the "modern equivalent of missions," reinforced by the fact that, now that the church was worldwide, "it could be said that the mission-ary task in the traditional sense had been completed"—a view Newbigin strongly disagreed with.[17] There was concern that this new source of fund-ing, which emphasized service, would undermine the previous efforts of missions to plant self-supporting churches, and that those churches would be detracted from the primacy of their "missionary task."[18]

The vigorous, well-funded intervention of service agencies into traditional "mission fields" also raised other concerns. Was the Western church losing confidence in traditionally held convictions about the gos-pel, and thus replacing the traditional role of missions in proclamation, with a more pervasive secular belief in the efficacy of development?

---

14. Newbigin, *Unfinished Agenda*, 150–51.

15. Previously, Newbigin had expressed this contentious view at Willingen and succeeded in getting the following text accepted into the draft statement: "Too large a proportion of the great volume of missionary giving and service which flows out from the older churches is at present required to prop up relatively static younger churches, rather than to make new advances for the Gospel." Ibid., 133–34.

16. Lesslie Newbigin, "Developments During 1962: An Editorial Survey," *IRM* 52 (1963) 6. Emphasis added.

17. Lesslie Newbigin, "Mission to Six Continents," in *The Ecumenical Advance*, vol. 2, ed. Harold E. Fey, 186.

18. Ibid., 182.

There was also the pernicious danger of service only being conceived of in terms of the things that the Western church was strong in, such as wealth, education, and technical skill.[19] Service agencies might then come to replicate the old paternalism of colonial mission rather than aid being truly *mutual* aid.

Rather than help, the Davos meeting of the Central Committee (1955) created confusion by failing to determine how mission and service could co-exist in a common field. The Central Committee then aggravated this problem further, as the expanded mandate allowed the DICA to enter *any* field by unilateral decision, irrespective of what was being done by mission organizations.[20] Newbigin recalled how, "Much friction was being generated by the increasingly vigorous intervention of the [DICA] in the areas hitherto the exclusive domain of the mission boards."[21] Davos "forced" the issue of relationship, requiring further rounds of meetings to clarify working relationships. The next meeting to tackle the issues, the Joint Committee of the WCC/IMC, was held at Herrenalb the following year.

The Herrenalb Joint Committee (20th–23rd July, 1956)

Prior to the Joint Committee meeting at Herrenalb, Charles Ranson had sought to press the IMC's concerns upon the executive of the WCC. Ranson recommended that, in the integrated council, DICA should join with the IMC to form a commission for world mission and service, and that the WCC Assembly and Central Committee be expanded to allow representatives from mission organizations, with persons appointed to the Central Committee to represent "missionary interests."[22] However, these proposals were rejected by the Joint Committee which concluded: "It was perhaps unwise to attempt at one and the same time to effect the integration of the two Councils and to make large alterations in their present internal organization."[23] With hindsight Ranson recognized that his proposal, for uniting service with mission, had been a "tactical error," presenting pre-

19. Newbigin "Mission of the Church to All the Nations," address given at the NCC General Assembly, San Francisco, 5/12/1960, section VI, WCC: electronic version.

20. Carpenter to Cooke, 24/7/1958, WCC 27.0012, 2–3.

21. Newbigin, *Unfinished Agenda*, 150.

22. Ranson to Visser 't Hooft, 9/8/1956, WCC 27.0015.

23. Van Dusen, Joint Committee Minutes (hereafter cited as JCM), Herrenalb, July 20–23, 1956, 13, SOAS: 270002, fiche 12.

mature plans for a united division which backfired. He recalled that "some WCC reactions were so vehement that the Joint Committee backed away from the idea of a single Division of Mission and Inter-Church Aid and has been shy of it ever since." Ranson suggested that the WCC objections, on practical grounds, veiled a more deep-seated resistance to reorganizing the WCC.[24]

Cooke had, in 1956, also promoted one division, "A Division of Ecumenical Mission and Service," which would bring the DICA "within the auspices of the mission." He recognized that service and mission impinged upon each other: "In fulfilling inter-church aid as a permanent obligation of the churches, a *World* Council cannot but move into the area of missions." And vice versa, for missions, in establishing churches, the "logic of the spirit" led them into service. Concerning integration Cooke was of the conviction that "a large gesture to the missionary interests will inspire their confidence and reassure them that the WCC means business"—that the IMC was not simply being incorporated into the WCC, but that the WCC was willing to undergo radical change as it embraced the IMC. To this end he further advocated that the director of the united division to be a "missions man."[25] Cooke was, at the time, therefore "disappointed" by the decision of the Herrenalb Joint Committee, considering it to be a "mistake."[26]

At Herrenalb, Visser 't Hooft reasoned that, with the complex relationship between the IMC and the DICA, it would be premature to bring them together, as there was the danger of missions then losing their distinctiveness.[27] Instead, he proposed, the creation of a commission for mission, modeled on the Faith and Order commission, continuing the function of the IMC within the WCC as a single division separate from the DICA.[28] This argument prevailed at Herrenalb, the assumption being that the problematic relationship between missions and service could only be dealt with after integration, not before.

The Joint Committee reached an uneasy compromise, categorizing the work of the expanded DICA, with the intention of thereby limiting its intervention into traditional mission fields. These became known as

24. Ranson to Carpenter, 6/8/1958, WCC 27.0015.

25. Cooke, "Some notes on methods of integration of the IMC and WCC," 9/4/1956, WCC: 27.0013.

26. Cooke to Newbigin, 14–16/8/1958, BUL: DA29/2/9/34.

27. Visser 't Hooft, JCM, 1956, 13.

28. Draft Statement on Integration containing two plans, JCM, 1956, 9.

the Herrenalb categories.[29] "They were organizationally understandable, but were eventually recognized as a bureaucratic hindrance to the service potential within the ecumenical movement."[30] For over a decade they were used to delineate the work of mission from service.

Inter-Church Aid Finances

The IMC, throughout its history, was advisory rather than administrative; the IMC did not have any centralized programs.[31] At the time of integration, not only did the IMC and DICA each have a different ethos and history, but they also existed with very different modes of operation. The advisory nature of the IMC contrasted with the considerable administrative and financial clout exercised by the DICA. The IMC's successor, the DWME, maintained the IMC practice of minimal centralized operations, with Newbigin often operating alone in Geneva whilst, at the same time, maintaining the old IMC offices in New York and London, and regularly commuting between the three.

In contrast, the DICA "developed a staff more than twenty times the size of the whole IMC operation, with specialists for each major area of the world and each specialized function."[32] By 1968 a quarter of the total workforce at the WCC headquarters was employed in the DICA. In addition to this, more than two hundred staff were employed by the DICA around the world. It was the largest single division of the WCC. The budget of the DICA was about 50 percent more that the entire general budget of the WCC, and "roughly $13,000,000 flowed through the Division every year," with most funding for service coming from the Western churches.[33] Most of the Western money came from the United States; the dramatic expansion of the work of the DICA beyond Europe had been made possible by new organizational arrangements with the US churches and their

29. For details of the categories, see Appendix D, JCM, 1956.

30. A. A. Brash, "Regional Responsibility: Its Joy and Pain," in *Hope in the Desert*, ed. Kenneth Slack, 47–48.

31. Except for the wartime orphan fund. The advisory nature of the IMC was changed with the advent of the Theological Education Fund, which was centrally organized, and originally had four million dollars committed towards its first mandate.

32. Newbigin, *Unfinished Agenda*, 200.

33. Murray, "Joint Service," 201–2. E.g., in 1956 Cooke estimated that the churches gave almost sixty-one million dollars in service, and sixty-four million dollars in 1957, whereas the income for the general budget of the WCC in 1959 was a little over $506,000. CCM, 1957, 30; CCM, 1958, 30; CCM, 1960, 106.

cooperative agencies from 1956.[34] Furthermore, DICA leadership was under "constant pressure from big donor agencies to expand . . . [the] programme."[35] Thus, at a practical level, the ethos and mode of operation of the IMC and the DICA were quite different, mitigating against their integration. The IMC was a minnow, the DICA a whale.

The Theological Relationship between Mission and Service

In a study (in 1955) on inter-church aid, the sub-committee of the Joint Committee concluded that "the Church's witness through the Word and its witness through service are inseparable from its witness as a Fellowship of the Spirit (koinonia)—its growth in a unity that is God's gathering together of His new people."[36] With the acknowledgement of that theological relationship the two councils were then faced with the task of creating structures which would allow for the suitable expression of the unity between *apostolate* and *diakonia*. They attested that the inseparability, of *apostolate* from *diakonia*, and of either from *koinonia*, became apparent when an attempt was made to separate one from the other in the "missionary" or "ecumenical" movement.[37] The recommendation to the Joint Committee was that "in order to manifest and exemplify the unity of these two functions of the Church, it is most desirable that the organizations of the churches concerned with mission and inter-church aid should be seen to be part of one integrated whole, so that the total task of the Church may be conceived and fulfilled in its unity";[38] that is, they recommended integration as a means to solve the problem of relationship between missions and service.

Inter-church aid became "a permanent expression of the mutual diakonia of Christian Churches. It was seen that this belongs to the nature of the Church"—this contribution by the ecumenical movement was deemed as "a new discovery" for ecclesiology. Furthermore, with a worldwide mandate, it was realized that inter-church aid was not limited

34. CCM, 1957, 109.

35. Newbigin, *Unfinished Agenda*, 200. E.g., in 1959 77 percent of funding for the DICA came from the United States; by 1962 this had dropped to 67 percent, CCM, 1963, 76.

36. "A statement submitted by the [the DICA and mission] sub-committee," St. Albans, 27–28/10/1955, WCC: 27.0012, 1.

37. Ibid., 4. It is interesting to note that these were perceived as being separate movements.

38. Ibid., 2.

to mutual service only *to the church*, but it was *diakonia* to the *world*.[39] "[Inter-church aid] therefore represents at the same time a *continuation* of the diakonia-tradition of historical Missions, a *widened* continuation and moreover a new *dimension* of the diakonia-aspect of historical Missions."[40] In the ecumenical movement, church and world had become dominant causing a *"re-thinking of mission (kerygma) and diakonia* as the two principal aspects of the Church's nature and calling."[41] Inter-church aid aided the recovery of ecclesiology, such that *diakonia* was no longer to be interpreted as a means to an end, but was understood to be integral to the apostolic nature of the church: *"ICA's significance is that diakonia* is not only (as in historical Missions) a paving of the way for the more successful preaching of the Gospel, but *the ecumenical expression of the nature of the Church towards and in the world."*[42]

Having recognized that mission and service were inextricably linked, various attempts, with resort to Greek nouns, were made to differentiate mission *from* service. A theological distinction between mission and service was sought as theological justification for the separation of the IMC from the DICA, or at least as ground for differentiating their operations.

Newbigin postulated that the primary witness is the Holy Spirit. "Marturia is the work of the Holy Spirit Himself, dwelling in the community, operating alike through preaching and action. . . . Both preaching and service, springing out of the new reality of the shared Holy Spirit (koinonia) can be used by the Spirit as vehicles of witness and can effect conversion." Newbigin suggested, diagrammatically, a model which maintained the primacy of the Holy Spirit, and the fellowship which he had bequeathed:[43]

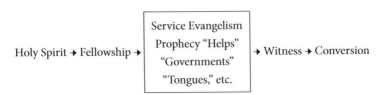

Holy Spirit → Fellowship → | Service Evangelism Prophecy "Helps" "Governments" "Tongues," etc. | → Witness → Conversion

39. Hendrick Kraemer, "Points of Address 'on the Significance of developments in lands outside Europe for the strategy of the churches in Inter-church aid and mission,'" Basel, 5–8/12/1959, WCC: 27.0012, 3.

40. Ibid.

41. Ibid., 4.

42. Emphasis in original, Ibid.

43. Newbigin to van Beyma, 28/11/1958, BUL: DA29/2/9/54.

Newbigin sustained an organizational model of integration, uniting mission with service, which was consistent with his theological convictions, and derived from his hermeneutic of the New Testament. He developed his argument more fully in his draft paper, "The Organization of the Church, Mission to the World."[44]

Newbigin's Proposal for Uniting the DICA with the IMC

"The Organization of the Church, Mission to the World"

In June 1958 Newbigin drafted the paper, "The Organization of the Church, Mission to the World," giving his theological rationale for the basis of integration, a paper which was discussed in both IMC and WCC circles. His major practical conclusion, based upon his theological argument, was that with integration, there should be one division in the integrated council which combined mission and inter-church aid.

Newbigin was concerned that much of traditional mission support was maintaining "younger churches" rather than bringing fresh missionary expansion. He argued that the "ends of the earth" dimension must be kept central; the church should be orientated towards the world rather than its own internal welfare. Related to this was the need to establish new channels of relationship between "younger" and "older churches" which discarded bilateral paternalism for multilateral partnership. With the recession of missions, and the simultaneous mushrooming of service organizations, Newbigin was concerned that inter-church aid would simply replace missions and perpetuate the support of introverted, static, "younger churches." Instead, "The purpose of our whole pattern of operations must be that it should enable the whole Church to help every part of the Church to remain in effective contact with the world," both locally and universally.[45] Therefore, "Our inter-church aid must be aid-for-missions." Service was not to be understood as superseding missions, with the demise of colonialism and the arrival of the ecumenical age. In examining the relationship between mission and service Newbigin reflected that, "The experience of the past few years has shown that it is impossible to draw a logically defensible line of demarcation between the sphere of mission boards and the sphere of interchurch aid. The two types of activity are, and

---

44. Newbigin, June 1958, BUL: DA29/2/9/2, 1–17.
45. Ibid., 12.

will increasingly be, inextricable [*sic*] intertwined."[46] This led Newbigin to a change of heart concerning the accepted plan for integration.

Previously, Newbigin had accepted the general consensus on integration in WCC circles, which was the addition of the IMC, as the mission wing, to the existing three-fold structure of WCC. But, as he drafted his paper, Newbigin came to seek a more radical reordering, uniting the IMC with the DICA. Otherwise, he claimed, the WCC would not fundamentally change its relationship to mission. He rejected the accepted consensus on integration because: first, it would not solve the practical problems that existed in relationship between the DICA and the IMC, but would perpetuate these problems within the integrated council; and second, it would not solve the problem of the existing one-track structure of relationships between individual mission boards and individual younger churches.[47] The multi-lateral patterns of relationship that Newbigin perceived as developing with the DICA had historical parallels, of mission boards cooperating regionally, initially in comity agreements. This regional emphasis, which was central to the history and ethos of the IMC, should continue to be developed as a corrective to the tendency of the WCC to centralize. Newbigin anticipated that increasing regionalism would raise questions for world confessional organizations. "The question whether the lineaments of the world-wide Christian fellowship are to be conceived in terms of a fellowship of regional churches, or a fellowship of globally organized denominations, may well be one of the key issues on which a decision has to be reached in the coming decade or two."[48]

Based upon the theological presuppositions that mission and church belonged together, and that the role of the DICA should not be confined to the strengthening of the church, but rather, should lead to mission, Newbigin was concerned that the mere incorporation of the IMC into the WCC was too cautious an approach, and would not evoke the desired re-evaluation, which Newbigin deemed, was as necessary for the church (as represented by the WCC), as it was for mission (represented the IMC). "If we confine ourselves to the changes proposed we are in danger of failing

46. Ibid., 14–15.

47. Ibid.

48. Ibid., 16. On this point Newbigin demonstrated considerable prescience, as this would later dominate ecumenical discussion. An important study on this was done by U. Duchrow, *Conflict over the Ecumenical Movement: Confessing Christ Today in the Universal Church*, trans. David Lewis (Geneva: WCC, 1981). See also Newbigin's review: Lesslie Newbigin, "Review of *Conflict over the Ecumenical Movement*, by Ulrich Duchrow, translated by David Lewis," *ER* 34:4 (1982).

altogether to evoke the response which we desire" which was "that the whole Church should be summoned afresh to a recognition of, and whole-hearted acceptance of its task as God's mission to the world."[49] To facilitate the changes Newbigin hoped for, he suggested four divisions for the integrated council: 1) Faith and Order; 2) World Mission and Inter-Church Aid; 3) Ecumenical Action; and 4) Study.[50]

The Joint Committee, Nyborg Strand
(14th to 17th August, 1958)

Newbigin's paper, with his radical proposal to re-order the WCC, promoted much discussion within the WCC and the IMC. Critical to the success of his proposition was the opinion of the general secretary. Newbigin sent Visser 't Hooft a copy of his paper prior to the Joint Committee meetings at Nyborg Strand in Denmark. Visser 't Hooft accepted the logic of Newbigin's argument—that the DICA and the IMC belonged together—but crucially he rejected Newbigin's chronology, instead adhering to an alternative chronology by which he subsequently governed and oversaw the course of integration.

Visser 't Hooft understood integration as being a process in three stages: first, of bringing the ecumenical movements of churches and missions together under one roof; second, to then lay the foundation for common strategic thinking on mission; and third, to coordinate and then unify the work of missions with that of inter-church aid.[51] For Visser 't Hooft, stage one would be achieved by integration in 1961. *Only after* that could there then be a progression to the subsequent stages. Visser 't Hooft, in maintaining the existing integrity of the WCC, was of the opinion that not all the problems of relationship between mission and church could be solved at once, at integration.

However, from the IMC perspective, leaving the WCC *unchanged* at integration gave the impression that it was also *unchallenged*, that the IMC was being *absorbed* into the WCC. Furthermore, "Once integration has happened, the motive for change in the WCC structure and the power to induce changes will be lessened."[52] The IMC outlook was that integration

49. Newbigin, *One Body*.
50. Ibid., 17.
51. Visser 't Hooft to Newbigin, 22/7/1958, WCC: 27.0015.
52. R. K. Orchard to Newbigin, 1/8/1958, BUL: DA29/2/9/26.

was the crucial time to secure radical change; afterwards the incentive for change would only dissipate.

These concerns were acutely felt by Charles Ranson, who, at the earlier Joint Committee meetings in 1956, had failed to sway the WCC in favor of a single division. The 1958 Joint Committee meetings presented a critical opportunity to again strive for a single division, as failure to deal with the issue of the relationship between the IMC and the DICA would be, in his opinion, a "disastrous mistake."[53] For Ranson, Newbigin's paper "was a powerful exposé of the underlying questions and a powerful reinforcement of the argument (on both theological and practical grounds) for a single Division," thus giving opportunity for the IMC to again press the WCC on this issue. Ranson wrote to Newbigin and Carpenter to encourage them to plead for a single division at Nyborg Strand. The alternative, of only minimal organizational change, would make procrastination easy: "We shall run on for another five or ten years without getting to grips with what is perhaps the most urgent issue in missionary strategy and operation."[54] And post-integration, the DWME, as a department of the WCC, would have a reduced mandate, its power to then effect change would be much more circumscribed: "If we plan to carry over into an integrated body the unresolved conflicts which integration was supposed to solve, then about all we are doing is to ensure continuing conflict, under conditions in which a Division of Missions will be at a greater disadvantage than an independent IMC."[55]

Significant to the outcome of the discussion at the Joint Committee was a volte-face by Leslie Cooke, the director of the DICA, who, in 1956 had backed the idea of a single division. In his paper prepared for the 1958 Joint Committee he now opposed a single division on the grounds that it: would be too large for the WCC, would result in unequal distribution of resources, would relegate inter-church aid concerns in Europe to a department of the mission division, and would prove difficult for the Orthodox churches, with their concerns about evangelical proselytism, to operate under the direction of the DWME.[56] He concluded that "the acceptance

53. Ranson to Newbigin, 11/8/1958, BUL: DA29/2/9/30; Ranson to Carpenter, (copy received by Newbigin) 6/8/1958, BUL: DA29/2/9/29, 1.

54. Ibid., 3

55. Charles Ranson, "Comments on Newbigin's paper the Organization of the Church," August 1958, WCC: 26.0042, 4.

56. Cooke, "Reflections concerning the relationship between ICA and Mission and their organizational expression in the integrated council of the WCC after 1961," 13/8/1958, BUL: DA29/2/9/31, 4.

of two Divisions without prejudging whether they should ultimately be one would appear to be the right frame of mind in which to approach this problem."[57]

During the Joint Committee, Cooke also gave a private response to Newbigin's paper: "I am horrified by the affirmation that . . . mission is Inter-Church Aid, or that Inter-Church Aid is mission . . . ICA is not mission—at least not mission as I have always understood it."[58] He urged Newbigin, "Please do not go too far out on a limb in your commitment to one Division."[59] Similarly, in a letter to A. A. Brash, the secretary of the East Asia Christian Conference (EACC), Cooke elaborated more on his objection to one division in the integrated council. The WCC, as a fellowship of churches, mainly expressed fellowship through the agency of inter-church aid. After integration fellowship would continue to be expressed through inter-church aid but also through mission bodies of churches. One division would be too large for the current structure of the WCC due to the size of the DICA and would bring disruption to the present plan of integration. Joining the IMC with the DICA would precipitate a "discussion which in certain quarters would exacerbate apprehension already felt about integration as a whole"; that is, the suspicions held by some associated with the IMC about the wisdom of uniting with the WCC.[60]

At the discussion at Nyborg Strand, Newbigin defended his proposal to unite the DICA with the IMC, "the integrated structure should reflect as completely as possible the larger issues at stake." He maintained that for years mission organizations had devoted much of their resources to what in effect *was* inter-church aid. For Newbigin, the crucial question about mutual aid, irrespective of the channel through which it was delivered to the churches, was whether it was *aid for survival* or *aid for mission*.[61] Besides the hostility to his proposal from WCC circles, from IMC quarters, Professor Walter Freytag voiced concern that a single division would alarm European mission boards and would be interpreted as confusing the different functions of the DICA and the IMC. This view was supported by Swedish, Norwegian, and British mission representatives.[62]

---

57. Ibid., 6
58. Cooke to Newbigin, 14–16/8/1958, BUL: DA29/2/9/34.
59. Ibid.
60. Cooke to Brash, 18/9/1958, WCC: 27.0012.
61. JCM, 1958, 7. Italics in original.
62. Ibid., 8.

Only one person voted in favor of Newbigin's proposal. Newbigin was thus bound by the decision of the Committee. The Joint Committee recommended that a sub-committee be established to study the relationship between the DICA and the IMC. It also recommended that Newbigin's paper be published in *International Review of Missions* and *Ecumenical Review* as a personal statement, to promote wider discussion.[63] Newbigin was forced to admit defeat: "In the debate . . . I pled for . . . [a single division] but was defeated. . . . For this reason I agreed to alter the first draft of the paper so as to exclude the original last two pages, which argued for a single Division. At the time of the Nyborg debate I said that while I was obviously bound to accept the decision and act on it, I remained convinced that eventually the separation of the two divisions would prove unworkable."[64]

IMC Staff Conference, Oxford (16th to 18th September, 1958)

The next major discussion of Newbigin's proposals for integration took place at the IMC Staff Conference in Oxford (16–18/9/1958). Response from the various IMC councils had been collated and was fed back to the conference. Whereas the leadership of the IMC advocated a single division, it became apparent that the constituency did not share the same enthusiasm. "The consensus of comment is against this" before integration, with no clear opinion whether it would be advisable after integration.[65] Some of the reasons given against forming a single division were that the DICA was already too large to combine with DWME, the two divisions were not homogenous enough to be integrated, and that the DWME needed to "find itself" in WCC first. One of the aims in integration was that the DWME might remind other divisions of the missionary dimension within their own divisions, instead "the mammoth Division might seem to contain within itself 'everything to do with mission'";[66] thus negating the pervasive role that the DWME should play within the WCC. Despite this Newbigin continued to reiterate his concern that inter-church aid should

63. Ibid., 10–12.

64. Newbigin, "Note on the preparation for *One Body, One Gospel, One World,*" September 1965, BUL: DA29/2/9/1.

65. Orchard, "Comments received on Bishop Newbigin's paper 'Organization of the Church,'" 3/9/1958, BUL: DA29/2/9/42, 4.

66. Conference of Missionary Societies in Great Britain and Ireland, "Review of the Relationship of Inter-Church Aid and Mission," 10/6/1959, WCC: 27.0012, 6.

empower churches for mission: "a very large proportion of the resources of missions are tied down in the on-going support of young churches. Is this a healthy and natural form of inter-church aid, or is it an improper dependence arising from a wrong missionary method?"[67]

One Body, One Gospel, One World

The central conclusion in Newbigin's draft paper "Organization of the Church" was that DICA and the IMC should be united into one division within the integrated council. After his rebuttal at the Nyborg meetings, and in deference to the will of the Joint Committee, Newbigin's proposal was entirely omitted from the publication *One Body, One Gospel, One World* (1958). This was in spite of the fact that Newbigin maintained his personal conviction and the booklet was published as a *personal* statement, rather than the official view of the IMC. The most significant change between the draft paper "Organization of the Church" and *One Body* was Newbigin's modification in his understanding of the relationship between mission and service. On the question of how the relationship, in an integrated council between the departments representing mission and inter-church aid, and within the total life of the church, can be adequately embodied, Newbigin was much more circumspect in *One Body* than before.[68]

Negatively, an acceptable relationship between the DICA and the DWME could not be expressed by defining the relationship geographically, as had been the case with the DICA being limited to Europe and the IMC having the remit of territory beyond Europe. Second, neither could they be distinguished by a "dividing line" between evangelism and service, as the two were intertwined both theologically and in historical practice. Third, Newbigin rejected maintaining the existing "structure of missionary operations," with all its confusion and inadequacies. Fourth, despite being tainted by colonialism Newbigin insisted that missions had an enduring role. The terminology of missions could not be simply dropped, and replaced by that of inter-church aid.[69]

On a positive note Newbigin offered three points which could help clarify the relationship. "It may well be that the deepest root of our perplexity at this point is simply the fact that we have corrupted the word

67. Newbigin to Secretaries of IMC member councils, 1/12/1958, WCC: 26.0042/4, 4.

68. Newbigin, *One Body*, 38ff.

69. Ibid., 40–41.

'Church' (and distorted the life of the churches) by constantly using it in a non-missionary sense." If the use of "church" always implied that it was missionary, "then inter-church aid would always be aid for mission and nothing else."[70] Second, in the integrated World Council there must be sufficient concentration upon missions "a place where the specifically missionary concern can be a matter of constant attention and study."[71] And third, Newbigin made a distinction between mission in a broad sense, which has always included service, and a narrower definition, which did not. Drawing upon the German distinction between "*sendung*" and "*mission*," mission in the narrower sense was to be understood as "part of an action of the Church in going out beyond the frontiers of its own life to bear witness to Christ as Lord among those who do not know Him, and when the overall *intention* of that action is that they should be brought from unbelief to faith."[72]

In "Organization of the Church," Newbigin maintained that evangelism was "always central" and "must be seen to be central to the whole mission"; service accompanied proclamation, and was thus subsidiary to evangelism.[73] But, in *One Body*, he modified his understanding of their relationship: "We have seen that service cannot be merely subordinated to evangelism; that acts of loving service to men in themselves have a proper place in the total witness to the presence of the Kingdom. We have also seen that the proper relation between the two is not a logical one but an ontological one—that they are properly related when they are rooted in the same reality of the new being in Christ."[74]

Newbigin's proposal—of forming one all-embracing division within the integrated council—was rejected in favor of two separate divisions, thus embodying within the integrated council the problem which had first driven them towards integration: the question of how mission could be differentiated from service.

70. Ibid., 42.

71. Ibid., 43.

72. Ibid., 43–44. Italics in original.

73. Newbigin, "Organization of the Church," 12.

74. Newbigin, *One Body*, 44.

Clarification of the Relationship between the DICA and the DWME

A lack of clarity in defining the focus and limits of each division continued to perturb the IMC membership in particular. The two directors corresponded extensively in an attempt to clarify the relationship between their departments—with candid admissions that (from Newbigin) this was of limited success. Cooke's attempt at delineation[75] alarmed the IMC, as the "definition of the Division's task [the DICA] seemed to be so all-inclusive as to cover what the new Division of World Mission would properly regard as its function."[76] In response, Newbigin acknowledged that both mission and service were permanent and worldwide obligations of the church. To delineate one from the other, it was therefore necessary to clarify the central focus of each, and then for each to limit their operations based upon their respective focus. Historically, missions had got involved in various forms of service, and would interpret those forms of service as being integral to mission.

The difference between the DICA and the DWME was not, therefore, to be understood in terms of their field or method of operation, but in terms of the substantial difference between service and mission. For mission Newbigin suggested as a definition the "crossing of the frontier between faith and unbelief with the intention to evoke faith"; whereas the concern of service was to meet human needs within and beyond the church. He acknowledged that they overlapped and that there was a natural relationship between the two.[77] For each this would lead to "foci of attention and could not be used to mark off limited and mutually exclusive territories."[78]

Newbigin "deeply believe in the fundamental unity of the two tasks, and it was [his] original hope that we could have one Division." However, having been convinced that two divisions were required for administrative purposes, he recognized the need for demarcation between them. Commenting on his ongoing correspondence with Cooke, Newbigin expressed

75. Appendix VII: "The Nature and Scope of the Task of the Division of Inter-Church Aid and Service to Refugees," CCM, 1959, 148–57. Original draft by Leslie Cooke, May 1959, WCC 27.0015.

76. Minutes of IMC Staff Conference, Westgate-on-sea, 25–29/4/1960, WCC: 26.0042/7, 15

77. Newbigin, "Comments on the Paper of the DICASR on the Nature and Scope of the Task of the Division," 10/6/1960, WCC: 27.0012, 5.

78. Ibid.

frustration that despite efforts to clarify the relationship between the two divisions, Cooke's response left "the matter as confused as it was before."[79]

Post-Integration Relationships between the DICA and the DWME

After integration Newbigin continued to press the Central Committee to re-examine the structure of the WCC and not allow the provisional nature of its structure to be accepted as permanent vis-à-vis the relationship between the IMC and the DICA. At the time of integration the assembly "explicitly recognized that the organization pattern there suggested will need early re-examination." Newbigin's report to the 1963 Central Committee communicated the resolution of the DWME, which sought to draw the attention of the Central Committee to that statement, and the need for the WCC to re-examine its structure.[80]

In the meantime, with the two divisions co-existing after integration, at an operational level, the members of each division had come to a position of growing mutual respect. From the inter-church aid side it was acknowledged that the "procedures" of the DICA "can never be a substitute for, though they may be complementary to, the continuing and sustained relationships of churches to one another which are established in the missionary enterprise." A statement which Newbigin found "a very moving signal of understanding from the 'other side.'"[81] Similarly, the DWME acknowledged its debt and appreciation of the DICA, in learning valuable lessons from a mode of operation which eschewed paternalism: "Missions have something immensely important to learn from the experience of . . . [DICA]. Inter-Church Aid has been able to enter into the fruits of Mission without having to take over the liabilities of the past. The pattern of mutual sharing on a basis of equality which has characterized Inter-Church Aid from the beginning is one form which Missions must learn."[82]

Newbigin recalled that "now that we were working together in one organization we were able—not without strain—to hammer out a stable relationship. . . . The critical point in practice was our relationship with the Division of Inter-Church Aid."[83] The fact that the relationship between

79. Newbigin to Goodall, 23/5/1960, WCC: 27.0012.

80. CCM, 1963, 139.

81. Newbigin, *Unfinished Agenda*, 172–73.

82. Newbigin, cited by Cooke, CCM, 1959, 149.

83. Newbigin, *Unfinished Agenda*, 200.

the two divisions was growing increasingly "close and cordial" was evident by the willingness of the DWME to "pass over" areas of responsibility to DICA "which would in the past have been regarded as the responsibility of mission boards or of the IMC."[84]

As noted, the Herrenalb categories had served as a "dyke," which delineated the relationship between the two divisions. For a decade these categories determined the operational relationship between missions and service within the WCC. But this "artificial boundary" between missions and service was having a damaging effect. Newbigin noted the twofold, detrimental impact. First, as a "dyke" to prevent inter-church aid getting involved in relations between mission boards and "younger churches," programs accepted under the Herrenalb categories were, by nature, *extra* to existing programs between churches and mission boards. This had the result that common strategic thinking, which combined mission and service, was confined to extras and not "permitted to penetrate the main work of the churches and missions." Second, there was organizational pressure to develop separate philosophies of service and mission "in order to rationalize the separation of these two patterns of activity." As inter-church aid pushed in the direction of emphasizing service, this increased the immobility of missions "since the new thinking and new resources were being channelled in the direction of 'service' defined as *other than* 'mission.'"[85]

With consent from DICA, the DWME requested the Central Committee that these categories be reformulated as their inadequacy was demonstrated in the increased cooperation between DICA and the DWME.[86] They were replaced in 1966 with DWME being responsible for long-term programs and the DICA for projects usually expected to become self-supporting within five years.[87] "It was a great liberation for both divisions when it was agreed that we would abandon the attempt to define which projects were 'missionary' and which were not."[88] Progress was made, but throughout Newbigin's tenure as general secretary of the IMC, and then as director of the DWME (which was extended until 1965), he recalled how

84. Newbigin to Visser 't Hooft, "Memo on staffing situation in DWME," 17/10/1963, WCC: 421.050.

85. Newbigin, "Working Paper for Committee on Questions of Structure and Relationships," CWME, Mexico City, no date, WCC: 421.052. Emphasis added.

86. DWME Report, CCM, 1965, par. 19.

87. Murray, "Joint Service," 218.

88. Newbigin, *Unfinished Agenda*, 200.

"the relation between mission and inter-church aid was still the subject of so much confusion and uncertainty."[89]

In Paul Löffler's opinion, the strength of Western donor agencies, which operated independent from mission organizations, was "the chief reason for the separate ways in which DICA and DWME worked within the WCC in spite of integration." Furthermore, he suggested that those within the other divisions of the WCC would have resisted the formation of a single division composed of the two largest units (the DICA and IMC) in terms of staff and funding: "Faith and Order, under Lukas Vischer, and Church and Society, under Paul Abrecht, would not have liked that at all and had an open ear [with the General Secretary]."[90]

After 1966, the WCC projects list was opened to include both mission and service. However, it was found that after almost a decade "missionary projects have not been taken up by inter-church aid funding agencies nor humanitarian projects by missionary societies on any large scale."[91]

Regionalization of Service

The evolution of the process and decision-making of inter-church aid resulted in the slow devolution of the power from the centre, in Geneva, to the regions. This process of decentralization brought the DICA closer to the mode of operation that the IMC had existed in prior to integration. A constant concern of Newbigin's was to battle against the centralizing tendency of the WCC by giving regions more autonomy.

The DICA became more regional in its decision-making as a result of frustration with the "Geneva process." Churches asking for aid needed to have their projects approved by the division in Geneva, which then authorized donor agencies to provide support. This could take considerable time. Some churches, faced with both an urgent need, and a considerable delay before they could respond to that need, chose to bypass this process (and their synods), and appeal directly to mission boards or service agencies. The bypassing of the vast majority of service around the division, whose *raison d'être* was to administer ecumenical service, naturally resulted in a re-evaluation of methods.[92]

89. Ibid., 211.

90. Paul Löffler, email to Laing, 02/08/2007.

91. Nissen, "Mission and Unity," 549–50.

92. Brash, "Regional Responsibility," 48.

Further impetus for regionalization was given with the new DICA mandate at the third assembly, which devolved operation of the DICA to the regions.[93] Taking the example of the EACC, which from the outset had combined mission and service,[94] Newbigin advocated that the EACC should serve as a model which could be replicated in other regions, and might be a future model for the integrated council.[95] Brash, as secretary of the EACC, was however more circumspect about the EACC serving as the ideal model of integration. Although the EACC had combined mission and service in its operations, he did not advocate this as a model which could be replicated centrally or regionally through the National Christian Councils, as the EACC model arose out of circumstances unique to that situation.[96]

As he had proposed at the Nyborg Strand Joint Committee before integration, Newbigin maintained that the central structure of the WCC be overhauled to "make the whole world council an organ of solidarity between the churches in mission and service. . . . [And to ensure] that the national councils [established by the IMC] were formally related to the whole WCC and not just to the DWME . . ."[97]

Joint Action for Mission (JAM)

Prior to integration Newbigin (and other IMC leaders) had failed to persuade the WCC that the DICA should become part of the DWME, which would have centrally united service and mission. But at the local and regional level Newbigin continued to press for such integration. Before the third assembly (New Delhi, 1961), Newbigin was developing the idea for Joint Action for Mission (JAM), which was subsequently endorsed at the assembly and the 1962 Central Committee.[98] JAM recommended the development of "proposals by which the churches and their related mission boards in a particular area could together survey their total task and plan

93. Murray, "Joint Service," 221.

94. Cooke, director of the DICA, offered funding to the EACC for a secretary. "The Asians . . . insisted on it being a secretary for mission *and* service." Brash, "Regional Responsibility," 47.

95. Newbigin, "Comments on DICASR," 10/6/1960, WCC: 27.0012.

96. Brash, "Mission and Inter-Church Aid," Enlarged Administrative Committee, 5–7/8/1959, Spittal, WCC: 27.0012.

97. Newbigin to Visser 't Hooft, 11/10/1963, WCC: 421.050.

98. Newbigin, "Developments During 1962," 4.

their total work in the context of a shared understanding of priorities."[99] These ideas, of replacing bilateral relationships between mission boards and "younger churches," for multilateral ones, had been inspired by the EACC, which at its inaugural meeting resolved to pursue "a more ecumenical pattern of relationships."[100]

Newbigin hoped that JAM might be the decisive step to move missions out of their immobility.[101] The "Paris Statement" on JAM which was endorsed by the Central Committee spoke of how missions must learn from "the pattern of ecumenical sharing of resources which the DICARWS has developed," the central aim being that "we believe that we have to find comparable ways of mobilizing the full resources of the churches for swift and effective response to the new openings for missionary advance which God is giving us."[102] Newbigin retained the emphasis that inter-church aid should further the mission of the church, rather than be limited only to humanitarian aid: "The Paris statement is a summons to all the churches to be as enterprising in mobilizing ecumenical resources for the task of world evangelization as they have been for the tasks of meeting human need."[103]

Further Developments in Inter-Church Aid

During 1966 two conferences were held to discuss and plan the future of the DICA. "At both of these the Churches were urged to align themselves more closely to governmental and intergovernmental programmes of development aid."[104] Significant changes beyond that have been the shift away from a centrally administered project system towards greater regional autonomy, and the change which allowed the priorities for service to be

99. DWME Report, CCM, 1963, 90. Proposals which Newbigin had previously sought to implement during his bishopric in Ramnad.

100. Cited by Newbigin, "Mission to Six Continents," 187. Newbigin would also draw upon his previous experience as bishop of Ramnad and Madurai where he sought to centralize the organization of mission work under the umbrella of the CSI. Details of this can be found in his extensive correspondence with Raymond Dudley, the India secretary of the American Board of Commissioners for Foreign Missions, BUL: DA29/2/1.

101. Ibid.

102. Cited by Newbigin, "Developments During 1962," 7.

103. Ibid., 8. Ideas which Newbigin developed in preparation for the first conference of the DWME, "Mexico Working Paper," WCC: 421.052.

104. Murray, "Joint Service," 229.

set by the recipients of aid.[105] Later issues which have dominated debate on the role and function of inter-church aid have been, first, a call for a moratorium on funds and personnel from the West; second, the search for a viable alternative to the project system to aid; and third, the political implications of aid. "As long as inter-church aid was understood as 'churches helping churches,' it was very normal, neutral, and readily acceptable."[106] During the seventies and eighties inter-church aid was concerned about its relationship with secular governments, and the role of inter-church aid in social action. It is significant to note that the debate had entirely moved away from discussing the relationship of inter-church aid with mission. The concerns which dominated integration had been dissipated to the extent that the CWME and DICA continued with separate mandates which, for both, were significant and life-giving activities.[107]

Conclusion

Missions and inter-church aid were very different in their origins, nature, and ethos, and (initially) in their field of operations. The enlarged mandate of the DICA set it on a collision course with the IMC, allowing the DICA to unilaterally enter what mission boards considered as their "fields." The attempt to resolve this conflict was *the* central reason for the call to integrate the two councils.

Missions had demonstrated a long-term commitment to the "younger church," but were tainted by colonialism, and were at times inflexible, paternalistic and embroiled in the affairs and governance of the "younger church." Inter-church aid by contrast, was temporary, multi-lateral, short-term, and encouraged mutuality between partner churches, but often lacked clarity as to its ultimate aim. The IMC was advisory and operated with a small leadership and was similarly constrained by budget, this contrasted with the burgeoning financial clout of the DICA, which soon became by far the largest division of the WCC. These differences made their union into one division improbable, and therefore Newbigin's advocacy for his plan of integration unrealistic, despite the strength of his theological argument.

105. J. E. Fischer, "Inter-Church Aid and the Future," in *Hope in the Desert*, ed. Kenneth Slack, 122.

106. Ibid., 126–27.

107. Conway to Laing, email, 06/09/2008.

Early theological reflections on the relationship between mission and service had acknowledged—at least at the level of the local congregation—that they were inextricably linked, and should be kept together. Mission and service exist in their own right and are yet interrelated and interdependent. Theological reflection on service led to the understanding that it was not simply a means to an end for missions; instead mission and service were understood as the two principal aspects of the church's nature and calling. Service was "*the ecumenical expression of the nature of the Church towards and in the world.*"[108]

The Joint Committee failed to deal with the fundamental problem for integration, the relationship between the DICA and the IMC, procrastinating decisions until after integration. Ranson had pressed the Joint Committee on this in 1956, as did Newbigin in 1958. Newbigin's central proposal in "Organization of the Church," which he presented at Nyborg Strand, was for one division. This was supported by IMC leadership, but overwhelmingly rejected by the WCC Central Committee. The letters exchanged before the meeting make it apparent that the minds of key people, such as Visser 't Hooft and Leslie Cooke, had already decided upon their plan for integration, and would not be dissuaded from it. At Oxford, whilst the IMC leadership supported Newbigin's plan, it became evident that the general IMC constituency also had concerns about the IMC being joined with the DICA. These concerns were mainly about maintaining the integrity and focus of mission within the integrated council.

The WCC Central Committee adopted a more cautious path towards integration, which resulted in the WCC incorporating the IMC into its existing structure without the existing WCC undergoing any substantial transformation. Just as missions were going through a major post-colonial re-evaluation, Newbigin argued that the WCC, as the international organ of the church, also needed to radically change, that it must be restructured to fully and adequately incorporate mission, to wholeheartedly reflect the fact that the church is "God's mission to the world." In both the IMC and the WCC Central Committee Newbigin was defeated on his vision of what integration could achieve for the WCC. The accepted alternative was, according to Newbigin, in "danger of failing altogether to evoke the response which we desire."[109]

At the time of integration the organizational decision was made to keep the DICA and the DWME as separate divisions within the integrated

108. Kraemer, "Inter-church aid and mission," 4. Italics in original.
109. Newbigin, "Organization of the Church," 16.

council. Those who were then involved in trying to keep them apart—and who had earlier acknowledged that mission and service were inseparable—sought, with limited success, to achieve theological justification for the delineation and ongoing partition of mission from service. The clue to solving the problem of relationship lay in starting with an understanding of the local congregation, and from there extrapolating to regional and international structures, rather than the reverse.[110] Newbigin's theological understanding placed *koinonia* as central, mission and service being inextricably linked in the local fellowship: "Both preaching and service, spring out of the new reality of the shared Holy Spirit (koinonia)"[111] Newbigin's case, that mission and service belonged together, and thus the DICA and the IMC should be united, remained the stronger case theologically. However, it was questionable whether that theological premise could adequately be translated into reality, given the profound historical differences between missions and inter-church aid. An adequate theological solution proved to be elusive because the organizational structure of the WCC forced its members to start theologizing from the central divisions of the WCC downwards to the local level, rather than the converse.

After integration Newbigin persisted in reminding the Central Committee of the need to overhaul the provisional nature of the WCC to "make the whole world council an organ of solidarity between the churches in mission and service."[112] This however did not take place, nor did Newbigin's other request, that the former IMC national councils become formally related to the *whole* WCC and not merely through the channel of the DWME. The WCC remained a council of *churches,* marginalizing the national councils bequeathed by the IMC. Procrastination over "the central issue" led to the dissipation of resolve, the inability to effect change, and contributed to the decline of mission concern within the WCC. This was exacerbated by the mushrooming of numerous programs within the WCC, thus diluting the influence of the DWME, which became one of but many departments.

The Herrenalb categories had for a decade delineated the relationship between mission and service. Newbigin correctly recognized that, although they had been an administrative necessity, they had the longer-term detrimental impact of artificially separating mission from service.

---

110. Newbigin shared this methodology with Ronald Orchard, "Inter-church aid and mission," Les Rasses Consultation, April 1956, WCC: 27.0012, 10.

111. Newbigin to van Beyma, 28/11/1958, BUL: DA29/2/9/54.

112. Newbigin to Visser 't Hooft, 11/10/1963, WCC: 421.050.

This was particularly injurious to missions as, at that time, service was receiving the lion's share of funding. It also limited the opportunity for the strengths and weaknesses of each to be respectively enhanced and corrected by the other. The damaging legacy of this polarization is apparent; a decade after their abolition the dichotomy was perpetuated with mission projects not receiving any significant funding from service agencies and vice versa.

Although defeated on the focal concern, Newbigin continued to hope that after integration the process of regionalization should counter the centralizing tendency of the WCC, and bring about the desired unity between mission and service. The administrative problems inherent with the "Geneva process" contributed to this process of regionalization. The example of the EACC, in uniting mission and service, inspired Newbigin to seek similar regional organization and initiate multi-lateral regional schemes which would combine mission and service (e.g., JAM).

Beyond the tenure of Newbigin, and the demise of Cooke, aid channeled through the WCC was increasingly understood in a secular sense, which could be devoid of any confessional stance, and could sit comfortably with the humanitarian work of secular governments. Newbigin's vision of aid being aid-for-missions, equipping churches to fulfill their calling to the world, was lost. This was certainly the experience of Myra Blyth as director of DICA during the 1990s.[113] She recalled how the relationship between CWME and DICA "were more separate than they should have been." At the level of the two commissions, centered in Geneva, "We never spoke as the development world and the mission world in terms of how do we integrate our projects," although there was more cooperation at regional and national level. The separation between mission and service was driven by the differing interests of the agencies. Mission agencies were, to a certain extent, defensive about being eclipsed by "stronger" service agencies, and sought to maintain their distinctive character, whilst service agencies eschewed any association with evangelism.[114]

Integration for Newbigin was not just the *reorganization* of mission; more fundamentally, he sought the *redefinition* of mission—mission free of colonial connotations and centered in the local church. Newbigin provided the theological basis for integration, rethinking the relationship between church and mission, moving from a colonial to a post-colonial

---

113. Blyth served in Geneva from 1988 to 2000, first as Europe secretary for DICA, then as director.

114. Myra Blyth, interview with Laing, 18/9/2008.

model in which the home base is everywhere, the church *is* the mission. Newbigin's theological arguments for integration are examined in the next chapter.

7

Newbigin's Theology of Integration

THIS CHAPTER SEEKS TO examine the theology Newbigin developed as a rationale for integration and to show how the debate on integration impinged upon his theologizing. Integration for Newbigin was not just the *reorganization* of mission—more fundamentally he desired the *redefinition* of mission—mission free of colonial connotations and centered in the local church. Newbigin recognized that a dichotomy existed between what was being said and what was being done; between the theological articulation of a recovered missionary ecclesiology and the satisfactory embodiment of that expression, in which the "church *is* the mission." The way forward for Newbigin was to change structures, to align them with theological presuppositions. Newbigin pressed for action, for implementation and embodiment of theological convictions. In his understanding, God had ordered the events and developments of the Protestant missionary movement and the ecumenical movement to bring the two councils to a crucial moment of decision and action.

The integration of the two councils was for Newbigin, but one expression, of the recovery and adequate expression of the relationship between mission and the church. His approach to integration was to emphasize the regional and local expressions of new relationships between church and mission, rather than expect a centralized hierarchy to be determinative for local ecclesiology.

The main means by which Newbigin initiated discussion on the redefinition of mission was through the various study papers he wrote. Newbigin's sequential draft papers are examined in this chapter to determine how the theological foundation for integration he provided evolved and developed as he moved from his analysis of the *structure* to the more fundamental level of the *substance* of mission. His first, "The Organization of the Church, Mission to the World,"[1] was discussed both by the Central Committee of the WCC and by the staff of the IMC. Its revised form, as the publication, *One Body, One Gospel, One World*,[2] served as a personal "manifesto" on integration, and was widely applauded, at least within IMC circles. In both Newbigin sought to address the issues of relationship, theologically between mission and church, and as expressed in the historical realities of mission agencies and churches.

In the study papers subsequent to that Newbigin made significant changes in his approach. He realized that the loss of morale and of momentum which had characterized the IMC assembly in Ghana was symptomatic of a more generalized malaise about mission. He wanted to address the essential reasons for that melancholy. In Newbigin's examination of the structure of mission, the relationship between mission and service as expressed vis-à-vis the IMC and the DICA, had dominated his thinking in preparation for integration (Ch 6). But Newbigin realized that, at a more fundamental level, there were considerable problems with the post-Tambaram church-centric model of mission. His initial papers, a "First tentative draft of a paper to follow the IMC paper 'One Body, One Gospel, One World,'" and his "Second draft . . ." were critical of the inadequacies of this church-centric model, but limited in their construction of an alternative. In his subsequent papers he developed a more adequate trinitarian foundation for mission.

"The Organization of the Church, Mission to the World"

Newbigin's study papers served as the focal point for extensive discussions on integration and what it meant. The first of these papers, "The Organization of the Church, Mission to the World," was a consequence of IMC discussions held in Montreal in 1958. In drafting his paper, Newbigin strove to address the issue of current relationships between mission and the church. Newbigin understood the vital issues for missions to be "the development of a pattern of relationships in which the present bi-lateral relation of sovereign mission boards to younger churches is

---

1. Newbigin, Draft paper "Organization of the Church, Mission to the World," June 1958, BUL: DA29/2/9/2.

2. Newbigin, *One Body*.

replaced by a multi-lateral relationship . . . on a basis of fundamental equality." And for the churches, "whether every congregation is or is not primarily a mission."[3]

To help bring focus to the thinking in the ecumenical movement in the late 1950s Newbigin sought a new "slogan." "I find that there is a widespread consensus of the conviction that the slogan 'One fellowship bearing one Gospel for one world' represents a real crystallization of our thinking about Church and Mission." Newbigin concurred with the acceptance of this slogan but was aware that it had not been yet been embodied in clear and simple terms in respect to theology and organization and administration.[4] To that end, Newbigin drafted "Organization of the Church," with the intention that it would promote discussion within both councils, with the IMC holding a staff consultation in September to discuss it.[5] Previously Newbigin had chaired the Drafting Committee which developed the theme for the second assembly of the WCC (1954). Evanston had showed him how preparation for the assembly was an excellent opportunity for an issue to penetrate into the life of the church, and to that end he proposed that the third assembly (New Delhi, 1961), which would enact integration, would take as the central theme the issues raised for the church by the fact that it is a mission to the world—this did not transpire.[6]

Visser 't Hooft was aware that Newbigin's leadership of the IMC would ensure sufficient discussion of that issue within the IMC, but Visser 't Hooft was concerned that this would not be mirrored by the corresponding breadth and depth of discussion within the WCC. "There is a danger that if the IMC leaders work out their policy of integration by themselves . . . we do not arrive at a really common mind and do not succeed in giving the same challenge in the two constituencies."[7] In preparation for the third assembly, there was the need for leaders of both councils to form a common mind, which could then help influence the

---

3. Newbigin to Visser 't Hooft, 4/6/1958, BUL: DA29/2/9/4.

4. Ibid.

5. Scheduling the IMC consultation in September prevented WCC involvement due to a conflict of dates, a proposal which displeased Visser 't Hooft. Joint Committee, 14–18/8/1958, WCC: 27.0003, 19.

6. Newbigin to Visser 't Hooft, 4/6/1958, BUL: DA29/2/9/4. The christo-centric theme adopted for New Delhi was, "Jesus Christ—The Light of the world." "The theme, however, was not given the same prominence as at previous assemblies, and served mainly as a sort of guiding principle." WCC Archives Web site: http://archives.oikoumene.org/.

7. Visser 't Hooft to Newbigin, 30/6/1958, BUL: DA29/2/9/6.

planning for the assembly. But this did not happen; Newbigin's theology of integration dominated the thinking within the IMC, and a corresponding self-analysis within the WCC did not take place.

In Newbigin's draft, his basic premise was that integration was the will of God in the same way that mission was. Newbigin sensed that there was the need to move the discussion on from the merely organizational level to engage with the deep underlying theological issues.[8]

"The Present Situation"[9]

Newbigin detailed the historical developments which had produced the dichotomy between mission and the church and had created a loss of momentum and a sense of hesitancy. There had been profound changes in the balance of political and cultural power between West and non-West; the rise of Communism and in particular the response of China, becoming "closed" to missions; the rise of "younger churches" and their co-partnership and demand for new relationships in the ecumenical movement with the "sending churches." The result, in Newbigin's words, was that "the sense of direction, the feeling of urgency, and the depth of conviction which underlay the slogan 'The Evangelization of the World in this Generation' are not present today in anything like the same measure in most of the bodies represented in the IMC and the WCC."[10]

At this juncture for mission and the church, Newbigin reiterated three potential outcomes for their relationship, which the integration of the two councils would symbolize.[11] First, the capitulation and death of missions; second, the perpetuation of colonial mission models; or third, the reconfiguring of mission and the church.[12]

To steer integration down the more difficult third path Newbigin suggested that a new slogan was required, as it was recognized that Mott's slogan, which had galvanized the generation from Edinburgh 1910, was now redundant.[13] Newbigin boldly hoped that a new slogan, which needed to

8. Newbigin, "Organization of the Church," 1.

9. The following four headings are those used by Newbigin in his draft paper.

10. Ibid., 1.

11. Newbigin derived this categorization from W. Freytag; see ch. 4.

12. Newbigin, "Organization of the Church," 2. The influence of Freytag is apparent when Newbigin describes possible outcomes for the IMC, citing Freytag's presentation at the IMC Ghana Assembly.

13. By 1910 the slogan was already waning from its earlier prominence.

encapsulate the new consensus of "one fellowship, one gospel one world," would evoke a similar response as Mott's had.[14] Newbigin interpreted integration as a critical moment in the history of the ecumenical movement, where decisive action was required to re-express a post-colonial form of mission. Newbigin used the metaphor of fruit, which ripens slowly but must be picked at once or else it will go rotten—ideas develop slowly but when the time comes action must be taken quickly.[15] Newbigin argued that 'One fellowship with one Gospel for the one world' would not be filled with meaning until the churches underwent repentance at this point, and learnt what it meant that the Church *is* a mission."[16] His hope was that integration of the two world councils would serve as a catalyst for similar integration in the local churches—especially in the West.

"Theological Questions Convictions"[17]

Newbigin presented his hope, that integration would precipitate a wide-ranging and radical reappraisal of ecclesiology. His hope was based upon his theological convictions derived from his reading of the New Testament.[18] "The Church's mission is none other than the carrying on of the mission of Christ Himself. 'As the Father has sent, me even so I send you.'"[19] Newbigin cited one of his key texts, John 20:21, as biblical foundation to the consensus of theological conviction, the acceptance of the *missio Dei* concept—the same text he had succeeded in introducing at Willingen. Already Newbigin was moving from a solely christological basis for mission and was developing a trinitarian basis which would become much more explicit later. "Strictly speaking, the agent of the mission is the Holy Spirit himself, and none other. . . . The Church participates in the mission only by virtue of its participation in the Holy Spirit."[20] Newbigin offered a threefold relationship between mission and church; the church

14. Newbigin, "Organization of the Church," 2, 3.

15. Ibid., 3.

16. Ibid., 4. Italics in original.

17. The original typed manuscript had "Theological Questions"; Newbigin amended this by hand, crossing out "Questions" to change the heading to "Theological Convictions." In *One Body* he further strengthened the heading, it becoming "The Unchanging Basis." Ibid., 5. Cf. Newbigin, *One Body*, 17.

18. Seldom does Newbigin make reference to any Old Testament text in support of his thesis.

19. Newbigin, "Organization of the Church," 5.

20. Ibid, 6.

as the community of the Holy Spirit is the place where the "fruit of Christ's mission is already present in foretaste"; "the powers of the Holy Spirit are available to serve"; and "witness is borne to that which is above and beyond the Church."[21]

"These three: fellowship, service and evangelism may be described as the three dimensions of the church's mission." But for Newbigin, "This work of explicit evangelism is central, and must be seen to be central to the whole mission. . . . works of love must accompany the proclamation of the word of the Gospel."[22] Newbigin, in his draft, attested that proclamation of the word is primary, "central," and deeds were understood as a necessary accompaniment to evangelism. The church "authenticates itself as truly the fellowship of the Holy Spirit when it points beyond itself" in mission; with mission being to the ends of the earth and the end of time, the end of mission being the *eschaton*, the summation of all human history.[23]

"Principles for Action"

The theological convictions that Newbigin developed, based upon his hermeneutic of the New Testament, led him to practical implications and to propose changes in mission policy to end the unbiblical dichotomy between mission and church.[24] New channels were needed to express the relationship of partnership rather than paternalism between "younger" and "older churches." The expression of a new relationship between mission and church needed to be locally determined rather than be imparted to the grassroots from some global headquarters, because the church is both universal and local. "It is universal because Christ is exalted as king and head of the whole creation. It is local because where two or three are gathered in His Name, there He is. A local congregation . . . is not, therefore, a 'branch' of the Church, deriving its authority from the larger body; it is the local manifestation of Christ's presence and the instrument of His mission."[25] For Newbigin the local form of organization was to precede and determine the central form, rather than vice versa; integration was not about "coordinating operations 'at the highest level.'" Rather, "[i]t is a question of the integrity of the Church's character and mission in every

21. Ibid.
22. Ibid., 6, 12.
23. Ibid., 6, 7.
24. Newbigin, "Organization of the Church," 8.
25. Ibid., 12.

place. What we are concerned about is that the Church should be—universally and locally—recognizable as one reconciled fellowship offering to all men everywhere the secret of reconciliation to God through Jesus Christ. . . . We must try to ensure that everything that can possibly be done locally and regionally is done. *And from there* we must go on to consider what are the things which must be done centrally."[26]

This repeated emphasis by Newbigin, on the local being determinative, undermined his argument that integration of the two international councils, as an ecumenical sign and symbol, would precipitate a wide-ranging transformation in local congregations. The local must precede the central; otherwise integration would merely become absorbed with questions of structure. The integration of the two councils was one expression of the proper relationship between mission and church. But it was not to be interpreted as a defining model which percolated from the top down to the constituent council members at the grass-roots. Rather, at the local and regional level, Newbigin recommended that fresh efforts and experimentation were required to embody the theological convictions that the church is the mission, and to express answers to the question, what kind of unity does God intend for us?[27] However, despite Newbigin's emphasis on the local, the methodology and process of integration was absorbed by concerns of the universal—marginalizing Newbigin's local concerns. The expectation was that integration at the level of the world councils would then provoke local and regional discussion—Newbigin did not foresee that the converse could happen, that centralization of the WCC would dominate thinking.

"Some Tentative Suggestions"

Newbigin concluded his paper by announcing that he had undergone an essential change in his thinking on integration (as detailed in chapter 6). Newbigin sought a more radical reordering of the WCC, otherwise, he claimed, the WCC would not fundamentally change its relationship to mission. There were two extremes of error, either of being too bold or of being too cautious. In Newbigin's estimate the latter was more probable: "I have become impressed with the danger that by making these minimal organizational changes, and leaving more radical issues untouched, one may defeat the main purpose [of integration]. . . . [T]hat the whole Church

26. Ibid., 12–13. Emphasis added.
27. Newbigin, "Organization of the Church," 13, 14.

should be summoned afresh to a recognition of, and wholehearted acceptance of its task as God's mission to the world."[28]

IMC Staff Conference: Oxford (16–18/9/58)

Newbigin's paper was the basis for discussion at the IMC Staff Conference in Oxford in September 1958. As with WCC meetings Oxford was predominantly composed of Western leadership.[29] Chairing the meeting, Newbigin raised various concerns which he hoped would guide their discussion. He reminded those gathered that the primary concern was not just integration, but Christian mission in this day, "The foremost concern out of which . . . [the] paper arose was simply the advance of the missionary cause in the 20th century."[30]

At the conclusion of the conference Newbigin suggested that the delegates had reached consensus on several points: "We are concerned primarily with the furthering of the missionary cause, our concern with integration is incidental to that"; the acceptance that the home base is everywhere; and the need for a fresh concentration on the "missionary task." The discussion sought to distinguish between what was perceived as the "eternally valid factor" for mission, from what was particular to the Protestant missionary movement. Three recurring distinctions were recognized: between evangelism and service; between missions at home and abroad; and between the sphere of "faith" and the sphere of "unbelief."[31] The latter, the crossing of a religious barrier, was understood as providing the essential and timeless factor: "the essence of mission as we understand it is the outreach of the Church beyond its own borders."[32]

Although Newbigin sought to initiate discussion beyond the merely organizational, to discuss the theological issues of relationship, the responses to his paper were fixated by structural concerns. Responses to

---

28. Ibid., 14.

29. Only two non-Western delegates were present. Report of IMC Staff Consultation, Regent's Park College, Oxford, 13–16/9/1958, WCC: 26.0042/4 (hereafter cited as Oxford Report). Freda Dearing highlighted the danger of only having consultants who could finance their travel, as the prohibitive cost of prevented from bringing people from the majority world. Dearing to Newbigin, 18/7/1958, WCC: 26.0042/1.

30. Oxford Report, 3.

31. It is notable that here Newbigin used problematic terms reminiscent of the medieval *fides* and *infides*, at least implying that all non-Christian faith is "unbelief," and that Christianity is the sole repository of "belief."

32. Oxford Report, 6, 15, 18, 51–53.

Newbigin's paper had been solicited and then reported back to the conference. Orchard's report of the responses from National Christian Councils and individuals showed that most did not discuss the theological convictions it propounded but accepted the main argument of the paper. Instead, most written feedback was devoted to the question of how the DICA would relate to the DWME after integration.[33]

Newbigin and Goodall also discussed the paper with WCC members in Geneva, incorporating their suggestions. In contrast to the affirmation on the enduring validity of mission, given in IMC circles at Oxford, in Geneva Newbigin recorded that "although there was a good discussion, I was made painfully aware of the deep scepticism with which some of the younger members of the staff viewed this attempt to rehabilitate a discredited concept. It was a signal to indicate some of the struggles to come."[34]

One Body, One Gospel, One World

On the basis of these discussions Newbigin revised his draft paper, "Organization of the Church." It was published by the IMC as *One Body, One Gospel, One World*. This booklet was widely translated and circulated in several editions.[35] As a personal statement by Newbigin, it was substantially unchanged from the draft except for important developments which are detailed below. Writing after the Oxford meeting to the secretaries of the IMC member councils, this "manifesto" was in turn circulated to them to promote discussion, the key aim being that "we should take the present time as an opportunity given by God for a serious and resolute attempt to think together about the missionary calling of the whole Church in this day and generation."[36]

Newbigin understood the Oxford consultation as clarifying and endorsing the essential change in mission understanding, from the directional model inherited from Christendom. There was a shift from an essentially geographic model, of mission emanating from the West, to understand, "that this differentium is the crossing of the frontier between

33. R. Orchard, Comments to Newbigin's paper prepared for staff consultation in Oxford, 3/9/1958, BUL: DA29/2/9/42.

34. Newbigin, *Unfinished Agenda*, 164–65, 197. The debate and subsequent polarization in definitions of "mission" in the ecumenical movement is discussed in ch. 10.

35. Ibid., 164.

36. Newbigin to the Secretaries of IMC Member Councils, Covering letter to introduce the aim of *One Body*, 1/12/1958, WCC: 26.0042/4.

faith and unbelief [regardless of geographic context] . . . with the intention of bringing men to belief; and that we must find ways in which, in any integrated structure, there is a proper point of concentration on the specific missionary task."[37] It was Newbigin's hope that the debate on integration would occasion the opportunity for each area to look at the unfinished task of evangelism "so that the proposed new Division . . . would start its work with the confidence that the whole constituency was ready for a fresh and vigorous advance in the world mission of the Church." To this end, Newbigin advocated that the IMC develop local experiments on the relationship between mission and the church, embodied in the relationship between mission agencies and those of inter-church aid. He proposed multilateral experiments in mission rather than bilateral relationships between individual mission boards and "younger churches."[38] The "younger church" was often characterized as being the "only child," having well-developed filial relationships to a particular mission organization which precluded the development of more appropriate relationships with similar neighboring "younger churches." To overcome this only-child syndrome, Newbigin recommended inter-visitation between IMC councils out of which might come the cross-fertilization of ideas and new expressions of relationship.

Discussion on "Organization of the Church" also brought to light the fact that, on several points, consensus had not been reached. Newbigin acknowledged that further discussion was required on several issues; besides the future relationship between the DICA and the IMC, there was the question of whether faithfulness to mission required a fresh approach to the problem of denominational differences, as well as questions of ecclesiology: "What are the implications for the ordinary life of the Church of the fact that it is a missionary body? This includes questions regarding the structure of congregational and parish life, the position of the ministry, and the content and method of theological training for the ministry."[39] Newbigin hoped that such questions would permeate the WCC after integration.

The emergent "new vision" understood mission as the "task" "of the whole church in every continent to the whole world," as the home base was now everywhere. As Newbigin had done in 1952, now, in 1958, *One*

37. Ibid.
38. Ibid.
39. Ibid.

Body "set out the theological basis for such a vision and formed a rationale for . . . integration."[40]

With recourse to Greek nouns, mission was defined as consisting of *koinonia, diakonia,* and *marturia.* There was the problem that this broad definition would undermine the specific role of missions taking the gospel to where it was not known: "If everything is mission, nothing is mission."[41] Newbigin sought to overcome this, making a distinction between missionary *dimension* and *intention.*[42] This was a development from the broad definition which pervaded "Organization of the Church." In *One Body,* Newbigin affirmed "the validity of missions as distinct activities within the total mission of the Church and to define their specific character in terms of intention. While all the activities of the Church have a missionary dimension, there are needed specific activities which have the intention of crossing the frontier between faith and unbelief."[43]

A further clarification from his earlier draft was his statement on the relationship between fellowship, service, and witness which before had been rather broadly understood as the three dimensions of the church's mission. Before Newbigin had maintained the primacy of witness. Service and evangelism are derived from and dependent upon the Spirit's primary work, the establishment of the fellowship. "The basic reality is the creation of a new being through the presence of the Holy Spirit. This new being is the common life (*koinonia*) in the Church. It is out of this new creation that both service and evangelism spring, and from it they receive their value."[44]

One Body had been widely applauded—at least within the IMC constituency—and had served its purpose of promoting discussion on relationships and the future pattern of mission. Later, however, Newbigin conceded that *One Body* had "made little impact beyond" IMC circles— that is, most crucially in changing and challenging the ecclesiological assumptions held within WCC circles.[45]

---

40. Newbigin, Curriculum Vitae, 1988, BUL: DA29/1/14/1.

41. S. Neill, *Creative Tension* (London: Edinburgh House, 1959) 81.

42. A distinction which continues to be accepted in mission theology. Goheen, *As the Father,* 56; Bosch, *Transforming Mission,* 373.

43. Newbigin, *Unfinished Agenda,* 164.

44. Newbigin, *One Body,* 20. Cf. Wainwright, *Newbigin,* 426 n. 22. By November 1958, Newbigin had changed his position, from then on maintaining that *koinonia* was primary.

45. Newbigin, "Integration," 250.

"First tentative draft of a paper to follow the IMC paper 'One Body, One Gospel, One World'"[46]

From Relationships to the Substance of Mission

In proposing a sequel to *One Body*, Newbigin recognized that the discussion had moved on and a new paper was required which examined the *substance* of the "missionary task." Although the discussion may have progressed, Charles Ranson raised practical questions as to what extent the discussion Newbigin had initiated had been translated into tangible change. How were mission boards implementing multilateral relationships: "[what] specific result in missionary planning and the pooling of resources can be traced to the very widespread discussion evoked by your pamphlet [*One Body*] . . . Unless they [mission boards] are pressed to decision . . . on this question, the process of 'carrying the discussion on a stage further' may simply be a convenient escape mechanism."[47] Newbigin conceded that despite much discussion on *One Body*, little had been done in practice to implement change.[48]

Newbigin identified four factors which prompted him to develop a sequel to *One Body*. First, reflection and discussion on a paper by Ronald Orchard given in Geneva on the theology of mission; second, the discussion provoked by Donald McGavran's book *How Churches Grow*;[49] third, the discussion held at the St. Andrew's Central Committee meetings on the role of the future DWME, and how sharper focus could be given on the DWME on taking the gospel to the "unbelieving world"—no longer just the non-Western world; and fourth, the response elicited by Newbigin's address at the San Francisco assembly of NCCUSA,[50] which encouraged him to believe that people were looking for a lead along those lines.[51] He proposed to write a sequel which he hoped would serve as a background document in preparation for the third assembly of the WCC.[52]

46. Newbigin, March 1961, WCC: 26.0042/10.

47. C. Ranson to Newbigin, 31/1/1961, WCC: 26.0042/11.

48. Newbigin, "First Draft," 3.

49. D. A. McGavran, *How Churches Grow: The New Frontiers of Mission* (London: World Dominion Press, 1959).

50. Newbigin, "Mission of the Church to All the Nations," address given at the NCC (USA) General Assembly, San Francisco, 5/12/1960, SOAS: 26–11–25/10.

51. Newbigin to IMC staff, 21/12/1960, WCC: 26.0042/11.

52. This did not happen. Due to the redrafting of his text, the final text was not published until 1963.

The paper began by Newbigin outlining the historical models of how the church was related to mission. In the history of the Protestant missionary movement, mission societies often had little concern for the church; mission and church were divorced from each other. Through the IMC, thinking moved from a mission-centered pattern to that of a church-centered pattern; but there were many problems inherent in that transition. Newbigin discerned various stages in the transition to that relationship. First was that of devolution of missions to the "younger churches." Second, when the problems of dichotomy between mission and church became apparent, this led to integration—mission organization operating in the field under the authority and the umbrella of regional or national churches. Third, from the Whitby conference, the term "partnership" was coined between the "younger" and "older churches." Fourth, with the need for pooling of resources to signify the fact that mission is the mission of the whole church to the whole world, Newbigin recommended the development of "multilateral patterns" in *One Body*.[53]

In this paper, rather than further the discussion on *patterns* of relationship Newbigin signaled his intention to move discussion to a more fundamental level to discuss the *substance* of mission. He was concerned by emerging trends he could perceive. Whilst missionary numbers were growing in the Roman Catholic Church and amongst conservative evangelicals, amongst the churches involved with the WCC there was not corresponding growth but rather decline. For Newbigin, the reason for this drop in numbers (and associated decline in other forms of commitment to mission), was due to a "failure of conviction" of the sufficiency and finality of Christ by traditional churches. "Do the churches recognise that fidelity to the missionary task, and belief in the truth of the Gospel are strictly interdependent?"[54] For Newbigin, the basis of the church's authority to engage in mission only came from Jesus Christ. He discerned that the loss of commitment to mission paralleled the discrediting of colonial mission with its misplaced confidence in "civilising" and "development."

Two factors were identified which served as correctives against placing missionary motivation in any other source that the authority of Christ. First, with the rise of the ecumenical movement, any formulation of missionary motive had to stand the "scrutiny of fellow-Christians in very different political and cultural situations."[55] In contrast to the more homo-

---

53. Newbigin, "First Draft," 1–3.

54. Ibid., 10.

55. Ibid., 11.

geneous expression of mission from the West, now the heterogeneity of the global church, as a hermeneutic for the gospel, served as a corrective. With the home base being everywhere, the motivation for mission must be universally applicable. This disqualified Western cultural factors such as colonialism and its continuation in the guise of development.

The second corrective was from the growing consensus on missionary ecclesiology. The Tambaram Conference marked the ascendancy of thinking of mission as *church-centric* mission. Although this model was strongly contested at Willingen,[56] consensus *had* been achieved which understood that mission was *God's* mission to the world; the authority was God's authority. "The Church as called and constituted by Jesus Christ *is* a mission to the world. . . . It is the continuing through history of Christ's mission to the world. . . . The Church, therefore, is at the centre of any true missionary thinking and—equally important—of any true missionary practice."[57] Newbigin urged that this consensus must be maintained, as he believed it to be true to the Bible and fruitful in practice.

Critique of the Post-Tambaram Church-Centric Mission Model

However, whilst Newbigin gave his support to this church-centric model of mission, he was not uncritical of it. He identified two issues which were not adequately dealt with and asked whether a corrective was not therefore required. First, Newbigin critiqued the post-Tambaram formulations on mission for being *too* church centered, thus too little attention was paid to the *world*. This had the consequence that mission was understood as a growth of the church, as a movement *within* history, rather than the very meaning of all history; in contrast, the Bible did not testify to any separation in God's dealing with the nations and the church.[58] The post-Tambaram formulations on mission were criticized by Newbigin as "too exclusively framed in terms of the life, growth and activity of the Church, and that they thereby run into the danger of making the events of secular history appear to be mere scenery for the history of salvation. In truth we cannot rightly think of the missionary task except in the context of God's

56. Even as this church-centric model was formulated at Tambaram, it was critiqued by E. Stanley-Jones, who proposed that the Kingdom of God should be central. For further discussion, see Kim, "Kingdom of God." At Willingen the attack against church-centricism was led by J. C. Hoekendijk, who advocated that the *world* should be central, not the church.

57. Newbigin, "First Draft," 21.

58. Ibid., 13.

cosmic purpose. It is His will to 'sum up *all things* in Christ, the things in heaven and the things upon earth.'"[59]

Writing in 1961, Newbigin employs language such as the world being "mere scenery" which closely resembles that used by Hoekendijk.[60] No doubt Hoekendijk's strident views would occupy a prominent place in Newbigin's thinking after their recent presentations at the Strasbourg Conference, 1960.[61] Newbigin was aware of the danger of simply grafting the motivation for mission onto secular ideas, as he discredited the idea of the indefinite terrestrial progress towards the Kingdom of God on earth. Rather, for Newbigin, the framework for understanding secular history must come from the New Testament apocalyptic passages. All history was thus understood as the convergence of all things upon the issues raised by the historical event of Christ's incarnation and the ultimate question "Jesus Christ, or antichrist?"[62] The end of history "is not a church but a kingdom."[63] Through a hermeneutic of the apocalyptic literature, Newbigin sought to discern God's movement in secular history; of how all things will be summed up in Christ.

The second defect Newbigin identified with the church-centric model was that it gave too little attention to the work of the Holy Spirit in mission. Witness was borne not primarily by the church but first and foremost by the Holy Spirit: "It [the church] is essentially the place where the sovereign Holy Spirit of God continues to bear *His own witness* to Christ as the revelation of God for man."[64] Newbigin looked to the book of Acts for confirmation that mission was the mission of the Holy Spirit. By contrast, in his evaluation of modern mission, "one is often compelled to ask whether all this is really in authentic succession from what we read in the 'Acts.'" Profoundly influenced by Roland Allen's thinking,[65] Newbigin con-

59. Ibid, 16. Italics in original.

60. Cf. Hoekendijk, "Church in Missionary Thinking," 324.

61. Discussed in ch. 8.

62. Newbigin, "First Draft," 15.

63. Ibid., 21.

64. Ibid., 21. Emphasis added.

65. Newbigin cited Allen in various publications around this time and endorsed his most famous work by writing a foreword to R. Allen, *Missionary Methods: St. Paul's or Ours?* (Grand Rapids: Eerdmans, 1962). Newbigin's first published reference to Allen occurred in "Our Task Today," a charge to be given to the fourth meeting of the Diocesan Council, Tirumangalam, 18–20/12/1951, NLS: ACC 7548/B45. This accords with George Hood's argument that Allen was only rediscovered by Western mission theorists in the wake of the China exodus. G. A. Hood, *Neither Bang nor Whimper: The End of a Missionary Era in China* (Singapore: Presbyterian Church in Singapore,

trasted Paul's methods: of trust in the Holy Spirit, and the establishment of self-propagating "adult" churches, reliant on the Spirit rather than being dependent on another church or mission; with current methods imbued with the legacy of colonialism, which had conflated mission with the quest to civilize. Newbigin predicted that, with the rapid decline of the colonial model, "The position of the Christian mission in the coming decades is likely to be nearer to that of St. Paul than to that of William Carey or David Livingstone. But the mental revolution which is required will not happen easily."[66]

Newbigin concluded his paper by stating that the authority for mission must be derived from a trinitarian basis, "the world mission of the church is rooted in the being of the triune God, Father, Son and Holy Spirit." The process of re-thinking the substance of mission therefore required a re-thinking of the meaning of that threefold name: "The threefold Name into which we are commanded to baptise all nations is the clue to the understanding of the nature and authority of the Christian mission. The re-thinking of the missionary task in our day must take the form of a fresh exploration of the meaning of that threefold Name."[67] Newbigin, in concurrence with Hoekendijk, identified the inherent flaws with a church-centric model of mission, that it had neglected the world due to its focus on the church, and that it neglected the role of the Holy Spirit. A model which was too christological was incapable of explaining the role of the Spirit, in bringing the kingdom of God outside of the church, in secular historical processes. Newbigin had identified the problem and knew that the "clue" to the solution lay in developing a trinitarian basis for mission. But, as yet, Newbigin could not map out the contours of an acceptable answer; his conclusion was a sign on the road directing him forward. Newbigin's theological quest for a sufficient basis for mission concurred with general sentiments which were being voiced. Later that year at the New Delhi assembly, he wrote:

> [I]t was clear that new questions were being raised and that the church-centric model which had dominated missionary thinking since Tambaram was breaking down. The report . . . spoke of

1991) 204–12.

66. Newbigin, "First Draft," 19. Newbigin's prescience again being echoed by similar sentiments from Andrew Walls: "It now seems increasingly likely that the bearers of the gospel will bring no gifts with them, except the gospel itself." A. F. Walls, *The Missionary Movement in Christian History: Studies in the Transmission of Faith* (Maryknoll, NY: Orbis, 1996) 261.

67. Newbigin, "First Draft," 22.

God's rule over the whole created world and said, "We have but little understanding of the wisdom, love and power which God has given to men of other faiths and of no faith," and in my own diary at the time I wrote: "It is clear that a Trinitarian, rather than a purely Christological understanding of the missionary task is more and more necessary."[68]

"Second draft of study booklet to follow 'One Body, One Gospel, One World'"[69]

The study booklet that Newbigin had suggested as background reading for the New Delhi assembly did not materialize in time for the assembly. In light of the fact that integration had now been enacted Newbigin desired to revise his first draft to prepare the discussion for the first conference of the DWME in New Mexico in 1963.

This second draft was substantially the same as Newbigin's first draft which sought to move the discussion from the patterns and relationships of mission to questions of the substance of mission. Newbigin acknowledged that the church-centric model of mission had been fruitful in developing the consensus that the church was called to mission and unity, and it was upon that presupposition that integration had proceeded. But Newbigin noted that at New Delhi, the issue which was hardest to find agreement upon was the question, what is God doing in our time?[70] "A purely 'church-centric' understanding of the missionary task has often caused us to take a wholly unbiblical view of the world."[71] As in his first draft, Newbigin recognized the limitations of a purely christological church-centric model for mission. As a development from his first draft, in which he was convinced of the need for a trinitarian basis, in his second draft, he now developed that basis more adequately.

A potential solution to understanding how Christ's work in the world was related to his work in the church was that proposed by extended

---

68. Newbigin, *Unfinished Agenda*, 192. It is significant that questions on Christianity's engagement with the non-Christian world are being raised at New Delhi, the first assembly convened outside the "Christian" West. Newbigin made the link between the context of the early church, and the emergence of the Trinity as a foundational missiological doctrine.

69. Newbigin, 1962, WCC: 421.050 (hereafter cited as "Second Draft").

70. Newbigin, "Second Draft," 12.

71. Ibid., 14.

christology; as Jesus is Lord of all, therefore we need to recognize his work in all things. This was problematic as it was an easy progression, from acknowledging divine initiative in secular events, to aligning oneself uncritically with these movements, and then equating that with God's will for the church.[72] Newbigin was critical of this syncretistic approach as it belittled the sharp command to leave everything and follow Christ.[73]

Newbigin contrasted the context of the early church, which existed as a small minority amongst many faiths and cultures, and was thus orientated towards the world, with that of Christendom, which was insular, existing as an assumed Christianized culture. Out of the former context the doctrine of the Trinity was first formulated, whilst in the latter, the doctrine was assumed but lacked any prominence or development.[74] Drawing from his experience as a missionary in South India, Newbigin found parallels between the context of Christianity in the non-West with that of the early church. In such contexts, where the church existed as a small minority, the doctrine of the Trinity was repeatedly a necessary starting point, a presupposition to preaching, not an intellectual capstone to be placed at the very end, "it is, on the contrary, what Athanasius called it, the *arche*, the pre-supposition without which the preaching of the Gospel in a pagan world cannot begin."[75]

But Newbigin continued to sound hesitant about his belief in the Trinity as the starting point from which to explicate a contemporary missiological agenda: "it may perhaps be accepted as at least a reasonable suggestion that a fresh articulation of the meaning of the missionary task . . . may require us likewise to acknowledge the necessity of a trinitarian starting point."[76]

For Newbigin, the answer to the distinction between what God is doing in Christ, and what God is doing in the world, came from a trinitarian understanding of the incarnation and the mission of the Son. Christ, rather than being revealed as the one who controls history, "appears as the Son who constantly looks up in love and obedience to the Father who

---

72. On this point, Newbigin was critical of M. M. Thomas for equating the processes of Indian nationalism with God's will, blurring the distinction between the secular and the sacred, and not answering acceptably how Christ's work in either was related or could be distinguished. Newbigin, "Second Draft," 15.

73. Ibid., 16.

74. Ibid., 17.

75. Ibid., 18.

76. Ibid., 18, 19. Cf. Lesslie Newbigin, *The Relevance of Trinitarian Doctrine for Today's Mission* (London: Edinburgh House, 1963) 84.

controls everything . . . [accepting] *the Father's ordering of events as the form in which His mission is to be fulfilled.*[77] Even if events appeared hostile to his ministry, the Son, through suffering demonstrated filial obedience. The Father is God, ordering world affairs; the Son is God, accepting the ordering of the Father. In Newbigin's study of the synoptic gospels he discerned, almost from the outset, a double movement of attraction and repulsion, people being polarized into a response for or against Christ. The church, in continuing the mission of Jesus, continued that process of polarization: "It [the church] continues to be the place where men are brought to the ultimate decision for or against God. . . . This is the message of the apocalyptic passages of the New Testament. In them we see the mission of the church as the continuance of this action of Jesus in precipitating decision and judgment. They show us the Church not as the body through which God controls history, but rather as the *sign* to men of God's control of history."[78]

"The Mission of the Triune God" and *The Relevance of Trinitarian Doctrine for Today's Mission*

Still not content, Newbigin revised his paper a third time to produce "The Mission of the Triune God."[79] This was very similar to his second draft, except that the study of eschatological passages was extended, especially of Mark's Gospel, to elucidate understanding of the relationship between eschatology and mission. Christ was understood as the centre for history—yet opposition to him and his church, the meager results from preaching the gospel, the immobilization of the church and the secularization of human life were causes for perplexity. Newbigin proposed that only a trinitarian framework for mission enabled an understanding of how Christ was fulfilling his mission through the agency of the church, in spite of the problems and setbacks internal and external to the church.

This was the first draft to be given a wider circulation being distributed to members of the DWME. However, the discussion on Newbigin's drafts subsequent to *One Body* did not generate nearly the same amount of feedback as *One Body* had generated. Newbigin hoped that his draft could serve as a background paper, to stimulate reflection, in preparation for the DWME Consultation in Mexico (1963). He wrote to ascertain whether

77. Ibid., 19. Italics in original.
78. Ibid., 22.
79. Newbigin, May 1962, WCC: 26.11.25.

DWME members thought "the main thrust of the enclosed paper is in the right direction?"—and if so, whether it could be used as a background paper for Mexico.[80] "The paper which I wrote . . . was intended to be a kind of manifesto for the DWME in the years following New Delhi, but Wims [Visser 't Hooft] and others did not like its theology and it therefore had to be relegated to the position of a 'Study Pamphlet.'"[81] The subsequent study booklet was published with the "appalling" title *The Relevance of Trinitarian Doctrine for Today's Mission.*[82]

In the booklet Newbigin reiterated his trinitarian framework as the basis for mission and the central agency of the church: "We are invited to become, through the presence of the Holy Spirit, participants in the Son's loving obedience to the Father. All things have been created that they may be summed up in Christ the Son. . . . The Spirit of God, who is also the Spirit of the Son, is given as the foretaste of that consummation, as the witness to it, and as the guide of the Church on the road towards it."[83] Newbigin's trinitarian framework is to be understood, "not [as] an alternative to be set over against a Christocentric orientation but rather [as] an elaboration and explication of it."[84]

Several years on Newbigin still believed that a fully trinitarian structure was needed to adequately answer the valid points being raised during the 1960s on the question of God's role in the world: "I deeply believe that only a Trinitarian doctrine of Mission can provide this perspective."[85] However, it was not until "nearly twenty years later that . . . I had the opportunity to develop its argument in a full-length book, *The Open*

---

80. Newbigin, draft letter to members of the Division, May 1962, SOAS: 26–11–25/8.

81. Newbigin to Thomas Wieser, Secretary to the North American Working Group, Department of Evangelism, 18/12/1975, WCC: 421.301. Newbigin did not specify the reasons for Visser 't Hooft's disapproval. Martin Conway suggested it may have been more to do with diplomacy than theology. Conway also contested that publication as a "Study Pamphlet" was in any way "downgrading" Newbigin's text; rather it was the normal and "most immediate" way for getting texts of that length into publication. Conway to Laing, email, 06/09/2008. That Visser 't Hooft disapproved of Newbigin's study was not just a private comment to his friend Wieser; Newbigin also went on the record by stating: "Wims disapproved of its theology, and my colleagues in the Division were not sufficiently persuaded to support me." Newbigin, *Unfinished Agenda,* 199.

82. Newbigin, *Trinitarian Doctrine.*

83. Ibid., 12, 78.

84. Goheen, *As the Father,* 119.

85. Newbigin to Wieser, 18/12/1975, WCC: 421.301.

Secret.[86] Even here Newbigin expressed hesitancy, the subtitle of the book being *Sketches for a Missionary Theology*. By 1978 he was at last able to set out "fully and persuasively what he had been trying to bring to bear on the puzzle of integration in the early 1960s."[87] His earlier drafts had been tentative and hesitant, as Newbigin struggled to formulate a theology which he was personally satisfied with and which could be endorsed by his peers in the ecumenical movement. As *Trinitarian Doctrine* had failed to convince key ecumenical leaders, it was thus not used as a preparatory study for the first conference of the DWME. In contrast, *Open Secret* was critically acclaimed.[88] In it Newbigin was much more certain in proposing a trinitarian approach to mission which held together the three aspects of God's work: the "proclamation" of the kingdom, the reign of the Father over all things; the mystery of the "presence" of the kingdom, which the church invites the world to partake of through its union with the Son; and the "prevenience" of the kingdom, through the ministry of the Spirit, the living foretaste of the kingdom.[89] "This threefold way of understanding mission is rooted in the triune being of God himself. If any of these is taken in isolation as the clue to the understanding of mission, distortion follows."[90]

Conclusion

This chapter has charted the progress of Newbigin's theology and sought to show how the debate on integration influenced it. Newbigin prepared various draft papers with which to focus the discussion on integration. He sought to centre discussion more on the theology he saw at the heart of the issue, and less on the distracting organizational matters, which he reasoned, could only be properly discussed subsequent to the theological debate.

86. Newbigin, *Unfinished Agenda*, 199. Lesslie Newbigin, *The Open Secret: Sketches for a Missionary Theology* (Grand Rapids: Eerdmans, 1978).

87. Conway to Laing, email, 06/09/2008.

88. *Trinitarian Doctrine* received only three reviews. In contrast, *Open Secret* had been reviewed at least twenty-six times, even being reviewed twenty years after publication.

89. Newbigin, *Open Secret*, 72. Newbigin's trinitarian basis for mission is made explicit in three chapters: ch. 4, "Proclaiming the Kingdom of the Father: Mission as Faith in Action; ch. 5, "Sharing the Life of the Son: Mission as Love in Action"; and ch. 6, "Bearing the Witness of the Spirit: Mission as Hope in Action."

90. Ibid.

The chapter demonstrates Newbigin's shift from examining the structure to exploring—at first rather tentatively—the substance of mission. In so doing, Newbigin returned to engage with issues which he had been first introduced to by Lehmann and Hoekendijk at Willingen—but, at that time, did not understand nor appreciate their concerns. Although critical of Hoekendijk, Newbigin utilized his theology to bring a critique of the post-Tambaram church-centric model.

The clue that Newbigin discerned to developing an adequate foundation for a theology of mission was that it must be trinitarian.[91] However, in contrast to his confidence in drafting a theology on the structure of mission, and his critique of past models, when Newbigin sought to construct an alternative model, he was much more hesitant.

One Body was the first revision of "Organization of the Church" and was hailed as a manifesto for integration—at least within IMC circles. In preparation for the third assembly of the WCC, which formalized integration and inaugurated the DWME, Newbigin had similar hopes, that his theology on the substance of mission would set the theme for the assembly on the relationship between mission and the church[92] and would then set the course of the DWME for the next decade. Previously, Newbigin had chaired the committee which prepared the theme for the second assembly (Evanston). That experience had taught him how a theme could shape and inspire the assembly and, like ripples in a pond, spread outward to inspire the local member churches. To this end, Newbigin hoped to influence the choice of theme for New Delhi.

But Newbigin's hopes were not realized at New Delhi. The process of revision delayed the production of his final draft. Even the term "tentative" was incorporated into his working title, which looked backwards rather than being inherently substantive.[93] Delayed, Newbigin transferred his hopes for New Delhi to Mexico and the first conference of the DWME in 1963. But Newbigin's personal hesitancy in his theologizing was mirrored by his failure to garner public endorsement. His draft failed to convince WCC leaders, with Visser 't Hooft expressing disapproval, and members of the DWME failing to support Newbigin's draft.

---

91. It can be concluded that Newbigin's trinitarian theology of mission arose as a result of his engagement on the issues raised by integration. He does not attribute any other sources influencing the development of his theology on this issue.

92. Newbigin to Visser 't Hooft, 4/6/1958, BUL: DA29/2/9/4.

93. The first draft for Newbigin's sequel was titled, "First tentative draft of a paper to follow the IMC paper 'One Body, One Gospel, One World.'"

It took nearly twenty years for Newbigin, in *Open Secret*, to reach a trinitarian formulation that he was content with.[94] Even here some think that Newbigin was "belaboring" his insistence on a trinitarian formulation. In *Open Secret*, "the trinitarian chapters seem almost to be forced into the picture."[95] Whilst there may still be some hesitancy in *Open Secret*, in his subsequent writing Newbigin is both certain and categorical on the necessity of a trinitarian understanding of mission. For example, in *Gospel in a Pluralist Society*, he wrote that "the mission of the Church is to be understood, *can only be rightly understood*, in terms of the trinitarian model."[96] Later, he elaborates:

> It seems to me to be of the greatest importance to insist that mission is not first of all an action of ours. It is an action of God, the triune God—of God the Father who is ceaselessly at work in all creation . . . of God the Son who has become part of this created history in the incarnation; and of God the Holy Spirit who is given as a foretaste of the end to empower and teach the Church. . . . Before we speak about our role . . . in mission, we need to have firmly in the centre of our thinking this action of God. This is the primal reality in mission; the rest is derivative.[97]

Primacy of God's action in mission modified the understanding of the agency of the church: "The Church is not so much the agent of the mission as the locus of mission."[98] Newbigin's engagement in the issues related to the integration of the two councils, and his efforts to provide a theological framework for integration, directly contributed to the development of Newbigin's trinitarian mission theology. Although the seeds of Willingen took many years to germinate and yield fruit.

A major new insight, introduced at Willingen, was to speak of "God's work in the secular world," that is, beyond the boundaries of the church. To discern the work of the Father in the world gave impetus to enlarge the focus of mission beyond that of the Son and his commission and a merely christological understanding of mission. The impact of secularization upon mission was to occupy Newbigin's thinking immediately after

94. Newbigin, *Unfinished Agenda*, 199.

95. Hunsberger, *Witness*, 241–42.

96. Lesslie Newbigin, *The Gospel in a Pluralist Society* (Geneva: WCC, 1989) 118. Emphasis added.

97. Ibid., 134–35.

98. Ibid., 119.

integration, in particular the quest for adequate missionary structures in secular society. This is the topic of chapter 8.

8

Integration and Secularization

The Quest for Missionary Structures

INTEGRATION OF THE IMC with WCC was always perceived to mean more than the administrative union of two world councils. Their international union was understood symbolically as a sign declaring that "the church is the mission." A recovery in the relationship between mission and the church implied that the ecclesiology before was defective, an incomplete or distorted understanding of the church.

Integration took place at a time when the process of secularization was reaching its zenith. "The collapse of colonialism, global westernization, resurgent secularism, and a revolutionary optimism provided a volatile mix that made . . . [the 1960s] 'volcanic.'"[1] The issue of secularization was not new having first been raised by J. H. Oldham at the 1928 Jerusalem conference of the IMC.[2] At Jerusalem the "questions were not radical enough and were not followed up."[3] At the Tambaram conference (1938) the IMC was distracted from the issue of secularism by the rise of totalitarian ideologies in Europe.[4] By 1952, at the Willingen conference, the

1. Goheen, *As the Father*, 66. For a good introduction to the changing context of ecumenism, see M. E. Marty, "The Global Context of Ecumenism 1968–2000," in *A History of the Ecumenical Movement*, vol. 3, *1968–2000*, ed. John H. Y. Briggs, Mercy Amba Oduyoye, and Georges Tsestis (Geneva: World Council of Churches, 2004).

2. Visser 't Hooft, *Memoirs*, 39.

3. Lesslie Newbigin, "Reflections on the History of Missions (Paper Prepared in Anticipation of San Antonio 1989)," in *A Word in Season*, ed. Eleanor Jackson (Grand Rapids: Eerdmans, 1994) 139.

4. Ibid., 134.

challenge was given by the American report "to break out of the Church-centered missiology of Tambaram and to speak of God's work outside the boundaries of the Church."[5] But it would be another decade before the world councils were ready to fully engage with secularism.

Issues raised by secularization affected the outcome of integration and raised key questions which the integrated council needed to grapple with. One of the perceived outcomes of secularization was the formation, for the first time, of a unified world civilization. As a fitting response to this integration sought to establish a "worldwide Christian fellowship committed to the task of mission to the whole world."[6] Traditionally missions had a "directedness" from the West. With a recovery in missionary ecclesiology came the related recognition that "the home base is everywhere."[7] Wherever the church is, it is in the "mission field," and must therefore be orientated towards the world.[8]

These concerns were explicitly addressed at the first conference of the DWME at Mexico (1963), which took as its theme, "mission in six continents." In addressing mission to the West the issues of secularism dominated the proceedings.[9] These issues were not limited to the West, but were of global importance and needed to be faced by the WCC. Secularization brought a critique to structures inherited from Christendom which failed to express the missionary nature of the church. In particular, the parochial organization of the church and the form of ministry were challenged.

This chapter begins by examining Newbigin's own critique of the structure of the church and form of ministry. This critique emerged not from his analysis of Western ecclesiology, but from Newbigin's experience as a missionary in South India. Reflecting on this Newbigin called for "bold experiment" in the form of ministry. Obvious parallels emerge between Newbigin's critique and that raised by secularization.

As an integrated council, the WCC responded to the issues raised by secularization. The chapter details how these issues were forcefully introduced to the agenda (at Strasbourg in 1960) and then, in subsequent programs, examined. The New Delhi assembly recognized the inherent problems with the traditional structure of the local congregation and

---

5. Ibid., 135.

6. Newbigin, "Summons to Mission," 186.

7. Newbigin, *One Body*, 25, 27.

8. Newbigin, "Mission to Six Continents," 193.

9. Ibid., 193–94.

inaugurated a program, "The Study of the Missionary Structure of the Congregation" (MSC), to address these issues, the findings being presented at the next assembly (Uppsala, 1968). Newbigin interpreted this as being a critical study of the form of the church, which would give "spiritual substance" to integration. The question that Newbigin repeatedly stressed was how abstract theological convictions could be properly made concrete and expressed.[10] Essentially it was at the level of the local congregation that integration of mission and church must be made real.

At the outset of this chapter it is important to make the distinction between "secularism" and "secularization." Newbigin interpreted the first as a "closed ideology, a final denial of God," "which in principle denies the existence or the significance of realities other than those which can be measured by the methods of natural science"; whilst the latter he interpreted to be an "opened-ended historical process" which offers the "possibilities both of new freedom and new slavery."[11] In Newbigin's estimation, aspects of secularization were positive; "it may be seen as the increasing assertion of the competence of human science and technics [*sic*] to handle human problems of every kind." But there were also negative aspects; secularization "is the withdrawal of areas of life and activity from the control of organized religious bodies, and the withdrawal of areas of thought from the control of what are believed to be revealed religious truths."[12]

Newbigin's Induction to Secular Issues

At Willingen, Newbigin had acknowledged that he did not comprehend the issues raised by Hoekendijk and Lehmann.[13] His initial exploration of secularism came as the result of a night flight in 1957 from Bombay to Rome. Newbigin was due to present a lecture at Bossey about the mission of the church in the contemporary world. Being unprepared, Newbigin spent the entire flight studying his Greek New Testament for occurrences of "the world." That night of study marked a significant shift in Newbigin's thinking: "My thoughts for the past decade had been centred in the

---

10. Ibid., 193.

11. Newbigin, "Mexico CWME Reflecting upon this meeting," 1964, BUL: DA29/5/3/27, 1. Cf. Newbigin, *Honest Religion*, 8.

12. Newbigin, *Honest Religion*, 8.

13. Newbigin, *Unfinished Agenda*, 153.

Church. This fresh exposure to the word of God set me thinking about the work of God in the world outside the Church."[14]

The thesis that Newbigin presented at Bossey was that "what we are witnessing is the process by which more and more of the human race is being gathered up into that history whose centre is the Cross and whose end is the final judgment and mercy of God."[15] By this Newbigin meant "the total shift from a cyclical to a linear way of understanding history, brought about by the impact of 'development.'"[16] The common goal and purpose set by "development" resulted, at least in Newbigin's interpretation, in "drawing together of all peoples into an irreversible movement in terms of the apocalyptic teaching of the New Testament."[17] Newbigin saw the force of secularization coalescing discreet histories into a single unified history, in which all civilizations now faced a common terminus: "in terms of the fact that world history is in the grip of Christ, is being propelled by him towards its ultimate issues."[18] Newbigin's lecture at Bossey was the catalyst for one delegate to develop a thesis on *Christianity in World History*,[19] in which secularization had united sacred with secular history: "The technological revolution is the evident and inescapable form in which the whole world is now confronted with the most recent phase of Christian history. In and through this form Christian history becomes world history."[20]

Although Newbigin embraced aspects of secularization in his theology from the outset of his "flirtation"[21] he was not uncritical of it.[22] Rather, secularization offered a distortion of Christianity which had "transmuted the hope of God's kingdom transcending history into the hope of a new

---

14. Ibid., 152–53.

15. Newbigin, "Gathering Up," 82.

16. Newbigin, *Unfinished Agenda*, 153.

17. Newbigin, "Gathering Up," 83.

18. Ibid., 82.

19. A. T. van Leeuwen, *Christianity in World History: The Meeting of the Faiths of East and West* (New York: Scribner, 1964). Van Leeuwen acknowledged inspiration from Newbigin and the need to address the question Newbigin raised. Van Leeuwen, *World History*, 16–17. With hindsight Newbigin conceded that he had been overly impressed by van Leeuwen's thesis. Newbigin, *Unfinished Agenda*, 254.

20. Van Leeuwen, *World History*, 408. Cf. Newbigin's adoption of van Leeuwen's thesis: "secularization was seen as the fruit of the gospel, and the advance of Western secular ideas into the old ontocratic societies was hailed as the contemporary form of the Christian mission." Newbigin, "History of Missions," 139; Newbigin, *Unfinished Agenda*, 153; Newbigin, "Mexico CWME," 2.

21. A term used by Wainwright, *Newbigin*, 341–54.

22. This will be considered in detail in ch. 9.

order within history to be achieved by man's progressive mastery of nature and of his own affairs." At the time of its global supremacy, Newbigin was aware of secularization's own bankruptcy. "[The] [f]ailure of secular faith [is] exposed by [the] totalitarianism of fascism and communism . . . by the outworking of its own inner falsity—it stands self-condemned in the lands of its origin."[23]

History was interpreted as converging towards a single, final issue: "Christ or Antichrist, the true Saviour of the world, or the bogus saviours."[24] In this historical process, Newbigin anticipated that "it will surely become more and more clear that it is in the Name of Christ alone that we can face the world, and that all those other names which we have added to the one Name . . . will drop into a secondary place."[25] "A universal Gospel demands as its sign and instrument a universal fellowship." The integration of the IMC with the WCC was seen as part of the "inner logic" of this movement, "one common organ for our growing fellowship as a worldwide Christian fellowship committed to the task of mission to the whole world."[26] Integration of mission with church would be symbolized at the international level by the joining of the IMC with the WCC. But, most critically, how was this relationship to be expressed at the level of the local congregation? Newbigin's experience and analysis of Protestant missions enabled him to proffer suggestions.

The Call for "Bold Experiment" in the Form of Ministry

In 1959, at the inaugural conference of the East Asia Christian Conference (EACC), in Kuala Lumpur, Newbigin's friend D. T. Niles instituted the John R. Mott memorial lectures and invited Newbigin to give two inaugural addresses.[27] In his presentations, Newbigin "argued for a style of mission on the lines sketched by Roland Allen and called for a radical reordering of the pattern of Church and ministry as the only way out of the dilemma. It was these ideas which I hoped to develop later in the WCC study on

23. Newbigin, "Summons to Mission," 183. Here Newbigin underestimated the religious (pagan) influences on Nazism.

24. Ibid., 185.

25. Ibid., 186.

26. Ibid.

27. Lesslie Newbigin, "The Pattern of Partnership," and "The Work of the Holy Spirit in the Life of the Asian Churches," in *A Decisive Hour for the Christian World Mission*, ed. N. Goodall and Lesslie Newbigin (London: SCM, 1960).

'The Missionary Structure of the Congregation.'"[28] As we shall see later, the process of secularization enabled Newbigin to critique the structure of the congregation and ministry inherited from Christendom. In these lectures, Newbigin raised similar issues, but in this instance he does so from a different angle—from his observation and experience of Protestant mission. Newbigin was critical of the form the "younger church" was taking as a consequence of the application of defective missiology, which was the consequence of the exportation of an inadequate Western ecclesiology.

In his lecture "The Pattern of Partnership," Newbigin examined the patterns and structures which colonial mission had created which "has been characterized by paternalism on the one hand, and by a wrong kind of dependence on the other." From his knowledge of the Indian church, Newbigin was alarmed that indigenous missionary organizations were also emulating those same patterns, which he thought to be highly defective. Newbigin maintained that no advance in the task of world evangelization would be possible "unless we are willing to make a radical break with the traditional pattern of missionary operations."[29]

This scenario contrasted with his understanding of St. Paul's methods of church planting, in which churches, free of dependency, were established, which were themselves self-propagating. The crucial difference between colonial patterns and those of St. Paul were, in Newbigin's understanding, "fundamentally a matter of our belief in the reality of the Holy Spirit, a belief which radically determines our understanding of what we are doing when we bring the Gospel to another people."[30] Newbigin's thinking here demonstrated dependency upon Roland Allen, and later he recalled, in a conversation with Wilbert Shenk, how he had sought to apply Allen's thesis: "Newbigin told me with some force 'I tried Rolland Allen's theories, *and they work* ."[31]

Newbigin's solution to remedy the problem was to insist that colonial patterns should be jettisoned on entering a post-colonial age. The inspiration for new patterns should come from the early church: "the pattern of the pre-Constantinian Church . . . is the proper pattern for this

---

28. Newbigin, *Unfinished Agenda*, 166. Newbigin had clear ideas of how he thought the study should proceed. However, Newbigin was not directly involved in this study, and it took a quite different direction from that which he had hoped.

29. E.g., that of creating dependency upon a paid worker placed by the missions. Newbigin, "The Pattern of Partnership," 40.

30. Ibid., 39.

31. Shenk, interview with Laing, 1/11/2006.

post-Constantinian era which we have now entered."[32] A key feature was the abandoning of bilateral relationships between "younger" and "older" churches" for the establishment of multilateral relationships which evidenced mutuality.

In his second lecture, "The Work of the Holy Spirit in the Life of the Asian Churches," Newbigin elaborated on the problem created by colonial patterns of mission. Reliance upon a professional agency controlled and paid by the mission has meant that the "basic pattern was not congregational but organizational," with the result that "the reality of the congregation as the basic unit of Christian existence . . . has not been really grasped. The congregation has been secondary, the agency primary."[33] This had the result of creating dependency of the "out-station" upon the "headquarters," with the consequence that such establishments were not self-propagating, rather a new congregation was viewed as "a liability and not an asset," and a major evangelistic opening was viewed as "a major financial disaster."[34]

Crucial to perpetuating colonial patterns, and therefore crucial for changing them, was the organization of the church around a paid, trained, full-time professional minister. Newbigin argued that this had sociological rather than theological origins. This pattern had arisen out of the atypical milieu of Christendom,[35] but had been assumed as normative, and thus the pattern for churches established by the Protestant missionary movement. Newbigin appealed for "bold experiment" in the form of ministry which would allow for greater flexibility: "I am sure that it is *not* part of the unchanging form of the Church that its ministry must be a professional class."[36]

The restoration of the relationship between mission and church was for Newbigin at the heart of integration. The most important arena for the expression of this relationship was not internationally, but at the level of the local congregation. To this end, Newbigin understood the role of the minister, in leading and shaping congregational life to be decisive. This was a topic Newbigin had previously considered from his Indian

32. Newbigin, "Pattern of Partnership," 40.

33. Lesslie Newbigin, "The Work of the Holy Spirit in the Life of the Asian Churches," in *A Decisive Hour for the Christian World Mission*, ed. N. Goodall and Lesslie Newbigin, 26.

34. Ibid., 27.

35. Newbigin overuses the term "Christendom" and is at times imprecise in his usage. For a discussion by Newbigin on "Christendom," see Newbigin, *Other Side of 1984: Questions for the Churches*, 32–37.

36. Newbigin, "Holy Spirit," 30. Italics in original.

experience[37]—and a topic he was soon able to raise with the Central Committee of the WCC. Towards the end of his life he continued to emphases the need for ministerial training to facilitate the growth of missionary congregations rather than mere maintenance: "The task of ministry is to lead the congregation as a whole in a mission to the community as a whole, to claim its whole public life, as well as the personal lives of all its people, for God's rule."[38]

A Tent Making Ministry

The concerns that Newbigin had highlighted in 1959 he was able to bring before the Central Committee of the WCC in 1962. At the Paris meetings he presented a report titled "A tent making ministry: towards a more flexible form of ministry."[39] This report was based upon the comment and criticism generated in response to an earlier study paper by Newbigin, "The Pattern of Ministry in a Missionary Church."[40] Newbigin began this paper by recalling how the IMC Willingen conference of 1952, advised that study should be made for developing a part-time ordained ministry. A decade on Newbigin presented his personal paper as a "starting point" for that study. Newbigin challenged the axioms of ordained ministry: that it must be a paid, full-time, professional service; and that it required a foundational theological education. These axioms, Newbigin declared, were "not rooted in a theological doctrine of Church and Ministry"; rather they had "sociological rather than theological roots," arising out of the context of Christendom when economic, and educational factors determined the pattern of ministry.[41] Returning to themes from his 1959 lectures, Newbigin was critical of the existing missionary pattern, a legacy of the nineteenth century, because "it has the effect of destroying . . . the proper character of a local congregation," creating instead "out-stations" which were dependent on a remote headquarters rather than the proper dependency upon the Holy Spirit.[42]

---

37. E.g., Newbigin, "The Ministry of the Church—Ordained and Unordained, Paid and Unpaid," March 1953, WCC: 29.19.07/88.

38. Newbigin, *Pluralist Society*, 238.

39. DWME Report, Appendix IX, CCM, 1962, 96–103.

40. Newbigin, 1961, WCC: 26.32.20.

41. Ibid., sections 2–3.

42. Ibid., section 4.

Newbigin concluded the report with a plea for action to reach the unreached with the gospel: "one has to conclude that a recovery of missionary mobility is greatly needed. . . . But we believe that the question must be asked whether this mobility can be recovered while the highly institutionalized and professionalized pattern of the ministry which has become traditional retains its present almost total dominance."[43] Newbigin was proposing to radically change the form of ministry which had endured and had been canonized by Christendom, to thus enable the church to be missionary.

Newbigin's report, however, received a rather muted response from the Central Committee. In the discussion on the report, Newbigin reiterated his plea for action; as the subject had been on the agenda of the IMC since 1952, action was urgent: "The point of integration was a point at which action might begin on some of the many ideas which had not so far been put into effect."[44] However, Russell Chandran found nothing very fresh in the statement of the DWME Committee which expressed the tasks of the division in terms of what had become common in recent years. In contradiction of Newbigin's plea, the Chairman of the Central Committee reminded the meeting that no action was demanded at the present time. On receiving the report, the Committee resolved only that the matter be discussed with member churches as may be appropriate.[45] On this occasion integration did not provide the platform for a radical review of church structures. These concerns would resurface later in the study of the Missionary Structure of the Congregation.

Although Newbigin's critique had been directed against Protestant missionary methods, with secular issues coming to the fore in the 1960s, this afforded opportunity for a similar critique of Western ecclesiology, this was first presented, with considerable vigor, at a conference in Strasbourg in 1960.

The Advent of the Secular

Strasbourg 1960

The World Student Christian Federation Conference on "The Life and Mission of the Church," which was held in Strasbourg in 1960, marked

---

43. DWME Report, CCM, 1962, 103.

44. CCM, 1962, 14.

45. Ibid., 14, 20.

the coming of age of secular missiology. The conference had been planned with two objectives: "the first was to make clear to the present student generation that by nature the Church is mission; the second was to look at the forms this mission should take at the present moment in world history. Many of us were surprised to discover at Strasbourg that the first required little attention."[46] At the conference the consensus on *missio Dei* was not questioned; "what was attacked was its imprisonment in the institutions of the Church."[47] Newbigin recorded that "there is a quite shattering degree of unanimity that the traditional missionary pattern cannot provide the pattern of obedience for our day," the harshest criticism coming from the West.[48] Newbigin's address at Strasbourg, titled "God so loved the world," was a traditional message which centered on the finality of the cross in history which brings both judgment and salvation.[49]

But it was Hoekendijk who captured the zeitgeist and won the approval of the delegates. At Willingen, Hoekendijk had tried, and failed, to dislodge the prevalent church-centric missiology; his audience at Strasbourg was more responsive to his thesis. Hoekendijk began his address by stating that "in God's plan of redemption Christ and the world are indissolubly bound together as messianic correlates. The coming of Jesus Christ in the flesh is a 'secular' event: an event in the world and for the world."[50] "And consequently this secular event and what was invited by it, the thing we usually call Christianity, *cannot be anything else, but a secular movement*, a movement in the world and for the world. It will always be a dangerous perversion of the truth to make Christianity into some sort of religion."[51]

However, as a consequence of developments within Western Christianity, and particularly the parochial system, the church had become increasingly isolated from, and antagonistic towards, the world.[52] The church had rejected its relationship with the world. Instead, the church's negative response to modernity had intensified its alienation from the

---

46. P. Maury, "Christ's Ministry to the World and Our Calling: Strasbourg 1960," *Student World* 54:1–2 (1961) 4.

47. Newbigin, "Recent Thinking," 260.

48. Newbigin cited by Niles, *Upon the Earth*, 29; Maury, "Strasbourg," 3.

49. Newbigin, "God so loved the world," Strasbourg 1960, unpublished notes, WCC Archives.

50. Hoekendijk, "Christ and the World in the Modern Age," Strasbourg, 1960, unpublished notes, WCC Archives, 1.

51. Hoekendijk, "Modern Age," 75. Emphasis added.

52. Hoekendijk, "Strasbourg," unpublished notes, 1.

modern world. In Hoekendijk's estimation, the parish church was beyond redemption: "it is completely inadequate and unfit to give expression to the life of a community which believes that Christ and this modern world are bound together, belong together."[53] To overcome this hurdle, and thus "make full identification with man in the modern world possible," Hoekendijk advocated that it was necessary "to move out of the traditional church structures in open, mobile, flexible groups"; to "desacralize" the church; and to "dereligionize" Christianity.[54] "*Christianity is a secular movement*, and this is basic for an understanding of it. We have no business to make it a religion again. The Christian is simply a man who is in the process of being restored to normal human manhood." [55] "The 'secular decade' had arrived."[56] Concepts from secularization were first embraced by students at Strasbourg but soon gained currency within the WCC. Hoekendijk's success at Strasbourg marked a decisive shift of focus from the church to the world—a shift which would dominate missiological reflection throughout the 1960s.[57]

New Delhi 1961

A year after the Strasbourg conference, at the third assembly of the WCC, the integration of the IMC with the WCC was ratified. Here Newbigin could raise concerns about the local congregation and the impact secularization was having upon its contemporary relevance. The local congregation located in the undifferentiated village remained an adequate form of the church, but its relevance was challenged by the differentiation of society that secularization brought. It was recognized that other effective units of congregation life were required. At the New Delhi assembly Newbigin succeeded in having a statement on unity endorsed. One particular paragraph, which Newbigin drafted, was particularly important because of its emphasis on the locality of the congregation, and the understanding of "place," which was being modified by the demands of secularization. Newbigin's statement read: "We believe that the unity which is both God's

53. Hoekendijk, "Modern Age," 81.

54. Hoekendijk, "Strasbourg," unpublished notes, 2.

55. Hoekendijk, "Modern Age," 81–82. Emphasis added. Cf. Newbigin, "Recent Thinking," 261. This is reminiscent of Bonhoeffer: D. Bonhoeffer and E. Bethge, eds., *Letters and Papers from Prison* (London: SCM, 1971).

56. Newbigin, *Unfinished Agenda*, 176.

57. Bassham, *Mission Theology*, 47.

will and his gift to his Church is being made visible as *all in each place* who are . . . reaching out in witness and service to all and who at the same time are united *with the whole Christian fellowship in all places and all ages* in such wise that ministry and members are accepted by all, and that all can act and speak together as occasion requires for the tasks to which God calls his people."[58]

The statement combined local with universal aspects of unity, although at New Delhi the emphasis was on local unity. At the Uppsala assembly (1968), the emphasis shifted to the universal.[59] Of course, the local is related to the universal and neither can be pursued to the neglect of the other: "The true catholicity of the Church, rooted in the being of the Triune God, is such that neither does universality cancel the particularity of each 'place,' nor does locality deny universality."[60]

In understanding how "place" was defined, the New Delhi report acknowledged the primary sense of local neighborhood, but also acknowledged that the "modern situation" required a broadening of definition; "place" thus also referred to different segments of society, such as the school, factory and office.[61] Newbigin further elaborated on how "place" was to be understood: "There is the world of work in industry or a profession, the world of kinship and a shared language, the world of shared political or ideological commitment and many others."[62] Drawing upon examples from church history, Newbigin demonstrated that although the "proper form of the congregation" had usually been determined by geographic location, it had not been exclusively so. Due to the exigencies of circumstances, the form of the church had at times also been determined by language, or in relation to a particular sector of society such as college chaplaincies. More questionable had been the organization of the church

---

58. WCC, *New Delhi Report*, 116. Emphasis added. Concerning this statement, Dr. Lukas Vischer recalled: "[It] is largely due to his [Newbigin's] initiative . . . The New Delhi statement had an enormous impact throughout my years in Faith and Order. Lesslie continued to emphasize that the unity of the local church was the real test of unity." Lukas Vischer to Wainwright, letter, 16/1/1998. Wainwright details the history of this paragraph, demonstrating that it was authored by Newbigin. Wainwright, *Newbigin*, 113, 421 n 60.

59. Lesslie Newbigin, "What Is a 'Local Church Truly United'?" in *In Each Place: Towards a Fellowship of Local Churches Truly United*, ed. Lesslie Newbigin et al. (Geneva: WCC Publications, 1977) 116.

60. Ibid., 120.

61. WCC, *New Delhi Report*, 118.

62. Newbigin, "Local Church," 119.

on ethnic basis, or according to the criteria of wealth and poverty, or else on the basis of differing confessional, liturgical, and spiritual traditions.[63]

Mexico 1963

The ability of the issue of secularization to dominate the agenda was evident in the planning and execution of the first DWME conference in Mexico in 1963. Newbigin, as general secretary, responsible for organizing the conference recorded that, "At the centre of its work was the effort to understand the process of secularisation from a biblical point of view."[64]

As preparatory material for the conference, Newbigin desired to revise his booklet *One Body*. In his second revision, Newbigin identified a fundamental question and related danger. Recognizing that in the post-colonial period secular processes were no longer "going our way" for missions, Newbigin asked, "[what] is . . . the relationship between what God is doing through the mission of His Church, and what He is doing in the totality of the affairs of men?"[65] The danger to be avoided was that of taking either extreme position, of conflating and thus equating God's will with historical forces, or else of maintaining " purely 'church-centric' understanding of the missionary task [which] has often caused us to take a wholly unbiblical view of the world."[66]

Through the process of secularization the issue of the structure of the congregation was again raised. "Within a generally christianised society, the local congregation provided the place where one withdrew for the specifically religious activities of worship, prayer and teaching. . . . The process of secularisation threatens it with the fate of becoming completely irrelevant."[67] Here Newbigin echoed the earlier sentiments of Hoekendijk in suggesting that the inherited parish model was no longer relevant for the city. As an alternative, Newbigin proposed "small cells" meeting in apartments, focusing on a particular problem, and out of which, it was anticipated, a worshipping congregation would emerge—citing his experience of living in Geneva.

Central to the form a congregation took was again the question of the ministry; a "rethinking of the sociological pattern of the ministry" would

63. Ibid., 120.
64. Newbigin, "Mexico CWME," 2.
65. Newbigin, "Second Draft," 1962, WCC: 421.050, 10.
66. Newbigin, "Second Draft," 14
67. Newbigin, "Mexico CWME," 2.

challenge the established norm of the church being centered around a paid professional. Newbigin believed this model to be anachronistic. Instead, drawing upon his experimentation in India, Newbigin proposed alternative forms of ministry, developing the role of the laity, which was akin to the practice of early Christianity.[68]

Uppsala 1968

In 1965 Newbigin left his job as director of the DWME to return to India, to take up a bishopric. In contrast to his earlier more rural ministry, in the large city of Madras he now sought to apply some the insights from his reflections on secularization: "Looking back in 1965 upon my earlier ministries in Kanchi and Madurai I felt that I had been too narrowly ecclesiastical in my concerns, and I resolved that I would challenge the strong churches of Madras City to think less of their own growth and welfare and more of God's purpose for the whole of the vast and growing city."[69] When Newbigin came to the fourth assembly of the WCC at Uppsala in 1968 he was no longer directly involved with the WCC but immersed with the issues of his bishopric in Madras.[70]

In many ways the fourth assembly marked the high point of the secular process, reflecting "the prevailing conviction that mission is concerned with the doing of God's will in the secular world."[71] Mission was "'for God's people everywhere' (including those already members of the churches)"[72] and was to be evaluated using the following criteria: "Do they place the church alongside the poor, the defenceless, the abused, the forgotten, the bored? Do they allow Christians to enter the concerns of others to accept their issues and their structures as vehicles of involvement? Are they the best situations for discerning with other men the signs of the times, and for moving with history towards the coming of the new humanity?"[73]

---

68. Ibid., 3.

69. Newbigin, *Unfinished Agenda*, 215.

70. An influence on Newbigin's thinking at this time may have been his reading of Herbert Marcuse. Murdoch Mackenzie, who worked with Newbigin in Madras, recalled that in 1968 Newbigin read Marcuse three times. Mackenzie, email to Laing, 23/5/2009. Mackenzie did not specify which work by Marcuse Newbigin had read.

71. Newbigin, "Recent Thinking," 262.

72. Ibid.

73. WCC, *The Uppsala Report, 1968: Official Report of the Fourth Assembly of the WCC, Uppsala July 4–20, 1968* (Geneva: WCC, 1968) 32.

At Uppsala mission was defined as genuine "humanization," which marked a shift away from the place traditionally held by conversion. Newbigin questioned how sustainable this model of mission would be for the future—now that development was being discredited as an extension of Western imperialism.[74]

At a personal level Newbigin found the Uppsala assembly a "shattering experience"; the report "seemed to reduce mission to nothing but a desperate struggle to solve insoluble problems. Obviously the Church itself was the major problem, and there was no enthusiasm for enlarging the membership of this dubious institution."[75]

Wainwright interprets Uppsala as "probably" sealing Newbigin's "disillusionment with secularizing theology."[76] Newbigin's response to Uppsala was more nuanced than a categorical renunciation. Instead, Newbigin recognized aspects of truth within "secular theology" and sought to retain their emphasis whilst still maintaining a critique of other aspects.[77]

By Uppsala Newbigin recognized that a new major "schism"—which was as serious as the schisms dividing the early church—had polarized the ecumenical movement between those who understood discipleship primarily "as the call to manifest the reign of God in the secular life of the nations, and those who see it primarily in terms of the offer of the gift of salvation to all men within the redeemed community."[78] The proof of tension between these two poles was the evidence that Christians have constantly capitulated to one or other extreme, from where they caricatured the other. This resulted in "social radicalism" becoming "divorced from the love of God"; or the other extreme of encouraging "complacent pietism." The difficult but only correct path was to avoid polarization and sustain the tension between both, as Newbigin maintained, both views

74. Newbigin, "The Congregation as a Missionary Agency," prepared for the study booklet to commemorate the 100th anniversary of the Church of Sweden Mission, BUL: DA29/4/3/12, 3. For details, see covering letter, Carl F. Hallencretuz to Newbigin, 20/6/1972, BUL: DA29/4/3/11.

75. Newbigin, *Unfinished Agenda*, 232.

76. Wainwright, *Newbigin*, 353.

77. This is discussed more fully in ch. 9.

78. Newbigin, "The Congregation," 4. Uppsala was also interpreted as marking a shift from the christo-centric universalism which had developed whilst Visser 't Hooft was general secretary, to a trinitarian model. K. Raiser, *Ecumenism in Transition: A Paradigm Shift in the Ecumenical Movement?* (Geneva: WCC Publications, 1991). Raiser's book was perceived to be his manifesto for his leadership as general secretary of the WCC in a way similar to how Newbigin's book *One Body* had served as a personal "manifesto" for integration. Raiser was general secretary from 1992 to 2004.

had biblical validation: "The Church is to be, therefore, *both* a task-force committed to the doing of God's will in the life of the secular world; *and* a family of those who know that they are God's dear children . . . It is of the very essence of the matter that the church is both these things, and if they are separated or set against each other, the Gospel has been denied."[79] How could this tension be creatively maintained in the church? This was the real test of integration. To address the question of the structure of the congregation for a secularized society, the WCC undertook a major study.

The Study of the Missionary Structure of the Congregation

The Study of the Missionary Structure of the Congregation (MSC) was a program which developed in the WCC Department on Studies in Evangelism. Newbigin hoped that this study would address many of the issues he had raised concerning the structure of the congregation and the form of ministry. The study was initiated by Hans Jochen Margull, the German secretary of the department.[80] At the New Delhi Assembly, the Central Committee was "convinced that one of the main hindrances in the pursuit of the evangelistic calling of the Church lies in the traditional structure of the local congregation."[81] As a consequence, the study was formalized, when the Central Committee asked "the Assembly to authorize the Department on Studies in Evangelism to carry out in the years between this [New Delhi] and the next Assembly a comprehensive study into the problems confronting the congregation in its evangelistic task. The title of this study should be 'The Missionary Structure of the Congregation.'"[82]

The issue of secularization was to dominate the MSC. At New Delhi the Report on "Witness" contained a section on "Reshaping the Witnessing Community."[83] At the outset of the MSC's inauguration it was acknowledged that "the secular causes," which made people impervious to preaching, must be taken seriously.[84] Rather than think of the church in conventional terms as the gathered congregation, the report proposed

---

79. Newbigin, "Congregation," 4–5. Italics in original. Evangelical responses to changes in the WCC's missiology will be considered in ch. 10.

80. Martin Conway, email to Laing, 06/09/2008.

81. WCC, *New Delhi Report*, 189.

82. Ibid., 189–90.

83. Ibid., 85–90.

84. Ibid., 86.

an alternative model, as "the laity scattered abroad in every department of daily life."[85] In each segment of society, the church should establish "cells," with the ordained ministry recovering its function as a "travelling apostolate." To avoid fragmentation the ministry would serve as a focus of unity, and the gathered congregation would be a "'congregation of congregations,' witnessing to the reality of the whole Church."[86]

It was originally envisaged that the study would be worldwide in scope,[87] but what transpired was limited to a European (including Eastern Europe) and a North American group. The rationale was that in these regions were the churches which most needed to learn about evangelism, whereas the non-Western churches were already active in evangelism.[88] Both groups of the MSC met several times with findings being disseminated to provoke further discussion.[89] The methodology of the two groups differed. The European group engaged in a "more traditional theological examination," whereas the North American group decided to "go into the field," and then theologize on the basis of their experience.[90] Charles West recalled the negative response by American churches to suggestions from the MSC that congregations be restructured to be "not only suburban but also urban," that is, that they would not be geographically centered in one or the other place, but stretch to them both: "This concept was thoroughly rejected by American Churches."[91]

The interim report acknowledged that "our service of Christ . . . is not to be confined to the ecclesiastical structures [as] the Lord is active *extra muros ecclesiae*"; and that the process of secularization should be given "a positive theological evaluation." Rather than emphasize discontinuity between the church and the world—as a church-centric missiology favored—the report stated that "the Church is a segment of the world and cannot be separated from it."[92] Hoekendijk sequentially influenced both

85. Ibid., 88–89.

86. Ibid., 89–90.

87. Ibid., 190–91.

88. Conway was a member of the European group from its beginning in 1962. Conway, interview with Laing, 17/8/2008.

89. For details of the meetings of the respective groups, see WCC, *Church for Others*, 3, 95–126. For interim publication details, see WCC, *1968 Central Committee Report*, 67.

90. "The Study on the Missionary Structure of the Congregation Report," in WCC, *1968 Central Committee Report*, 68.

91. Charles West, interview with Laing, 15/9/2008.

92. In the interim report, discontinuity was also acknowledged, but the report was

groups, as he moved from involvement with the European group to then join the North American group, providing continuity and helping to unify findings.[93] West opined that in the MSC, Hoekendijk had "radicalised his tendencies" and was "less compromising" than before.[94]

The Church for Others

The North American and the Western European working groups' reports were published jointly in 1967 in preparation for the Uppsala assembly. The goal of mission was identified as "shalom" by the European group and as "humanization" by the North Americans.[95] This placed the world at the centre of God's activity, the ordering of: God → world → shalom (or humanization) replacing the church-centric ordering of: God → church → world.[96] Thus, "[t]he world provides the agenda."[97]

Rather than be concerned "about increasing its own membership," the church was requested to participate in God's mission in the world: "If mission is basically understood as God working out his purpose for his creation, the church does not have a separate mission of its own. It is called to participate in God's mission."[98] "Participation in God's mission is entering into partnership with God in history, because our knowledge of God in Christ compels us to affirm that God is working out his purpose in the midst of the world and its historical processes."[99] Mission was being done irrespective of the church; the church was therefore summoned to "be where the action is." As the church aligned itself and participated in the various movements for humanization, "the church by what it is and does becomes part of [the gospel] proclamation."[100] This participation was a critical process for the church, in which the relevance

---

unclear as to its nature. T. Wieser, ed., *Planning for Mission: Working Papers on the New Quest for Missionary Communities* (London: Epworth, 1966) 7, 9.

93. His influence may have encouraged the publication of the two reports together as a united report; Conway, email, 06/09/2008.

94. West, interview, 15/9/2008.

95. WCC, *Church for Others*, 15, 77–78.

96. Ibid., 16–17. Although this reordering was not unanimously accepted within the MSC; Wieser, ed., *Planning for Mission*, 8.

97. WCC, *Church for Others*, 20.

98. Ibid., 19, 75.

99. Ibid., 14.

100. Ibid., 72–75.

of various forms of the church's mission would be appraised. Participation must be undertaken with the "readiness to change and [even] to disband at the right time."[101]

The combined report was adopted by the assembly at Uppsala.[102] The discussion it provoked was the most heated of the entire assembly, receiving the most attention of the six reports.[103] One of the salient points discussed at Uppsala was the report's critique of "the parish system as a hindrance to the missionary task of the Church." This was due to "morphological fundamentalism" in which "the existing forms of the life of the Christian community are taken as fixed once and for all; their historical nature—and that means their relativity and changeability—is ignored."[104] Much of the discussion was on the contentious slogan, "the world provides the agenda." "This slogan does not mean that the world tells us the Gospel, but it does mean that the Church must take seriously the exegetical *opinio communis*."[105] This was not to be interpreted as an agenda at variance with—or even against—the church. Rather, Hollenweger meant that the agenda, which the Holy Spirit is setting for the church, can only be adequately discerned in the world by meeting with people in their greatest need, rather than by meeting your fellow Christians in the church.[106]

Newbigin's Response to the MSC

In Newbigin's understanding the integration of the IMC with the WCC was symbolic of the greater reality that the church *is* God's mission to the world. A central concern for Newbigin was *how* each church was to be God's agent for mission, and how must the church change from its current status to embody that reality. With these personal concerns it was natural that Newbigin would be very interested in the outcome of the MSC—although he was not directly involved in the program. Writing in 1975 to Dr. Thomas Wieser, who had been the secretary to the North American

101. Ibid., 3.

102. WCC, *1968 Central Committee Report*, 66–71.

103. Martin Conway, interview with Laing, 17/8/2008.

104. A term introduced by Hoekendijk, WCC, *1968 Central Committee Report*, 69. In response to this "polysyllabic" slogan, Newbigin proffered his own, "a judicious combination of morphological radicalism with evangelical fundamentalism." Newbigin, "Call to Mission," 264.

105. The slogan was from Walter Hollenweger, WCC, *1968 Central Committee Report*, 69.

106. Conway, interview, 17/8/2008.

working group, Newbigin explained his hopes for the program: "It is obvious that the basic conviction behind the IMC/WCC integration was that the Church itself is God's mission to the world. . . . It can only mean that every congregation is itself an agent of mission. I therefore felt at that time that this study [the MSC] was perhaps *the most important single element in the effort to give spiritual substance to the formal action on integration.*"[107]

There were obvious parallels between Newbigin's own missiological agenda, shaped by his missionary experience, and that of the MSC. Newbigin drew from his own "very vivid experiences . . . of 'spontaneous expansion' among the small village congregations where I had been working in South India."[108] As noted, Newbigin's reflection was profoundly influenced by Roland Allen, particularly Allen's most famous book, *Missionary Methods.*[109]

Newbigin's observations and reflection led him to critique Protestant missionary methods and the inherent ecclesiology from which this missiology had evolved. When he came to India in 1936, Newbigin quickly saw that the old classical form of missions was bankrupt. Shenk recalls from conversation with Newbigin that "he refused to do things in the old way as much as possible . . . He self-consciously stood against the old system and tried to begin doing things in a new way . . . In that sense he was subversive, he was not patient with the old system at all."[110] In India Newbigin had experienced "spontaneous [church] expansion" and had experimented with new forms of congregational life, such as home groups based around an extended family (or families), training the laity, and allowing them to administer sacraments. With the MSC Newbigin hoped that this study would develop along similar lines, but with the possibility of global impact, in particular the renewal of the vitality of the Western church.[111]

It was, however, to be a lifelong disappointment that the MSC did not develop along the lines he envisaged: "When I became part of the WCC staff, I proposed the study on the missionary structure of the congregation precisely with the hope that Roland Allen's ideas might penetrate the older

---

107. Newbigin to Wieser, 18/12/1975, WCC: 421.301. Emphasis added.

108. Ibid.

109. Which Newbigin endorsed with his foreword; Allen, *Missionary Methods,* i–iii.

110. Wilbert Shenk, interview with Laing, 1/11/2006.

111. Newbigin, *Unfinished Agenda,* 206.

churches. But the 'paradigm shift' of the 1960s ensured that the study was hijacked in the interests of the dominant ideology of the secular."[112]

Newbigin was disappointed by the report of the MSC, in which mission was defined as "participation in secular programmes for urban renewal, for civil rights, for community organization, etc. In this perspective 'the Church is a happening on the road from one event to the next' and the events are events in secular programmes for human liberation."[113] More candidly, in his letter to Wieser, Newbigin recalled, "However, the study did not go the way I expected. I did not foresee the tremendous power of the coming emphasis on the secular which was to dominate our thinking during the sixties. These powerful currents carried the whole study in a direction which was almost entirely concerned with the question, 'What is God doing in the secular world and how can we get with it?' . . . [T]he basic thrust of . . . the study got lost because it got carried away in that theological current which has now spent itself."[114]

Newbigin rejected the report of the MSC because it uncritically adopted secular processes, interpreting them as God's mission. In the report the church lost any distinctive or prophetic voice with which to critique secular processes. Instead, the church has to align itself to the world's agenda, "be where the action is," and thus become "part of [the gospel] proclamation." There was a sharp divergence between the report and the ecclesiology Newbigin was developing. In the report the church was entirely at the mercy of the world, and concerns dear to Newbigin were not mentioned, such as the role of revelation, that the church was the firstfruit, the *arrabon*, a sign of the kingdom, and was bearing the witness by the Spirit. The report did not have a developed eschatology, which was so central to Newbigin's understanding of the role of the church in history—witnessing to the ends of the earth, and the end of time—instead there was the assumption of a gradual evolution to achieve the kingdom of God through secular processes.

In railing against church-centric missiology—which Hoekendijk had done from Willingen—the report had lurched to the other extreme: "A line of thought which had begun with the conviction that 'the Church is

112. Newbigin's terminology is confusing in that he did not "propose the study"; rather this was his personal hope for the study. Lesslie Newbigin, "Reply to Konrad Raiser," *IBMR* 18:2 (1994) 52. Cf. Newbigin, *Unfinished Agenda*, 166.

113. Newbigin, "Recent Thinking," 261.

114. Newbigin to Wieser, 18/12/1975, WCC: 421.301.

the Mission,' had led into a missiology from which the Church was practically eliminated."[115]

Almost three decades after the publication of the report Newbigin reiterated his earlier concerns: "In reaction against an overly church-centered missiology, we had a missiology that found God's redeeming action almost everywhere except in the preaching of the Gospel. It was a sad period."[116] From the above it can be established that Newbigin's expression of disappointment with the MSC was not a rash outburst privately disclosed to his friend. Rather, both publicly and privately, over several decades, Newbigin consistently expressed disappointment that the process of secularization had been too influential upon the study.

Despite his personal disappointment with the MSC, Newbigin continued to believe, write, and speak on missionary ecclesiology.[117] And he beseeched Wieser to resurrect the study: "I would like to *plead very strongly* that the study be taken up again in a fresh and more fully balanced theological perspective. I deeply believe that only a Trinitarian doctrine of Mission can provide this perspective."[118]

Although Newbigin personally rejected the theology of the MSC report, the majority of the assembly endorsed it at Uppsala.[119] Bosch notes that this missiology then became the "received view" in WCC circles, in which the "distinction between church and world has, for all intents and purposes, been dropped completely."[120] The polarization of theological positions concerning the *missio Dei* concept, which had first emerged within the IMC at Willingen, had, by Uppsala, become institutionalized.[121]

At least within the Western church, this polarization of understanding has led to the ongoing, and largely unresolved, schism between "evangelical" and "ecumenical" Christians that has dominated the latter half of

---

115. Newbigin, "Recent Thinking," 261.

116. Newbigin, "Reply to Raiser," 52.

117. E.g., Newbigin, "The Congregation as a Missionary Agency," June 1972, BUL: DA29/4/3/12.

118. Newbigin to Wieser, 18/12/1975, WCC: 421.301. Emphasis added.

119. Although in his later life Newbigin was outspoken in his criticism of the report of Section II, at the plenary discussion he had remained silent. Conway, email, 06/09/2008.

120. Bosch, *Transforming Mission*, 383.

121. Flett understands the "supposed exaggeration" of the MSC to be "a legitimate outworking of
Willingen's articulation of Trinity doctrine." Flett, "God Is a Missionary God," 230.

the twentieth century.[122] Whereas many within the WCC endorsed the position that Hoekendijk had maintained, evangelical reaction crystallized into what later became the Lausanne Movement, which sought to maintain a central and distinctive role for the church.[123] "For Hoekendijk, it appeared, *missio Dei* had become identified with a process of historical transformation whereby humankind would gradually achieve the goals of the messianic kingdom through the processes of secular history."[124] This historical-eschatological approach was in distinct contrast to the salvation-history ecclesiological approach which sought to maintain the centrality of the church as God's primary channel of mission to the world. Newbigin again faced the discord in theological positions that he first encountered at Willingen. He attempted to resolve the tension between these positions by examining the relationship between sacred and secular history—this will be considered in the next chapter.

Conclusion

The logic of integration operated at various levels. The act of unification of the councils created a world council which united church and mission, representing a global reality of a fundamental theological conviction. A crucial question posed at the time of integration was: Is there a centre on which humanity can seek unity? Secularism proposed to be such a centre, whilst the Christian gospel was also claiming to be the basis for the unity of humanity—a claim based on the atonement, wrought out in history and expressed in a visible community. What then was the proper form and expression of this one visible global community—and what form should a representative world council take?[125] These were questions which had exercised Newbigin since before the second assembly of the WCC at Evanston, in 1954.

122. W. Richebächer, "Missio Dei: The Basis of Mission Theology or a Wrong Path?" *IRM* 92:367 (2003) 593–94.

123. E.g., "The Church is at the very centre of God's cosmic purpose and is his appointed means of spreading the gospel." The Lausanne Covenant, par. 6; http://www.lausanne.org/lausanne-1974/lausanne-covenant.html.

124. Scherer cited by T. Engelsviken, "Missio Dei: The Understanding and Misunderstanding of a Theological Concept in European Churches and Missiology," *IRM* 92:367 (2003) 489.

125. JEL Newbigin, "The Quest for Unity through Religion," *Journal of Religion*, no. 35 (1955): 30–31.

Van Leeuwen's thesis in particular proposed that the forces of secularization were unifying world civilizations into one civilization. Secularization was "hailed" *as* Christian mission, unifying sacred with secular histories. At the time the assumption that a single world civilization was emerging gave impetus to integration. And a world civilization required a single world Christian body as a sign and witness. But secularism's erroneous assumption was a false dawn which beguiled many, including, for a time, Newbigin. The secular was not neutral but another ideology. With hindsight—which Newbigin obviously lacked at the time—we can interpret the globalization of secularism as the final throes of Western enlightenment, exported through the conduit of colonialism, and then continued in the guise of "development."

To a large extent the ideological foundation for "Christian development" was assumed from secularist models. A key thesis, applicable to both capitalist and socialist economies, is that presented by Walter Rostow in *Stages of Economic Growth*.[126] Rostow proposed that "nations could reach a stage of 'take-off' towards economic and social prosperity if sufficient technical skills, financial support and economic organization were made available."[127] However, such secular assumptions concerning development were increasingly challenged within the ecumenical movement, the critique of Rostow's model coming most pointedly from non-Western sources. M. M. Thomas, at the Geneva Church and Society conference of 1966, and two years later at the Uppsala assembly, led the challenge on the nature of the church's role in development. The work on development by the Indian economist Samuel Parmar further undermined the validity of a secularist model of development which had largely been assumed within ecumenical circles.[128] The ideological basis for development came under further scrutiny with the acknowledgement that the first UN Development Decade (1960–70) had failed. This led to radical questioning, and the identification of several shortcomings in the concept, particularly by non-Western critics.[129] Within ecumenical circles, a shift away from secularist models of development could be discerned which instead embraced

---

126. W. W. Rostow, *The Stages of Economic Growth: A Non-Communist Manifesto* (Cambridge: Cambridge University Press, 1960).

127. Dickinson, "Development," 298.

128. Parmar emphasized economic growth, self-reliance, and social justice. Cited by Dickinson, "Development," 299.

129. Ibid., 300.

"participation of the people" with a "commitment to solidarity with the poor."[130]

The logic of integration was, most significantly, expressed (and tested) at the local level of the church. How was the local congregation to embody the relationship between mission and church? The issue of the secular was first raised at Willingen by Hoekendijk and Lehmann but gained prominence at Strasbourg. The process of secularization exposed the inadequacies of Christendom's ecclesiastical legacy. The inherited structure of the congregation did not reflect recoveries in ecclesiological understanding, namely, that the church is missionary. Instead, due to "morphological fundamentalism," the parochial model continued to live on anachronistically in the modern city. Related to this was the sociological assumption about the form of the ministry—that each congregation should be centered around a full-time, theologically trained specialist. Secularization also challenged the assumed definition of "place," in which the primacy of geographic location and "neighbourhood" were undermined. Instead, in a society which was highly segmented and differentiated, it was necessary for the church to be visible in these different segments of society. To do so meant changing the basic form of the congregation. Newbigin is rightly critical of the relevance of the parochial model of Western Christianity for the secularized city. But in his construction of alternative models, Newbigin remained frustratingly sketchy.

The WCC sought to respond to these issues raised by secularization, which then dominated their agenda from Strasbourg, reaching a climax at Uppsala. The most important study which ran through this period was the MSC. Acceptance of the study by the majority at Uppsala exposed the unresolved polarization within the ecumenical movement. The issues first raised at Willingen became institutionalized. Uppsala marked a decisive a shift from the church-centric model which had dominated since Tambaram. Dissonant voices on the role of the church vis-à-vis the world could not be reconciled, and opinion diverged on the church's continuity or discontinuity with the world. There was a schism between those who understood mission as bringing God's reign in the secular life of the nations. This "social radicalism" became dominant within WCC circles. Conservative "evangelical" Christians, in contrast, understood mission as offering salvation, not humanization, with the goal of gathering people

130. Ibid., 301.

into the visible redeemed community.[131] The theology of Lausanne became polarized from that of Geneva.

The MSC was asking the right questions of the church, but for many the results were a disappointment. Newbigin is right in his assessment of the study, that it was "hijacked in the interests of the dominant ideology of the secular."[132] In the West, mission had become a remote reality, both geographically—being done in foreign lands far removed from the home base—and in the memory of the people. With the establishment of a Christianized society, the West no longer faced the issue of how Christianity should relate to other faiths, which was the daily reality for many Christians in the majority world.

It is somewhat surprising, therefore, that whilst the MSC correctly diagnosed that the problem lay with the Western church, they overlooked the non-Western church, by *also* looking to the West to provide the solution. All the resource people in the study were Western[133] and therefore influenced by Enlightenment thinking and secularization. The non-Western churches were excluded from the study as it was assumed they were already active in evangelism and subsequently had less need of reform. Since they were closer to the reality of the church being missionary, both geographically and in terms of their recent experience, it was surprising that the benefit of their wisdom was not incorporated into the study, either through analysis of the non-Western church, or at least by resourcing insights from non-Western church leadership.

At a personal level Newbigin did incorporate insights from the non-Western world, bringing a critique of Western ecclesiology by repeatedly comparing it with his missionary experience in India. Newbigin argued that where the church exists amongst dominant non-Christian religious cultures practical questions are raised about the church's relationship to the world, this in turn has led to an appraisal of the true nature of the church. From the premise of his own experience, Newbigin broadened his argument to state that the missionary encounters of Western Christianity with the non-Western world have been one of the main sources

---

131. The question of the relationship between salvation and humanization was the basis of a protracted debate, primarily between M. M. Thomas and Newbigin (although involving others). Related to it was how to determine the legitimate boundary and form of the church in any cultural "place." The correspondence on this debate can be found at: BUL: DA29/3/5/1–26. See also G. R. Hunsberger, "Conversion and Community: Revisiting the Lesslie Newbigin-M. M. Thomas Debate," *IBMR* 22:3 (1998).

132. Newbigin, "Reply to Raiser," 52.

133. For a list of members, see WCC, *Church for Others*, 53–54, 56.

enabling a recovery of ecclesiology.[134] His hope was that the ecumenical movement would be an international conduit to disseminate and develop these finding. It is therefore disappointing that the MSC in their quest for a solution examined the problem, the Western church, but failed to draw upon potential solutions from beyond the West.

After Uppsala Newbigin's own position was to eschew polarization between understanding salvation in terms of fighting for God's action in the world versus celebrating the salvation he gives. Rather he insisted that the church is *both* a task force committed to the doing of God's will in the life of the secular world, *and* a family of those reconciled and gathered in Christ as a visible community. In seeking to reconcile the two positions, Newbigin maintained that both were biblical. He sought to maintain a creative tension between both positions and avoid capitulation to either extreme. Instead, he proffered an image of the church which is seldom used but which he thought was appropriate to the situation: the apocalyptic image of "the Church as the company of those who follow the Lamb in the way of the Cross."[135] The next chapter, which looks in detail at Newbigin's own engagement with the secular, will examine his theological attempt to reconcile these positions and his practical suggestions to embody them in appropriate church structures.

---

134. The two other main sources are the demise of Christendom and rise of the ecumenical movement. Newbigin, *Household of God*, 1–25.

135. Newbigin, "Congregation," 7.

9

Secularization and the Missionary Structure of the Church

INTEGRATION OF THE IMC with the WCC challenged "all Christians to recognize the intrinsically missionary character of their churchmanship, and to reflect afresh upon the way in which this is to be expressed in the changed conditions of the twentieth century"—particularly in response to the process of secularization.[1]

At the heart of integration was the reunification of church with mission. It was Newbigin's hope that this would be expressed at all levels of the church's existence, the ecumenical movement serving as a catalyst for this process. By the time of formal integration there was convergence in Newbigin's critique of the structure of the congregation inherited from Western Christianity. His practical experience, and experimentation within the Indian church, now confirmed the analysis brought by secularization, that a major fault of the Western church was its failure to be missionary.

With the acknowledgement that mission was now to six, not just three continents, the particular need of the West, as a mission field, came into focus. And with it came the admission that the church had to move from redundant structures inherited from Christendom which did not express the missionary nature of the church. To this end the study initiated by the WCC, the Missionary Structure of the Congregation, sought to deal with secularization and propose new and appropriate church structures for the twentieth century (see chapter 8). From Newbigin's perspective the study "was perhaps the most important single element in the effort

---

1. Lesslie Newbigin, *A Faith for This One World?* (London: SCM, 1961) 8.

to give spiritual substance to the formal action on integration."[2] But the study did not develop as Newbigin had hoped. This present chapter now focuses on Newbigin's particular contribution to these issues. Newbigin's own engagement with secularism can be understood in three stages, his initial introduction to the issues, the middle period characterized by his endorsement of secularization, and the late period of increasing disenchantment. This staging risks oversimplification, distorting Newbigin's nuanced engagement, as already during his early encounter Newbigin demonstrated an ambivalence towards secularization which contrasted with the endorsements given by his more optimistic peers.[3]

Newbigin understood secularization to have impact upon society, and upon the church. One aspect of secularization's impact upon society is briefly considered at the start of this chapter. Secularization was understood to bring a "prophetic attack" upon "ontocratic" societies[4]—ancient civilizations which maintained a cyclical interpretation of history. It was assumed that the result of secularization's impact on ancient societies was to transform such societies to a linear understanding of history; this enabled them to coalesce into a "single world civilization," with a unified history culminating in a common terminus.

There are two main sections to this chapter. The first examines Newbigin's understanding of how secularization affected the structure of the congregation. Secularization critiqued the form of the church inherited from Christendom, in particular the parochial system. Having established that the parochial form was inadequate for the modern city, Newbigin then explored alternative forms of church which could maintain the inherent tension between the congregation being gathered out of society and yet being sent into the world. The second major section of the chapter assesses the stages of Newbigin's engagement (and ultimate disenchantment) with secularization and the implications for the structure of the congregation.

---

2. Newbigin to Wieser, 18/12/1975, WCC: 421.301.

3. Wainwright refers to Newbigin's secular "flirtation." This term is perhaps inadequate, as this was not a brief distraction; rather, Newbigin engaged seriously with the issues raised over many years. Wainwright, *Newbigin*, 341ff.

4. A term Newbigin adopted from A. T. van Leeuwen; e.g., Newbigin, *Honest Religion*, 27–28.

A Single Civilization: From a Cyclical
to a Linear View of History

One of the expected outcomes from the process of secularization was the creation, for the first time, of a unified world civilization: "There is emerging a single world culture which has its characteristic expression in the rapidly growing cities in all parts of the world, and which has as its common substance the science and technology which have been developed in the West, and as its driving power the belief in the possibility of rational planning for total human welfare."[5]

This had several implications. If a "single world culture" was emerging, what could be the unifying centre for such a civilization? Newbigin proposed that this secularized civilization could not remain religiously neutral but would instead force concentration to a single issue, the acceptance, or rejection, of Jesus Christ as the organizing locus of history.[6] He suggested that if his thesis was true—"that what we are witnessing is the drawing together of the human race into that history whose centre is the Cross—then the issue of Christian unity is the most central and critical one for the mission of the Church."[7]

It was reasonable to assume that a single world civilization needed one visible sign and servant, the WCC, to bear the gospel to the world. At the heart of this quest for unity was the ecumenical movement. Integration of the IMC with the WCC could be interpreted as a consequence of these developments, the "inner logic" of integration being to establishment a "worldwide Christian fellowship committed to the task of mission to the whole world."[8]

How was secularization forming a single civilization? Reflecting upon his missionary experience in rural India, Newbigin recalled the impression that J. L. Myres's book *The Dawn of History*[9] had made upon him as a student. The first chapter, "The Peoples which have no History," reminded Newbigin of Myres's assumption that the majority of humanity lived without history;[10] that is, they live with a cyclical worldview, in

5. Newbigin, *One World*, 109.

6. Ibid., 27–28.

7. Newbigin, "Gathering Up," 90.

8. Newbigin, "Summons to Mission," 186.

9. J. L. Myres, *The Dawn of History* (London: William & Norgate, 1911).

10. Ibid., 13–28, Newbigin, *One World*, 26. C.f. Newbigin, *Honest Religion*, 13. Newbigin here is uncritical in his adoption of Myres although, during the 1960s, these antiquated views were losing currency.

a "static situation," perpetually repeating the life of their predecessors, without any conception of development or progress.[11] Newbigin made the assumption that for people such as Indian villagers, their encounter with Western civilization resulted in a "dawning," a change from a cyclical to a linear understanding of history. "One can say that these villages belong to prehistory rather than to history. Or perhaps one should say that they are just emerging into history."[12] This oversimplification led Newbigin to assume that the disruption of their worldview was a consequence of India engaging with secularization, the secular democracy emerging and embarking upon a series of "five-year plans." With as many as twelve such plans proposed, this displaced a cyclical view of time with a linear one, enshrining the concept of "purposive change" and development.[13] Newbigin argued that the process of secularization, which was bringing about a "scientific world civilization," had emerged in the West as a consequence of Christianity. Hence the dissemination of this secularization could be understood as India encountering the gospel:

> I believe that this great new upreach [*sic*] of vital power which is expressing itself in the whole life of the country—in rural development, in industry and technology, in politics and social change—is in the last analysis the fruit of the meeting of the Gospel with the soul of India . . . the Gospel reflected and refracted in a thousand ways—yes, and distorted too—in the civilization of the West within its literature, its service, its jurisprudence, its political ideas and in many other ways. *India is responding to that contact now for the first time with her whole strength.* . . . From the terrific experiments of this decade, India must surely go on to faith in Christ as the sole Redeemer, or into godless scepticism.[14]

Newbigin believed that his decades of missionary experience in India and his work with the IMC gave him "an angle of vision," enabling

---

11. That modernity was initiating such progress was not a new concept to Newbigin. He had first publically presented the "idea of progress" in a series of lectures at United Theological College, Bangalore, in 1941. "The Kingdom of God and the Idea of Progress," in Newbigin, *Signs Amid the Rubble*, 3–55. However, in contrast with when church-centric missiology had become dominant, in these lectures "there is very little explicit ecclesiology." Wainwright in Newbigin, *Signs Amid the Rubble*, x.

12. Newbigin, *India Diary*, 44.

13. Newbigin, *One World*, 19–20.

14. Lesslie Newbigin, "A Time for Decision," in *Revolution in Missions*, ed. Blaise Levai (Vellore: Popular, 1957), appendix. Emphasis added.

greater insight to interpret secularization than could be achieved "from a purely western point of view."[15] From the particularity of India, Newbigin extrapolated globally to propose that humanity was "not being unified on the basis of a common religious faith or even of a common ideology, but on the basis of a shared secular terror and a shared secular hope."[16]

When Newbigin described his understanding of the emerging "scientific world civilization," the most crucial feature was that it "is indissolubly related to the belief that by its means human life can be made better, fuller, healthier, richer than it has been in the past, and that human history ought to be understood in terms of the effort to make it so."[17] The world civilization which Newbigin discerned was characterized first by "an essential ingredient," "the fact of purposive change" which made it incompatible with the cyclical view of history inherent in Eastern religious traditions. Second, Newbigin asserted that this sense of purpose and linear concept of time had been incubated during the period of Christendom, and "have found their way into western civilization from the Bible."[18]

The emergence of a single world civilization implied a unified history and a concentration on the question, what could be the legitimate basis for the unity of humanity? Newbigin asserted that "the centre point of all history is the invasion of the End into the midst of the story, in the man Jesus in whom the word was made flesh. By that invasion, the crisis of history is precipitated. Slowly but inexorably all men and all nations are brought within the range of that event and are faced with issues for which natural religion has no place—the issue of the ultimate consummation of all things."[19]

These assumptions, and Newbigin's disenchantment with them, will be assessed in the latter part of this chapter.

Secularization and the Structure of the Church

Prior to Newbigin's engagement with the issues raised by secularization, his favored model was the church as the gathered congregation, the visible body in the midst of the community, as a sign of the kingdom. This was

15. Newbigin, *Honest Religion*, 7–8.

16. Ibid., 13.

17. Newbigin, *One World*, 18.

18. Ibid., 20.

19. Lesslie Newbigin, "Jesus the Servant and Man's Community," in *Christ's Call to Service Now*, ed. Ambrose Reeves (London: SCM, 1963) 29.

the repeated model he had experienced in his missionary career in Tamil Nadu, the church in an Indian village; the congregation often gathering in the square, as they did not have a church building, with Hindu and Muslim onlookers gathering to observe the spectacle.[20] "That pattern still has validity wherever the local community remains the fundamental form of human relationships."[21] However, by the 1960s Newbigin had realized that this model was no longer tenable when society was complex, fragmented, and had developed beyond a simple agricultural structure.[22] Newbigin's main work on secularization during this time was the 1964 Firth Lectures at the University of Nottingham, which were published as *Honest Religion for Secular Man*[23]—his response to John Robinson's *Honest to God*.[24] The negative legacy of church structures was now being critiqued by secularization—these aspects will be considered in turn.

The Negative Impact of Christendom

Christendom had profoundly damaged the relationship between church and mission. Newbigin identified five ways in which ecclesiology had been damaged. Christendom had resulted in an introverted form of Christianity which defined itself in relationship to its various factions rather than in orientation to the non-Christian world.[25] Second, this theological orientation was manifest in the patterns of churchmanship which were prioritized with the maintenance of the institution, the church being the guardian of civilization, the chaplain of society. "It was in this period, when the dimension of the ends of the earth had ceased to exist as a practical reality in the minds of Christians, that the main patterns of churchmanship were formed . . . The Church had become the religious department of European society rather than the task force selected and appointed for a world mission."[26] The third factor concerned the church in relation to

20. E.g., Newbigin, *India Diary*; Newbigin, "Unity and Mission," 3.

21. Newbigin, *Honest Religion*, 108.

22. Lesslie Newbigin, *The Good Shepherd: Meditations on Christian Ministry in Today's World* (Leighton Buzzard: Faith, 1977) 88.

23. Newbigin's writings on this topic are to be found in "Gathering Up"; "Summons to Mission"; "Holy Spirit"; *One World*; "Jesus the Servant"; *Trinitarian Doctrine*; and *Honest Religion*.

24. J. A. T. Robinson, *Honest to God* (London: SCM, 1963).

25. Newbigin, *Household of God*, 11–12.

26. Newbigin, *Honest Religion*, 102–3.

culture. With the uniting of church and state came the assumption of responsibility for the maintenance of cultural values. This is "[t]ypical of a national Church, which accepts a certain responsibility for the whole life of the community, but fails to make it clear that the Church is a separate community marked off from the world in order to save the world." Recognizing that some churches chose to quietly acquiesce to the demands of culture, other types of churches, in reaction to this, had culturally isolated themselves, repudiating their need for cultural engagement.[27]

Fourth, the ingrown introversion of Christendom had anaesthetized the church to the "anomaly" of disunity. A persistent critique against this arose from the "younger churches" who reacted against the imported denominational divisions of Christendom, finding them detrimental to their witness to the world. The effort of the "younger churches" to overcome imposed practical problems led to theological reflection in which it was recognized that "at the centre of the whole missionary enterprise stands Christ's abiding promise, 'I, if I be lifted up, will draw all men unto myself,' and its goal is 'to sum up all things in Christ.'"[28] The fifth negative legacy of Christendom was the loss of the eschatological horizon. The church itself fills the horizon, the goal of mission being to pluck "souls" out of the world. The church, as a receptacle for the saved, was introverted and viewed the world negatively. The church had lost its pilgrim character and understood itself as a static institution. "When this becomes dominant the Church thinks primarily of its duty to care for its own members, and its duty to those outside drops into second place."[29] Other factors, such as missionary encounters with non-Western civilizations and the emergence of the ecumenical movement, aided the recovery of ecclesiology, a key aspect of which is the acknowledgement that the church is missionary in its very essence.

Secularization's Critique of Christendom

One of the major consequences of secularization was the impact that it had upon the form of the church. Secularization broke the "sacral unity of the Christendom society," the link between church and society.[30] A missional understanding of the church flatly contradicted the ecclesiology of

27. Newbigin, *Household of God*, 16.

28. Ibid., 17.

29. Ibid., 146.

30. Newbigin, *Honest Religion*, 104.

the Reformers who defined the church without reference to its mission.[31] Secularization forced a re-examination of this erroneous model of church as a gathered institution at the centre of society. In a secularized society such a model was no longer tenable, as the church was no longer central to society. Those who gathered to worship were in fact separating themselves from society, and were marginalized by society.

Christendom's ecclesiology emphasized "coming" to the static institution, to the neglect of "going." But the church is the community of God *and* the mission of God. Secularization exposed Western Christianity's preference for the former to the neglect of the latter. The demise of Christendom enabled the recovery of a "pre-Constantinian" understanding of "the Church as a missionary community"[32]—now the normative context of most Christians. Furthering this understanding and helping to disseminate it was the experience that Western missionaries brought back to the West.[33] In comparing primitive Christianity with its expression during Christendom, Newbigin noted that for early Christians, their self-understanding was expressed by their adoption of the secular term *ecclesia* for their assembly rather than the more obvious religious choice, *synagogos*: "[*Ecclesia*] referred to the public assembly of all the citizens gathered to discuss and settle the public affairs of the city. In other words, the early Church did not see itself as a private religious society competing with others to offer personal salvation to its members; it saw itself as a movement launched into the public life of the world, challenging the *cultus publicus* of the Empire, claiming the allegiance of all without exception."[34]

Alternatives to the Parochial System

The particular critique against the ecclesiology assumed by Christendom was against the parochial system. In the rural situation the parochial model was still tenable where the concepts of "locality" and "neighbour" retained their meaning. But in the urban setting, "[l]ocality has been abolished. Neighbourhood is no longer a word that refers to a place. Man is no

---

31. Ibid.

32. Ibid.

33. Ibid.

34. Lesslie Newbigin, *Your Kingdom Come: Reflections on the Theme of the Melbourne Conference on World Mission and Evangelism, 1980* (Leeds: John Paul the Preacher's Press, 1980) 27–28.

longer a neighbour; he is at best the point of intersection of two or three unrelated worlds."[35]

The parochial model of the church, as a legacy from Christendom, failed in the secular city because it "appears to be neither relevant to the life of a secularized society, nor true to the biblical picture of the Church as a missionary community."[36] Furthermore, based upon his exegetical studies on the New Testament, Newbigin was critical of the church forms inherited from Christendom; that the form of the church was wrong in "the matter of the size and character." In the New Testament, groups "were small enough and intimate enough to enable the members to take a real responsibility for one another."[37]

The form of the congregation is determined by theology, but it is also sociologically defined (and refined) by the realities of the society in which it is set.[38] This meant for Newbigin that in each locality the church must be visibly present. "The Church, in other words, can only be a sign of God's intention for all humankind if it is in each segment of society a relevant sign of God's intention for that segment."[39] Tradition had established the local church as the "sole definitive form of the Church's existence," relegating other structural forms, which were missionary, to the status of "non-ecclesiastical," or at best, "para-ecclesiastical activities."

Newbigin limited his analysis to the Protestant church and did not engage with, for instance, the Roman Catholic position and their claims of catholicity where missionary orders are very much a part of the church. Also, for Catholics, the local unit of the church is the diocese rather than the congregation. At this level the church, through the leadership of the bishop, can take real responsibility for society, with the laity understanding the primary expression of their witness in society to be through their daily work.

In his continued critique of Western church models, Newbigin again resorted to his understanding of the ministry in the early church—in a non-secular world—to sustain his argument:

---

35. On Newbigin's use of "place," see Newbigin, *Honest Religion*, 107.

36. Ibid.

37. JEL Newbigin, "Church Union: Which Way Forward?" *NCCR*, no. 89 (1969): 358–9.

38. Newbigin, "The Congregation as a Missionary Agency," BUL: DA29/4/3/12, p5.

39. Newbigin, "Forms of Unity," 10.

In particular it does seem that the early church acknowledged two forms of ministry: the settled ministry of bishops (elders) and deacons, and the mobile ministry of apostles, prophets, and evangelists. These are all listed as part of the ministry of the one body, but they have different roles. I wonder whether or not the split in our contemporary thinking between "church" and "mission" has something to do with the disappearance of the second (mobile) element in the ministry from our acknowledged church orders. Missionary societies and other specialized agencies have begun to provide in our day something of what these mobile ministries provided for the early church, but they have never been integrated theoretically into our ecclesiologies or practically into our church orders.[40]

Newbigin therefore asked, "Is the Church only truly the Church when it is in camp, and not when it is on the march? Is mission not as truly churchly as congregation? Are these goings forth, these self-emptyings, these fallings into the ground, not as truly of the life of the Church as the settled local congregation?"[41] From the premise of New Testament example, Newbigin widened the base of his argument, drawing upon his missionary experience in South India, to state that "para-church" cell groups which meet in schools, universities, factories, and offices should be sacramental in character.[42] Rather than the "come" structures which invite people to separate into a "holy huddle," calling them away from their civic duties, the church should be "an affair of small teams formed to deal with the living issues of the city. The congregation should 'take shape around' these issues."[43]

This has implications also for the ministry, challenging the image of a pastor drawing a congregation together—and apart from the world. Instead, the role of the minister is understood as leading the congregation for radical change in the world.[44] The church in a secularized society can-

40. Newbigin, "Cross-Currents," 150.

41. Newbigin, *Honest Religion*, 112.

42. Ibid., 114. A conviction he again reiterated over a decade later; Newbigin, *Melbourne*, 39–40.

43. Newbigin, "Missionary Agency," BUL: DA29/4/3/12, 2. The practical application of this would be the ordination of "shop-floor" industrial workers, as a parallel to Newbigin's experiments in ordaining Indian agricultural laborers. Newbigin, *Melbourne*, 40.

44. Newbigin, "Missionary Agency," BUL: DA29/4/3/12, 2. A major expression of this was Newbigin's initiatives in urban-industrial mission whilst bishop in Madras. Murdoch Mackenzie, email to Laing, 25/5/2009.

not therefore exist in one definitive form. The rather surprising correlate which Newbigin proposed was that a Christian would belong to more than one congregation—representing the different segments of his or her secular life.[45] The fragmentation of society was to be reflected in the fragmented life of the individual.

Secularization and the Development of Missionary Structures

Newbigin extended his argument further. Secularization has critiqued the parochial system inherited from Christendom. He now added that secularization *itself* should be understood as being used as a divine force, analogous to the scattering of the early church in Jerusalem—secularization being used to "break up old patterns of community . . . and to scatter Christians in ones and twos throughout the manifold and varied sectors of a complex society, God is scattering in order that he may gather."[46] The fragmenting of established church structures required a *kenosis*, a self-emptying, "which mirrors and in a true sense re-enacts the self-emptying of the Son of God."[47] As the grain of wheat falls to the ground and dies, "the particular fruit of *that* ground may be brought to perfection for Christ."[48] By this Newbigin meant that churches should be willing to die to their particular denominational heritage to be re-born in a form appropriate for the new context. As a fitting image of the church, Newbigin drew on the seldom-used image in the book of Revelation: "the Church as the company of those who follow the Lamb in the way of the Cross."[49]

The critique of Christendom's ecclesiology provided by secularization caused Newbigin to ask, "Does the very structure of our congregations contradict the missionary calling of the Church?"[50] To remedy this situation, Newbigin had called for "bold experiment" with regard to the forms of ministry and congregational life.[51] He recognized that "nothing

---

45. Newbigin, *Honest Religion*, 114. Now evident in some expressions of the emerging church; Mackenzie, email, 25/5/2009.

46. Ibid., 122.

47. Ibid., 118.

48. Ibid., 111. Italics in original.

49. Newbigin, "Missionary Agency," BUL: DA29/4/3/12, 7.

50. Newbigin, "Developments During 1962," 9.

51. Newbigin, "Holy Spirit," 30, 32.

is more important in the long run for the life of the church than the quality of its ministry."[52]

At the time of integration, Newbigin, as general secretary of the IMC, had called for local experimentation to embody a recovered relationship between mission and church.[53] Two decades on from his call for "bold experiment" in church structure, Newbigin acknowledged three (relatively) new structural forms which were providing alternative structures for the problems inherited from Christendom. First, there were "Programme agencies" "which exist to carry on work in the fields of evangelism, education and social and political action."[54] Focused on a particular issue, these agencies may be denominational or ecumenical. Second, there were "Sector Ministries." These were usually ordained ministers who, instead of pastoring a local congregation, related "to some sector of secular life such as industry, education or healing" as chaplains.[55] "Sector Ministries" could also function as a cell group of believers within a particular segment of society. Third, there was the "para-church" which was formed "on the basis of a common vision for the Church, or of a common concern about Christian action in the world."[56] Each of these groups met apart from the "traditional gatherings of the 'local church.'" Taking a lead from the Medellin Conference of Latin American bishops, which spoke of the Basic Community as the "primary and fundamental ecclesial nucleus," Newbigin interpreted these groups as "the local congregation in its most vivid form." These groups were "integrated into the life of the parish so that the parish is seen as 'a confederation of basal ecclesial communities.'"[57]

These three structures have arisen as attempts to overcome the privatization of Christianity and enable the mission entrusted to the church to be fulfilled in public, and as such, "[t]hey are important growing points for the mission of the Church." However, for all three, "[t]heir weaknesses arise precisely at the point of their separation from the local congregation."[58] The isolation of congregation from agency is detrimental for both, as "on the one hand, the local congregation is not challenged to remember that

52. Newbigin (from 1962) cited by Goheen, *As the Father*, 84.

53. Newbigin to the Secretaries of IMC Member Councils, Covering letter to introduce the aim of *One Body*, 1/12/1958, WCC: 26.0042/4.

54. Newbigin, *Melbourne*, 35.

55. Ibid.

56. Ibid.

57. Ibid., 38.

58. Newbigin, *Melbourne*, 36.

it exists for the sake of its neighbourhood; it is rather encouraged to exist as a society for its own members because the wider responsibilities are carried by another agency. On the other hand the work of the agency is not seen to spring right out of the life of worship and fellowship in the Gospel. It is not seen as an overspill of a charismatic experience."[59]

These insights were distilled from years of ministry in Madras. As bishop Newbigin consciously sought to maintain the connection between congregational ministry and service to the city, as to sever their interconnectedness would be fatal for both. The ministry would become "irrelevant," "looking after selfish and introverted congregations" with little concern for their neighbor. Service, devoid of its sacramental nature, would lose its character as witness. Although the service provided by a local congregation might appear pitiably small in comparison to the gigantean needs of a city such as Madras, "But as signs which point beyond what is now visible and create the possibility of hope, they are infinitely precious."[60] Thus Newbigin's practical endeavors in Madras to link church and mission, congregation and service, fostered a vision beyond the parochial, creating a "coherent body of people concerned about the City as a whole"[61]—albeit an embryonic one. The "signs" of service pointing beyond the remit of the congregation cultivated an understanding of how the local related to the universal.

The statement on unity, which Newbigin had drafted and succeeded in being adopted at New Delhi, emphasized both the local and universal aspects of church unity. The local, "'all in each place' is a committed fellowship which is also recognizable as one universal fellowship in all times and places."[62] That tension between those two poles needed to be maintained in the local congregation, as there was the danger of being pulled towards an unbalanced position at either pole. Emphasis only on "each place" would result in fragmented, introverted congregations "which give little sign that they have any organic connection with Jesus Christ"—which would be demonstrated by links to the global church and continuity with the church's historical traditions.[63] The opposite danger, of emphasizing the universal to the neglect of the local, would result in the bureaucratiza-

---

59. Ibid., 37.

60. Lesslie Newbigin, "Reflections on an Indian Ministry," *Frontier* 18 (1975) 26–27.

61. Ibid., 25.

62. Newbigin, "Cooperation and Unity," 73.

63. Ibid., 73–74.

tion of the church such that it would then bear little resemblance to the New Testament model.[64]

Newbigin's Disenchantment with Secularization

Early Ambivalence towards Secularization

Even at the time when Newbigin first embraced secularization, his assessment was more measured and critical than other protagonists. Whilst Newbigin "frankly accept[ed] van Leeuwen's biblical interpretation of the process of secularization," he was not so accommodating of the analysis proffered by others.[65] In chapters 2 and 3 of *Honest Religion for Secular Man*, he was critical of Rudolph Bultmann, Paul van Buren, Harvey Cox, and John A. T. Robinson.[66] "In each of the cases . . . Newbigin is noting the loosening of the ties between the 'prophetic attack' on all ontocratic patterns and the foundation of authority upon which that prophetic attack was first made, the reality of a personal God. This contained grave dangers which began to point out the illusion of thinking that an 'ideological vacuum' is possible."[67] In his critique of other Christian scholars' responses to secularization, Newbigin concluded

> that if the mastery which is given to man through the process of secularization is not held within the context of man's responsibility to God, the result will be a new slavery; that if the dynamism of "development," the drive to a new kind of human society, is not informed by the biblical faith concerning the nature of the Kingdom of God it will end in totalitarianism; and that if the secular critique of all established orders is not informed and directed by the knowledge of God it will end in a self destructive nihilism.[68]

Later Newbigin would be unequivocal in his rejection of secular theology. But, even as he embraced it, he demonstrated ambivalence towards it. Hunsberger identified three areas of early ambivalence which subsequently gained clarity, enabling Newbigin to later utilize

---

64. Ibid., 73.
65. Newbigin, *Honest Religion*, 69.
66. Ibid., 44–99.
67. Hunsberger, *Witness*, 147.
68. Newbigin, *Honest Religion*, 38–39.

his understanding of secularization to give a missiological critique of Western culture.[69]

The first area Newbigin was equivocal about was the *Western* nature of secularization.[70] Whilst he accepted that secularization came from the crucible of Christendom, Newbigin proposed that pure secularization could be distilled, as an ideologically neutral concentrate, uncontaminated by Western civilization. Yet, elsewhere Newbigin conceded that the concepts of development and progress were very much imbued with Western ideology. Newbigin proposed that whilst Western colonialism was discredited, the ideological seed of progress, which contributed to the dynamism of colonialism, could take root in other soils: "What has happened then is that while the cultural and political and economic advance of the Western world has been halted, while the West's claim to world leadership has been repudiated, something has come into being which is recognized as a world civilization, something which, while it is indubitably a product of the West, is regarded as *a detachable and potentially independent product*, something potentially the property of all men equally."[71]

This becomes problematic when the abstract notion of "progress" was given greater substance in the more concrete application of "development." Development can be ideologically neutral, yet, as was the case during the 1950s and 1960s, it "might almost be described as the substitution for the traditional cultural values of a set of values derived from Western Europe and North America."[72] Later, Newbigin was more explicit in linking development with a continuation of colonial values and ideals: "What is called development is (though we often forget this) the substitution by the peoples of Asia and Africa of a new hierarchy of values for that which has ruled them hitherto."[73] The concept of "development" was a fragile one, and with hindsight, Newbigin could recognize the "hollowness" of the ideal, which strove to bringing the "'under developed' countries up to the level of the 'developed.'"[74] Direct colonial rule had simply been substituted by ideological domination in which "[t]he prevalent values were

---

69. Hunsberger, *Witness*, 149.

70. Ibid.

71. Newbigin, *One World*, 14. Emphasis added.

72. Newbigin, "Jesus the Servant," 27.

73. Lesslie Newbigin, "From the Editor," *IRM* 54 (1965) 418.

74. Lesslie Newbigin, "Which Way for 'Faith and Order'?" in *What Unity Implies: Six Essays after Uppsala*, ed. Reinhard Groscurth (Geneva: WCC, 1969) 129.

those of the Western nations."[75] This of course undermined the claim that the notion of progress was culturally neutral, a "detachable . . . independent product," which could thus migrate without Western baggage.

The second area of ambivalence was highlighted by the "paradox" of Asia accepting Western technology and science but rejecting Western presuppositions which had fostered these developments.[76] Newbigin was troubled by the fact that "non-Western peoples are eager to master every element in the science and techniques of the Western world, but are almost totally uninterested in enquiring into the roots of the tree on which these fruits have grown."[77] In fact, they could consume vast quantities of the "fruits" without ever suffering from any "indigestion." "Hindu pantheism seems to be able to absorb modern science and technology without even suffering from mild indigestion."[78] This undermined Newbigin's thesis that scientific civilization would displace a cyclical understanding of history with a linear, teleological one. Instead, Asians were cherry-picking from the West, their own worldview being uncompromised as they embraced Western technology.

It was only much later that Newbigin could provide a satisfactory solution to this problem. This came from his analysis of Western culture in which he identified the "abandonment of teleology" as the most critical assumption of the Enlightenment.[79] Western civilization, through the Renaissance and then the Enlightenment, had eliminated purpose, an ideological position which was already inherent to Hinduism. A contributing factor, which may help explain this "paradox," is Hinduism's

---

75. Newbigin, *Open Secret*, 104.

76. Hunsberger, *Witness*, 150.

77. Newbigin, *Honest Religion*, 25. That "modernisation does not necessarily lead to secularisation" continues to be attested by more recent studies. Concerning the rise of secularization and the decline of Western Christianity, the case of Europe is better understood to be an "anomaly" rather than a paradigm to predict the future of other nations. Furthermore, the ability of secularization to displace religion in Europe is contested. Under the surface, Europe is "less secular than is popularly conceived," although religious expression has become less institutionally rooted. J. A. Kirk, "Secularisation, the World Church and the Future of Mission," *Transformation* 22:3 (2005) 2, 7.

78. Newbigin, "Gathering Up," 81. A point Newbigin noted on several occasions: e.g., Newbigin, *One World*, 17; Newbigin, *Trinitarian Doctrine*, 45; Newbigin, *Honest Religion*, 25.

79. Newbigin, *Foolishness*, 34. Cf. Hunsberger, *Witness*, 150.

intrinsic adaptability to reconstitute itself in response to eternal challenges—to absorb and evolve, as Newbigin's metaphor of the sand bank had demonstrated.[80]

The third reason for Newbigin's early ambivalence towards secularization Hunsberger termed the "the ghost of Christopher Dawson," the scattered references that Newbigin made to Dawson.[81] Dawson proposed that for the West, "the loss of this faith that God acts in history could in the long run destroy the dynamic of modern western civilization and leave it to sink back again into the timeless monism of the ancient pagan religions of Asia."[82] Initially, Newbigin was rather skeptical of Dawson's thesis, but with time became more convinced that Dawson's "prophecy" was being fulfilled.[83] Newbigin's ultimate endorsement of Dawson's thesis coincided with Newbigin's return, in "retirement," to the United Kingdom. His decades of missiological engagement with Indian culture led him to conclude that he must now engage missiologically with Western culture— and that this would be a far more difficult task.[84]

Here was a great irony. Whilst Newbigin (and van Leeuwen in particular) had in the 1960s assumed that Western science was changing Eastern minds to a linear, purposeful view of history, the converse was happening. Eastern worldviews remained immutable to Western ideology. Instead, Western worldviews were adopting mindsets analogous to those in the East. Newbigin had highlighted the danger of the "prophetic attack" brought by secularization being cut asunder from the foundation and authority for such an attack. The Enlightenment, with the "abandonment of teleology" had driven out the concept of a personal God giving meaning to history. With God expelled, the house swept clean, the demons of "new slavery," "totalitarianism," and "self-destructive nihilism" came to inhabit the ideological vacuum in the West.[85]

Newbigin later realized that secularization was not ideologically neutral. "I think that what has come into being is not a secular society but a pagan society, not a society devoid of public images but a society which

---

80. This was to counter Alexander Duff's metaphor of Hinduism being a mine. Newbigin, "Gathering Up," 82.

81. Hunsberger, *Witness*, 150–51.

82. Newbigin, *Honest Religion*, 56.

83. Lesslie Newbigin, "The Centrality of Jesus for History," in *Incarnation and Myth: The Debate Continued*, ed. Michael Goulder (Grand Rapids: Eerdmans, 1979) 210. Cf. Hunsberger, *Witness*, 151.

84. Newbigin, *Unfinished Agenda*, 249.

85. Cf. Ibid.

worships gods which are not God."[86] Western society, having thrown off Christianity, has returned to its pre-Christian paganism, adopting a worldview which paralleled Asian monism.

Rejection of a Secular Ideological Vacuum

By 1975 Newbigin conceded that the enchantment with secularization had ended "more quickly than most theological fashions." It had been "an illusion" to assume that secularization would create an "ideological vacuum."[87] The anticipated revolution in African and Asian worldviews had just not materialized. A decade later Newbigin conceded that he had been beguiled by theories of secularization, particularly van Leeuwen's thesis in *Christianity and World History*: "I do not now believe that the 'modern' secular culture of the post-Enlightenment west has an assured future. It seems to me to show all the signs of disintegration."[88] And with this came the penitential realization that, as a Western missionary, Newbigin had himself been a force for secularization.[89]

Previously, in the 1960s, Newbigin had believed that the forces of secularization were unifying all civilizations into one world civilization. He had, with van Leeuwen, accepted "the process of secularization as a form of liberation made possible by the Christian gospel"—that the process of secularization would create "a space free of all ideological or religious control."[90] But, from the 1980s onwards, he came to believe that secularization was itself just another ideology, a "myth." Newbigin meant "myth" in the popular sense, as mistaken, false belief, and in the technical sense, "an unproved collective belief that is accepted uncritically to justify a social institution."[91]

Wainwright suggests that Newbigin's disenchantment with secularization "may have been less a chronological than a geographical one, occasioned by what he had seen since his final return to the United Kingdom in 1974 of the disastrous results of Christendom's collapse in British

86. Newbigin, *Pluralist Society*, 220.

87. Newbigin, "Reflections on an Indian Ministry," 27.

88. Newbigin, *Unfinished Agenda*, 254.

89. Ibid. Although not to the extent that Newbigin originally thought—in the sense that he now realized that non-Western societies did not uncritically adopt Western ideology along with its technology.

90. Newbigin, "History of Missions," 149.

91. Newbigin, *Pluralist Society*, 211.

society."[92] Newbigin's colleague and friend M. M. Thomas explained that "with the dehumanizing effect of modernization on the western and non-western peoples becoming stronger . . . positive theology of modern secular culture as an ally of the Christian mission . . . has got weakened considerably."[93]

In his disenchantment Newbigin convincingly deconstructed the early secularizing thesis presented by Max Weber and the more contemporary one by Denis Munby in his book *The Idea of a Secular Society*.[94] With secularization, it was argued that the processes of rationalization, industrialization, and bureaucratization would create a society with less and less room for the supernatural, magical, and transcendent. In reality, the converse has transpired; in both East and West, despite technological advancement, people remain resolutely religious.[95] The so-called "'secular' society is not a neutral area into which we can project the Christian message. It is an area already occupied by other gods."[96]

Recapitulation to the Parish Model

Newbigin accepted that the church's form is both theologically and sociologically determined. He believed that "the structural forms of the Church are determined by the secular reality, and not by the internal needs of the Church" and that this was attested both by church history and scripture.[97] In the fragmented, differentiated, secular world, the form of church has been made manifest by various denominations. "The sociologists of religion have pointed out to us that the denomination is precisely the visible form that the Church takes when a secularized society privatizes religion."[98] Newbigin was critical of denominationalism[99] and interpreted

92. Wainwright, *Newbigin*, 354.

93. Thomas cited by Wainwright, ibid., 445–46 n. 29.

94. D. L. Munby, *The Idea of a Secular Society and Its Significance for Christians* (London: Oxford University Press, 1963); Newbigin, *Pluralist Society*, ch. 17.

95. Newbigin, *Pluralist Society*, 211.

96. Newbigin, "History of Missions," 150.

97. Lesslie Newbigin, "Does Society Still Need the Parish Church?" in *A Word in Season: Perspectives on Christian World Missions*, ed. Eleanor Jackson (Grand Rapids: Eerdmans, 1994) 53.

98. Ibid., 63.

99. In his critique of denominationalism, Newbigin mainly interacts with the writings of John Macquarrie and Russell Richey. Lesslie Newbigin, "All in One Place or All of One Sort: On Unity and Diversity in the Church," in *Creation, Christ, and Culture:*

it as a product of secularization, which demonstrated how the church had capitulated to the dominant cultural forces: "the denomination cannot be the bearer of the challenge of the gospel to our society, because it is itself the outward and visible form of an inward and spiritual surrender to the ideology of that society."[100] However, the quite unsatisfactory solution Newbigin proposed for the problem of secularization was to restate his belief in the parish principle.[101]

In his early reflections on the impact of secularization, Newbigin was categorical in his criticism of the parish principle—that it was only sustainable in an undifferentiated situation, for example, the rural situation of low mobility, such as the Indian village, but had become an anachronistic irrelevance in the modern city. Newbigin's criticism of the parochial model was twofold: it failed both sociologically and theologically. Critique of the parish system came both from Western sociology and from the experience of the "younger churches" in which the West's problematic dichotomy between mission and church was exposed.

After a further twenty years of reflection—which included his experience as bishop in the large metropolis of Madras—Newbigin modified his position from that of outright rejection: "I do not think that the geographical parish can ever become irrelevant or marginal."[102] But that was amended with the reiteration of his earlier realization, that "alongside these geographically defined units of the Church's corporate life, there is need for other basic Christian congregations shaped by the other kinds of neighbourhood."[103] Urban residents belong to several "places" or "neighbourhoods" simultaneously. Therefore Newbigin recognized the necessity of the church being present in each of these spheres of life: "The 'neighbour' is not just the one so defined by geographical propinquity of residence. There is therefore need that the forms of the church should include congregations which are based on these other neighbourhoods"[104]—not just as an extension of the church, or as a para-church organization, but

---

A Festschrift in Honour of Professor Thomas F. Torrance, ed. Richard W. A. McKinney (Edinburgh: T. & T. Clark, 1976); Lesslie Newbigin, "Review of *Denominationalism*, edited by Russell E. Richey," *ER* 30:2 (1978); Newbigin, "Forms of Unity"; Newbigin, *Foolishness*, 144–46.

100. Newbigin, "Parish Church," 64.

101. Ibid.

102. Newbigin, *Melbourne*, 39.

103. Ibid.

104. Ibid. Sentiments which were also expressed in Newbigin, *Good Shepherd*, 88; Newbigin, "Forms of Unity," 10.

as an actual visible congregation. Because "the primary witness to the sovereignty of Christ must be given, and can only be given, in the ordinary secular work of lay men and women in business, in politics, in professional work, as farmer, factory workers and so on."[105]

There is a progression in Newbigin's thinking on the parish model. In his early thinking he accepted the parish model. In the middle period (during the 1960s) he initially rejected it as an outdated product of 18th- and 19th-century Christendom, but then altered his position. He re-accepted it as the local expression of the congregation, but recognized that it needed to be modified by the forces of secularization, and that it could not be the exclusive expression of the church's form, alternatives were required.

It is rather disappointing that Newbigin does not maintain and develop this position. Rather, in his later reflection, he recapitulated to again endorse the parish model—but now without providing any of the alternatives demanded by secularization.[106] Also, in Newbigin's use of the term "parish," he does not distinguish the different ways this term is understood—although it can be assumed that by "true parish," Newbigin meant one which exists missiologically for the totality of life and persons within the parish.[107]

For his predominant model of the church he returned to that which he had experienced in the Indian villages: "[t]hat scene, repeated hundreds of times, etches in one's mind a picture of the church."[108] Having earlier rejected this model because of its inadequacies, exposed by secularization, he now re-embraced it as his predominant model of the church, without re-engaging in his early critique of it. Here Newbigin was inconsistent in his application of sociological analysis. He has accepted that the parish model, as a gathered institution, isolates people religiously from the world. It was thus an inadequate structure to express the missionary nature of the church. Whilst on the one hand he accepted sociology's critique of denominationalism—that it is a product of secularization—he retracts away from its similar critique of the parish system—that the parochial model, as a legacy from Christendom, fails in the secular city. The parochial legacy emphasized "coming" to the static institution, to the neglect of the "going" of the church—its "sentness."

105. Newbigin, "Holy Spirit," 28.

106. See, e.g., Newbigin, "Parish Church."

107. E.g., Congregationalists, Baptists, and Methodists understand their responsibilities to relate to their own people within the parish, whereas the Church of Scotland see their vocation as related to all the people living in a parish.

108. Newbigin, *Mission in Christ's Way: Bible Studies*, 23.

Whilst re-endorsing the parochial model, Newbigin is disappointing in not providing clues for the restructuring of the church which would enable it to be the community of God *and* the mission of God. Instead Newbigin attempted to combine the inherent tension between the "coming" and the "going" of the congregation, by reiterating the Indian village church as his defining paradigm for the structure of the congregation. Returning to that image of the church etched in his mind from his Madurai diocese, when more than half of the congregations had no buildings of their own, he spoke of the church as "a movement launched into the public life of the world. It has no life except in this sending. . . . [It exists] not as a body drawn out of the world into a secure place, but as a body thrust out into the world to draw all people to Christ. The church's being is in that sending."[109] Earlier he had realized that the parochial model emphasized "coming" to the neglect of "going," and was thus "not true to the biblical picture of the Church as a missionary community." In re-endorsing the parochial model, Newbigin does not deal with this theological criticism by offering a solution of how "sending" can be expressed in the parochial system. Nor does he deal with the problem of how his Indian paradigm of the church can be reconciled with the Western form of parish church and applied to the context of the city.

The solution Newbigin proposed was rather enigmatic: "I don't think we will recover the true form of the parish until we recover a truly missionary approach to our culture. I don't think we will achieve a truly missionary encounter with our culture without recovering the true form of the parish. These two tasks are reciprocally related to each other, and we have to work together on them both."[110] Newbigin has created a catch-22 solution, as reciprocally linking both could prevent progress on either.

The "true form" of the parish church can be taken to mean the church "which exists for the neighbourhood and not just its members" who are drawn out from that neighborhood.[111] But the prevalent form of the parish church was the product of 18th- and 19th-century Western Christianity, which understood mission as almost exclusively *foreign* mission and which, rather than engage missiologically with Western culture, had become acritically syncretized with it.[112] The parochial system served its

109. Ibid., 22, 23. Cf. Newbigin, "Parish Church," 55.

110. Newbigin, "Parish Church," 65.

111. Newbigin, *Pluralist Society*, 236.

112. Mission to the inner-city poor was often an expression of the parish model. E.g., this was the case with Thomas Chalmers' Glasgow experiment. A. L. Drummond and J. Bulloch, *The Scottish Church, 1688–1843: The Age of the Moderates* (Edinburgh:

purpose when the link between church and society was sustained within Christendom; now that it has been severed, an alternative model of the church is required. But "at the most crucial point in his thought, Newbigin fails to be contextual . . . he does not take into account the effects of western culture, namely individualism and differentiation."[113] In rejecting the impact of secularization upon his thinking, it is regrettable that Newbigin also rejected the theological insights that he developed on the structure of the congregation during this period. For example, when writing in 1990 about "Evangelism in the Context of Secularization,"[114] he is silent on the structural issues that secularization raised for the congregation and does not allude to his earlier thinking on evangelism and secularization. The church is "the hermeneutic of the gospel,"[115] but Newbigin is silent on how that is to be structurally expressed. In returning to his Indian paradigm of the church, his recapitulation does not do justice to his earlier critique of the sustainability of this model in a secularized society.

A solution to how the congregation can be missionary may lie with the minister who leads the congregation into the world, "enabling," "sustaining," and "nourishing" them rather than merely "teaching"—the prevalent Protestant model of the ministry, which resulted in both minister and congregation having "their backs turned to the outside world."[116]

Conclusion

At the IMC conference in Willingen theological impulses were introduced which demanded a shift away from the church-centric model which had hitherto dominated Protestant missionary thinking; orientation must be towards the world. Circumstances within the missionary movement, and at large, were necessitating a redefinition of mission. Mission had lost its "directedness." It was acknowledged that "the home base is everywhere," and that mission was now to six, not just three continents, the church, rather than sending, is being sent into the world. At the time of integration it was important that these slogans be translated into action. The historic pattern of missions to Asia and Africa needed transformation. With the

---

St. Andrew Press, 1973), ch. 8.

113. Vandervelde cited by Goheen, *As the Father*, 234.

114. Lesslie Newbigin, "Evangelism in the Context of Secularization," in *A Word in Season*, ed. Eleanor Jackson (Grand Rapids: Eerdmans, 1994).

115. Newbigin, *Pluralist Society*, 222–33.

116. Ibid., 240.

demise of Christendom, it was now recognized that the West was also a mission field. To think on how mission could be done in the West meant taking the issue of secularization seriously.

Christian theologians in the 1960s—Newbigin amongst them—were very positive in their interpretation of secularization. The main impact of secularization upon society was perceived to be the forging of a single civilization which united the world into one linear history, replacing cyclical interpretations. Based upon this assumption, it was logical to conclude that integration of the IMC with the WCC was necessary—the creation of a worldwide fellowship committed to mission to the whole earth. With hindsight we recognize the announcement of a single civilization as quite erroneous. Newbigin was wrong in his interpretation of the impact of secularization upon society. But, compared to his peers, in his critical assessment of secularization, Newbigin exhibited uncanny prescience about the demise of Western culture.

Newbigin was uncomfortable with aspects of van Leeuwen's thesis which were contradicted by his own observations. With time Newbigin came to recognize that the Western linear interpretation of history was being rejected by the East. Instead, because the West had abandoned teleology, it was experiencing an ideological implosion which allowed the invasion of concepts akin to Asian monism. Newbigin, albeit ahead of the pack, was quite wrong in his attempt to interpret God's action in history, conflating secularization with a biblical "prophetic attack." This is a salutary lesson when we accept Christ as the "clue" to history, and that the process of discerning God's action in history comes through committing "oneself to constructive action in history."[117]

Integration of the two world councils was the logical outcome of the theological conviction that the church was God's mission to the world. Whilst the integration of the two councils expressed this at a universal level, it was at the local level that a recovered missional ecclesiology was to be most critically expressed. Secularization enabled Newbigin (and others) to recognize the failure of Western patterns of church, the inadequacy of the parochial model, and the need, in the secularized city, for new expressions of church.

But Newbigin became disenchanted with secularization. He came to recognize the hollow declaration of secularization to provide an ideologically neutral platform on which the claims of Christ could be presented to the world. In particular, Newbigin recognized that the West was not

117. Lesslie Newbigin, *The Finality of Christ* (London: SCM, 1969) 80.

secular but "pagan"—a conviction which was strengthened by his "retirement" to England.[118]

The main WCC study to examine the missionary structure of the congregation in a secularized society was rejected by Newbigin because it became captive to the forces it sought to master. With his rejection Newbigin capitulated in the opposite direction away from secularization. In doing so, he reiterated his favored model of the church, that of the Indian village, which had been exposed as redundant in the secularized city.[119]

The myth of a secular ideological vacuum was the seed which germinated into Newbigin's later missiological engagement with Western culture. Newbigin had previously called for "bold experiment" in the expression of missionary ecclesiology, anticipating a plethora of responses. But, with his rejection of secularization, Newbigin then became silent on the structural embodiment of the missional church. For example, this issue is not addressed in his manifesto which gave birth to the Gospel and Our Culture Movement.[120] The movement predominantly focused on how, at an intellectual level, to engage missiologically with a syncretized, "pagan" Western culture[121]—the question of how this was to be structurally embodied only

---

118. Newbigin, *Unfinished Agenda*, 249.

119. The question of the church's relationship to the secular state has been revisited in the recent work of Charles Taylor, who argues that a secularist regime needs to integrate diversity rather than manage religion. Taylor's work demonstrates the inherent problems with exclusive humanism, namely, that it fails to provide an adequate (and satisfying) answer to what it means to be human, as transcendence beyond the immanent is barred: "[t]he door is barred against further discovery." C. Taylor, *A Secular Age* (Cambridge: Belknap Press of Harvard University Press, 2007) 769. C. Taylor, "The Necessity of Secularist Regimes: Gifford Lecture 21/5/2009," (University of Glasgow: 2009). It is at this point of weakness that Andrew Kirk sees opportunity for the church's missiological engagement on two fronts. First, that "Christian mission . . . has the task of challenging the propensity of our culture to try to explain all human behaviour in terms of our alleged evolutionary past." The second opportunity concerns the concept of "human flourishing," which exclusive humanism has distorted, making it an unrestrained and hedonistic pursuit of personal happiness. Instead, Kirk offers an alternative, that human flourishing can be "understood as the transformation of human nature by the grace of God." J. Andrew Kirk, "'A Secular Age' in a Mission Perspective: A Response to Charles Taylor's Magnum Opus." Conference paper, in *Responding to Secularism: Christian Witness in a Dogmatic Public Culture*, 9–10. Cambridge, 24/4/2009.

120. Newbigin, *The Other Side of 1984: Questions for the Churches*.

121. Hunsberger, *Witness*, 4–8. Later, for the North American wing of the movement, the "cutting edge" became their "focus on the formation of the missional character of the church." Hunsberger, *Witness*, 5. This was expressed through such publications as D. L. Guder, *The Continuing Conversion of the Church* (Grand Rapids: Eerdmans, 2000); D. L. Guder, ed., *Missional Church: A Vision for the Sending of*

coming to the fore much later than Newbigin's foundational input into the movement. The movement is also criticized—at least the North American incarnation—because its work is directed towards mainline churches neglecting other churches beyond that remit, and because the theology of the laity, an important concern of Newbigin's, has been neglected.[122]

Newbigin's quiescence on the structural form of the church is perhaps reflected by his own ministry. His re-endorsement of the parish model paralleled his own ministry in retirement to the local United Reformed Church at Winson Green in Birmingham, and can be contrasted with his earlier bishopric in Madras in which he experimented with what it meant for the church to have a vision of the gospel for the city as a whole.[123]

---

the Church in North America (Grand Rapids: Eerdmans, 1998); C. Van Gelder, ed., *The Missional Church in Context: Helping Congregations Develop Contextual Ministry* (Grand Rapids: Eerdmans, 2007).

122. Michael Goheen, interview with Laing, 28/8/2008.

123. Newbigin, *Unfinished Agenda*, 248-49; Newbigin, *Updated Autobiography*, 243-44. Aware of the problems of "success," in which Christians migrated from the inner-city to the "leafy suburb," Newbigin insisted that the congregation should remain "intimately" engaged with secular concerns. Yet, in his later writing, he did not return to the issue of the structure of the congregation. Lesslie Newbigin, "The Pastor's Opportunities: VI. Evangelism in the City," *Expository Times* 98 (1987) 357. Being a minister of a local congregation, rather than a bishop of a diocese, as he was in Madras, limited Newbigin's opportunities for service, but there is evidence that he maintained a citywide vision—e.g., in his contribution to the concluding chapter of *Faith in the City of Birmingham: An Examination of Problems and Opportunities Facing a City*, ed. R. O'Brien (Exeter: Paternoster, 1988) 133-48.

10

Conclusion

The Outcome of Integration

THE POST-COLONIAL QUEST TO reorganize and restructure missions became focused on the question of how the IMC should relate to the WCC, as international symbols of a recovered relationship between mission and church. The desire to rehabilitate missions led to the more fundamental questioning of how mission should be *redefined*. This thesis has demonstrated, through a study of Newbigin's involvement in the integration of the IMC with the WCC, how, after Tambaram (1938), church-centric missiology was redefined. The integration of the IMC with the WCC was a decisive moment in ecumenical history, the culmination of years of reflection on the missionary nature of the church. The thesis has sought to ascertain what Newbigin contributed to integration; and secondly, how the process of integration affected Newbigin's theological reflection on the nature of mission. The thesis has also elucidated the contours of Newbigin's theological journey, as he engaged with others, as a consequence of his involvement in the course of integration.

As noted, prior studies on Newbigin have focused almost exclusively on his published work, treating his theology in isolation as a fixed entity, without due concern for the evolution of Newbigin's thought, nor his historical context. A further problem with many prior studies is that they do not bridge the gap between Newbigin's theological construction and the actual embodiment of that theology in historical entities.

In contrast this study takes seriously the fact that Newbigin was a task theologian. In doing so this study reveals how Newbigin's early experiences in the SCM and as a missionary in south India imbued him with convictions which would influence his leadership of integration. An important contribution of this study has been to bridge the gap between Newbigin's theologizing and his attempts to embody his convictions in reality, coming to terms with the historical structures the church has created.

In the first section of this concluding chapter, the overarching link between Newbigin's theology and the organizational embodiment of his convictions is examined through four key themes which are interwoven throughout the core of the thesis. First, how the early influences upon Newbigin's ecclesiology became expressed in integration. Second, throughout his life Newbigin had to contend with various polarizations and dichotomies, his response to these is considered. Third, Newbigin's *method* of theologizing is assessed. And fourth, the importance and role of the local congregation in Newbigin's theologizing is appraised.

The second section of the chapter examines the outcome of integration, in particular the factors which impacted the role of the D/CWME within the WCC. The effect of the ongoing dichotomy between "evangelical" and "ecumenical" in the ecumenical movement at large is considered. Finally, the chapter concludes by returning to Newbigin's assessment of integration.

Embodying the Church's Call to Mission and to Unity

The Shaping of Newbigin's Ecclesiology

First, the thesis has shown that three factors, which influenced Newbigin's ecclesiology, were determinative in shaping Newbigin for his crucial responsibility in integration. These were the SCM, his experience of the south Indian church and the formation of the CSI. How these factors influenced Newbigin's aim for integration has also been explained. At the start of his Christian experience Newbigin had a vision of a world-wide cross embracing the earth and reaching to heaven. This vision is analogous to the form of Christianity he derived from the SCM, centered on Christ but with an ecumenical vision of the world as its boundary. The creative and dialectical tension between this core and boundary characterized Newbigin's life. He remained acutely aware of the danger of capitulating to one pole to the detriment of the other. From the SCM Newbigin imbibed the crucial concern for the health of the smallest unit of an organization. This influenced his priorities on integration, his approach being to emphasize the regional and local expressions of new relationships between church and mission, rather than allow a centralized hierarchy to determine organization. And this emphasis set him at odds with the centralizing bureaucracy of the WCC.

The thesis has argued that Newbigin's vision of the church was formed through his experience of the "spontaneous" expansion of south India village churches. These experiences were crucial, giving Newbigin an enduring model of the church, to which he would consistently return.

Through the formation of the CSI, and Newbigin's defense of reunion, he came to understand that the church was defined not just historically in terms of its essence, but also dynamically in terms of what it was *becoming*. The church was defined by looking back to the cross and forward to the *eschaton*. Newbigin maintained that the recovery of relationship between mission and unity which he first experienced in south Asia was applicable worldwide. At a personal level Newbigin was ideally equipped to lead integration having inculcated the theological integration between mission and church. A fact which, for ecumenical leaders such as Visser 't Hooft, made him the obvious choice to be the IMC general secretary: "It was in no small measure due to his [Newbigin's] vision that integration took place. . . . For he believed deeply that the missionary-evangelistic concern and the concern for church-unity are both rooted in the same mandate."[1]

As the CSI was a sign to the churches that reunion was possible, Newbigin understood integration in an analogous way as a sign to the world. The reunion process stressed the concept of time in theologizing and the need for enactment. In integration there was a need to act upon the growing consensus in the ecumenical movement that the church is missionary and called to unity.

But Newbigin's non-Western vision of the church set him at odds with a Western dominated WCC—as his defense of the CSI had done with Anglo-Catholics. Integration brought a rehabilitation and redefinition of mission. But this was not matched by a corresponding resolve to renew the WCC. The quest to embody the acknowledged recovery in ecclesiology could be deferred until after integration. This decision enabled the WCC executive to accept the integration of the IMC without an analogous reformation of the structures of the WCC. This was reflected in the incorporation of the IMC into the WCC rather than the complete overhaul of the structure of the WCC at integration which Newbigin had, unsuccessfully, pressed for.

1. Visser 't Hooft, "Statement on Newbigin," February 1974, WCC: 994.1.09/10.

Contending with Dichotomies

Second, throughout his career Newbigin had to contend with various theological dichotomies. A key characteristic of Newbigin's life was his holistic grasp of the gospel and his strenuous efforts to retain a creative tension between conflicting poles without capitulating to either. Through the schism in the SCM Newbigin was first introduced to the tension and polarization in the ecumenical movement, fault lines opening up to create the institutional chasm between "ecumenicals" and "evangelicals." Efforts to bridge this chasm would occupy Newbigin throughout his life.

As a Church of Scotland missionary Newbigin was introduced to the "intolerable dichotomy" between mission and church created by the Protestant missionary movement. More adequate relationships were sought between the "younger" and "older" churches reflected in a gradual shift of the IMC as it became increasingly church-centric in its thinking. The parallel co-existence of the IMC and the WCC at least gave the appearance that the two mandates of mission and church unity could be pursued in exclusion and without reference to the other. And the term for the councils' relationship, "in association with," became so over-laden with meaning that it broke down as an adequate expression of their inter-connectedness.

In this context Newbigin was repeatedly called upon to draft statements arising out of ecumenical conferences. This demonstrated the public acknowledgment of his ability to preserve creative tension, to build consensus and bridge different ecclesiological positions—as was evident in his drafting of statements at Willingen.

Willingen first introduced Newbigin to the concerns of Hoekendijk and Lehmann with their critique of church-centric missiology. The tension between a church-centric missiology versus one centered on the world was to dominate both Newbigin's theological reflection from Willingen onwards and the larger canvas of the ecumenical movement. Uppsala marked a decisive a shift away from the church-centric model which had dominated since Tambaram. Dissonant voices on the role of the church vis-à-vis the world could not be reconciled and opinion diverged on the church's continuity or discontinuity with the world. This led to the unresolved tension, between two conflicting ecclesiologies, between "salvation" and "humanization."

In the 1960s the church sought to respond to the forces of secularization. On the role of the local congregation in a secularized society the thesis shows how Newbigin sought to sustain a position between polarities, insisting that the church is *both* a task force committed to the doing of God's will in the life of the secular world; *and* a family of those reconciled and gathered in Christ as a visible community. But in this instance Newbigin was less successful in maintaining equilibrium. In Newbigin's beguilement with secularization he rejected the parish model of the gathered community. Then, with his ultimate rejection of secular ideology as an inappropriate vehicle for Christianity, Newbigin capitulated in the opposite direction, away from secularization. In doing so, he reiterated his favored model of the church, that of the Indian village, which has been shown to be an inadequate model for the secularized city.

At the heart of the ecumenical movement another dichotomy loomed large. The problem of the relationship between mission and service became concentrated by the enlarged mandate of the DICA, which allowed it to expand beyond the confines of Europe into traditional "mission fields." The quest to resolve this problem had been *the* reason to pursue integration. Theological reflection on service led to the understanding that it was not simply a means to an end for missions; instead mission and service were understood as the two principal aspects of the church's nature and calling to the world. Service was "the ecumenical expression of the nature of the Church towards and in the world."[2] Newbigin's theological understanding held *koinonia* as central, mission and service being inextricably linked in the local fellowship: "Both preaching and service, spring out of the new reality of the shared Holy Spirit (koinonia)."[3]

Newbigin's case, that mission and service belonged together, and thus the DICA and the IMC should be united at integration, remained the stronger case theologically. However, it was questionable whether that theological premise could be adequately translated into reality, given the profound historical differences between mission and inter-church aid agencies. The IMC was advisory and operated with a small leadership and was similarly constrained by budget. This contrasted with the burgeoning financial clout of the DICA, which became by far the largest division of the WCC. These differences made their union into one division improbable, and therefore Newbigin's advocacy of his plan of integration unrealistic. The Joint Committee failed to deal with this fundamental problem that had originally prompted calls for integration, delaying decisions until after integration. This limited the effectiveness of integration and led to a dissipation of resolve to tackle this issue.

2. Kraemer, "Inter-church aid and mission," 5–8/12/1959, WCC: 27.0012, 4.
3. Newbigin to van Beyma, 28/11/1958, BUL: DA29/2/9/54.

Newbigin's Method of Theologizing

The third recurring theme in this thesis concerns Newbigin's method of theologizing. Newbigin operated with confidence and a sense of urgency to respond to what he perceived as divine imperative—often in the face of a loss of confidence and inertia. Due to the obsession with structures, and the growing association between the two councils, there was the danger of interpreting integration only at a structural level. One of the reasons Newbigin was recruited as general secretary was because of his ability to see beyond the structural issues and facilitate more fundamental theological debate.

Newbigin consistently argued from theological presuppositions to organizational expression—insisting that theology must be embodied.[4] He started from his interpretation of theological ideals rather than from the historical realities which had evolved—and yet he was shaped by the historical processes he encountered, his experiences in India being particularly determinative. At times he tended to be idealistic and clashed with those for whom historical realities were more decisive—such as Max Warren.

Integration of the two world councils was the logical outcome of the theological conviction that the church was God's mission to the world. For Newbigin the clue to solving the problem of relationship always lay in starting with an understanding of the local congregation, and from there extrapolating to regional and international structures, rather than the reverse—a methodology at odds with the WCC's centralizing ethos. Integration was about translating theology into action so Newbigin consistently pressed for concrete action and local and regional experimentation.

Newbigin was rather naive in his expectation of integration. His emphasis on the local and regional, mirrored in the IMC's ethos of regionalization meant that insufficient pressure was brought to counter the centralizing tendency of the WCC in Geneva. There was no person within WCC circles who, as Newbigin had done in the IMC, would ensure adequate discussion on integration. In contrast, the Western church continued to dominate the WCC offices, WCC funding and thus its agenda. This, coupled with Newbigin's acknowledged inadequacies as an administrator, led Newbigin to concede that his administrative failure had impacted the

---

4. Newbigin's ability to move from theory to the practical details of the life of the church "excited" emerging leaders such as Emilio Castro. Castro, interview with Laing, 10/9/2008.

effectiveness of bringing the concern of mission into the centre of the WCC's agenda, limiting the success of integration.

Newbigin's critique of the inadequacies of the church-centric model led him into more constructive theologizing on the trinitarian basis of mission; making the significant shift from addressing the *structures* of mission to exploring the *substance* of mission. This thesis has demonstrated how the process of integration enabled Newbigin to move from reflecting upon the *reorganization and rehabilitation* of mission to more fundamental issues of how mission should be *redefined*. But during this period of theologizing, rather than Newbigin's characteristic confidence, he exhibited personal hesitancy, mirrored by his failure to garner public endorsement from ecumenical leadership.

Compared to his peers Newbigin exhibited an uncanny prescience on many matters. But he was quite wrong in his application of secularization, conflating secularization with a biblical "prophetic attack" on non-Western civilizations. That Newbigin could be so wrong is a salutary lesson to the church which accepts Christ as the "clue" to history, and acknowledges that the method of discerning God's action in history comes through committing "oneself to constructive action in history."

The Importance of the Local Congregation

The fourth theme running throughout this thesis has been the importance Newbigin placed upon the local congregation, *the* place to express the recovery in the relationship between mission and church. The act of unification of the councils created a world body which united church and mission, representing a global reality of a fundamental theological conviction. But the logic of integration was, most significantly, expressed (and tested) at the local level of the church. Newbigin's concern was not primarily with the two world councils but at the local level of the congregation—how was the local congregation to embody this relationship? The pursuit of an adequate answer led to the study, the MSC, which unfortunately ignored lessons from the non-Western church and became captive to the forces of secularization with which it had sought to reckon.

Newbigin's critique of the church-centric model led him to appreciate the primacy of God's action in mission, that the Holy Spirit is the primary missionary. These convictions were reinforced by Newbigin's early experience of the "spontaneous" growth of rural village churches. This modified his understanding of the agency of the church: "The Church is not so much the agent of the mission as the locus of mission."[5] However, with his rejection of secularization, Newbigin became silent on how the missional church was to be structurally embodied. Instead, he returned uncritically to his model of the Indian village church.

The Outcome of Integration: An Analysis

Post-Integration Developments

There were several factors which impacted the outcome of the integration of the IMC with the WCC. As already noted, the councils were quite different in their *modus operandi* and ethos. Newbigin "was proud" of the decentralized, advisor nature of the IMC, which operated as a think tank.[6] In contrast Löffler is correct in his assessment of the centralizing tendencies of the WCC, which understood itself as the "privileged instrument of the ecumenical movement" and "operated as an international powerhouse . . . initiating activities and radiating impulses from the centre to the ecumenical periphery."[7] This made the IMC organizationally incompatible with the WCC.

The administrative resolve to reconcile this incompatibility was considerably weakened by the transition in leadership which occurred soon after integration. Newbigin left office in 1965 and Visser 't Hooft retired in 1967. Their departure marked a critical shift to a younger generation of ecumenical leadership, who did not share the concerns which had first prompted calls for integration, nor concern for the ongoing issues which integration had not resolved—such as the relationship between mission and service. In fact, the question of integration was "never re-opened."[8]

Despite organizational differences, several factors lead to the conclusion that integration was a "success." The CWME through its publications and continuing world mission conferences "greatly influenced the direction of the ecumenical movement."[9] The concerns and ethos of the CWME was transmitted to the whole of the WCC through the appointment of Philip Potter and then Emilio Castro as general secretaries, both of whom

---

5. Newbigin, *Pluralist Society*, 119.
6. Paul Löffler, email to Laing, 17/08/2007.
7. Löffler, email to Laing, 28/9/2007.
8. Castro, interview, 10/9/2008.
9. Löffler, email, 17/08/2007.

had been schooled in the CWME.[10] At the height of its influence, the CWME was an influential department within the WCC "with considerable overlaps in the field of studies (inter-religious dialogue, proselytism), in ecumenical cooperation (with Rome after Vatican II), [and] in the field of ecumenical action."[11]

But changes were afoot internal and external to the WCC which limited the long-term effectiveness of integration. The 1960s and 1970s represent the zenith of the twentieth-century ecumenical movement. After this period, the administration of the WCC, centered in Geneva, shrank to a third of its size, and changed from having an executive function to being "reduced to a knowledge based organization."[12] Contraction of the whole obviously impacts each constituent member of the WCC. Furthermore, in the 1960s the WCC was *the* ecumenical organ operating at a world level. Since then there has been a multiplication of organizations, world confessional families, service agencies and looser confederations operating internationally, such as the Lausanne Movement and the World Evangelical Fellowship, diluting the international impact of the WCC.

The WCC shrank as a whole, but so too did the CWME in relation to the WCC: "One could say there has been a certain diminishing influence [of mission] from 1961 'til now."[13] The D/CWME "has been constantly reduced in its importance in the WCC due to financial and restructuring factors."[14] This was the result of a change in ethos which understood "traditional items like mission and Faith and Order as belonging to the old past."[15] The impact of the CWME was further diluted by the mushrooming of numerous small units within the WCC during the 1970s, each with a commission and budget, and each appealing directly to the churches— the most notable of these being the Program to Combat Racism.[16] This program marked a radical departure for the WCC, from supporting the agency of the church, to directly supporting action (and even violent struggle) by secular agencies against racism.

10. Potter was general secretary from 1972 to1984, Castro from 1985 to1992.

11. Löffler, email, 17/08/2007.

12. Jacques Matthey, director of WCC program for Unity, Mission, Evangelism and Spirituality, interview with Laing, 20/8/2008.

13. Matthey, interview, 20/8/2008.

14. Ibid.

15. Ibid.

16. Castro recalled that sixteen or seventeen units emerged. Castro, interview, 10/9/2008.

Newbigin stressed that "*only* the local congregation, which believes and lives the Gospel, can be a bearer of mission," and that the "missionary church is a community of first fruits of the kingdom with a prophetic task."[17] For Newbigin, the church was therefore not necessarily a social and political agent. In maintaining this narrow understanding of mission, centered on the church, Newbigin shrank back from endorsing political action as a legitimate aspect of mission, setting him at odds with its general endorsement within the WCC: "[T]aking that position . . . meant not to be on the ecumenical bandwagon at the time."[18] Newbigin's view had ramifications for the perception of mission in the WCC, reinforcing its outmoded image. In contrast, the general endorsement of political action *as* mission within the WCC was also later approved by the CWME, under Potter's tenure.[19] But Newbigin was right to insist that Christian witness cannot be detached from the life of the local community. As is Löffler, who is of the opinion that this disassociation of mission from the church contributed to "the ultimate decline of DWME in the WCC."[20]

Newbigin's emphasis on the centrality of the *local* congregation was further undermined after integration by the rise in prominence of world confessional families. Most notably the changes wrought in the Roman Catholic Church after Vatican II required a realignment of relationships for the WCC. The shift away from local expressions of unity, to an emphasis on the relationship between world confessional bodies, with a resultant hardening their separate identities, meant that the "dynamic of the New-Delhi-formula has been lost."[21]

The direction and evolving ethos of the WCC is profoundly influenced by the incumbent general secretary. Whilst Potter and Castro had come from the CWME fold, Konrad Raiser presented a vision for the ecumenical movement at odds with Newbigin's. As Newbigin's *One Body* had served as a personal "manifesto" for integration, Raiser's book *Ecumenism in Transition*[22] was perceived to be his manifesto for his leadership as general secretary.[23] Raiser discerned a shift from the christo-centric universal-

17. Löffler, emails, 17/08/2007 and 28/9/2007. Emphasis added.

18. Löffler, email, 28/9/2007.

19. Ibid.

20. Löffler, email, 17/08/2007.

21. Ibid. Here Löffler is referring to the statement, "All in each place," drafted by Newbigin. WCC, *New Delhi Report*, 116.

22. K. Raiser, *Ecumenism in Transition: A Paradigm Shift in the Ecumenical Movement?* (Geneva: WCC, 1991).

23. Raiser was general secretary from 1992 to 2004.

ism which was developed under Visser 't Hooft, to a trinitarian model which came to the fore at the Uppsala assembly. Newbigin was critical of Raiser, asking whether Raiser was not replacing or obscuring the old model—trinitarianism did not relativize Christ.[24]

Newbigin's major criticism of Raiser's book was in its "total amnesia in respect of the missionary and evangelistic work of the churches. . . . To allow the worldwide missionary and evangelistic calling of the church to disappear from the agenda of the WCC (as this book effectively does) is much more than a 'paradigm shift.'"[25] Newbigin was concerned that Raiser's vision for the future development of the ecumenical movement would be realized under his leadership as general secretary: "I have to confess to a deep personal concern here, for if the vision for the WCC that this book represents were to be realized, then the bringing of the [IMC] . . . into the WCC would have to be judged as having been a mistake."[26] Although Newbigin's disquiet continued throughout Raiser's tenure, afterwards (and beyond Newbigin's death) there is general consensus that, on the place of mission in the WCC, there has been movement in the direction of which Newbigin would have approved of.[27]

The Evangelical/Ecumenical Dichotomy

Reflecting on his tenure at the WCC, Newbigin was penitent that "the adjectives 'evangelical' and 'ecumenical' should have come in our time to stand for two mutually opposed positions."[28] At times the communication between the two camps was reduced to the level of warfare.[29]

Newbigin's hope, in uniting mission with church in the integration of the two councils, was the rebirth of missionary concern within the

24. Newbigin, "Ecumenical Amnesia."

25. Ibid., 5.

26. Ibid. On the Newbigin/Raiser debate, see Goheen, "Future of Mission." The acrimonious nature may have been exacerbated by misunderstandings. Martin Conway recalls a conversation with Raiser in which Raiser said that "he just didn't know how to write back to Lesslie when the latter had so grievously misunderstood what he had been trying to say." Conway, email to Laing, 06/09/2008.

27. Conway, email, 06/09/2008; Wilbert Shenk, interview with Laing, 1/11/2006.

28. Newbigin, "Cross-Currents," 146.

29. This was even the case *within* the Lausanne movement, with Donald McGavran and Peter Wagner and their detractors lobbing metaphorical "hand grenades at one another." J. R. W. Stott, "Twenty Years after Lausanne: Some Personal Reflections," *IBMR* 19:2 (1995) 50.

WCC and its member churches. Two decades after integration he acknowledged that the hoped-for changes had not transpired, although, in his opinion, integration remained the right decision: "If . . . the transformation in the life of the WCC and of its member churches which we hoped for has not happened, yet I must affirm that it was right, and that it created the context in which a true rebirth of the missionary concern of the churches can take place."[30]

A major reason the rebirth of the churches failed to develop was due to the ongoing dichotomy between ecumenicals and evangelicals. The divergent paths taken in their history after integration was a stark contradiction to the theological foundation for integration. By Uppsala Newbigin conceded that "These two words [mission and unity] no longer seem to belong together. They pull in opposite directions. On one side the call is to leave the 'institutional Church' behind in order to evangelise the unconverted; on the other it is to leave the 'institutional Church' in order to express one's solidarity with the total humanity."[31]

Both movements, in their pursuit of mission, neglected the centrality of the church as the crucial agent of mission, thus spurning an opportunity for the church's reformation. Yet they did so for diametrically opposite reasons. For conservative evangelicals their driving compulsion to evangelize the unreached people groups of the world distracted them from reforming their deficient ecclesiology. The slow turning behemoth, the "institutional church," could be nimbly sidestepped by fleet-footed missionary organizations and appeased to ensure an uninterrupted flow of funding. In ecumenical missiology, loyalty to the slogan "the world sets the agenda," increasingly relegated the role of the church, as God's actions were to be discerned in secular movements.

By quite different paths both movements came to the same conviction: "that the present institutional structures of the Church are not appropriate to its missionary calling. The Church as we know it is simply not built for mission."[32] Both movements faced the obstacle of the church on their road; they swerved in opposite directions around the obstacle, leaving the church behind, unreformed. In many ways the development of their contrasting missiologies were mirror images of the other, a strength

---

30. Newbigin, "Integration."

31. Newbigin, "Call to Mission," 257.

32. Ibid., 263.

in ecumenical missiology representing a corresponding weakness in evangelical concerns—and vice versa.[33]

The theological impetus for integration was the belief that the church is called both to mission and unity. But the outcome of integration has been an ecumenical/evangelical polarization in which the call to mission has been heard "on both sides—as a call not to unity but to separation."[34] Integration sought to solve the theological problem of relating mission to the church. The events which evolved from that act have been a bitter and protracted missiological "confrontation." Both parties (largely) bypassed the church, as the church was problematic or irrelevant to the pursuit of their missiology. Evangelicals perpetuated the Western historical dichotomy between church and mission; their concern was mission, not the church. For ecumenicals, from Uppsala onwards, the distinction between church and world was blurred (or obliterated) as the world assumed priority. However, after a period of pronounced polarization, Matthey is of the opinion that the WCC and Lausanne movement are both now more moderate, and "have come into the middle," with extremes now on either side, rather than running through and defining them.[35]

Throughout his life, both publically[36] and privately, Newbigin affirmed that integration had been the right decision at the time, although he conceded that he had been disappointment by the outcome. He maintained that only in the context which had overcome the false dichotomy between mission and church, could an adequate, post-colonial understanding of mission, be developed.[37] Integration had contributed to that understanding, and the general acceptance of missionary ecclesiology, recovering the missionary dimension of each church.[38]

There was sadness that although integration was the right decision, the outcome had not transpired as Newbigin had hoped.[39] Newbigin was critical of the failure of the WCC to give mission the central place that

33. D. J. Bosch, "Evangelism: An Holistic Approach," *Journal of Theology for Southern Africa* 36 (1981) 43–63. S. Barrington-Ward, "The Marriage of North and South," *IRM* 73:289 (1984) 51.

34. Newbigin, "Call to Mission," 257.

35. Matthey, interview, 20/8/2008.

36. E.g., in response to questioning by Gerald Anderson during a public lecture at Divinity School of Samford, University of Birmingham, Alabama, c. 1992. Anderson, interview with Laing, 21/8/2008.

37. Newbigin, "Integration," 250–51.

38. Ibid., 255.

39. Shenk, interview, 1/11/2006.

he believed it deserved. There were "no lack of critical voices" raising the charge that "evangelism has a very small place in the programs of the WCC, and that while the word 'mission' is freely used, it has been robbed of its classical reference to the bringing of the Gospel to those outside the Church"—a charge which Newbigin could not simply "shrug off."[40] Although fully engaged in the ecumenical movement Newbigin became increasingly estranged from the WCC. This can be catalogued in his publication record, which showed that he was increasingly publishing elsewhere rather than with the WCC press, as he had done formerly.[41]

As with the formation of the CSI and the international calls for organic unity, so too the integration of the IMC with the WCC marked the passing of an epoch. Newbigin, at the centre of these events, compelled by his convictions about the gospel, sought to seize these moments and garner the momentum they generated. Many anticipated that the next phase of Christianity would be conciliar in character.[42] But the WCC (and Lausanne) have shrunk in size and influence and the Roman Catholic Church has returned to being progressively more monarchical. Moreover, this is not happening against a backdrop of general decline, but during the tremendous growth of non-Western Christianity. It is both sobering and ironic to note that on the eve of the centenary celebrations of Edinburgh 1910 the quest for unity which arose in the modern ecumenical movement, reaching its zenith in integration, has now been eclipsed by other concerns. The drive behind the ecumenical movement has dissipated and an alternative movement is yet to emerge to inspire, unite and engage Christians around the world in a manner similar to that witnessed in the twentieth century.

40. Newbigin, "Integration," 248.

41. Darrell Guder, interview with Laing, 19/8/2008.

42. E.g., Andrew Walls, interview with Laing, 24/4/2009.

Appendix 1

A Chronology of Newbigin's Life with Other Key Events[1]

1909	8 December: Born, Newcastle upon Tyne
1909–28	Early life
1928–31	Cambridge University
1931–33	Student Christian Movement Intercollegiate Secretary (Glasgow)
1933–36	Theological training at Westminster College, Cambridge University
1936	20 August: Marriage to Helen Henderson
1936	22 October: Landed at Madras
1936–37	Missionary in India with Church of Scotland
1937	5 October: Returned to Edinburgh due to leg injury
June 1938–July 1939	Missionary Candidates Secretary for Church of Scotland
1939–46	District missionary of Kanchipuram, Madras (arrived 18 October)

1. Based on Lesslie Newbigin, *Unfinished Agenda: An Updated Autobiography* (Geneva: WCC, 1993); Thomas F. Foust, "Lesslie Newbigin," *The Bible in TransMission: Special Issue* (1998).

Appendix 1

1946	10 June: Arrived in United Kingdom on furlough
1947	27 September: Inauguration of the CSI, Madras; Newbigin consecrated as bishop
1947–59	Bishop in the CSI at Madurai and Ramnad
1948	2 August: Inauguration and first assembly of the WCC, Amsterdam; Newbigin attends as delegate of the CSI
1959–61	London: General Secretary of the IMC
1961	Third Assembly of the WCC, New Delhi, 19 November–5 December, 1961; integration of the IMC with the WCC
1962–65	Geneva: seconded to the WCC Division of World Mission and Evangelism
1965–74	Bishop in Madras, India
1974	Awarded CBE (Commander of the Most Excellent Order of the British Empire)
1974–79	Lecturer in Theology at Selly Oak Colleges, Birmingham
1977–78	Moderator of the General Assembly of the United Reformed Church
1980–88	Minister with United Reformed Church, Winson Green, Birmingham
1983–98	Retired; active with The Gospel and Our Culture Movement, writing, advising, and teaching
1998	30 January: Died, West Dulwich, London

Appendix 2

Methodology

A MAJOR AIM OF this study is to put the integration of the IMC under the microscope in a unique way with Newbigin at the centre. This study has sought to produce a theological history of this important event and demonstrate that Newbigin's theologizing on mission arose directly from his reflections on integration. A central method of this study has been the uncovering of unpublished documents, researching their contextual background, and integrating those findings with Newbigin's published works. This study sees considerable merit in this method, the use of primary sources, particularly that of personal correspondence, in an attempt to understand Newbigin.

Previous Research

By any standard, Newbigin was a major theological and missiological thinker of the twentieth century, a pivotal figure in the rise of the ecumenical movement. Reflecting upon Newbigin's importance, Geoffrey Wainwright has written a major "theological biography" of him.[2] Wainwright identifies ten themes which characterized Newbigin's life and work and organizes his book around these themes. Wainwright's major contribution serves as a useful map through the contours of Newbigin's published work, but he leaves the reader adrift from the historical anchors that a more chronological work would give.

Of particular relevance to this thesis is Wainwright's fifth chapter, "The Missionary Strategist," which details Newbigin's involvement with the IMC and WCC. Here Wainwright largely draws upon Newbigin's

2. G. Wainwright, *Lesslie Newbigin: A Theological Life* (Oxford: Oxford University Press, 2000).

autobiography as his primary source. But in a book which aims to deal exhaustively with Newbigin's theological life Wainwright can devote only a few pages to integration.[3]

A major attempt to wrestle with Newbigin's missiology for Western culture is found in the book *A Scandalous Prophet: The Way of Mission after Newbigin*.[4] For the purposes of this study, what is perhaps most useful in this book is the extensive (although not exhaustive) bibliography on Newbigin.[5] As well as cataloguing Newbigin's published work, the editors have also catalogued selected unpublished manuscripts and important audio and video material by Newbigin. The bibliography also contains an extensive list of the various reviews of Newbigin's publications and a final section on "Selected Engagements with Newbigin's Thought."

Previous postgraduate research on Newbigin has focused primarily on his work in "retirement" when he sought to develop a missiological engagement with Western culture. Research has thus tended to orbit around the topics of pluralism, inter-faith dialogue, and developing missiological approaches to Western culture. Recent examples of this approach to the study of Newbigin include those by Veldhorst,[6] Thomas,[7] Wood,[8] Keskitalo,[9] Foust,[10] and Weston.[11] Although for Newbigin the area of Christian encounter with other faiths was increasingly important from his Indian years onwards, this thesis of necessity has not been able to devote

3. Ibid., 164–77.

4. T. F. Foust, et al. *A Scandalous Prophet: The Way of Mission after Newbigin* (Grand Rapids: Eerdmans, 2001).

5. T. F. Foust and George R. Hunsberger, "Bishop J. E. Lesslie Newbigin: A Comprehensive Bibliography," in ibid., 249–323.

6. B. J. Veldhorst, "A Christian Voice in a World without God" (PhD diss., State University of Utrecht, 1990).

7. J. M. Thomas, "The Centrality of Christ and Inter-Religious Dialogue in the Theology of Lesslie Newbigin" (PhD diss., University of St. Matthew's College, 1996).

8. N. J. Wood, "Confessing Christ in a Plural World: A Missiological Approach to Inter-Faith Relations with Particular Reference to Kenneth Cragg and Lesslie Newbigin." (DPhil diss., Oxford University, 1996).

9. J. Keskitalo, "Kolmiyhteisen Jumalan Missio: Lesslie Newbigin Lähetyskäsityksen Teologinen Perusta" (MTh, University of Helsinki, 1988); J. Keskitalo, "Kristillinen Usko Ja Moderni Kulttuuri: Lesslie Newbigin Ksitys Kirkon Missiosta Modernissa Lnsimaisessa Kulttuurissa" (ThD, Suomalainen Teologinen Kirjallisuusseura, 1999).

10. T. F. Foust, "The Missiological Approach to Modern Western Culture according to Lesslie Newbigin and Dean E. Walker" (PhD diss, University of Birmingham, 2002).

11. P. D. A. Weston, "Mission and Cultural Change: Critical Engagement with the Writings of Lesslie Newbigin" (PhD diss., King's College, London, 2002).

more than occasional attention to this theme that was so prominent in Newbigin's thinking for the remainder of his life.

In contrast to the majority of studies which focus on Newbigin's later writing, two works have sought to follow the development of Newbigin's missiology from his early writings to his retirement. Michael Goheen's doctoral study of Newbigin's missionary ecclesiology, published as *As the Father Has Sent Me, I Am Sending You*,[12] follows the contours of Newbigin's evolving ecclesiology. In the first part of his thesis, Goheen, through an historical approach to Newbigin's *published* work, identifies the major "shifts" in Newbigin's evolving ecclesiology. From historical analysis, Goheen then presents a systematic synthesis of Newbigin's ecclesiology.

The second doctoral study on Newbigin's earlier writings is that by George Hunsberger, which was published as *Bearing the Witness of the Spirit*.[13] Hunsberger follows the enduring theme of election as a thread through the chronology of Newbigin's work. Hunsberger argues that Newbigin's "notion of election provides a foundation for a theology of cultural plurality."[14] Newbigin's missionary experience in India served as a crucible in which he had to counter Hindu objection to the apparent offensiveness of the particularity of election. Newbigin argues that the doctrine of election provides the essential link between the particularity of God's actions and the universality of his intentions. Election reflects God's personal nature and provides the "fit" between that and the social character of human life and the mediation of divine salvation.[15]

The short *akzessarbeit* study by Maria Klopfeusfein is of more relevance to this thesis. Klopfeusfein focuses on Newbigin's contribution to the integration of the IMC with the WCC.[16] The study follows the historical and theological processes contributing to the case for integration and the respective cases against as presented by Canon Max Warren, the Norwegian mission organizations, and the Orthodox Churches. Using the published minutes of IMC and WCC committee meetings, Klopfeusfein then details Newbigin's argument for integration with particular attention

12. M. W. Goheen, *As the Father Has Sent Me, I Am Sending You: J. E. Lesslie Newbigin's Missionary Ecclesiology* (Zoetermeer: Boekencentrum, 2000).

13. G. R. Hunsberger, *Bearing the Witness of the Spirit: Lesslie Newbigin's Theology of Cultural Plurality* (Grand Rapids: Eerdmans, 1998).

14. Ibid., 112.

15. Ibid.

16. M. Klopfeusfein, "Lesslie Newbigin: Mission Und Einheit Der Kirche" (Akzessarbeit, University of Berne, 1984).

to his manifesto *One Body, One Gospel, One World*.[17] As a short study—just ninety pages—based on the *published* material available, it gives a useful overview of Newbigin's particular contribution. But the study is limited to published material and does not therefore include the archival materials such as draft papers, correspondence, and unpublished lectures that Newbigin gave around the time of integration.

Previous studies have limited the scope of their research to that of Newbigin's published corpus. This study seeks to advance knowledge by assessing Newbigin's role in integration, primarily using archival sources, which include a vast amount of correspondence, unpublished lecture notes, draft papers and sermon notes.

Archival Sources

The location of Newbigin's archives reflects his international career, repositories being held in Edinburgh, Birmingham, London, and Geneva. Although some are fully catalogued, and the catalogue is available online, for other materials the researcher needed to travel to the archive just to ascertain the contents and potential usefulness of the archival materials.

The main repository of archives on Newbigin is held in the Special Collections of the Main Library of the University of Birmingham. This is organized as a collection *on* Newbigin and contains correspondence, unpublished lecture notes, draft papers and sermon notes from throughout his life. Other repositories include: the Foreign Mission Records of the Church of Scotland, held at The National Library of Scotland; the Archives of the World Council of Churches, held in Geneva; and a microfiche copy of the International Missionary Council Archives, held at the School of Oriental and African Studies in London.

Apart from the Newbigin collection in Birmingham, which is organized around Newbigin, all the other repositories are organized around the respective institution. Relevant material by Newbigin, held in these repositories therefore required a thorough search as some are only partly catalogued.

Archival sources used in this thesis are from the four repositories listed below. Each archival reference begins with a prefix referring to its source:

BUL: Birmingham University Library

---

17. Lesslie Newbigin, *One Body, One Gospel, One World: The Christian Mission Today* (London: IMC, 1958).

NLS: The National Library of Scotland

SOAS: School of Oriental and African Studies

WCC: World Council of Churches

Each library (except the NLS) allowed me to take digital copies of archival resources. This has allowed me to check with the original sources to maintain accuracy when writing up the thesis.

The Use of Newbigin's Personal Letters

Throughout his long career, Newbigin was an indefatigable letter writer who was meticulous in storing his correspondence. In contrast to his published work, his unpublished correspondence, as would be expected, is often extremely candid as he shares concerns and observations which were absent from, or suitably tempered for, publications.

Besides extensive personal letters to various organizational administrators there is also a large repository of letters between Newbigin and his immediate family. It was Newbigin's expectation that these letters would be kept private within the family, and as such they add color and texture to the more bland canvas painted by the official documents.[18] David Arnold and Robert Bickers, in their introduction to a book concerned with methodological issues in the use of missionary archives, comment that "the introspection and self-analysis that characterizes Protestantism is a boon to the researcher."[19] On the use of letters as resource material for history, Max Warren, in a letter to his son-in-law, Roger Hooker, makes an amusing yet valid observation when he contrasts the value of minutes and official documents to the revelations evident in personal letters. Commenting on the work of Gordon Hewitt, who was researching a history of the Church Missionary Society,[20] Warren stated: "There is no escaping a man's letters if you want to get near him, feel a personal touch. Gordon Hewitt, bless him, did in my judgment make a real mistake in his History 'The Problem of Success' by taking committee minutes seriously. They really are of minimal importance. It is the covering letters and the personal explanations, and how they were understood at the other end that matters.

18. The Newbigin family, and the Newbigin Estate, in depositing his archives in Birmingham University Library, have allowed their use for private research purposes.

19. D. Arnold and R. A. Bickers, "Introduction," in *Missionary Encounters: Sources and Issues*, ed. Robert A. Bickers and Rosemary Seton (Richmond: Curzon, 1996) 2.

20. G. Hewitt, *The Problems of Success: A History of the Church Missionary Society, 1910–1942*, 2 vols. (London: SCM, 1971).

That is the stuff of history. Minutes are rarely of any great significance and chiefly serve the purpose of confusing the historian!!"[21]

A major aim of this study is to recover "the stuff of history" through Newbigin's personal correspondence, to develop a contextual understanding of Newbigin's theology and demonstrate how that evolved through his engagement with others, and as a consequence of circumstances.

Newbigin's personal correspondence must be read with a hermeneutic of suspicion, partly because the record is incomplete but also because his voice has a particular accent. Newbigin's initial correspondence from India is in the genre of evangelical missionary correspondence. It goes without saying that the "missionary is, by nature and vocation, biased"; consequently, this then raises the question of "the utility of studying this type of material."[22] This bias however is not "insurmountable." "In fact . . . the biases of the missionary reporter are often much more clearly acknowledged and better known than those of other writers, which adds to their usefulness."[23]

Newbigin wrote during the rise of Indian nationalism and the advent of British de-colonization. Given the historical association of Protestant mission with colonialism, questions must then be raised concerning Newbigin's understanding of the relationship between the British Raj and missionary enterprise, and how that colored his perspective. This is pertinent given Newbigin's missionary experience in India, the first nation to throw off British rule. Prior to integration it was acknowledged that missions were discredited due to their colonial association and needed to be rehabilitated. During this time mission agencies entered a period of profound self-analysis and loss of confidence, in contrast to their somewhat unquestioning self-assurance and poise during the colonial period.

An associated issue is that of "critical distance" in reading and accessing the documents. This is twofold: distance between Newbigin and his respective correspondent, and critical distance between that body of correspondence and myself as a researcher. In both relationships, it must be asked if there is adequate "critical distance" for valid, substantive analysis to be made from the correspondence, which is respectful of the writers but not uncritical of them. As a methodological guide on the use of personal correspondence a parallel can be made between this study and that of

21. Warren cited by G. Kings, *Christianity Connected: Hindus, Muslims and the World in the Letters of Max Warren and Roger Hooker* (Zoetermeer: Boekencentrum, 2002), 170. Emphasis added.

22. Arnold and Bickers, "Introduction," 4.

23. Ibid.

Graham Kings' thesis, in which he analyses the correspondence between Max Warren and Roger Hooker.[24]

Another valuable primary resource has been qualitative interviews with those who knew and worked with Newbigin.[25] Permission was obtained to record and use these interviews. Often, subsequent email correspondence was used to augment interviews.

Newbigin's Historiography

In a study which seeks to undertake a historical analysis of Newbigin's archives, it is pertinent to ask, what was Newbigin's own historiography?[26] And, in particular, how did Newbigin relate sacred to secular history, how did he understand the history of Christianity in relationship to the history of humanity? Robert Frykenberg provides a typology of historical interpretation. He details three categories of presuppositions about the nature of historical understanding:[27] firstly, the "triumphalist" presupposition, which may be doctrinal or ideological. This reflects a recognition that "every historical understanding is a vehicle for conveying some belief system. . . . Events can be understood *only* in the light of, and can *only* be informed by, convictions about ultimate verities already held."[28] The second of Frykenberg's models is termed the "positivist" presupposition, a product of the Enlightenment. The underlying assumption is that "no valid understanding of any event is possible which does not come to us directly from empirical observation."[29] Third in the typology is the "nihilistic" presupposition. This model questions the "reality of any valid links between understandings and events."[30]

Whilst accepting this triad, Kings goes on to suggest other labels for Frykenberg's typology: "pre-modern," "modern," and "post-modern" or,

---

24. Kings, *Warren and Hooker*.

25. Listed in Appendix 3.

26. A major source for this is the collection of early lectures by Newbigin, published as Lesslie Newbigin, *Signs Amid the Rubble: The Purposes of God in Human History*, ed. Geoffrey Wainwright (Grand Rapids: Eerdmans, 2003).

27. R. E. Frykenberg, *History and Belief: The Foundations of Historical Understanding* (Grand Rapids: Eerdmans, 1996) 312–28.

28. Ibid., 313. Italics in original.

29. Ibid., 316.

30. Ibid., 318.

alternatively, "teleological," "objectivist," and "subjectivist."[31] As with any such typology, the advocates are not proposing watertight categories but an aid to the analysis of historical interpretation. Newbigin would be located in the first category. Newbigin understood Christ as the "clue to history." "Here—in the self-disclosure of God's purposes within history—are to be found the events that are determinative for the meaning of the whole."[32] This, according to Newbigin, is the basis for the church to meaningfully engage with the world and take action within history. Newbigin thus eschews any dichotomy between salvation history and secular history, but argues that the latter is determined by, and interpreted by the former.[33]

Style and Definition of Terms

Key terms in the thesis are defined at their first occurrence. Throughout the thesis, a distinction is made between "mission" and "missions" to maintain the distinction Newbigin made. Mission is used "to denote the totality of that for which the church is sent into the world," whereas missions denotes "particular enterprises within the total mission that have the primary intention of bringing into existence a Christian presence in a milieu where there was previously no such presence."[34] Mission is thus used mainly in a theological sense, whereas missions is used mainly in a historical sense to refer to mission agencies.

The terms "evangelical," "conservative evangelical," and "evangelicalism" are defined where they first occur. "Ecumenical," from the Greek *oikoumene*—the whole inhabited earth—is used to describe "everything that relates to the whole task of the whole Church to bring the Gospel to the whole world."[35] Where a contradistinction to "evangelicals" is sought for those actively involved in the ecumenical movement, rather than use the

---

31. Kings, *Warren and Hooker*, 71.

32. P. D. A. Weston and Lesslie Newbigin, *Lesslie Newbigin, Missionary Theologian: A Reader* (London: SPCK, 2006) 54.

33. This is further discussed in ch. 9. A detailed analysis of Newbigin's understanding of history in relation to the kingdom of God is given in the ongoing doctoral research of Jürgen Schuster, "The Significance of the Eschatological Tension of the Kingdom of God in the Theology of Mission of Lesslie Newbigin," (Trinity International University: Deerfield).

34. Lesslie Newbigin, "Cross-Currents in Ecumenical and Evangelical Understandings of Mission," *IBMR* 6:4 (1982) 146.

35. J. A. Mackay, "What the Ecumenical Movement Can Learn from Conservative Evangelicals," *Christianity Today* 10 (1966) 20. Cf. Newbigin, "Cross-Currents," 146.

clumsy term "non-evangelicals," the term "ecumenicals" is used in reference to conciliar Protestants.[36]

For stylistic consistency throughout the thesis, the term "church" has been lowercased, although its original use in quotations has been preserved. For accuracy, all quotations are reproduced as they originally occurred without grammatical corrections. All abbreviations are listed in a table. The necessary biographical details of correspondents, as they are introduced, can be found at their first occurrence.

36. The terms "evangelicals" and "ecumenicals" are of course not "mutually exclusive." G. Vandervelde, "Evangelical Ecumenical Concerns," in *Dictionary of the Ecumenical Movement*, ed. N. Lossky et al. (Geneva: WCC, 2002) 437.

Appendix 3

Interviews

	Place	Date Held
Dr. Gerald Anderson	Balaton	21/8/2008
		22/8/2008
Dr. Dan Beeby	Birmingham	3/11/2005
Rev. Myra Blyth	(By Skype)	18/9/2008
Rev. Dr. Robin Boyd	Edinburgh	7/8/2008
Rev. Dr. Jan van Butselaar	Balaton	18/8/2008
Rev. Dr. Emilio Castro	(By Skype)	10/9/2008
Dr. Martin Conway	Balaton	17/8/2008
Prof. Duncan Forrester	Edinburgh	27/9/2005
Dr. Tom F. Foust	(By Skype)	17/9/2008
Bishop C. L. Furtado	Pune	21/9/2006
Dr. Michael Goheen	(By Skype)	28/8/2008
Dr. Darrell Guder	Balaton	19/8/2008
Dr. George Hunsberger	(By Skype)	27/8/2008
Dr. Eleanor Jackson	Radstock	30/7/2005
Rev. Dr. Steven Mackie	Edinburgh	12/9/2008
Rev. Murdoch Mackenzie	Connel	13,14/8/2005
	Larbert	14/11/2005
	Larbert	23/1/2006
Rev. Jacques Matthey	Balaton	20/8/2008
Prof. Wilbert Shenk	Pune	1/11/2006
Dr. Charles West	(By Skype)	15/9/2008
Rev. Dr. Paul Weston	(By Skype)	11/9/2008

Bibliography

Archives

Foreign Mission Records of the Church of Scotland (Acc 7548)
    The National Library of Scotland
    George IV Bridge, Edinburgh EH1 1EW, Scotland, UK
    Catalogued at: http://www.nls.uk/catalogues/online/mss/index.html

The International Missionary Council Archives (IMC)
    Archives, Manuscripts and Rare Books Division, The Library, SOAS
    Thornhaugh Street, Russell Square, London WC1H 0XG, UK
    Catalogued at: http://www.idcpublishers.com/ead/138.xml

The Papers of Lesslie Newbigin (DA29)
    Special Collections, Main Library, University of Birmingham
    Edgbaston, Birmingham B15 2TT, UK
    Catalogued at: http://calmview.bham.ac.uk/default.aspx

Max Warren, Travel Diaries, West Africa, vol. 3, 1957–58, CMS/Unofficial Papers (Acc 882)
    Special Collections, Main Library, University of Birmingham
    Edgbaston, Birmingham B15 2TT, UK
    Catalogued at: http://calmview.bham.ac.uk/default.aspx

World Council of Churches Archives
    World Council of Churches Ecumenical Library and Archives
    Ecumenical Center, 7, route des Morillons, 1211, Genève 2, Switzerland
    Catalogued at: http://archives.wcc-coe.org/query/

Reports and Minutes

Church of Scotland

"Report of the Foreign Mission Committee." In *Reports to the General Assembly with the Legislative Acts*. The General Assembly of the Church of Scotland. Edinburgh: W. Blackwood, 1935–1946.

Bibliography

International Missionary Council

Jerusalem (1928)

IMC. *Jerusalem Meeting March 24th–April 8th: The World Mission of Christianity: Messages and Recommendations.* London: IMC/Oxford University Press, 1928.
———. *Jerusalem Meeting Report: The Younger and Older Churches.* Vol. 3. London: Oxford University Press, 1928.

Tambaram (1938)

IMC. *Addresses and Other Records: Tambaram, Madras, December 12th to 29th, 1938.* Vol. 7. London: IMC/Oxford University Press, 1939.

Willingen (1952)

Minutes of the Enlarged Meeting and the Committee of the IMC: Willingen, Germany, July 5th to 21st, 1952. London: IMC, 1952.
Goodall, Norman, editor. *Missions under the Cross: Addresses Delivered at the Enlarged Meeting of the Committee of the IMC at Willingen, in Germany, 1952.* London: Edinburgh House, 1953.
"A Statement by Delegates from the Younger Churches." In *Missions under the Cross,* edited by Norman Goodall, 233–35. London: Edinburgh House, 1953.
"The Theological Basis of the Missionary Obligation (an Interim Report)." In *Missions under the Cross,* edited by Norman Goodall, 238–45. London: Edinburgh House, 1953.

Ghana (1957–58)

Minutes of the Assembly of the IMC, Ghana: December 28th, 1957 to January 8th, 1958. London: IMC, 1958.
Orchard, Ronald K., editor. *The Ghana Assembly of the International Missionary Council.* London: IMC/Edinburgh House, 1958.

New Delhi (1961)

IMC. *IMC Minutes, November 17–18, 1961 at New Delhi.* London, 1962.

Minutes of the Joint Committee of the WCC and the IMC

1956, 20th–23rd July, Herrenalb, Germany, SOAS: 270002, fiche 12.
1958, 14th–17th August, Nyborg Strand, Denmark, WCC: 27.0003.

World Council of Churches

Evanston Assembly (1954)

Newbigin, J. E. Lesslie, and Willem Adolf Visser 't Hooft. "The First Report of the Advisory Commission on the Theme of the Second Assembly of the World Council of Churches." *ER* 4:1 (1951) 71–79.

"Report of the Joint Committee." In *The Evanston Report*, edited by Willem Adolph Visser 't Hooft, 322–27. London: SCM, 1955.

"Social Questions: The Responsible Society in a World Perspective." In *The Evanston Report*, edited by Willem Adolph Visser 't Hooft, 112–30. London: SCM, 1955.

Visser 't Hooft, Willem Adolph, editor. *The Evanston Report: The Second Assembly of the World Council of Churches 1954*. London: SCM, 1955.

New Delhi Assembly (1961)

WCC. *The New Delhi Report: The Third Assembly of the World Council of Churches, 1961*. London: SCM, 1962.

Uppsala Assembly (1968)

WCC. *The Church for Others and the Church for the World: A Quest for Structures for Missionary Congregations*. Geneva: WCC, 1967.

———. *New Delhi to Uppsala 1961–1968: Report of the Central Committee to the 4th Assembly of the WCC*. Geneva: WCC, 1968.

———. *The Uppsala Report, 1968: Official Report of the Fourth Assembly of the WCC, Uppsala July 4–20, 1968*. Geneva: WCC, 1968.

WCC Central Committee Minutes, published by WCC, Geneva

1951, 4th–11th August, Rolle, Switzerland, 4th meeting
1955, 2nd–9th August, Davos, Switzerland, 8th meeting
1956, 28th July–5th August, Galyatető, Hungary, 9th meeting
1957, 30th July–7th August, New Haven, USA, 10th meeting
1958, 21st–29th August, Nyborg Strand, Denmark, 11th meeting
1959, 19th–27th August, Rhodes, Greece, 12th meeting
1960, 16th–24th August, St. Andrews, Scotland, 13th meeting
1961, 17th–18th November, New Delhi, India, 14th meeting
1961, 6th–7th December, New Delhi, India, 15th meeting
1962, 7th–16th August, Paris, France, 16th meeting
1963, 26th August–2nd September, Rochester, USA, 17th meeting
1965, 12th–21st January, Enugu, Nigeria, 18th meeting

Books and Articles by Newbigin

Newbigin, J. E. Lesslie. "The Student Volunteer Missionary Union." In *The Christian Faith Today*, 95–104. London: SCM, 1933.

————. *Living Epistles: Impressions of the Foreign Mission Work of the Church of Scotland in 1938*. Edinburgh: Church of Scotland Foreign Missions Committee, 1939.

————. "Ordained Foreign Missionary in the Indian Church." *IRM* 34 (1945) 86–94.

————. *The Reunion of the Church: A Defence of the South India Scheme*. London: SCM, 1948, reprinted 1960.

————. "Comments on 'the Church, the Churches and the World Council of Churches.'" *ER* 3:3 (1951) 252–54.

————. *A South India Diary*. London: SCM, 1951.

————. "The Christian Layman in the World and in the Church." *NCCR* 72 (1952) 185–89.

————. "The Christian Hope." In *Missions under the Cross*, edited by Norman Goodall, 107–16. London: Edinburgh House, 1953.

————. "A Statement on the Missionary Calling of the Church." In *Missions under the Cross*, edited by Norman Goodall, 188–92. London: Edinburgh House, 1953.

————. *The Household of God: Lectures on the Nature of the Church*. London: SCM, 1953.

————. "The Quest for Unity through Religion." *Journal of Religion* 35 (1955) 17–33.

————. "A Time for Decision." In *Revolution in Missions*, edited by Blaise Levai. Vellore: Popular Press, 1957.

————. *One Body, One Gospel, One World: The Christian Mission Today*. London: IMC, 1958.

————. "The Gathering Up of History into Christ." In *The Missionary Church in East and West*, edited by Charles C. West and David M. Paton, 81–90. London: SCM, 1959.

————. "The Summons to Christian Mission Today." *IRM* 48:190 (1959) 177–89.

————. "The Pattern of Partnership." In *A Decisive Hour for the Christian World Mission*, edited by Norman Goodall and J. E. Lesslie Newbigin, 34–45. London: SCM, 1960.

————. "The Work of the Holy Spirit in the Life of the Asian Churches." In *A Decisive Hour for the Christian World Mission*, edited by Norman Goodall and J. E. Lesslie Newbigin, 18–33. London: SCM, 1960.

————. *A Faith for This One World?* London: SCM, 1961.

————. "Unity and Mission." *Covenant Quarterly* 19 (1961) 3–6.

————. "The Mission of the Triune God," 1962. (WCC, Ecumenical Centre Library: Geneva). Electronic version.

————. "The Missionary Dimension of the Ecumenical Movement." *ER* 14:2 (1962) 207–15.

————. "Missions in an Ecumenical Perspective," 1962. (WCC, Ecumenical Centre Library: Geneva). Electronic version.

————. "Report of the Division of World Mission and Evangelism to the Central Committee." *ER* 15:1 (1962) 88–94.

————. "Developments during 1962: An Editorial Survey." *IRM* 52 (1963) 3–14.

————. "Director's Report." In *Minutes of the Second Meeting of the CWME, Mexico City, December 8th–19th, 1963*, 76–89. London, New York: The Commission, 1963.

———. "Jesus the Servant and Man's Community." In *Christ's Call to Service Now*, edited by Ambrose Reeves, 23–33. London: SCM, 1963.

———. *The Relevance of Trinitarian Doctrine for Today's Mission*. London: Edinburgh House, 1963.

———. "Editor's Notes." *IRM* 53 (1964) 248–52.

———. "From the Editor." *IRM* 54 (1965) 417–27.

———. *Honest Religion for Secular Man*. London: SCM, 1966.

———. "Anglicans, Methodists and Intercommunion: A Moment for Decision." *Churchman* 82:4 (1968) 281–85.

———. "The Call to Mission—A Call to Unity?" In *The Church Crossing Frontiers*, edited by Peter Beyerhaus and Carl F. Hallencreutz, 254–65. Lund: Gleerup, 1969.

———. "Church Union: Which Way Forward?" *NCCR* 89 (1969) 356–63.

———. *The Finality of Christ*. London: SCM, 1969.

———. "Which Way for 'Faith and Order'?" In *What Unity Implies: Six Essays after Uppsala*, edited by Reinhard Groscurth, 115–32. Geneva: WCC, 1969.

———. "Cooperation and Unity." *IRM* 59:233 (1970) 67–74.

———. "Mission to Six Continents." In *The Ecumenical Advance: A History of the Ecumenical Movement*, edited by Harold E. Fey, 2:171–97. London: SPCK, 1970.

———. "Reflections on an Indian Ministry." *Frontier* 18 (1975) 25–27.

———. "All in One Place or All of One Sort: On Unity and Diversity in the Church." In *Creation, Christ, and Culture: A Festschrift in Honour of Professor Thomas F. Torrance*, edited by Richard W. A. McKinney, 288–306. Edinburgh: T. & T. Clark, 1976.

———. *"The Good Shepherd": Meditations on Christian Ministry in Today's World*. Leighton Buzzard: Faith Press, 1977.

———. "Recent Thinking on Christian Beliefs: VIII Mission and Missions." *Expository Times* 88:9 (1977) 260–64.

———. "What is a 'Local Church Truly United'?" In *In Each Place: Towards a Fellowship of Local Churches Truly United*, edited by J. E. Lesslie Newbigin et al., 14–29. Geneva: WCC, 1977.

———. *The Open Secret: Sketches for a Missionary Theology*. Grand Rapids: Eerdmans, 1978.

———. Review of *Denominationalism*, edited by Russell E. Richey. *ER* 30:2 (1978) 189.

———. "The Centrality of Jesus for History." In *Incarnation and Myth: The Debate Continued*, edited by Michael Goulder, 197–210. Grand Rapids: Eerdmans, 1979.

———. *Your Kingdom Come: Reflections on the Theme of the Melbourne Conference on World Mission and Evangelism, 1980*. Leeds: John Paul the Preacher's Press, 1980.

———. "Integration—Some Personal Reflections 1981." *IRM* 70:280 (1981) 247–55.

———. "Cross-Currents in Ecumenical and Evangelical Understandings of Mission." *IBMR* 6:4 (1982) 146–51.

———. Review of *Conflict over the Ecumenical Movement*, by Ulrich Duchrow, translated by David Lewis. *ER* 34:4 (1982) 428–30.

———. *The Other Side of 1984: Questions for the Churches*. Geneva: WCC, 1983.

———. "The Basis and the Forms of Unity." *Mid-Stream: The Ecumenical Movement Today* 23 (1984) 1–12.

———. "Faith and Faithfulness in the Ecumenical Movement." In *Faith and Faithfulness: Essays on Contemporary Ecumenical Themes*, edited by Pauline Webb, 1–7. Geneva: WCC, 1984.

―――. *Unfinished Agenda: An Autobiography.* Grand Rapids: Eerdmans, 1985.

―――. *Foolishness to the Greeks: The Gospel and Western Culture.* Grand Rapids: Eerdmans, 1986.

―――. *Mission in Christ's Way: Bible Studies.* Geneva: WCC, 1987.

―――. "The Pastor's Opportunities: VI. Evangelism in the City." *Expository Times* 98 (1987) 355–58.

―――. *The Gospel in a Pluralist Society.* Geneva: WCC, 1989.

―――. *Unfinished Agenda: An Updated Autobiography.* Geneva: WCC, 1993.

―――. "Does Society Still Need the Parish Church?" In *A Word in Season: Perspectives on Christian World Missions,* edited by Eleanor Jackson, 48–65. Grand Rapids: Eerdmans, 1994.

―――. "Ecumenical Amnesia." *IBMR* 18 (1994) 2–5.

―――. "Evangelism in the Context of Secularization." In *A Word in Season,* edited by Eleanor Jackson, 148–57. Grand Rapids: Eerdmans, 1994.

―――. "Reflections on the History of Missions (Paper Prepared in Anticipation of San Antonio 1989)." In *A Word in Season,* edited by Eleanor Jackson, 132–47. Grand Rapids: Eerdmans, 1994.

―――. "Reply to Konrad Raiser." *IBMR* 18:2 (1994) 51–52.

―――. "Union, Organic." In *Dictionary of the Ecumenical Movement,* edited by N. Lossky, J. M. Bonino, and J. Pobee, 1028–30. Geneva: WCC, 2002.

―――. *Signs Amid the Rubble: The Purposes of God in Human History,* edited by Geoffrey Wainwright. Grand Rapids: Eerdmans, 2003.

Books and Articles by Others

Aagaard, Johannes. "Trends in Missiological Thinking during the Sixties." *IRM* 62:245 (1973) 8–25.

―――. "Mission after Uppsala." In *Crucial Issues in Mission Today,* edited by Thomas F. Stransky and Gerald H. Anderson, 13–21. New York: Paulist, 1974.

Allen, Roland. *Missionary Methods: St. Paul's or Ours?* Grand Rapids: Eerdmans, 1962.

Andersen, Wilhelm. *Towards a Theology of Mission: A Study of the Encounter between the Missionary Enterprise and the Church and Its Theology.* London: SCM, 1955.

Anderson, Gerald H. *The Theology of the Christian Mission.* London: SCM, 1961.

Arias, Mortimer. "That the World May Believe." *IRM* 65:257 (1976) 13–26.

Arnold, David, and Robert A. Bickers. "Introduction." In *Missionary Encounters: Sources and Issues,* edited by Robert A. Bickers and Rosemary Seton. Richmond: Curzon, 1996.

Barclay, Oliver R., and Robert M. Horn. *From Cambridge to the World: 125 Years of Student Witness.* Leicester: InterVarsity, 2002.

Barrington-Ward, Simon. "The Marriage of North and South." *IRM* 73:289 (1984) 48–56.

Bassham, Rodger C. "Seeking a Deeper Theological Basis for Mission." *IRM* 67:267 (1978) 329–37.

―――. *Mission Theology, 1948–1975: Years of Worldwide Creative Tension— Ecumenical, Evangelical, and Roman Catholic.* Pasadena, CA: William Carey Library, 1979.

Bebbington, D. W. *Evangelicalism in Modern Britain: A History from the 1730s to the 1980s.* London: Routledge, 2002.

Berkhof, Hendrikus. "Berlin versus Geneva: Our Relationship with the 'Evangelicals.'" *ER* 28:1 (1976) 80–86.

Berkouwer, G. C. "What Conservative Evangelicals Can Learn from the Ecumenical Movement." *Christianity Today* 10 (1966) 17–23.

Beyerhaus, Peter. "Mission and Humanization." *IRM* 60:237 (1971) 11–24.

———. *Missions: Which Way? Humanization or Redemption.* Grand Rapids: Zondervan, 1974.

———. "Mission and Humanization." In *Crucial Issues in Mission Today*, edited by Thomas F. Stransky and Gerald H. Anderson, 231–45. New York: Paulist, 1974.

Blauw, Johannes. *The Missionary Nature of the Church: A Survey of the Biblical Theology of Mission.* London: Lutterworth, 1962.

Bonhoeffer, Dietrich. *Letters and Papers from Prison.* Enl. ed. Edited by Eberhard Bethge. London: SCM, 1971.

Bosch, David J. *Witness to the World: The Christian Mission in Theological Perspective.* London: Marshall Morgan & Scott, 1980.

———. "Evangelism: An Holistic Approach." *Journal of Theology for Southern Africa* 36 (1981) 43–63.

———. "'Ecumenicals' and 'Evangelicals': A Growing Relationship?" *ER* 40:3–4 (1988) 458–72.

———. *Transforming Mission: Paradigm Shifts in Theology of Mission.* Maryknoll, NY: Orbis, 1991.

Boyd, Robin H. S. *The Witness of the Student Christian Movement: "Church Ahead of the Church."* London: SPCK, 2007.

Brash, Alan A. "Regional Responsibility: Its Joy and Pain." In *Hope in the Desert*, edited by Kenneth Slack, 44–51. Geneva: WCC, 1986.

Briggs, John H. Y., Mercy Amba Oduyoye, and Georges Tsestis. *A History of the Ecumenical Movement.* Vol. 3, *1968–2000.* Geneva: WCC, 2004.

Burgess, Stanley M., and E. M. Van der Maas. *The New International Dictionary of Pentecostal and Charismatic Movements.* Grand Rapids: Zondervan, 2002.

Carpenter, Joel A. *Revive Us Again: The Reawakening of American Fundamentalism.* New York: Oxford University Press, 1997.

Castro, Emilio. "Editorial." *IRM* 70:280 (1981) 233–39.

———. "Mission and Evangelism: An Ecumenical Affirmation." *IRM* 71:284 (1982) 421.

———. "Editorial." *ER* 40 (1988) 1–3.

———. "Ecumenical Social Thought in the Post-Cold War Period." *ER* 43:3 (1991) 305–7.

Clements, K. W. *Faith on the Frontier: A Life of J. H. Oldham.* Edinburgh: T. & T. Clark, 1999.

Central Committee, WCC. "The Church, the Churches and the World Council of Churches: The Ecclesiological Significance of the World Council of Churches." *ER* 3:1 (1950) 47–53.

Coote, Robert. "The Uneven Growth of Conservative Evangelical Missions." *IBMR* 6:3 (1982) 118–23.

Cox, Harvey Gallagher. *The Secular City.* London: SCM, 1965.

Daughrity, Dyron B. *Bishop Stephen Neill: From Edinburgh to South India*. Oxford: Peter Lang, 2008.

————. "Researching Bishop Stephen Neill: Engaging History, Methods, and the 'Reconstruction.'" Henry Martyn Paper. Online: http://131.111.227.198/CDaurighty.htm. Accessed 14/5/2010.

Dayton, Donald W. "Yet Another Layer of the Onion: Or Opening the Ecumenical Door to Let the Riffraff In." *ER* 40:1 (1988) 87–110.

Denney, James. *St. Paul's Epistle to the Romans*. In vol. 2 of *The Expositor's Greek Testament*. London: Hodder & Stoughton, 1901.

Dickinson, Richard D. N. "Development." In *Dictionary of the Ecumenical Movement*, edited by N. Lossky, J. M. Bonino, and J. Pobee, 298–303. Geneva: WCC, 2002.

Douglas, J. D., editor. *Let the Earth Hear His Voice*. Minneapolis: World Wide Publications, 1975.

Drummond, Andrew Landale, and James Bulloch. *The Scottish Church, 1688–1843: The Age of the Moderates*. Edinburgh: St. Andrew Press, 1973.

Duchrow, Ulrich. *Conflict over the Ecumenical Movement: Confessing Christ Today in the Universal Church*. Translated by David Lewis. Geneva: WCC, 1981.

Dudley-Smith, Timothy. *John Stott: The Making of a Leader*. Leicester: InterVarsity, 1999.

Engelsviken, Tormod. "Missio Dei: The Understanding and Misunderstanding of a Theological Concept in European Churches and Missiology." *IRM* 92:367 (2003) 481–97.

Fenton, Horace. "Mission and Social Concern." In *The Church's Worldwide Mission: Proceedings of the Congress, Wheaton, April 9–16*, edited by Harold Lindsell, 193–203. Waco, TX: Word, 1966.

Fischer, Jean E. "Inter-Church Aid and the Future." In *Hope in the Desert*, edited by Kenneth Slack, 119–32. Geneva: WCC, 1986.

Foust, Thomas F., and George R. Hunsberger. "Bishop J. E. Lesslie Newbigin: A Comprehensive Bibliography." In *A Scandalous Prophet: The Way of Mission after Newbigin*, edited by Thomas F. Foust et al., 249–325. Grand Rapids: Eerdmans, 2001.

Foust, Thomas F., et al. *A Scandalous Prophet: The Way of Mission after Newbigin*. Grand Rapids: Eerdmans, 2001.

"The Frankfurt Declaration." In *Missions: Which Way? Humanization or Redemption*, by Peter Beyerhaus, 107–20. Grand Rapids: Zondervan, 1974.

Frykenberg, Robert Eric. *History and Belief: The Foundations of Historical Understanding*. Grand Rapids: Eerdmans, 1996.

Glasser, Arthur F. "Reconciliation between Ecumenical and Evangelical Theologies and Theologians of Mission." *Missionalia* 7:3 (1979) 99–114.

————. "The Evolution of Evangelical Mission Theology since World War II." *IBMR* 9 (1985) 9–13.

————. "Mission in the 1990s: Two Views." *IBMR* 13 (1989) 2–10.

Glasser, Arthur F., and Donald A. McGavran. *Contemporary Theologies of Mission*. Grand Rapids: Baker, 1983.

Goheen, Michael W. *As the Father Has Sent Me, I Am Sending You: J. E. Lesslie Newbigin's Missionary Ecclesiology*. Zoetermeer: Boekencentrum, 2000.

———. "The Future of Mission in the World Council of Churches: The Dialogue between Lesslie Newbigin and Konrad Raiser." *Mission Studies* 21:1 (2004) 97–111.

Goodall, Norman. "'Evangelicals' and WCC-IMC." *IRM* 47:186 (1958) 210–15.

———. "Evangelicalism and the Ecumenical Movement." *ER* 15:4 (1963) 399–409.

———. "WCC and IMC: Some Considerations Bearing on Their Relationships."

Goodhew, David. "The Rise of the Cambridge Inter-Collegiate Christian Union, 1910–1971." *Journal of Ecclesiastical History* 54:1 (2003) 62–88.

Guder, Darrell L. *The Continuing Conversion of the Church*. Grand Rapids: Eerdmans, 2000.

_____, editor. *Missional Church: A Vision for the Sending of the Church in North America*. Grand Rapids: Eerdmans, 1998.

Hedlund, Roger E. *Roots of the Great Debate in Mission*. Madras: Evangelical Literature Service for Church Growth Research Centre, 1981.

Henry, Carl F. H. *The Uneasy Conscience of Modern Fundamentalism*. Grand Rapids: Eerdmans, 1947, reprinted 2003.

———. "Report on New Delhi." *Christianity Today* 6:22 (1961) 3–7.

———. "Evangelicals and Ecumenism." *Christianity Today* 10 (1966) 17–23.

Henry, Carl, and Stanley Mooneyham, editors. *One Race, One Gospel, One Task*. 2 vols. Minneapolis: World Wide Publications, 1967.

Hewitt, Gordon. *The Problems of Success: A History of the Church Missionary Society, 1910–1942*. 2 vols. London: SCM, 1971.

Hitchen, John M. "What It Means to Be an Evangelical Today—An Antipodean Perspective. Part One, Mapping Our Movement." *Evangelical Quarterly* 76:1 (2004) 47–64.

Hoedemaker, L. A. "The People of God and the Ends of the Earth." In *Missiology: An Ecumenical Introduction*, edited by Frans J. Verstraelen et al., 157–71. Grand Rapids: Eerdmans, 1995.

———. "Mission and Unity: The Relevance of Hoekendijk's Vision." In *Changing Partnership of Missionary and Ecumenical Movements: Essays in Honour of Marc Spindler*, edited by Leny Lagerwerf, Karel Steenbrink, and Frans J. Verstraelen, 26–35. Leiden-Utrecht: Interuniversity Institute for Missiological and Ecumenical Research, 1995.

Hoekendijk, Johannes C. "The Call to Evangelism." *IRM* 39 (1950) 162–75.

———. "The Church in Missionary Thinking." *IRM* 41 (1952) 324–36.

———. "Christ and the World in the Modern Age: Strasbourg 1960." *Student World* 54:1–2 (1961) 75–82.

———. *The Church Inside Out*. London: SCM, 1967.

Hoekstra, Harvey T. *The World Council of Churches and the Demise of Evangelism*. Wheaton: Tyndale House, 1979.

Hogg, William Richey. *Ecumenical Foundations: A History of the International Missionary Council and Its Nineteenth Century Background*. New York: Harper, 1952.

———. "Role of American Protestantism in World Mission." In *American Missions in Bicentennial Perspective*, edited by R. Pierce Beaver, 354–402. South Pasadena, CA: William Carey Library, 1977.

Hollenweger, Walter J. *The Pentecostals*. London: SCM, 1972.

Hood, George A. *Neither Bang nor Whimper: The End of a Missionary Era in China.* Singapore: Presbyterian Church in Singapore, 1991.

Hopkins, Charles Howard. *John R. Mott, 1865–1955: A Biography.* Grand Rapids: Eerdmans, 1979.

Hunsberger, George R. *Bearing the Witness of the Spirit: Lesslie Newbigin's Theology of Cultural Plurality.* Grand Rapids: Eerdmans, 1998.

———. "Conversion and Community: Revisiting the Lesslie Newbigin–M. M. Thomas Debate." *IBMR* 22:3 (1998) 112–17.

Kim, Sebastian. "The Kingdom of God versus the Church: The Debate at the Conference of the International Missionary Council, Tambaram, 1938." In *Interpreting Contemporary Christianity: Global Processes and Local Identities*, edited by Ogbu U. Kalu and Alaine M. Low, 131–47. Grand Rapids: Eerdmans, 2008.

Kings, Graham. *Christianity Connected: Hindus, Muslims and the World in the Letters of Max Warren and Roger Hooker.* Zoetermeer: Boekencentrum, 2002.

Kirk, J. Andrew. "Secularisation, the World Church and the Future of Mission." *Transformation* 22:3 (2005) 1–22. Electronic version.

———. "'A Secular Age' in a Mission Perspective: A Response to Charles Taylor's Magnum Opus." Conference paper, Cambridge, 24/4/2009. In *Responding to Secularism: Christian Witness in a Dogmatic Public Culture*, 1–10.

Kraemer, Hendrik. *The Christian Message in a Non-Christian World.* London: Edinburgh House, 1938.

Künneth, Walter, and Peter Beyerhaus, editors. *Reich Gottes Oder Weltgemeinschaft? Die Berliner Ökumene-Erklärung Zur Utopischen Vision Des Weltkirchenrates [Kingdom of God or World Community? The Berlin Ecumenical Manifesto on the Utopian Vision of the WCC].* Bad Liebenzell: Liebenzeller Mission Press, 1975.

Laing, Mark T. B. "The Advocates and Opponents of Church Union in South India: Perceptions and Portrayals of 'the Other.'" In *Yale-Edinburgh Group on the History of the Missionary Movement and Non-Western Christianity.* New College, University of Edinburgh, 2008.

———. "The International Impact of the Formation of the Church of South India: Bishop Newbigin versus the Anglican Fathers." *IBMR* 33 (2009) 18–24.

Latourette, Kenneth Scott. "Ecumenical Bearings of the Missionary Movement and the International Missionary Council." In *A History of the Ecumenical Movement, 1517–1948*, edited by Ruth Rouse and Stephen Neill, 351–402. London: SPCK, 1954.

"The Lausanne Covenant." In *Let the Earth Hear His Voice*, edited by J. D. Douglas, 3–9. Minneapolis: World Wide Publications, 1975.

Leeuwen, Arend T. van. *Christianity in World History: The Meeting of the Faiths of East and West.* New York: Scribner, 1964.

Lehmann, Paul L. "Editorial: Willingen and Lund: The Church on the Way to Unity." *Theology Today* 9:4 (1953) 431–41.

Lossky, Nicolas, Jose Miguez Bonino, and John Pobee. *Dictionary of the Ecumenical Movement.* Geneva: WCC, 1991.

———. *Dictionary of the Ecumenical Movement.* 2nd ed. Geneva: WCC, 2002.

Lyall, Leslie T., and Lesslie Newbigin. *The Church Local and Universal.* Things We Face Together 2. London: World Dominion, 1962.

Mackay, John Alexander. "What the Ecumenical Movement Can Learn from Conservative Evangelicals." *Christianity Today* 10 (1966) 17, 20–23.

Marty, Martin E. "The Global Context of Ecumenism 1968–2000." In *A History of the Ecumenical Movement*, edited by John H. Y. Briggs, Mercy Amba Oduyoye, and Georges Tsestis, 3:3–22. Geneva: WCC, 2004.

Maury, Philippe. "Christ's Ministry to the World and Our Calling: Strasbourg 1960." *Student World* 54:1–2 (1961) 1–18.

McCaughey, John Davis. *Christian Obedience in the University: Studies in the Life of the Student Christian Movement of Great Britain and Ireland, 1930–1950.* London: SCM, 1958.

McGavran, Donald A. *How Churches Grow: The New Frontiers of Mission.* London: World Dominion, 1959.

———. *Conciliar-Evangelical Debate: The Crucial Documents, 1964–1976.* South Pasadena, CA: William Carey Library, 1977.

———. "My Pilgrimage in Mission." *IBMR* 10:2 (1986) 53–54, 56–58.

"The Missionary Task of the Church: Theological Reflections, Report of Meeting in Bossey, July 1961." *Bulletin of the Division of Studies, WCC* 7:2 (1961) 3–17.

Munby, D. L. *The Idea of a Secular Society and Its Significance for Christians.* London: Oxford University Press, 1963.

Murray, Geoffrey. "Joint Service as an Instrument of Renewal." In *The Ecumenical Advance*, edited by Harold E. Fey, 2:201–231. Geneva: WCC, 1986.

Myres, John Linton. *The Dawn of History.* London: William & Norgate, 1911.

Neill, Stephen. *Creative Tension.* Duff Lectures; 1958. London: Edinburgh House, 1959.

———. *The Church and Christian Union.* Bampton Lectures; 1964. London: Oxford University Press, 1968.

Niles, Daniel T. *Upon the Earth: The Mission of God and the Missionary Enterprise of the Churches.* London: Lutterworth, 1962.

———. *Ideas and Services: A Report of the East Asia Christian Conference, 1957–1967.* Christchurch: National Council of Churches, 1968.

Nissen, Karsten. "Integration in Nordic Missions." In *Missions from the North: Nordic Missionary Council, 50 Years*, edited by Carl F. Hallencreutz, Johannes Aagaard, and Nils Bloch-Hoell, 123–46. Oslo: Universitetsforlaget, 1974.

———. "Mission and Unity: A Look at the Integration of the IMC and the WCC." *IRM* 63 (1974) 539–50.

O'Brien, Richard, editor. *Faith in the City of Birmingham: An Examination of Problems and Opportunities Facing a City.* Exeter: Paternoster, 1988.

Oldham, J. H. "Faith in God and Faith in Man." In *The Christian Faith Today*, 54–75. London: SCM, 1933.

Payne, Ernest A., and David G. Moses. *Why Integration?* London: Edinburgh House for the Joint Committee, 1957.

Potter, Philip A., and Jacques Matthey. "Mission." In *Dictionary of the Ecumenical Movement*, edited by N. Lossky, J. M. Bonino, and J. Pobee, 783–90. Geneva: WCC, 2002.

Potter, Philip A., and Thomas Wieser. *Seeking and Serving the Truth: The First Hundred Years of the World Student Christian Federation.* Geneva: WCC, 1997.

Raiser, Konrad. *Ecumenism in Transition: A Paradigm Shift in the Ecumenical Movement?* Geneva: WCC, 1991.

Richebächer, Wilhelm. "Missio Dei: The Basis of Mission Theology or a Wrong Path?" *IRM* 92:367 (2003) 588–605.

Robinson, John A. T. *Honest to God.* London: SCM, 1963.

Rosin, H. H. *"Missio Dei": An Examination of the Origin, Contents and Function of the Term in Protestant Missiological Discussion*. Leiden: Interuniversity Institute for Missiological and Ecumenical Research, Department of Missiology, 1972.

Rostow, W. W. *The Stages of Economic Growth: A Non-Communist Manifesto*. Cambridge: Cambridge University Press, 1960.

Rouse, Ruth, Stephen Neill, and Harold E. Fey. *A History of the Ecumenical Movement, 1517–1968*. 4th ed. Geneva: WCC, 1993.

Saayman, W. A. *Unity and Mission: A Study of the Concept of Unity in Ecumenical Discussions since 1961 and Its Influence on the World Mission of the Church*. Pretoria: University of South Africa, 1984.

Shenk, Wilbert R. "Rufus Anderson and Henry Venn: A Special Relationship?" *IBMR* 5:4 (1981) 168–72.

Sittler, Joseph A. "Called to Unity." *ER* 14 (1962) 177–87.

Smith, Eugene L. "The Conservative Evangelicals and the WCC." *ER* 15:2 (1963) 182–91.

———. "Wheaton Congress in the Eyes of an Ecumenical Observer." *IRM* 55:220 (1966) 480–82.

Smith, George. *The Life of Alexander Duff*. London: Hodder & Stoughton, 1879.

Stanley, Brian. *The Bible and the Flag: Protestant Missions and British Imperialism in the Nineteenth and Twentieth Centuries*. Leicester: Apollos, 1990.

———. "Twentieth-Century World Christianity: A Perspective from the History of Missions." In *Christianity Reborn: The Global Expansion of Evangelicalism in the Twentieth Century*, edited by Donald M. Lewis, 52–83. Grand Rapids: Eerdmans, 2004.

———. "The Remedy Lies with Themselves: Edinburgh 1910 on the Self-Supporting Indigenous Church." In *Yale-Edinburgh Group on the History of the Missionary Movement and Non-Western Christianity*, 1–13. Edinburgh, July 2004.

———. *The World Missionary Conference, Edinburgh 1910*. Grand Rapids: Eerdmans, 2009.

Stott, John R. W. "The Biblical Basis of Evangelism." In *Let the Earth Hear His Voice*, edited by J. D. Douglas, 65–78. Minneapolis: World Wide Publications, 1975.

———. "Significance of Lausanne." *IRM* 64:255 (1975) 288–94.

———. "Response to Bishop Mortimer Arias." *IRM* 65:257 (1976) 30–34.

———. "Twenty Years after Lausanne: Some Personal Reflections." *IBMR* 19:2 (1995) 50–55.

Stransky, Thomas F. "Mission Power in the 1980s." *IRM* 69:273 (1980) 40–48.

Sundkler, Bengt. *Church of South India: The Movement Towards Union, 1900–1947*. London: Lutterworth, 1954.

Tatlow, Tissington. *The Story of the Student Christian Movement of Great Britain and Ireland*. London: SCM, 1933.

Taylor, Charles. *A Secular Age*. Cambridge: Belknap Press of Harvard University Press, 2007.

———. "The Necessity of Secularist Regimes: Gifford Lecture 21/5/2009." University of Glasgow, 2009.

Taylor, John V. "Small Is Beautiful: Thoughts Arising from *Can Churches Be Compared?*" *IRM* 60:239 (1971) 328–38.

Temple, William. *The Church Looks Forward*. London: Macmillan, 1944.

Templeton, Elizabeth. *God's February: A Life of Archie Craig, 1888–1985*. London: BCC/CCBI, 1991.

Thomas, Jacob. *From Lausanne to Manila: Evangelical Social Thought*. Delhi: ISPCK, 2003.

"Those with Evangelical Concerns at the World Council of Churches' Conference at San Antonio to the Lausanne II Conference at Manila." *IBMR* 133 (1989) 132, 134–35.

Tomkins, Oliver S. *The Church in the Purpose of God: An Introduction to the Work of the Commission on Faith and Order of the World Council of Churches, in Preparation for the Third World Conference on Faith and Order to Be Held at Lund, Sweden, in 1952*. London: SCM, 1950.

Vandervelde, George. "Evangelical Ecumenical Concerns." In *Dictionary of the Ecumenical Movement*, edited by N. Lossky, J. M. Bonino, and J. Pobee, 437–40. Geneva: WCC, 2002.

Van Gelder, Craig, editor. *The Missional Church in Context: Helping Congregations Develop Contextual Ministry*. Grand Rapids: Eerdmans, 2007.

Vicedom, Georg F. *Missio Dei: Einfuhrung in Eine Theologie Der Mission*. Munich: Chr. Kaiser, 1958.

———. *The Mission of God*. Translated by Gilbert A. Thiele and Dennis Hilgendorf. St. Louis: Concordia, 1965.

Visser 't Hooft, Willem A. *Memoirs*. London: SCM, 1973.

———. *The Genesis and Formation of the World Council of Churches*. Geneva: WCC, 1982.

———. "Inter-Church Aid: How It All Began." In *Hope in the Desert*, edited by Kenneth Slack, 1–11. Geneva: WCC, 1986.

Wainwright, Geoffrey. *Lesslie Newbigin: A Theological Life*. Oxford: Oxford University Press, 2000.

Walls, Andrew F. "Missionary Societies and the Fortunate Subversion of the Church." *Evangelical Quarterly* 60 (1988) 141–55.

———. *The Missionary Movement in Christian History: Studies in the Transmission of Faith*. Maryknoll, NY: Orbis, 1996.

———. *The Cross-Cultural Process in Christian History: Studies in the Transmission and Appropriation of Faith*. Maryknoll, NY: Orbis, 2002.

Walvoord, John F. "The Theological Basis for Foreign Missions." In *Facing the Unfinished Task: Messages Delivered at the Congress on World Missions*, edited by Mary Bennett and J. O. Percy, compiler, 244–50. Grand Rapids: Zondervan, 1961.

Warren, Max A.C. *The Sevenfold Secret*. London: SPCK, 1962.

———. *Crowded Canvas: Some Experiences of a Life-Time*. London: Hodder & Stoughton, 1974.

———. "The Fusion of IMC and WCC at New Delhi: Retrospective Thoughts after a Decade and a Half." *OBMR* 3:3 (1979) 104–8.

WCC. "Mission and Evangelism: An Ecumenical Affirmation." *IBMR* 7:2 (1983) 65–71.

WCC, Central Committee. "The Calling of the Church to Mission and to Unity." *ER* 4:1 (1951) 66–71.

Weston, P. D. A., and J. E. Lesslie Newbigin. *Lesslie Newbigin, Missionary Theologian: A Reader*. London: SPCK, 2006.

"Wheaton Declaration." In *The Church's Worldwide Mission: Proceedings of the Congress, Wheaton, April 9–16*, edited by Harold Lindsell, 217–37. Waco, TX: Word, 1966.

Wieser, Thomas, editor. *Planning for Mission: Working Papers on the New Quest for Missionary Communities.* London: Epworth, 1966.

Winter, Ralph D. "Ghana: Preparation for Marriage." *IRM* 67:267 (1978) 338–53.

"World Council Diary." *ER* 19:1 (1967) 89.

Yates, Timothy E. *Christian Mission in the Twentieth Century.* Cambridge: Cambridge University Press, 1994.

———. "Edinburgh Revisited: Edinburgh 1910 to Melbourne 1980." *Churchman* 94:2 (1980) 145–55.

Theses

Flett, John G. "God Is a Missionary God: Missio Dei, Karl Barth, and the Doctrine of the Trinity." PhD, Princeton Theological Seminary, 2007.

Foust, Thomas F. "The Missiological Approach to Modern Western Culture according to Lesslie Newbigin and Dean E. Walker." PhD, University of Birmingham, 2002.

Keskitalo, Jukka. "Kolmiyhteisen Jumalan Missio: Lesslie Newbigin Lähetyskäsityksen Teologinen Perusta." MTh, University of Helsinki, 1988.

———. "Kristillinen Usko Ja Moderni Kulttuuri: Lesslie Newbigin Ksitys Kirkon Missiosta Modernissa Lnsimaisessa Kulttuurissa." ThD, Suomalainen Teologinen Kirjallisuusseura, 1999.

Klopfeusfein, Maria. "Lesslie Newbigin: Mission Und Einheit Der Kirche." Akzessarbeit, University of Berne, 1984.

Philip, Thollayirakuzayil Varughese. "Mission and Unity: Factors Contributing to the Integration of the International Missionary Council and the World Council of Churches." PhD, Hartford Seminary Foundation, 1967.

Schuster, Jürgen "The Significance of the Eschatological Tension of the Kingdom of God in the Theology of Mission of Lesslie Newbigin." PhD, Trinity International University, in process.

Thomas, Joe Matthew. "The Centrality of Christ and Inter-Religious Dialogue in the Theology of Lesslie Newbigin." PhD, University of St. Matthew's College, 1996.

Veldhorst, Berend J. "A Christian Voice in a World without God." PhD, State University of Utrecht, 1990.

Weston, Paul D. A. "Mission and Cultural Change: Critical Engagement with the Writings of Lesslie Newbigin." PhD, King's College, London, 2002.

Wood, N. J. "Confessing Christ in a Plural World: A Missiological Approach to Inter-Faith Relations with Particular Reference to Kenneth Cragg and Lesslie Newbigin." DPhil, Oxford University, 1996.

Web and Electronic Resources

"CWME Statement on Edinburgh 1910." http://www.oikoumene.org/en/who-are-we/organization-structure/consultative-bodies/world-mission-and-evangelism/history.html#c16564, accessed 21/5/2009.

"God's Reign and Our Unity: The Report of the Anglican-Reformed International Commission, 1981–1984." http://warc.jalb.de/warcajsp/news_file/3.pdf.

The Lausanne Covenant. http://www.lausanne.org/lausanne-1974/lausanne-covenant. html.

"Lausanne III." http://www.lausanne.org/cape-town-2010.

Oxford University Press. *Oxford Dictionary of National Biography.* [Oxford]: Oxford University Press, 2004–9, http://www.oxforddnb.com.ezproxy.webfeat.lib.ed.ac. uk/index.jsp.

————. *Oxford English Dictionary.* [Oxford]: Oxford University Press, 2000, http:// dictionary.oed.com/.

Newbigin.net: Online Bibliography and Documents, http://www.newbigin.net/.

The *Newbigin.Net CD-Rom*, available from http://www.newbigin.net/.

"Rev. Alexander S. Kydd Obituary." *The Scotsman*, 19/7/1950, p. 3; digital archive, http://edu.archive.scotsman.com/article.cfm?id=TSC/1950/07/19/Ar00307.

WCC Archives Web Site. http://archives.oikoumene.org/query/Detail.aspx?ID=40915.

Index

Allen, Roland, 14, 181, 195–96, 210
American Board of Commissioners for Foreign Missions, 21, 161
Anderson, Gerald, 256
Anglican, 22, 24, 27, 45
Anglo-Catholic, 20–23, 71, 246
Apostolic, 17, 26, 36, 72–73, 147
Arias, Mortimer, 132

Baptist, 56–57, 68
Barth, Karl, 14, 78–80
Bebbington, David, 3, 46–47, 56
Beyerhaus, Peter, 129–30
Blauw, Johannes, 83
Bosch, David, 47, 78, 99, 132, 212
Brash, A. A., 152, 160

Calvinism, 11
Cambridge, xx, 3–11, 30, 99, 134
Cambridge Inter-Collegiate Christian Union (CICCU), 3–5, 7
Castro, Emilio, 54, 56, 123, 132, 249, 251–53
Carpenter, George, 102, 151
Catholic, 17, 23, 25, 35, 49, 56, 96, 118, 122, 127, 131–32, 179, 202, 226, 253, 257
Central Committee of the World Council of Churches, xx, 42, 46, 53, 57, 60–63, 65–67, 85–86, 87–89, 100, 104–5, 107, 113–17, 119, 121, 134, 138, 143, 157–58, 160–61, 163–64, 168, 178, 198–99, 206
Ceylon scheme, 23–24
Christendom, xiii–xiv, xxii, 20–21, 23, 30, 35–36, 43, 105, 175, 184, 192, 196–99, 215, 217–19, 222, 223–26, 228–29, 232, 235, 238, 240–241

Church of Scotland (CofS), xx, 1, 9, 11–12, 15, 17–21, 29, 30, 40, 238, 247, 264
Church of South India (CSI), xx, 1–2, 9–10, 20–25, 27–28, 30–31, 44, 51, 61–62, 64, 107, 114, 161, 245–46, 257
church-centric, xvi, xx–xxi, 14–19, 40–41, 51, 59, 62, 71–73, 83, 92, 112, 123, 168, 180–83, 188, 200, 203, 207–8, 211, 215, 221, 240, 244, 247, 250
Colonialism, 34, 43, 58, 76, 106, 148, 154, 162, 180, 182, 191, 214, 232, 266
Comity, xiv–xv, 23–24, 30, 149
Commission of World Mission and Evangelism (CWME), 94, 122–25, 130–33, 162, 165, 245, 251–53
Communism, xiii, 76, 118, 170, 195
Conway, Martin, 135, 186, 207, 254
Cooke, Leslie E., 139, 144–45, 151–52, 156, 163, 165
conservative evangelicals, xx, 29, 32–33, 46–54, 57–59, 63, 68, 90, 126–27, 130, 179, 255, 268
Craig, Archie, 6–7

Denney, James, 11
Division of World Mission and Evangelism (DWME), 69, 94, 100–101, 112, 118–21, 124–25, 133, 136, 139, 145, 151, 153–54, 156–64, 175, 178, 183, 185–88, 192, 199, 203–4, 253
Duff, Alexander, 35, 234
East Asia Christian Conference (EACC), 39, 117, 152, 160–61, 165, 195

Index

Enlightenment, 9, 36, 64, 214, 216, 233–34, 267

Episcopal, 20, 22–24, 27, 44

Eschatology, Eschatological, xvii, 1, 26, 28, 30, 35, 63–64, 68, 72, 75, 185, 211, 213, 224

Eschaton, 24, 26, 30, 64, 73, 98, 172, 246

Evangelicalism, 3–4, 10, 29, 47–48, 52, 56, 127, 131, 268

Evangelical Foreign Missions Association(EFMA), 50, 55, 126

Evanston Assembly (1954), 62–63, 68, 74, 140, 169, 188, 213

Farmer, Herbert, 2

Faith and Order, 27, 37, 41, 57, 66, 99, 107, 116, 144, 150, 159, 202, 252

Freytag, Walter, 35, 67, 106, 126, 152, 170

Fundamentalist, 3, 42, 48–49, 51–52, 55, 106, 109, 126

Ghana (1957–58), xxi, 1, 83, 86, Ch4, 112–13, 116, 118–19, 123–24, 168, 170

General Assembly, 12–13, 17, 19, 143, 178

general secretary, xix–xxi, 1–2, 12, 29, 31, 38, 44, 57, 63, 87–88, 99–109, Ch5, 139, 150, 158–59, 203, 205, 229, 246, 249, 252–54

Globalization, 214

Glasgow, 5–7, 25, 239

Glasser, Arthur, 47

Goodall, Norman, 49, 71, 78, 101–2, 175

Graham, Billy, 49, 127–28

Henderson, Helen, 6

Hendry, Carl, 48, 52

Herrenalb categories, 143–45, 158, 164

Hindu, Hinduism, ix, 14, 223, 233–34, 263

Hollis, Michael, 102

Hoekendijk,Johannes Christiaan, 62, 66–69, 71, 72–76, 79, 83–86, 92, 135, 180–82, 188, 193, 200–201, 203, 207–9, 211, 213, 215, 247

Household of God, The, 25–28

Humanization, 85, 129, 205, 208, 215–16, 247

Indian independence, 19, 34

Indigenous, 13–19, 29, 40, 50, 92, 196

Interdenominational Foreign Mission Association (IFMA), 50, 55, 126

International Review of Mission(s), xvi, 9, 153

Inter-Church Aid, xxi, 42, 106, 114, 137, Ch6, 176, 248

Inter Varsity Fellowship (IVF), 4, 10

Islam, 36, 76

Jerusalem (1928), xvi, 40–41, 191, 228

Joint Aid for Mission (JAM), 160–61, 165

Kingdom of God, 40, 51–52, 64, 75, 180–82, 211, 221, 231, 268

Koinonia, 37, 146–47, 164, 177, 248

Kydd, Alexander S, 12–15, 29, 40

Kraemer, Hendrik, 8, 13, 29, 147

Lambeth, 23, 27–28

van Leeuwen, AT, 194, 214, 219, 231, 234–35, 241

Lausanne (1974), 59, 126–27, 130–33, 213, 216, 252, 254, 256–57

Lehmann, Paul, 53, 62, 69, 71, 73, 75, 79, 83, 188, 193, 215, 247

Life and Work, 37, 41

Löffler, Paul, 2, 111, 136, 159, 251, 253

Lyall, Leslie, 132

Mackay, John Alexander, 38, 43, 88–89, 95, 98, 100–102, 104, 108

Mackenzie, Murdoch, xi, 204

Mackenzie, Robert P., 19

Maclean, J. H., 21

Matthey, Jacques, 132, 252, 256

McGavran, Donald A, 128–30, 178, 254

McIntire, Carl, 52, 55

missio dei, 60, 62, 69, 78–80, 84, 112, 126, 171, 200, 212–13

Missionary Structure of the Congregation (MSC), The, xxii, 82, 84, 129, 193, 196, 199, 206–12, 215–17, 218, 242, 250

Mott, John R., xv, 8, 37–38, 41, 101, 170–71, 195

Muslim, 223

National Christian Council (NCC), 92, 98, 143, 160, 175

Neill, Stephen, xvi, 5, 49, 57, 67, 93, 99, 121–22
New Delhi (1961), viii, xvi, xxi, 32, 46, 119, 120–123, 160, 169, 182–83, 186, 188, 192, 201–2, 206, 230
Niles, D. T., 54, 83, 195
Non-episcopal, 20, 22–24, 44
North India scheme, 23

Oldham, J. H., xv–xvi, 8–9, 37–38, 191
Oman, John, 2
Orchard, Ronald K, 164, 175, 178
organic union, xv, 27, 97
Orthodox, xiii, 103, 109, 118
Orthodox Church(es), 33, 42, 56, 113, 114–17, 122–23, 151, 263
Oxford, 8–9, 37, 44, 118, 134, 153–54, 163, 174–75

Paton, William, 38, 71,
Payne, E. A., 56–57, 86, 89
Pentecostal, Pentecostalism, 26, 36, 63, 68, 70, 96, 103, 109, 122
post-colonial, xiii, 114, 121, 135, 138, 163, 165, 171, 196, 203, 244, 256
Post-Enlightenment, 9, 235
Potter, Phillip A, 137, 251–53
Protestant, Protestantism, xiv, xv, xix, 22–23, 25, 30, 33–35, 42, 44, 49–51, 56, 58, 64, 90, 98, 100, 105, 117–18, 122, 126–27, 135, 138, 140–41, 167, 174, 179, 195–97, 199, 210, 226, 240, 247, 265–66, 269,

Quaker, 5

Raiser, Konrad, 124, 205, 211, 253–54
Ranson, Charles, 67, 88, 100, 143–44, 151, 163, 178
Reunion of the Church, The, 23–25
Rolle, xx, 60, Ch3, 89, 104, 112, 120
Russia, xiii, 42, 76, 123
Secularism, secularization, ix, xiii, xviii, xxii, 35, 51, 55, 125, 185, 189, ch. 8, ch. 9, 247–48, 250–51
Shaw, Ellis O., 19
Smith, Eugene, 48, 55, 127
South India, xiv, xviii, xx, 1, 12, 20–23, 25, 33, 40, 44, 93, 97, 102, 107, 184, 192, 210, 227, 245–46
South India Scheme for Church Union (SIS), 21–24, 27, 30
Stott, John RW, 57, 128, 130–32

Strasbourg (1960), 84, 181, 192, 199–201, 215
Student Christian Movement (SCM), xx, 1–11, 20, 29, 105, 134, 245, 247
Student Volunteer Movement, xv, 7
Student Volunteer Missionary Union (SVMU), 3, 7, 65

Tambaram (1938), xvi, xx–xxi, 9, 13, 33, 38–41, 51, 59, 62, 71–72, 83, 90, 108, 112, 123, 168, 180–83, 188, 191–92, 215, 244, 247
Temple, William, 8, 37–38
Theological Education Fund, 100, 145
Thomas, MM, 9, 53–54, 107, 135, 184, 214, 216, 236
three-selfs, 17
Toronto statement, 58, 116
Trinitarian, x, xvii, xx, xxii, 59, 77–80, 83, 112, 168, 171, 182–89, 205, 212, 250, 254

Uppsala (1968), 53, 84, 128–30, 135, 193, 202, 204–6, 208–9, 212, 214–15, 217, 247, 254–56

Van Dusen, H. P., 89–90, 114
Vatican II, 56, 122, 126, 252–53
Visser 't Hooft, Willem Adolph (Wims), 37, 44, 63, 65, 97–98, 101–4, 113–15, 121–23, 133–34, 139, 144, 150, 163, 169, 186, 188, 205, 246, 251, 254

Walls, Andrew, ix–x, xi, xviii, 182
Warren, Max, xxi, 5, 47, 49, 66–67, 70, 76, 88, 91, 93, 94–100, 108, 125–26, 249, 263, 265–67
West, Charles, 53, 135, 207
Western ecclesiology, 22, 192, 196, 199, 216
Wieser, Thomas, 186, 209, 211–12,
Willingen (1952), xx–xxi, 40–41, 51, 53, 60, Ch3, 89, 92, 103, 124, 126, 142, 171, 180, 188–89, 191, 193, 198, 200, 211–13, 215, 240, 247
Winter, Ralph D, 91, 94, 126
World Missionary Conference, Edinburgh 1910, xv, xviii, 37, 94, 126, 130, 133, 170, 257
World Student Christian Federation (WSCF), 8, 53, 84, 199